Capabilities and Happiness

Capabilities and Happiness

Edited by
Luigino Bruni, Flavio Comim,
and Maurizio Pugno

OXFORD
UNIVERSITY PRESS

OXFORD
UNIVERSITY PRESS

Great Clarendon Street, Oxford OX2 6DP

Oxford University Press is a department of the University of Oxford.
It furthers the University's objective of excellence in research, scholarship,
and education by publishing worldwide in

Oxford New York

Auckland Cape Town Dar es Salaam Hong Kong Karachi
Kuala Lumpur Madrid Melbourne Mexico City Nairobi
New Delhi Shanghai Taipei Toronto

With offices in

Argentina Austria Brazil Chile Czech Republic France Greece
Guatemala Hungary Italy Japan Poland Portugal Singapore
South Korea Switzerland Thailand Turkey Ukraine Vietnam

Oxford is a registered trade mark of Oxford University Press
in the UK and in certain other countries

Published in the United States
by Oxford University Press Inc., New York

British Library Cataloguing in Publication Data

Data available

Library of Congress Cataloging in Publication Data

Data available

Typeset by SPI Publisher Services, Pondicherry, India
Printed in Great Britain
on acid-free paper by
Biddles Ltd., King's Lynn, Norfolk

ISBN 978–0–19–953214–8

1 3 5 7 9 10 8 6 4 2

Contents

Contents

List of Contributors

Sabina Alkire, Oxford Poverty & Human Development Initiative (OPHDI), Oxford University.

Erik Angner, University of Alabama at Birmingham.

Luigino Bruni, University of Milan-Bicocca and Econometica.

Flavio Comim, Capability and Sustainability Centre, University of Cambridge.

Edward L. Deci, University of Rochester.

Ed Diener, University of Illinois.

Richard A. Easterlin, University of Southern California.

Carol Graham, The Brookings Institution.

Johannes Hirata, Institute for Business Ethics of St. Gallen University.

Pelin Kesebir, University of Illinois.

Maurizio Pugno, University of Cassino.

Richard M. Ryan, University of Rochester.

Amartya Sen, Harvard University.

Robert Sugden, University of East Anglia.

Maarten Vansteenkiste, University of Leuven.

Introduction[*]

Luigino Bruni, Flavio Comim, and Maurizio Pugno

Capability and Happiness: Two Different Approaches to Understanding and Assessing Well-Being and Human Development

Is the road to human development paved with wealth? For a long time econo-mists and other social scientists were convinced that promoting opulence was the best (and sometimes the only) way to achieve well-being. However, this conventional thought has been disputed during the last three decades by two different approaches that put forward distinct philosophies and method-ologies to measure, evaluate, and promote human well-being and develop-ment. The conventional economic approach of *homo oeconomicus* or of the rational choice theory to individual utility is undoubtedly a powerful element within a scientific method that has heuristic value and a broad range of applications. However, its theoretical drawbacks and empirical anomalies cannot be ignored in the present state of economic theory. Exploring these shortcomings and the nature of the alternatives is an important step towards better guidance about evaluating human well-being and thinking about strategies for promoting quality of life.

The seminal contributions of Amartya Sen (1980, 1985, 1992, and 1999) and Martha Nussbaum (1999, 2000), within the context of political and moral philosophy and human development, shaped the main tenets of what has become the Capability Approach (CA). More recently, the approach has expanded with a substantial body of applications and refinements (for a

[*] This volume is the result of the international conference "Capability and Happiness" held in Milano-Bicocca in June 2005. We would like to thank Saint Elmuth College of Cambridge, Pier Luigi Porta and the Dipartimento di Economia Politica of the University of Milano-Bicocca, Enrica Chiappero and the HDCA—Human Development and Capability Association. Thanks also to Benedetto Gui and Stefano Zamagni for the scientific contribution in organiz-ing the conference. Luigino Bruni thanks Econometica for financial support.

sample, see Comim, Qizilbash, and Alkire 2007). Sen (1985, 1992) criticizes the use of income and utility as appropriate informational spaces for carrying out adequate well-being analysis. According to him, resources are imperfect indicators of human well-being, because human diversity makes conversion rates (of resources into realizations) different for distinct individuals. Thus, one particular level of opulence could be related to totally different levels of well-being if the individuals' personal or social circumstances are associated with different abilities of converting resources into valuable states of being. In addition, Sen argues that reliance on subjective metrics is also open to distortions due to the problem of adaptive preferences.

As a result, the CA emerges as an objective and multi-dimensional framework for assessing and measuring individual well-being and development that sees income mostly as a means to achieve higher human ends, such as being healthy or educated. The CA has been specially applied to issues of poverty and inequality and to designs of welfare policies. Ultimately, the CA argues that autonomy and agency are important elements in contextualizing human well-being. These concepts lay down the theoretical foundations for the human development paradigm, where human beings are the ends of development and the economic activity simply a means to achieve these ends.

Another relatively new approach to well-being that has emerged as an alternative to the economic literature is the Happiness Approach (HA) (see Kesebir and Diener, Ch. 3, Bruni 2006; Bruni and Porta 2005, 2007; Frey and Stutzer 2002; Layard 2005). The approach was originally conceived by Easterlin (1974)[1] and by Scitovsky (1976), and it is now fast developing, by drawing insights from psychology, and in particular from positive psychology (Argyle 1987; Diener et al. 1999; Myers 1993; Ryan and Deci 2001; Seligman 2002).[2] Despite the exponential growth of the HA literature, it is possible to summarize its main methodological contributions into essentially two tenets, namely, to consider subjective data as valuable, and to raise paradoxes, that is, unexpected evidence with respect to received theory.

Easterlin's early applied researches showed that self-reported well-being, also called subjective well-being (SWB), has not systematically increased with income in the most developed countries, whereas richer households report higher well-being everywhere. This appears as a paradox since economists are used to taking individual and national income as a good proxy for well-being. Subjective well-being has been surveyed on large samples of the population in many countries by asking respondents to rate their happiness or satisfaction of their lives on a fixed-points scale.

---

[1] Also Cantril (1965) can be considered as a pioneer of the empirical studies on happiness.
[2] Kahneman, who also contributed to this approach, is a psychologist but a Nobel prize winner in Economics.

Recent literature has largely confirmed the paradox (Frey and Stutzer 2002; Layard 2003; Clark et al. 2008), even finding cases of a declining trend in subjective well-being, such as in the US (Blanchflower and Oswald 2004). This subjective measure has been tested on various grounds, experimentally and in the field, against objective as well as other subjective measures, but survived as embodying valuable information (see Frey and Stutzer 2002; Konow and Earley 2003; Bertrand and Mullainathan 2001; Myers and Diener 1995; and Clark et al. 2008).

Scitovsky anticipated this paradox in his *Joyless Economy* (1976). He observed that boredom and violence could be pervasive in an opulent country like the US, and attempted to find reasons for this apparently paradoxical phenomenon. By drawing from psychology research, he argued that one fundamental biological need is the need for stimulation. Unfortunately, opulence distracts people's choice towards material comfort, which tends to produce boredom. Violence would appear as an abnormal reaction from the need for stimulation (see also Scitovsky 1986).

The HA has been developed both as applied research and as theoretical analysis. Subjective measures have been used to examine many new problems, which essentially derive from the observation that individuals' choices do not reflect preferences. This observation contrasts with the received economic theory of revealed preferences, whereas empirical psychology has produced an amount of research on this account.

Two variants of the HA can be envisaged, both in economics and in psychology (Bruni 2006; Ryan and Deci 2001). The "hedonic" variant attempts to lay more solid foundations for the utilitaristic tradition (from Bentham to Edgeworth), which has preceded modern economic theory. According to the "hedonic" approach, pleasures and pains would guide the individual's decision-making, but they may be measured objectively (Kahneman et al. 1999). An alternative variant of HA has been developed from the Aristotelian tradition and it is called the "eudaimonic" variant. In this case, decision-making is guided by the evaluation of what constitutes a "good life". Both material and non-material rewards become valuable, and choices do not emerge as necessarily self-regarding.

It is important to note that the CA and the HA come from different traditions. Nevertheless, they both aim to overcome the rigid boundaries of the conventional economic approach to well-being. Such a comparison appears even more interesting once we consider that the two approaches have been developed independently, with very few cross-references. A first step in bringing together the two approaches has been taken by the 2005 *Review of Social Economy* special edition on "Capabilities and Happiness", but much remains to be done.

This book provides a focused attempt to reflect on the joint significance of the two strands of research, and it is to our knowledge the first attempt of this kind. It includes contributions from leading authors of both approaches, as well as contributions which evaluate them and contrast one with the other. The book is also a result of an interdisciplinary effort to tackle contributions from different disciplines, in particular, economics and psychology. A preliminary exploration of the similarities and differences between the two approaches, as carried out in what follows, is useful in highlighting some potential cross-fertilization areas and synergies.

What CA and HA Have in Common

A proper interpretation of the approaches should recognize the original contexts in which they were elaborated and the use to which they can be put when jointly considered. While the CA emphasizes human well-being as a dimension of moral thought and political philosophy, the HA stresses the role of psychological (and even neurological) aspects in understanding descriptive features of human behavior.

However, it is important to acknowledge that both approaches share a similar general objective, namely, an investigation of human well-being that goes beyond the concept of *economic* well-being, as defined from Pigou onwards. The qualification of "human" reminds us that the analysis explicitly considers well-being as a prime end of human actions, and it does not limit itself to the material instruments used to pursue well-being, like, typically, income. Both theories rely at least partially on individuals' own evaluations of their own well-being. This is a consequence of the psychological work on both the HA and the CA origins in moral philosophy.

As supported by both theories, the instruments to achieve well-being and development are empirically laden and often measurable by necessity. Both the CA and the eudaimonic version of HA aim at identifying the fundamental contributing factors to autonomous aspects of well-being and development, while the hedonic version of HA seems to focus more on subjective attempts to measure well-being as nominally felt by humans. Secondly, the interplay between instruments for well-being and actual experience of well-being becomes crucial for both approaches, so that an investigation of specific concepts becomes quite important: the relevance of capabilities and functionings in the CA, and of intrinsic and extrinsic motivations in the HA depends on their particular realizations. Thirdly, these concepts help the approaches to evaluate how welfare policies can promote actual human well-being, distinguishing those categories that are feasible from those that are merely theoretical possibilities.

Identifying these aims makes finally evident the difference between the two approaches and the standard economic approach. Both approaches go beyond a resource-based view of well-being, observing that material quality of life, as represented by, for example, per capita income, is an insufficient indicator of well-being. From both CA and HA also emerges the tenet that decision-making is a complex process, where, at least, the standard concepts of preferences and constraints should be extended and reformulated. It is not the objective of this introduction fully to scrutinize the commonalities and differences between the approaches (for more see Comim 2005), but to emphasize that there are potential synergies to be explored by looking jointly at them.

Differences between CA and HA

The origin of the CA, as it can been seen in the works of Sen and Nussbaum, is intrinsically related to applications of the approach to an investigation of empirical issues such as those of poverty, inequality, discrimination, and even famines around the world, mostly in the developing countries. By pointing out the relevance of functionings and capabilities in assessing human well-being, the CA shows how different forms of deprivation and exclusion involve not only material scarcity but also short life expectancy, illnesses, illiteracy, gender discrimination, and other constraints to individuals' rights and liberties. In other words, emphasis is not limited to "entitlements" but go beyond what people are really able to be and to do. Alternatively, the origin of HA, that is, the "Easterlin paradox", refers not to poverty but to the lack of well-being increases in rich countries, especially in the US and EU. Income and material resources, besides rights and liberties, appear to be insufficient to make people happy. It is thus interesting to note that although motivated by contrasting empirical problems, that is, poverty vs. opulence, both approaches have reached similar conclusions about the complex "technology" of transforming resources into human well-being.

However, the difference in the origin and original applications between the two approaches reflects also a difference in their analytical frameworks. The CA's analysis is basically normative, focusing on the issue of substantive freedoms, using functionings and capabilities to provide the main informational basis for evaluating the necessity and adequacy of policy actions. Conversely, the HA's analysis stresses instead the interpretative problem of why individuals are not able to use existing abundance of material resources and freedoms efficaciously, if not efficiently, for improving their own well-being.

Both approaches, in observing a gap between availability of material resources and enjoyment of well-being, delve into what really makes a good life for different people. However, the two approaches take the question from rather different points of view. The CA privileges the category of "equality" across people as essential in allowing them to pursue and live a good life. Differences between Sen's and Nussbaum's approaches are related to the relative importance that both attach to universal values in orientating public reasoning processes. Yet, both agree on the relevance of a "normative anchor" for assessing human well-being derived from Aristotelian and Kantian concerns. On the other hand, the HA follows a rather empirical approach for defining what human well-being is about. Its main strategy consists in searching for the economic, social, demographic, and psychological variables that can better account for subjective well-being. It is interesting to note that recent econometric studies show that capabilities or functionings, and self-reported satisfaction might be significantly correlated (Anand et al. 2005; Anand and van Hees 2006).

The most difficult obstacle in bringing together these two approaches emerges from their different assessments about the role of subjective information in providing a reliable characterization of individuals' well-being. In the HA, subjective information coming from individuals is actually the only source of reliable information in examining human well-being. In the CA, "public reasoning" plays a role that might transcend the individual and might confer objectivity that might overcome possible biases present in subjective evaluations. However, the ultimate question about the confidence that one can have or not on subjective metrics is what constitutes the main watershed between the two approaches.

Amartya Sen (1979, 1992, 1999) has advanced a series of criticisms related to the "informational famine" promoted by utilitarianism in economics. In particular, he has criticized the use of subjective metrics due to the problem of adaptive preferences (Comim, Ch. 6). The concept of adaptation has a tradition in psychology, and it is based on the argument that individuals develop a set-point of psychological well-being, toward which they revert after favorable or unfavorable external events (see Easterlin, Ch. 2, for a discussion on this point). Under these circumstances, a third party is a better observer of external conditions. The HA and various studies in psychology rejoin that adaptation takes time, and it is hardly complete (Kesebir and Diener, Ch. 3). It also differs across conditions and shocks. For example, Easterlin (2005) points out that individuals' adaptation to financial shocks is almost complete, whereas their adaptation to marriage and divorce is significantly less than complete. These results corroborate HA's findings based on subjective reports over and above individuals' fixed effects. However—Sen and Nussbaum would argue—the bias due to adaptation remains, and it should be determined case by case, with the use of additional informational spaces (such as the space of capabilities) to help in determining individuals' level of well-being.

Subjective well-being is biased—according to Sen (1992) and Nussbaum (1999)—because it relies excessively on individuals' feelings and mental states, rather than on an objective evaluation, and underestimates the key role of preferences adaptation. Kahneman (1999) has shown, in particular, that individuals' memories of past events form a biased basis for maximizing decision-making, and the so-called "behavioral economics" has shown how other contextual factors bias individuals' evaluations and choices. However, other studies in both psychology and economics counter-argue that emotions and happiness may contribute to efficient decision-making (Kesebir and Diener, and Graham, Chs 3 and 4 respectively). This argument is consistent with the fact that the role of emotions in shaping our normative judgments is a permanent topic in Nussbaum's philosophy (1990, 1999).

Another criticism of the use of subjective well-being measures in policy-making is that they provide self-centered, or even self-regarding metrics, while an assessment of society's advantage would include public goods. This point has not been particularly studied in the HA at country or community level, although Frey and Stutzer (2000) show that democratic participation matters for subjective well-being. At the individual level, many experimental studies confirm other-regarding preferences (Kolm and Ythier 2006), and psychology studies show that the individuals' well-being includes the internalization of social norms and conducts (Deci and Ryan 2000), but much remains to be done.

A further criticism to subjective reports points to their unreliable use in inter-individual comparisons. This criticism has a long history in the utilitarian welfare tradition. While the CA gives an answer to this problem by referring to objective indices, the HA has largely overlooked the problem in the econometric studies on happiness, but attention appears to rise towards objective indices of well-being which are strictly correlated to subjective reports, like suicides (Helliwell 2003) and hypertension (Blanchflower and Oswald 2007).

The above critical remarks of the HA don't mean that the CA is devoid of criticism. On its side, the problems of who is the evaluator and what are the features of evaluation in the CA are not trivial. Two methodological points are worthy of consideration: the role that the CA gives to democratic participation in carrying out normative evaluations, and how it considers "reason and scrutiny" in the choice of valuable functionings and capabilities. It is interesting to note that democratic participation could be often imperfect, offering challenges to individual's freedom, with an intrusion of democratic evaluations onto personal matters. The individual may own private valuable information, which, if it were to become publicly diffused, would be very costly. The consequences of some choices may be even greatly uncertain for psychological or contextual reasons. But even if the individual and the public are symmetrically informed, the risk of paternalism may pose a serious challenge to the CA (see Sugden, Ch. 12).

The appeal to careful reasoning appears indisputable, since irrationality and noise are not desirable features of any form of evaluation. Even the HA often uses self-reports on satisfaction, which implies a more reasoned evaluation than straightforward happiness reports. However, again, studies in behavioral economics and psychology show that emotions may contribute to efficient decision-making, and studies in neuroscience also show that affect generally is essential to effective decision-making (Damasio 1994). For example, it has been found that happiness, which is well correlated with positive and negative affects (with obvious opposite sign), has helped people to find better partners, and even a better career and personal success (Kesebir and Diener, Ch. 3).

An emphasis on democratic participation and on careful "reason and scrutiny", as sensible and relevant as they may be, may distance the CA from its possibilities of operationalization (Sugden 1993). The difficulties in moving from its theoretical underpinnings to different operational methodologies have been constantly reiterated by critics of the CA. Contrary to that, Sen himself defends the presence of some vagueness in using the CA, allowing an opportunity to tailor particular methodologies to the nature and context of specific problems and cases at hand.

On the whole, the problems of evaluator and evaluation emerge as not yet properly solved by both the CA and the HA. More criticisms are leveled against the HA, but much research has been effectively undertaken, suggesting new ways of tackling these issues, as shown here in this book.

Are There Synergies between the CA and the HA?

Both the CA and the HA pursue the same aim of understanding well-being and human development with multidisciplinary tools, but they follow two different lines of inquiry. Going beyond their particular features, and stressing their common points, such as their emphasis on individuals' own evaluations, their criticism of a "resource-based" view of well-being, their attachment to values of participation and democracy, their recognition of the importance of autonomy and self-determination in shaping human well-being, their concern with procedural fairness and emotions and their methodological pluralism, we can explore their synergies and potential insights.

To a certain extent, their differences can be complementary in identifying obstacles to the pursuit of well-being and human development. Whereas the CA's literature focuses on social issues of inequality, poverty, and rights violations, the HA's centers its efforts on examining obstacles to unique personal growth and flourishing through the study of both the rational and the affective components of people's thought and behavior. Indeed, these "informational spaces" seem to be complementary as much as individual dimensions of autonomous behavior are related to broad general inequality and injustice issues. As a matter of fact, using broader informational spaces in assessing individuals' well-being seems to be a strategy welcomed by both approaches.

Complementarities also appear in the range and nature of applications that have been explored by the two different approaches. While the CA has shown that problems of functionings and capabilities in the less developed countries (LDCs) cannot be properly ranked according to income, the HA has shown that income does not necessarily lead citizens in rich countries to more happiness. Furthermore, while the CA can help in understanding limitations in liberties in these same countries, the HA helps in understanding unhappiness in unemployment over and above income losses.

Conflicts between the two approaches arise rather as a result of their different views about the degree of reliability and adequacy of subjective reports, while the operationalization of objective indices does not appear straightforward. One of the dangers to which the CA is open is that by skipping the subjective evidence, it tends to overlook problems of people's psychological uneasiness when capabilities can be hardly observed. One should also note that people decide on the basis of what they perceive, however biased their perceptions could be. Think about decision in voting, or whether to migrate or not. This is an important issue for the CA when one applies to "reasons to value" new options to include in the option set. This is also important to the HA that relies in large part on individuals' own evaluations of their own well-being.

In deciding how to negotiate between subjective and objective spaces, the use of both the CA and the HA seem to provide a useful starting point. The use of the CA can throw light on how different social contexts and deprivation conditions can bias subjective evaluations. Binding traditions, old discriminatory customs, violent practices in the families and communities can clearly bias subjective evaluations. One could also extend this consideration to modern social competition fueled by television and advertising. Addressing the problem of adaptive preferences should be at the heart of the agenda for handling well-being and human development issues.

The synergies between the two approaches are multiple, and the contributions in this volume witness this complementarity.[3]

Overview of the Chapters of the Book

Amartya Sen's contribution opens the book, by offering an extremely clear and concise account of his theoretical thought on the weaknesses of the concept of happiness, as conceived and used in the economic tradition, and on the merits of the CA. Sen interchangeably discusses happiness and utility, remarking that the utilitarian tradition regards happiness as the only goal for both welfare policies and individuals' decision-making. He thus criticizes utilitarian happiness on a number of grounds. By contrast, Sen argues, the

---

[3] See how Schokkaert's (2007) methodological attempt goes in this same direction, while Gasper (2007) maintains skepticism.

CA does not suffer from these weaknesses because it considers individuals' objective and specific conditions, and because it uses a multidimensional informational space, which can be enlarged and evaluated explicitly in public informed and reasoned debates.

Richard Easterlin, the forerunner of happiness studies in economics, shows in Chapter 2 how economics can benefit from psychology's insights, but only after careful examination. In fact, he rejects the psychological "set point theory" of well-being, which argues that happiness is primarily determined by personality and genetic factors, and that adaptation leads individuals' shocks from the various life events to the set point level. However, Easterlin takes up psychology's insight that happiness can vary depending on different life domains, testing for constancy of overall happiness over people's life cycle. Therefore, he retains the concept of adaptation, contrary to the economists, who usually assume individuals' ability to anticipate future outcomes, but he also observes that adaptation is neither complete nor rapid. More specifically, Easterlin finds that overall happiness is almost flat over the life cycle, although with a small rise until the mid-forties, and then a small decline. But he also finds that these changes are due to a composition effect among the different life domains. In particular, people report increasing satisfaction in the financial domain even after working age, thus exhibiting a strong adaptation, whereas they report decreasing satisfaction in the health domain, thus exhibiting a weak adaptation.

Pelin Kesebir and **Ed Diener** provide in Chapter 3 a thorough review of the recent literature, mainly psychological, on happiness. Their main claim is the need to build a measure of happiness on a country basis to inform public policy. The arguments revolve around three points. First, national income is not an accurate approximation of well-being, or even worse, affluence may have some negative effects on well-being. Secondly, subjective well-being is a more valid and interesting measure of well-being than simple objective indicators, like infant mortality, life expectancy, crime, and literacy rates. In fact, it is important to note that objective indicators have also problems of measurement, in particular because they do not indicate the most desirable states to be achieved by different societies. The third argument in support of a national measure of happiness is the most original and intriguing. Diener collects many results of empirical psychology, which indicate *positive effects* of happiness, in particular on decision-making accuracy, mastery of information, leadership and ratings of managerial performance, problem solving, creativity, and on chance in succeeding in work life.

Carol Graham's chapter, Chapter 4, complements the previous chapter, both because it mainly surveys economic literature on happiness, and because it pays special attention to empirical literature on LDCs and transition economies, which are of special interest in the comparison with the CA. Starting from the "income–happiness paradox", the author shows that subjective well-being adds important information to standard measures of economic development. She takes, from her own research, the cases of Peru and Russia, but the results suggest that new economic research is also valuable for rich economies. Her approach is to combine objective and subjective information in a dynamic way. Graham discusses "frustrated achievers", those who appear to be characterized by less satisfaction with the market as well as with democracy, high fear of being unemployed in the future, and stronger inclination toward redistributive policies against the rich. Contrasting this evidence with that for Britain, where people with greater income variance are *more* tolerant of inequality, makes evident that the effect of income inequality on well-being differs, depending on how it is perceived.

Luigino Bruni, in Chapter 5, discusses critically some issues of the debate on happiness in economics. In particular, his chapter deals with the relationship between happiness and sociality. In fact, in contemporary "economics and happiness" literature, a new interest in interpersonal relationships can be registered, due to the huge empirical evidence that genuine sociality is one of the heaviest components of people's self-reported happiness. At the same time, mainstream economics is a badly equipped discipline for studying sociality, because it treats interpersonal interactions as elements to be taken into account in terms of externality. The intuition originating the chapter is the conviction that if researches on happiness want to take into account non-instrumental interpersonal relations, scholars will profit by a reconsideration of the rediscovery of the Aristotelian tradition of happiness as *eudaimonia*.

Flavio Comim, in Chapter 6, delves into the foundations of the capability critiques of subjective informational spaces. In particular, he investigates Amartya Sen's and Martha Nussbaum's critiques of utility, happiness, preferences, and desires as appropriate informational spaces for normative evaluations. Attention is given to the problem of adaptive preferences and how subjective information could be used in a broader informational perspective. This revision provides specific information about the precise reasons why the CA is critical of the HA. Moreover, it highlights the "sources of the informational exclusions and constraints" that pervade contemporary economics and lay down the foundations for a revised view of happiness. Ultimately, this chapter tries to put forward an "empirical agenda" about how to operate within a multiplicity of informational spaces, combining capability and subjective informations in order to produce a coherent account of human well-being.

Johannes Hirata, in Chapter 7, argues that the capability and the happiness perspectives are both guided by an ethical concern for good development, but they do not represent a complete account of development ethics, neither individually nor combined. The capability perspective identifies substantive freedoms as the major informational basis for the clarification of questions of justice. As such, it identifies morally relevant inequalities, but it does not specify how to judge whether an instance of capability inequality is also unjust. It also provides no orientation with respect to the distinction between those capabilities that are more and those that are less valuable contents of a good life. The happiness perspective, by contrast, provides orientation with respect to the good life, but it does not address questions of justice. Both perspectives therefore complement each other, but still need to be complemented by a conception of legitimacy. A comprehensive conception of development ethics should be conceived of as a division of labor between the capability perspective, the happiness perspective, and discourse ethics.

Maarten Vansteenkiste, **Richard Ryan**, and **Edward Deci**, in Chapter 8, provide interesting theoretical arguments and empirical information that make the HA a more solid approach, with evident complementarities with the CA. They synthesize a thirty-year-old stream of research initiated by Deci and Ryan, which is essentially based on experimental data and on fieldwork evidence. Putting it in a single statement, they claim that well-being is not simply due to individuals' trying to maximize their utilitarian goals, because both the kind of goals and the underlying motivations change the effects on well-being. Their main argument is that tangible rewards may undermine intrinsic motivations, which are yielded from the actions themselves, with negative effects on well-being. Deci and Ryan's explanation is that tangible distinct rewards may exert a control on the individual, thus undermining her/his autonomy, which is meant as the inner locus of causality of her/his own actions.

Maurizio Pugno, in Chapter 9, starts by observing the different contexts where the CA and the HA are usually applied, and suggests a way for a reconciliation between them by drawing from social psychology research (also from Deci and Ryan's research). The author argues that, according to the CA, deprivation in functionings is usually due to observable constraints, like physical impediments, social and political constraints, as it is frequently in LDCs. By contrast, the HA has arisen from the "Easterlin paradox", which especially applies in the case of rich countries, where those constraints are far more relaxed. Besides the indicator of subjective well-being, other indicators of mental well-being, like depression, anxiety, and addiction point to an even marked and objective deterioration in rich countries. Social psychology suggests considering the special functioning of the self as responsible for individuals' ability to evaluate and to choose. Pugno argues that the self is a useful construct in the analysis, since it changes in ability by collecting new information on preference and beliefs, through both conscious and non-conscious processes.

In Chapter 10, **Sabine Alkire** reviews subjective quantitative measures of human agency at the individual level. Sen's writings have articulated the importance of human agency, and identified the need for information in agency freedom to inform our evaluation of social arrangements. This chapter introduces large-scale cross-cultural psychological studies of self-direction, of autonomy, of self-efficacy and self-determination. Such studies and approaches have largely developed along an independent academy path from economic development and poverty reduction literature. The scope of this chapter is to note avenues of collaborative inquiry that may be fruitful to develop.

In Chapter 11, **Erik Angner** makes explicit fundamental theoretical commitments of the effort to develop subjective measures of well-being. The chapter's main thesis is that increased attention to these commitments—which can also be called philosophical foundations—can help us improve our understanding of the nature, strengths, and weaknesses of these measures. Angner argues that although it is perfectly reasonable for social and behavioral scientists to be wary of spending too much time thinking about the philosophical foundations of their enterprise, there are moments when it is eminently useful to do so. In this case, the chapter maintains, the philosophical foundations of the enterprise are directly relevant to the assessment of subjective measures, and attending to those foundations is therefore well worth the effort.

Robert Sugden in the final chapter argues that one of the most salient features of welfarism is that it accepts each individual's own judgments about how to run her own life as decisive in assessing the relative well-being she derives from alternative options. Economists have traditionally treated this feature of welfarism as an important merit of the approach—the merit of respecting "consumer sovereignty", of not being paternalistic in evaluating individuals' well-being. Sugden argues that neither the capability approach nor the happiness approach has this feature. In different ways, each of these new approaches allows the individual's own judgments about her own life to be subordinated to judgments that are imposed from outside, whether by normative analysts, by supposed "experts" in decision-making, or as the outcome of some political process. Sugden tries to show that each of us, as citizens, should be wary of allowing our own judgments to be overridden in this way.

This book intends overall to give a critical presentation of both happiness and capability approaches, and to discuss most of the key issues raised by considering both research projects as part of a single attempt at "complicating economics", and evaluating more effectively human well-being.

References

Anand, P., Hunter, G., and Smith, R. (2005) Capabilities and well-being: evidence based on the Sen–Nussbaum approach to welfare, *Social Indicators Research* 74, 9–55.
—— and van Hees, M. (2006) Capabilities and achievements: an empirical study, *Journal of Socio-Economics* 35, 268–84.

Argyle, M. (1987) *The Psychology of Happiness*, London: Methuen.

Bertrand, M. and Mullainathan, S. (2001) Do people mean what they say? Implication for subjective survey data, *American Economic Review* 91(2), 67–72.

Blanchflower, D.G. and Oswald, A.J. (2004) Well-being over time in Britain and the US, *Journal of Public Economics* 88(7–8), 1359–86.

—— —— (2007) Hypertension and happiness across nations, NBER Working Papers 12934, National Bureau of Economic Research.

Bruni, L. (2006) *Civil Happiness: Economics and Human Flourishing in Historical Perspective*, London: Routledge.

Bruni, L. and Porta, P.L. (eds) (2005) *Economics and Happiness: Framing the Analysis*, Oxford: Oxford University Press.

—— —— (eds) (2007) *A Handbook of Happiness in Economics*, London: Elgar.

Cantril, H. (1965) *The Pattern of Human Concerns*, New Brunswick: Rutgers University Press.

Clark, A., Frijters, P., and Shields, M. (2008) Relative income, happiness and utility: an explanation for the Easterlin Paradox and other puzzles?, *Journal of Economic Literature*, Vol. 46, No. 1, March.

Comim, Flavio (2005) Capabilities and Happiness: potential synergies. *Review of Social Economy*, vol. LXIII, n. 2, June, 161–76.

—— Qizilbash, M. and Alkire, S. (eds) (2008) The Capability Approach: concepts, measures and applications. Cambridge: Cambridge University Press.

Damasio, A.R. (1994) *Descartes' Error: Emotion, Reason and the Human Brain*, New York: Avon Books.

Deci, E.L. and Ryan, R.M. (2000) The "what" and "why" of goal pursuits: human needs and the self-determination of behaviour. *Psychological Inquiry* 11, 227–68.

Diener, E, Suh, E.M., Lucas, R.E., and Smith, H.I. (1999) Subjective well-being: three decade of progress. *Psychological Bulletin* 125(2), 276–302.

Easterlin, R.A. (1974), Does economic growth improve the human lot? Some empirical evidence. In P.A. David and M.W. Reder (eds) *Nations and Households in Economic Growth* (pp. 89–125). New York: Academic Press.

—— (2005) Building a better theory of well-being. In L. Bruni and P. Porta (eds) *Economics and Happiness*, Oxford: Oxford University Press.

Frey, B.S. and Stutzer, A. (2000) Happiness, economy and institutions, *Economic Journal* 110, 918–38.

—— —— (2002) *Happiness and Economics: How the Economy and Institutions Affect Well-being*, Princeton, N.J.: Princeton University Press.

Gasper, D. (2007) What is the capability approach? Its core, rationale, partners and dangers, *Journal of Socio-Economics* 36, 335–59.

Helliwell, J.F. (2003) How's life? Combining individual and national variables to explain subjective well-being. *Economic Modelling* 20(2), 331–60.

Kahneman, D., Diener, E., and Schwarz, N. (1999) (eds) *Well-Being: The Foundations of Hedonic Psychology*, New York: Russell Sage Foundation.

Kolm, S. and Ythier, J.M. (eds) (2006) *Handbook of the Economics of Giving, Altruism, and Reciprocity*, Amsterdam: North-Holland.

Konow, J. and Earley, J. (2003) The hedonistic paradox: is homo oeconomicus happier?, MPRA Paper 2728, University Library of Munich, Germany.

Layard, P.R.G. (2003) Happiness has social clue? Lionel Robbins Memorial Lectures 3–5 March. London School of Economics.

—— (2005) *Happiness; Lessons from a New Science*, New York: Penguin Press.

Myers, D.G. (1993) *The Pursuit of Happiness*, New York: Avon.

—— and Diener, E. (1995) Who is Happy? *Psychological Science*, 6, I, 10–19.

Nussbaum, M. (1990) *Love's Knowledge*, Oxford: Oxford University Press.

—— (1999) *Sex and Social Justice*, Oxford: Oxford University Press.

—— (2000) *Women and Human Development*, Cambridge: Cambridge University Press.

—— (2003) Capabilities as fundamental entitlements: Sen and social justice, *Feminist Economics*, 9(2–3), 33–59.

Review of Social Economy (2005).

Ryan, R.M. and Deci, E.L. (2001) On happiness and human potentials, *Annual Review of Psychology* 52, 141–66.

Schokkaert, E. (2007) Capabilities and satisfaction with life, *Journal of Human Development*, Vol. 8, No. 3, November (on-line version).

Scitovsky, T. (1976) *The Joyless Economy*, New York: Oxford University Press.

—— (1986) *Human Desire and Economic Satisfaction: Essays on the Frontiers of Economics*, New York: New York University Press.

Seligman, M.E.P. (2002) *Authentic Happiness*, New York: Free Press.

Sen, A. (1979) Informational Analysis of Moral Principles. In R. Harrison (ed.) (1979) *Rational Action: Studies in Philosophy and Social Science*. Cambridge: Cambridge University Press.

—— (1980) Equality of what? In S. McMurrin (eds.), *The Tanner Lectures on Human Values*, Salt Lake City: University of Utah Press.

—— (1985) *Commodities and Capabilities*, Oxford: Oxford University Press.

—— (1992) *Inequality Re-Examined*, Oxford: Oxford University Press.

—— (1999) *Development as Freedom*, Oxford: Oxford University Press.

—— (2005) Human rights and capabilities, *Journal of Human Development* 6(2), 151–66.

Sugden, R. (1993) Welfare, resources and capabilities: a review of 'Inequality Reexamined' by Amartya Sen, *Journal of Economic Literature*, 31, 1947–62.

1

The Economics of Happiness and Capability

Amartya Sen

1

Economists are often seen as terrible killjoys who want to drown the natural cheerfulness of human beings in an artificial sea of gloom. Thomas Carlyle's famous description of economics as "the dismal science" points to a bleak discipline that is firmly entrenched in dreariness. It certainly cannot be doubted that the subject matter of economics is often rather grave and sometimes quite dispiriting. Given that subject matter, it may well be hard to retain one's natural cheerfulness, for example in studying famines or hunger or exploitation, or in trying to understand the causes and effects of devastating unemployment or dreadful poverty.

There is, however, no way of escaping the subject matter of economics if that is the form that economic problems often take. The discipline of economics can hardly be blamed for the existence of these phenomena—famines, poverty, unemployment, and other maladies that afflict humanity. Indeed, the hope is that if economic analysis is successful and illuminating, then it can even help to eliminate these ailments and sufferings, thereby contributing to the generation of happiness.

The questions with which I want to begin this chapter concern the way economics *treats* happiness. Does the discipline show much interest in human happiness and in its far-reaching importance? Economics may not be rightly described as being "killjoy", but does it at least recognize the importance of joy, and view it with adequate interest? Then, later on, I shall also consider an alternative perspective, that of capability and human freedom.

2

Happiness has, in fact, been a very central concern in economics. At least the discipline of "welfare economics", which is the part of economics that is concerned with assessment of states of affairs and the appraisal of policy as well as their consequences, has had a long history of placing happiness at the very centre of the discipline of evaluation. Indeed, for a long time—for well over a century—welfare economics was dominated by one particular approach, to wit, utilitarianism, initiated in its modern form by Jeremy Bentham, and championed by such economists as Mill, Edgeworth, Sidgwick, Marshall, and Pigou, among many other leading economists. It gave happiness the status of being uniquely important in assessing social states as well as public policy. Utilitarianism was for a very long time the "official" theory of welfare economics in a unique way. Indeed, a substantial part of even contemporary welfare economics is still largely utilitarian.

Utilitarians, such as Bentham, or Edgeworth, or Marshall, or Pigou, saw no great difficulty in asserting that the ranking of social goodness and the selection of what is to be chosen must be done simply on the basis of the *sum* of individual welfares. They also took individual welfare as being represented by individual "utility", and in its classic formulation saw utility simply as individual happiness.

The definition of utility has varied over the years. While Bentham's hedonistic view of utility as pleasure still survives in welfare economics and in political philosophy, other ways of seeing utility have also become common, including desire fulfillment and preference satisfaction, and different alternative formulations of preference-based utilities, explored in various ways by Frank Ramsey, Kenneth Arrow, John Harsanyi, James Mirrlees, Peter Hammond, John Broome, James Griffin, and others. In the different utilitarian approaches, all alternative states were judged by the respective sum-totals of utilities they generated. The approach of assessing all achievements by the sum-totals of happiness, or of indicators of preference fulfillment, remained firmly in place.

To take social welfare to be exclusively dependent on individual utilities is often called "welfarism". To aggregate the utilities simply by summing them together (an arithmetic addition) is called "sum-ranking". Utilitarianism is a species of *welfarism* that relies on *sum-ranking* for the purpose of aggregation and for overall evaluation.

3

Welfarism in general—including the particular approach championed by the utilitarians—yields a very special approach to social ethics. One of the major limitations of this approach lies in the fact that the same collection of individual welfares may go with very different social arrangements, opportunities, freedoms, and consequences, and welfarism demands that the evaluation pay no direct attention to any of these different features—only to utility or happiness. But the same set of utility numbers may go, in one case, with serious violations of accepted individual rights, but not in another. Or it may involve the denial of some important individual freedoms in one case but not in another. No matter what happens in these other respects, welfarism would still demand that those differences be ignored in the evaluative exercises, with each alternative being judged only by the utility totals respectively generated. There is something quite peculiar in the odd insistence that no intrinsic importance at all is given to anything other than utility in the assessment of alternative states or policies.

The neglect applies both to "overall" freedoms, including what are called "positive" freedoms (for example, the freedom to have free or affordable elementary education, the right to have unemployment insurance, or the freedom to have basic health care), which may entail claims on the state or the society. The neglect applies also to "negative" freedoms which demand the absence of intrusive interference by others (e.g. the right to personal liberties). The indifference of welfarism to so-called "negative freedoms" (such as libertarian immunities) may be obvious enough, but the effective freedoms to do this or be that ("positive freedoms", as they are sometimes called) are also equally neglected in the exclusive concentration on welfare achievements. Welfarism entails a very limited view of normative evaluation and welfare economics. It is one thing to see utility or happiness as important, but it is quite another to insist that nothing else matters. In particular, we may have much reason to want that substantive note be taken of considerations of freedom in assessing social arrangements.

Second, the informational limitation is made even stronger by the particular utilitarian interpretation of individual welfare, seeing it simply as happiness, or as the fulfillment of desires and longings. This narrow view of individual well-being can be particularly restrictive when making *interpersonal* comparisons of deprivation. For example, comparisons of happiness, or of the strength of desires, can be very misleading as a guide to interpersonal contrasts of how well we are respectively doing, since our expectations and inclination for enjoyment tend to adjust to circumstances, particularly to make life bearable in adverse situations.

The utilitarian calculus based on, say, happiness can be deeply unfair to those who are persistently deprived, such as the traditional underdogs in stratified societies, oppressed minorities in intolerant communities, precarious sharecroppers living in a world of uncertainty, sweated workers in exploitative industrial arrangements, subdued housewives in deeply sexist cultures. The hopelessly deprived people may lack the courage to desire any radical change and often tend to adjust their desires and expectations to what little they see as feasible. They train themselves to take pleasure in small mercies. The practical merit of such adjustments for people in chronically adverse positions is easy to understand: this is one way of making deprived lives bearable. But the adjustments also have the incidental effect of distorting the scale of utilities.

In the metric of pleasure or desire fulfillment, the disadvantages of the hopeless underdog may seem much smaller than would emerge from a more objective analysis of the extent of their deprivation and unfreedom.

Third, there are special limitations of utilitarianism related to "sum-ranking", that is, the procedure of aggregating collections of utilities simply by *addition*. Utilitarianism cannot differentiate between two distributions of the same total utility. For example, it makes no difference in utilitarian evaluation whether one person has 100 units of utility and another has 2, or they have 51 units of utility each. This lack of concern with the distribution of welfares is a further limitation of utilitarianism. It adds to the problems posed by the total reliance on utility—in the form of happiness or desire fulfillment—for assessing each individual's respective situation.

4

The subject of welfare economics suffered a big blow in the 1930s when economists came to be persuaded by arguments presented by Lionel Robbins and others (influenced by "logical positivist" philosophy) that interpersonal comparisons of utility have no scientific basis and cannot be sensibly made. One person's happiness, it was argued, could not be compared, in any way, with the happiness of another. Robbins invoked Jevons in denying that there could be any "means whereby such comparisons can be accomplished": "Every mind is inscrutable to every other mind and no common denominator of feelings is possible."

Since economists came, by and large, to be convinced—far too rapidly—that there was indeed something methodologically wrong in using interpersonal comparison of utilities, the fuller version of the utilitarian tradition soon gave way, in the 1940s and the 1950s, to what can be called "mutilated welfarism". It came to be known as "the new welfare economics". This took the form of continuing to rely on utilities only, but of dispensing with interpersonal comparisons altogether. The "informational basis" of welfare economics remained narrowly confined to utilities, but the permitted ways of using the utility information were further restricted by the ban on interpersonal comparisons. Welfarism without interpersonal comparisons is, in fact, a very restrictive informational basis for social judgments.

An important part of the new welfare economics used only one criterion of social improvement, namely, the Pareto criterion, which relied on taking note of utilities of each person *separately*, without any interpersonal comparisons. According to this criterion, social state x is better than social state y if at least one person has more utility in x than in y and everyone has at least as much utility in x as in y. A state is described as "Pareto optimal" or "Pareto efficient" if and only if there is no other feasible state that is superior to it in terms of the Pareto criterion. A good deal of subsequent welfare economics confined attention to Pareto optimality only, and that practice is very common even today.

It would be bizarre to see Pareto optimality as an adequate criterion for a good society. Pareto optimality only requires that no one's utility can be raised without someone's utility having to be reduced, and thus it is an extremely limited condition of efficiency in the generation of happiness or desire fulfillment.

Pareto optimality is silent on the *distribution* of utilities (including inequalities of utilities), and it takes no direct note of anything *other than* utilities (such as freedoms, or liberties, or rights, or opportunities). A society in which some people lead lives of great luxury while others live in acute misery can still be Pareto optimal if the agony of the deprived cannot be reduced without cutting into the ecstasy of the affluent. A state can be Pareto optimal and still be thoroughly revolting and nasty.

It has become, for this reason, more common to argue that Pareto optimality is a necessary condition for social optimality, even though not sufficient. If Pareto optimality is not sufficient (though necessary), we need some *further* criteria to make judgments about different distributions, and the question arises how that supplementation may be done. The need for using systematic procedures for this supplementation was discussed by Abram Bergson, and extensively explored by Paul Samuelson in his classic treatise *Foundations of Economic Analysis*.

5

It was in the context of the on-going search for acceptable formulations of social welfare that Kenneth Arrow presented his well-known "impossibility theorem". His book *Social Choice and Individual Values* (published in 1951) launched the new subject of social choice theory. Arrow considered a set of very mild-looking conditions relating social choices or judgments to the set of individual preferences. Arrow showed that it is impossible to satisfy those apparently undemanding conditions simultaneously. The "impossibility theorem" precipitated a major crisis in welfare economics, and it is, in fact, a landmark in the history of social and political study as well as economics.

In formulating the problem of social choice based on individual preferences, Arrow took the viewpoint—following what was by then the dominant tradition—that "interpersonal comparison of utilities has no meaning" (p. 9). He took the social choice to be determined by the set of individual preferences, and this functional relationship between the set of individual preferences and the social ordering he called the "social welfare function". While welfarism was not explicitly invoked as a condition on its own, it is in fact—in a particular form—entailed by the conditions that Arrow imposed (the analytical process that yields this result is investigated and assessed in my *Choice, Welfare and Measurement*, 1982).

The combination of this specific welfarism result and the ruling out of interpersonal comparisons of utility makes the resulting system—axiomatized by Arrow—extremely undiscriminating. Let me illustrate. Consider, for example, the problem of choosing between different distributions of a cake between two or more persons. In the informational framework characterized by Arrow, we cannot, in effect, be guided by any equity consideration that would require the identification of the rich vis-à-vis the poor. If "being rich" or "being poor" is defined in terms of *income or commodity holdings*, then that is a non-utility characteristic of which we cannot take any direct note in the Arrow system, thanks to welfarism. But nor can we identify "being rich" or "being poor" with having a high or a low level of happiness, since that would involve interpersonal comparison of happiness or utilities, which is also ruled out. Equity considerations, thus, lose their applicability in this framework. The extent of happiness as an indicator of a person's situation is applied to individuals separately—without any comparison between the levels of happiness of two different persons—and no use can be made of the happiness metric to assess inequality and to take note of the demands of equity.

This is how Arrow's impossibility result emerges, and it is useful to see how it works. The only acceptable information as specified by *welfarism* (to wit, utility or happiness) has to be used in an extremely restricted form because of the insistence on *non-comparability* of utilities. This leaves us with a class of decision procedures that are really some variant or other of *voting* methods (like majority decision). Since they do not need any interpersonal comparison, these voting procedures do remain available in Arrow's informational framework. But these procedures have consistency problems, as had been noted more than two hundred years ago by French mathematicians such as Condorcet and Borda.

We are left, then, with the unattractive possibility of having a dictatorial method of social judgment (i.e. handing it over to one person—"the dictator"—whose preferences could then determine the social rankings). This is clearly an unacceptable method of decision making. It is, in fact, ruled out explicitly by one of Arrow's conditions (that of "non-dictatorship"). This is how Arrow's impossibility result emerges.

The crisis really arises from demanding welfarism (in line with utilitarianism), overlooking everything other than happiness or utility, and—at the same time—ruling out interpersonal comparability of happiness and utility (on which utilitarianism in fact relies). After happiness has been given a unique position in the assessment of social states (through welfarism), its ability to discriminate is largely wiped out by the added assumption of no interpersonal comparisons. This generates the remarkable impasse which is reflected in Arrow's mathematical result.

6

There is a vast literature dealing with the significance and robustness of Arrow's result and exploring various ways of getting round the "impossibility theorem" established by him. "Ways out" have been sought through relaxing each of Arrow's conditions, but each alleged "solution" has some considerable difficulty. I have argued elsewhere that despite the interesting possibilities rightly explored in each direction, the most likely route of escaping the Arrow dilemma in making social welfare judgments lies not in any marginal modification of one or other of the detailed Arrow axioms, but in the general direction of enriching the informational input into that analysis. Making use of interpersonal comparisons of utility has much to offer in this respect.

As it happens, Arrow had ruled out not only interpersonal comparison of utilities, but also the use of the so-called "cardinal" measures of utility or happiness, which would permit us to go beyond people's utility rankings to comparisons of such things as utility *differences*, and *differences of differences*, and so on. Cardinal utility can be invoked for each person separately, without interpersonal comparison, and it can be asked whether an escape from the Arrow impossibility result can be found if we admit cardinal utility, without introducing interpersonal comparisons. The answer is no. It is, in fact, possible to show that Arrow's impossibility result will hold even in the case in which cardinal utility measures are fully admitted for each person separately (without interpersonal utility comparisons being also allowed).

Indeed, in this respect, the critical difference is made by the use or non-use of interpersonal comparison of utility, not cardinality. It is, in fact, easy to show that all of Arrow's conditions can be fulfilled if the axioms are redefined to admit interpersonal comparison of utilities, even if the comparisons do not admit cardinality. An important example that meets this demand can be derived from adapting the philosopher John Rawls's "Difference Principle".[1] This approach concentrates on making the worst-off individual as well off as possible. If stricter interpersonal comparisons are admitted, then other types of social welfare rules also become usable (including, of course, the utilitarian one).

---

[1] It must, however, be noted that Rawls's own formulation applies to judging individual advantage by holdings of "primary goods", rather than enjoyment of utilities. Thus, the welfarist recharacterization of the Difference Principle is not strictly a "Rawlsian" rule.

Once interpersonal comparisons are systematically admitted, the problems faced by modern welfare economics change radically. Instead of Arrow's impossibility, we have to face choices over various *different* rules of social decision (e.g. the utilitarian rule of maximization of utility sum-total vis-à-vis the Rawlsian rule of maximizing the position of the worst-off individual). This applies both to the general evaluative frameworks and also to specific welfare-economic exercises, for example, comparison of inequality or poverty (e.g. in the work of A. B. Atkinson). Instead of being denied these comparisons, at a loss about how to compare inequalities or poverty levels, we can then use various different informational bases for demanding different types of interpersonally comparable information.

The problem of interpersonal comparisons of *welfare* is, in fact, broader than that of interpersonal comparisons of *utility* or *happiness*, since there are also other ways of seeing individual welfare, rather than relying entirely on the calculus of happiness or desire satisfaction. The two questions were not distinguished in traditional and "new" welfare economics, because under utilitarian influence, utility and welfare were thoroughly identified. When Lionel Robbins delivered his influential critique of the foundations of welfare economics (to which reference was made earlier), he did not feel the necessity to go beyond disputing the viability of interpersonal comparison of utilities as such.

To deny the possibility of interpersonal comparison of welfare, it was adequate for Robbins, given his own utility-based outlook, to argue that "no common denominator of *feelings* is possible."

But comparative assessments of welfare are not just matters of comparison of "feelings". The "rules" that we follow in describing someone as being better off than another have many other elements, and the possibility of welfare comparisons cannot be reduced simply to the scrutability of our *feelings*. The problem of comparing the well-being of people has to be dissociated from the insistence on sticking to the utilitarian straitjacket of comparisons of happiness or desires.

7

One route that some of us have tried to explore relates to Aristotle's pointer, in the *Nicomachean Ethics*, to the achievement of valuable *functionings* and to the ability to generate and enjoy such functionings. That ability to achieve combinations of functionings, which is often called "capability", is really an expression of *freedom*, and can be interpreted as the freedom to attain different kinds of alternative lives (between which a person can choose).

One of the basic issues to consider in the analysis of effective freedom is the choice of variables in terms of which achievement is to be judged. For example, freedom to buy *commodities* can be expressed by what economists call a "budget set", namely, the set of alternative bundles of commodities which are all within one's budget and from which any one bundle can be chosen. But commodity ownership is rarely sought for itself, since commodities are means to other ends. The importance of commodities is typically instrumental rather than intrinsic. For example, having food helps us to be nourished, to enjoy eating, to entertain friends, and so forth. The extent of the different "functionings" we can achieve with the same bundle of commodities can vary greatly from one person to another. For example, the extent of nourishment that a person is able to get from a given amount of food depends on the person's basal metabolic rate, body size, age, gender, whether (or not) one is pregnant, the presence or absence of parasitic diseases, climatic conditions, and so on. There is, thus, a need to go beyond commodity holdings or real incomes to judge individual advantage.

Functionings are part of the condition of a person—in particular the various things that he or she manages to do (or be) in leading a life. The *capability* of a person reflects the alternative combinations of functionings the person can attain, and from which he or she can choose one collection. The assessment of welfares and of freedoms can be related to the functionings achieved and to the capability to achieve them.

Some functionings are very elementary, such as being adequately nourished, being in good health, and so on, and these may be strongly valued by all, for obvious reasons. Others may be more complex, but still widely valued, such as achieving self-respect, or being socially integrated. Individuals may, however, differ a good deal from each other in the weights they attach to these different functionings—valuable though they may all be—and the assessment of individual and social advantages must be alive to these variations.

The capability perspective also differs from the important ethical approach championed by John Rawls of concentrating on what he calls "primary goods". These are general-purpose means for pursuing various different ends, and include such diverse things as "rights, liberties and opportunities, income and wealth, and the social bases of self-respect". While this concentration serves Rawls's purpose, holdings of primary goods are indicators neither of well-being, nor of freedom. A disabled person, or one who is more prone to illness for genetic or epidemiological reasons, can quite possibly achieve much less with the same bundle of primary goods than another person without that problem. There are systematic differences related to gender, age, proneness to disease, and so on, and they make the holding of primary goods an inadequate indicator of a person's advantage. Focusing instead on functionings and capabilities has, in this respect, some obvious merit.

In the context of some types of social analysis, for example in dealing with extreme poverty, we may be able to concentrate, to a great extent, on a relatively small number of centrally important functionings and the corresponding basic capabilities (e.g. the freedom to be well-nourished, well-sheltered, and in good general health, the capability of escaping avoidable morbidity and premature mortality, the ability to move about freely, the possibility to participate in the life of the community, and so forth). In other contexts, the list may have to be longer and more complex.

Choices have to be faced in the delineation of the *relevant* functionings. The format always permits additional "achievements" to be defined and included. Many functionings are of no great interest to anyone. There is no escape from the problem of evaluation in selecting a class of functionings in the description and appraisal of capabilities, and this selection problem is, in fact, one part of the general task of the choice of *weights* in making normative evaluation.

The need for selection and discrimination is neither an embarrassment, nor a unique difficulty, for conceptualizing functionings and capabilities. A similar problem exists in evaluating commodity bundles, namely how to weigh the different commodities vis-à-vis each other. This valuation is often done in terms of market prices, and it might thus give the impression of being rather unproblematic and perhaps even "objective" (since market prices are simply observable). But weighting at market prices also involves implicit valuation (namely that those market prices provide the right weights for normative evaluation). This procedure may, of course, be very misleading for a number of reasons, including the influence of one person's consumption on another person's well-being (what are called "externalities"), and the fact that a rich person's dollar may reflect a very different level of urgency compared with a poor person's dollar. In the case of functionings and capabilities (unlike commodities that exchange in the market), the weighting exercise has to be done in terms of *explicit* valuations, drawing on the prevailing values in a given society.

This explicitness is not, in itself, a bad thing. It is, in fact, an important condition of public reasoning, and that is, of democracy in the broad sense. It gives the public a clear opportunity to discuss, scrutinize, and question the values that are being invoked, and also to debate the decisions that are being taken. The scope for rational arguments on valuation can be quite considerable, and informed public discussions and debates can be crucially important for plausible and transparent use of this approach.

8

In the light of the preceding discussion, we can now reexamine what we can say about the relevance and reach of happiness as a criterion of assessing individual well-being and also social achievement. A few conclusions would seem to be clear enough.

First, in so far as happiness is used as a criterion of social evaluation, there is much to be said for using it in an interpersonally comparable form. The path of the so-called "new welfare economics", initiated in the middle of the twentieth century takes us very little distance, and can even land us in the impasse of "impossibility theorems", in one form or another. There is little case for relying on Paretian evaluation as one's principal guide.

Second, armed with interpersonal comparisons of happiness and utility, welfarism has much greater plausibility than the narrow perspective of utilitarianism, since utilitarianism pays no attention to the interpersonal distribution of happiness and utilities. Even if happiness is what we would come to rely entirely on (a sad prospect, as it is), there would still be little case for the axiom called "sum-ranking", with its insistence that distribution among persons makes no difference—all that matters is the aggregate sum of utilities.

Third, even though welfarism is less restrictive than full-fledged utilitarianism, nevertheless even on its own, welfarism is a very limiting approach, since it insists that nothing other than utilities or happiness matters. People have good reason to be interested in many other things, for example the freedoms that they enjoy, the rights that are fulfilled (rather than violated), the actual opportunities in society that are available to them, and so on. Also, in social evaluation, there are grounds for being concerned about the interpersonal distribution of these freedoms, rights, and opportunities.

Fourth, the capability to achieve functionings that we have reason to value provides a different—and in many ways a richer—perspective on the evaluation of individual well-being and freedom, and for assessing the deals that the individuals get. And through this connection with individual advantage, capabilities tend to provide a plausible informational basis for a large part of social evaluation.

Fifth, happiness, however, is extremely important, since being happy is a momentous achievement in itself. Happiness cannot be the only thing that we have reason to value, nor the only metric for measuring other things that we value, but on its own, happiness is an important human functioning. The capability to be happy is, similarly, a major aspect of the freedom that we have good reason to treasure. The perspective of happiness illuminates one critically important element of human living.

Finally, aside from the recognition that happiness is valuable in itself, we must take note of the fact that the achievement of other things that we do value (and have reason to value) very often influences our sense of happiness—generated by that fulfillment. It is natural to take pleasure in our success in achieving what we are trying to achieve. Similarly, on the negative side, our failure to get what we value can be a source of disappointment. So happiness and frustration relate, respectively, to our success and failure to achieve the fulfillment of our objectives—no matter what these objectives are. This can be of great "evidential" interest in checking whether people are succeeding or failing to get what they value and have reason to value.

Despite this connection, it is very important to recognize that we value the things that we do value not just *for the reason that* not getting them would lead to frustration, or getting them would make us happier. Rather, the connection goes the other way.

The reasons that we have for the valuation of our objectives (no matter how remote these objectives are from merely seeking happiness) actually help to explain why we may sensibly feel happy about achieving what we are trying to achieve. Happiness, thus, has "evidential" merit in being, typically, related to our successes and failures in life. This is so even though happiness is not the only thing we seek, or have reason to seek.

It is also important to be clear that the evidential role of happiness does not entail that a thing is valuable only to the *extent* that it yields happiness. Happiness may be linked with success, but the metric of happiness need not be a particularly good guide to the force and extent of our valuations in general. To confound the two was part of the old utilitarian trap into which we have reason not to fall. We have to keep distinct issues separate, and yet we must take note of the way the achievement or failure of what we have reason to value may in fact influence our happiness.

So there is much of interest and significance in the perspective of happiness even for post-utilitarian economics, provided we do not confuse the causal connections. Happiness is not all that matters, but first of all, it does matter (and that is important), and second, it can often provide useful evidence on whether or not we are achieving our objectives in general. As empirical scientists, economists have good reason not to ignore the value of relevant evidence, but we must also be careful not to fall into the illusion that what are ultimately evidential concerns actually have intrinsic and unique importance.

The role of happiness in economic and social evaluation demands serious engagement as well as skeptical scrutiny.

2

Life Cycle Happiness and Its Sources: Why Psychology and Economics Need Each Other*

Richard A. Easterlin

At what stage of life are people happiest—when they are on the threshold of their adult lives, at midlife when families are complete and many are close to the peak of their working careers, or in the "golden years" of retirement? What are the factors responsible for the life cycle pattern of happiness; do major transitions over the life course in areas such as work, family, and health leave their imprint on happiness? These are the questions to which this chapter is addressed. The answers point to a need for greater collaboration between psychology and economics in the study of subjective well-being (SWB).[1]

Background

As Mroczek and Kolarz (1998) have pointed out, conclusions of work in psychology about the nature of life cycle happiness are ambiguous. (In the following review happiness, life satisfaction, and affect balance, though not identical, are treated as reasonably interchangeable measures of SWB.) Since the time of their study the situation has become even more confused. For example, David G. Myers (2000, p. 58), in the special issue of the *American*

* Adapted in part from *Journal of Economic Psychology*, vol. 27(4), Easterlin, Richard, "Life Cycle Happiness and Its Sources", pp. 463–82, (2006), with permission from Elsevier. This paper has benefited from exceptional research assistance and comments by Pouyan Mashayekh-Ahangarani, Olga Shemyakina, and Anke Zimmermann. Helpful ideas were suggested by David Cutler, Daniel T. Gilbert, Bob Osborne, and Steven J. Sherman. Financial support was provided by the University of Southern California.
[1] Two economists, Bernard M.S. van Praag and Ada Ferrer-i-Carbonell, come to a similar conclusion in their recent book (2004, p. 321).

Psychologist on positive psychology, offers the most commonly found generalization: "Although many people believe there are unhappy times of life—times of adolescent stress, midlife crisis, or old age decline—repeated surveys across the industrialized world reveal that no time in life is notably happiest and most satisfying." But the work of Carstensen and her collaborators (2000) implies that well-being increases with age, a conclusion consistent with the empirical results that Mroczek and Kolarz (1998, p. 1345) themselves obtained (cf. also Argyle 1999, 2001). Research in economics, reporting a U-shaped relation with age, compounds the ambiguity. In a volume synthesizing much of the recent economics literature, Bruno S. Frey and Alois Stutzer conclude that "much care should be taken when claiming that old age leads to unhappiness, or that the old are happier than the young.... [T]he economic studies just referred to reach a more differentiated conclusion—namely, that the young and the old are happier than the middle-aged" (2002a, p. 54). Finally, a new study by Mroczek and Spiro (2005) turns the economists' result upside down—they find an inverted U-shape with age.

Though not well-recognized, an important reason for these varying conclusions on life cycle happiness is a difference in the question being addressed. Is the aim to generalize about the change in well-being as people progress from youth through midlife to retirement experiencing life's various joys and vicissitudes—what one might think of, in the words of Mroczek and Spiro (2005, p. 190), as the "overall trend" in life cycle satisfaction? Or is the purpose to identify what might be called the "pure effect" of age itself? Carstensen's socioemotional selectivity theory is a perfect example of the "pure effect" idea. Her hypothesis about rising well-being over the life cycle is based on a mechanism that is triggered entirely by the process of aging; as persons get older, years of remaining life expectancy decline. The consequent shortening of time horizons is thought to induce an emotion regulation change that *by itself* would raise well-being. Note, however, that even if this change in emotion regulation actually occurs it does not follow that older people would be happier than younger, because other factors may differentially impact the happiness of young and old. One such factor is physical health—if well-being is positively related to health and older people are less healthy than younger, then the effect of health *by itself* would be to lower the relative well-being of older persons. Not surprisingly, Carstensen and her collaborators, in testing socioemotional selectivity theory, estimate the relation of affect to age, after controlling for health. Similarly, the empirical results of Mroczek and Kolarz (1998) that support Carstensen's theory include a control for health.

The research of economists reported by Frey and Stutzer is also directed towards identifying the pure effect of age, although economists are often unclear on this point. The economists' finding of a U-shaped relation of happiness to age, on which the Frey–Stutzer quotation above is based, comes from a multivariate regression in which age is just one regressor along with numerous others—gender, race, education, health, income, work status, marital status, and so forth. Thus, the U-shaped association of happiness with age is, in effect, what emerges after eliminating differences between young and old in numerous social and economic circumstances. The difference between the economists' findings on the pure effect of age and those of Carstensen (2000) and Mroczek and Kolarz (1998) is no doubt due to the economists' inclusion of many more "control" variables.[2]

In contrast, in studies seeking simply to identify the "overall trend" in life cycle happiness rather than the pure age effect, no controls for life circumstances are needed. If one wants to know whether people are happier in their golden years than when forming families, one would not want to set aside the facts that older people are likely to be less healthy than younger and more likely to be living alone. Rather, one is interested in how happiness varies as people progress through the life cycle, *all things considered*, including both changes in life circumstances and psychological functioning. Thus, because they seek to answer different questions, there is no contradiction between the results reported, on the one hand, by Carstensen and her collaborators, Mroczek and Kolarz, and Frey and Stutzer, and, on the other, by Myers (2000) and Mroczek and Spiro (2005).[3]

But among studies that seek to answer the question of how happiness varies across the life cycle, all things considered, the conclusion continues to remain uncertain. As mentioned, the most common generalization about the overall trend is "no change", represented by the Myers quotation above. The empirical support usually cited for this pattern is data that show little difference in happiness between younger and older persons at a point in time, and Myers himself refers specifically to such evidence. Point-of-time studies, however, are an uncertain basis for generalizing about life cycle experience, because the young and old in such comparisons are persons from different birth cohorts with different life histories. When data, say, for the year 2000 for happiness classified by age are used to infer change over the life cycle, the implicit assumption is that those born in 1980 (who are 20 years old in 2000) will follow the same life course trajectory as did those born fifty years earlier (and are 70 years old in 2000). The unease created by this assumption is

---

[2] A puzzling aspect of the sample studied by Carstensen and her associates is the treatment of work status. Their report that blue or white collar status in the sample is "distributed evenly across age" raises questions about the treatment in their analysis of both retired persons and those who have never worked, categories for which blue- or white-collar status is ambiguous or nonexistent.

[3] When Mroczek and Spiro state that "our findings are at variance with reports, *including some of our own*, which indicate that well-being improves with age" they are perhaps being unduly hard on themselves, because they have not distinguished between the overall trend in life satisfaction and the pure effect of age (2005, p.197, emphasis added).

compounded when one realizes that cross sectional studies in the 1950s revealed a negative, not constant, association of happiness to age (Campbell 1981, pp. 175, 245).

Panel studies in psychology that follow the happiness of the same individuals as they grow older are usually limited to only a few years of the life span; one of the longest, that of Costa and others (1987), extends over nine years and reports no trend in affect balance. Demographic research following 10-year birth cohorts over up to 24 years of the life cycle (sometimes described as a "synthetic panel") also concludes that life cycle happiness is constant (Easterlin and Schaeffer 1999). But, as noted, a new panel study by Mroczek and Spiro (2005) following 1900 men for 22 years reports an overall trajectory that is curvilinear, with a peak in life satisfaction at age 65.[4]

If one turns to theories of life cycle well-being, the literature is equally ambiguous, especially as regards the role of life circumstances. For purposes of contrast it is useful to distinguish two extreme views, one prevailing in economics, the other commonly found in psychology. Economists tend to adopt the view—what one might call the "strong" economic model—that well-being depends on one's objective circumstances alone. The multivariate regressions performed by economists—of happiness on a variety of demographic, economic, social, and even political characteristics—are an implementation of this theoretical view (Frey and Stutzer 2002a, 2002b).

In contrast, psychologists typically view the effect on well-being of objective conditions as being mediated by psychological processes in which people adjust to the ups and downs in their life circumstances.[5] At the extreme, this adjustment process, termed "hedonic adaptation", has led to the notion that people are on a hedonic treadmill (Brickman and Campbell 1971; Kahneman 1999, pp. 13–15). This view, sometimes called the "set point model" sees individual happiness as essentially determined by personality and genetics. Life events, such as marriage, loss of a job, and serious injury or disease, may deflect a person above or below this set point, but hedonic adaptation will fairly quickly return an individual to the baseline level. In this "strong" set point model hedonic adaptation to life events is rapid and complete. It is exemplified by recent statements such as the following: "Our human capacity for adaptation . . . helps explain a major conclusion of subjective well-being

---

[4] The panel study by Costa and others (1987) actually has a similar pattern. If one plots the mean level of affect balance (with or without the "health concerns" component) against age for the five successive life cycle segments represented by the cohorts in the study, there is a suggestion that the overall trend in mean level peaks around age 65.

[5] The issue was put succinctly by psychologist Angus Campbell (1972, p. 442) over three decades ago: "I cannot feel satisfied that the correspondence between such objective measures as amount of money earned, number of rooms occupied, or type of job held, and the subjective satisfaction with these conditions of life, is close enough to warrant accepting the one as replacement for the other" (cf. also Lyubomirsky 2001).

research, as expressed by the late Richard Kammann (1983): 'Objective life circumstances have a negligible role to play in a theory of happiness' " (Myers 2000, p. 60; cf. also Csikszmentmihalyi and Hunter 2003, pp. 185–6; Lykken and Tellegen 1996, p. 189).[6]

Not all economists view well-being as depending solely on objective conditions. There is a line of work, some of it extending back over fifty years, that brings into consideration psychological processes such as social comparison and habituation (Duesenberry 1949; Modigliani 1949; Pollak 1970, 1976), and these concepts have been applied in economic research on SWB (Easterlin 1995, 2001a; Layard 2005; Stutzer 2003; van Praag and Frijters 1999). In psychology, although "[t]he assumption that happiness set points exist has guided much of the current theory and research on SWB" (Lucas et al. 2004, p. 8), few researchers these days adhere to the strong set point model.[7] At a minimum, allowance is usually made for the possibility of individuals improving their well-being through various psychological measures (Seligman 2002). Beyond this, there is often recognition that at least some life circumstances may have lasting effects on happiness. Myers (1992, 2000) makes a specific exception to the hedonic treadmill in the case of family and social relationships. Lucas and others (2003) report that while adaptation to marriage is, on average, rapid and complete, adaptation to widowhood may take, on average, eight years. Elsewhere, they conclude that the effect on well-being of unemployment is even more enduring, changing the "happiness set point" (Lucas et al. 2004). A clear implication of this line of research is that life circumstances, rather than being lumped together in a portmanteau generalization, might better be considered separately with regard to their effects on well-being, as is done by Diener and Seligman (2004) in their thoughtful proposal for a national well-being index. Recent research by Kahneman and others (2004), making clear that all life circumstances are not hedonically equal, underscores the importance of looking separately at different life circumstances (see Robinson and Godbey 1997, chapter 17 for a similar analysis of a broader population sample).

---

[6] Themes of this type have been taken up by the popular media. See, for example, the *New York Times Magazine* article on the "futile pursuit of happiness" (Gertner 2003) and the quotation attributed to Daniel Kahneman in *Time* magazine's special issue on the science of happiness, "Circumstances don't seem to have much effect on happiness" (2005, p. A32).

[7] Cf. e.g. Fujita and Diener 2005. Headey and Wearing were among the first to reject the strong set point model, arguing from their longitudinal data that "life events influence SWB over and above the effects of personality" (1989, p.731; cf. also Headey, Holmström, and Wearing 1984; Diener 1996). However, life events in the Headey–Wearing empirical analysis are not specific circumstances but aggregative measures that combine a number of favorable and/or unfavorable experiences, each experience being assumed to have equal weight in determining satisfaction.

The Present Investigation

On the empirical side, the aim of this study is to clarify first, and most importantly, the overall trend in life cycle happiness; secondly, the pure effect of age. On the theoretical side, the purpose is to consider implications of the analysis for the strong economic model versus the strong set point model of the determinants of well-being.

The conceptual framework here is the domain satisfaction approach pioneered by Angus Campbell and his collaborators (Campbell, Converse, and Rodgers 1976; Campbell 1981; for a wide-ranging recent study employing the domain approach see Saris et al. 1995). In economics this tradition has been taken up by Bernard M.S. van Praag and Ada Ferrer-i-Carbonell (2004; see also van Praag, Frijters, and Ferrer-i-Carbonell 2003; Rojas 2005). In this approach, responses on global happiness are seen as the net outcome of reported satisfaction with various domains of life. Statements about satisfaction in each domain are, in turn, viewed as reflecting the extent to which objective outcomes in that domain match the respondent's goals or needs in that area.[8]

An advantage of the domain satisfaction approach is that it encompasses a variety of life circumstances and groups them into a tractable set of realms that accord closely with people's principal everyday concerns (material living conditions, family life, health, work, and so on; cf. Cantril 1965; Herzog, Rodgers, and Woodworth 1982; Layard 2005), and people are generally able to make judgments on their degree of satisfaction in each domain. In the domain of family life, for example, one's goals, simply put, might be a happy marriage with two children and warm family relationships. Satisfaction with family life would reflect the extent to which objective circumstances match these goals— the greater the shortfall, the less the satisfaction with family life. Over time, goals, objective circumstances, or both may change, and thereby alter judgments on domain satisfaction. Given objective conditions, goals may be adjusted to accord more closely with actual circumstances in line with the process of hedonic adaptation emphasized by psychologists. Given goals, objective circumstances may shift closer to or farther from goals, altering satisfaction along the lines stressed by economists. Thus, the life cycle pattern of judgments on domain satisfaction offers the possibility for insight into the relative merits of the mechanisms determining well-being proposed in both the strong set point model and the strong economic model. The scope of the present analysis makes it possible to derive some qualitative impressions, but not quantitative conclusions about the comparative value of the two approaches in explaining satisfaction within individual domains.

---

[8] This conceptual approach to explaining SWB is sometimes termed multiple discrepancy theory (Michalos 1986, 1991; cf. also Diener et al. 1999; Solberg et al. 2002).

Richard A. Easterlin

The domains of life included here are financial situation, family life, health, and work, and overall happiness is viewed as a weighted average of these domains. Exactly what realms of life are conceptually preferable, and whether one should study life domains, psychological needs, or both together as determinants of life satisfaction is a matter of continuing research (Cummins 1996; Salvatore and Muñoz Sastre 2001; Saris et al. 1995). The choice here is constrained by the data set in which a total of seven life domains is identified—financial situation, family life, work, health, friends, place of residence, and hobbies. The most economical explanation of life cycle happiness was obtained here with the first four domains and the analysis is consequently confined to these areas.

Methodologically, the present approach comes closest to that of Mroczek and Spiro (2005). As in that study, a statistical generalization is derived of the overall trend in life cycle happiness. It is estimated here by averaging the experience of numerous closely overlapping birth cohorts, some younger, some older, as they age over up to thirty years of the life cycle. The technique is essentially a statistically refined variant of demographers' birth cohort analysis that draws on the economists' regression approach. Overall trends are similarly estimated for satisfaction with one's financial situation, family life, health, and work. A regression of global happiness on satisfaction in the individual domains is then derived, and using this regression, an attempt made to predict the life cycle pattern of happiness from the life cycle patterns of domain satisfaction. Finally, the pure effect of age on happiness is estimated by controlling for changes over the life cycle in life circumstances, as reflected in domain satisfaction.

Birth cohort data are from a nationally representative social survey conducted almost annually over the period 1972 to 2002. Persons born in 1954, for example, who were age 18 in the first survey year, 1972, are followed year by year as they grow older up to age 48 in 2002; persons born in 1953 are followed as they age from 19 to 49; and so on. In any given year, however, the individuals actually surveyed differ from the previous year—the survey provides a random sample year after year of persons from the same birth cohort, but not the responses of exactly the same members of the cohort; thus it is a "synthetic" panel. An important advantage of this approach is that the data encompass the entire population, and hence avoid the problem of possible bias due to sample selectivity. But while it is possible to infer the overall trend for birth cohorts it is not possible to perform the second important stage of the Mroczek and Spiro (2005) empirical analysis and examine individual variation around the mean—this can be done only when exactly the same persons are followed as they age. Nevertheless, clarification of the typical pattern as a birth cohort ages is a step forward.

Method

Data Source and Sample

The survey data are from the United States General Social Survey (GSS) conducted by the National Opinion Research Center (Davis and Smith 2002). This is a nationally representative survey conducted annually from 1972 to 1993 (with a few exceptions) and biannually from 1994 to 2002. For happiness, which is reported in every survey over the 30-year span, there are three response options. The domain satisfaction variables comprise financial satisfaction (3 response options), job satisfaction (4 options), family satisfaction (7 options), and health satisfaction (7 options). The specific question for each variable is given in Appendix A. The response of an individual to each question is assigned an integer value, with a range from least satisfied (or happy) equal to 1, up to the total number of response options (e.g. 3 for happiness, 7 for health satisfaction). The analysis here for the domain satisfaction variables is based on data for 1973–94, because family and health satisfaction were included in the GSS only during this time span.

Statistical Analysis

The overall trend of happiness from ages 18 to 89 is established by regressing happiness on age controlling for year of birth (birth cohort), gender, race, and education. The control for birth cohort means, in effect, that segments of life cycle experience for numerous overlapping birth cohorts are combined to infer the typical life cycle pattern. The total number of birth cohorts included in the analysis is 102. Each of the 42 cohorts born from 1913 to 1954 is followed over the full 30-year time span (those born in 1913 starting at age 59; those in 1954, at age 18). For the other 60 cohorts the time span covered ranges from 29 years (for the cohorts of 1912 and 1955) down to 1 year (for the cohorts of 1883 and 1984), with a mean time span for these 60 cohorts of 15 years.

Gender, race, and education are characteristics that are either fixed throughout the adult life cycle, or, in the case of education, fixed early on for almost all persons. The controls for these characteristics are because older persons and older cohorts differ somewhat in their demographic composition from younger, with somewhat larger proportions of females, non-blacks, and more educated persons. As a result, comparisons made without controls that seek to generalize about happiness differences over the life course will be distorted because happiness or domain satisfaction varies by gender, race, and education (Argyle 1999; Blanchflower and Oswald 2004; Easterlin 2001b, 2003b; Frey and Stutzer 2002a).

A dichotomous variable for education is used here—12 years or less or 13 years or more, but the results would be virtually the same if, instead, highest grade completed were the variable. A dichotomous variable is used because

35

education is viewed as dividing the population in much the same way as the gender and race variables—into two distinctive social groups, in this case, those who go to college and those who do not. Each of these subdivisions may be thought of as identifying classes of the population whose overall trend in life cycle happiness may differ significantly from average. Differences among these subgroups are a research issue for the future; in the present analysis the focus is on the pattern typical of the population as a whole, and gender, race, and education are treated only as control variables.

The same procedure—a regression on age, controlling for birth cohort, gender, race (black or non-black), and education (some vs. no college)—is followed to obtain the life cycle pattern for each domain satisfaction variable. Descriptive statistics for all variables are presented in Appendix B. The regression technique used throughout is ordered logit, because responses to the several variables are categorical and number three or more. Ordinary least squares regressions yield virtually identical results, suggesting that the findings are robust with regard to methodology. Various linear and quadratic combinations have been tried for the age and cohort variables. The regression yielding the best fit for each variable is used here, because there is no reason to suppose that life cycle and cohort effects would be the same from one domain to another or for global happiness. The overall trend in life cycle happiness and in each domain satisfaction variable is the estimated value at each age 18 to 89 when mean values for all independent variables other than age are entered in the regression equation.[9]

The relation of global happiness to the individual domain satisfaction variables is then derived by regressing global happiness on the four domain satisfaction variables—financial, job, family, and health. Predicted happiness at each age is obtained by entering in this regression equation the value at each age 18 to 89 for each domain satisfaction variable, as estimated from the overall trend for that variable. Finally, the pure effect of aging on happiness is derived from a regression of happiness on age, controlling not only for cohort, gender, race, and education, but also for satisfaction in the various domains.

Results

The Overall Trend in Life Cycle Happiness

Happiness is greatest at midlife, but only barely so. It rises slightly, on average, as people progress from age 18 to 45 and then declines slowly thereafter

---

[9] More specifically, this estimation procedure yields probabilities for each response category—in the case of happiness, for example, the probabilities that happiness equals 1, 2, or 3 respectively. The mean predicted value is obtained by multiplying the category value (1, 2, or 3) by the probability for that category, and summing the products.

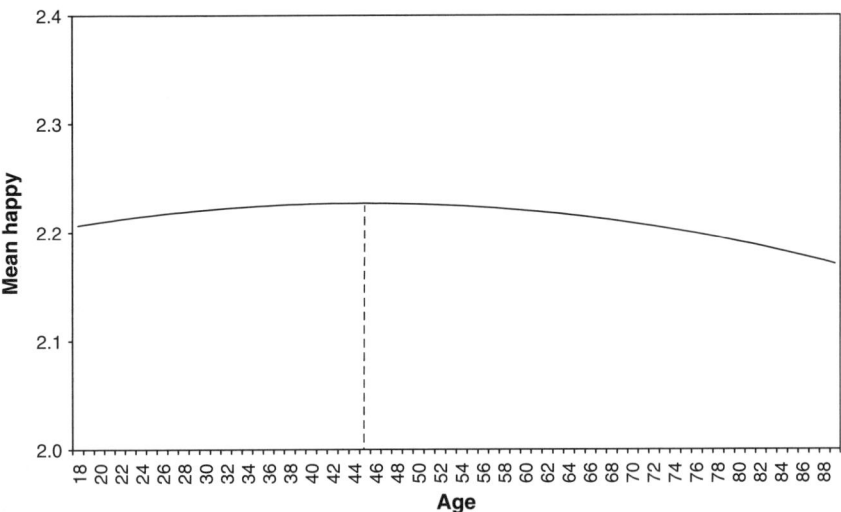

Figure 2.1. The overall trend in life cycle happiness

Source: Appendix C, column 1.

(Figure 2.1; the underlying equation is given in Appendix C, column 1). The size of the life cycle swing in happiness is so small as to be barely perceptible, but it is statistically significant. On the three option happiness scale—very happy, pretty happy, not too happy—the increase from age 18 to 45 is equivalent to an upward shift over 27 years of only 2 percent of the population by one response category, say from "not too happy" to "pretty happy." In the ensuing 27 years happiness drops at the same rate as it previously rose. Thereafter, the rate of decline picks up slightly and by age 89 happiness is below the level at age 72, but by an amount equivalent to a downward shift of one response category for only 4 percent of the population.

As mentioned, Mroczek and Spiro (2005) also find an inverted U for the overall trajectory of life cycle satisfaction. The amplitude of movement that they report appears somewhat larger and the peak later in life at age 65. The difference in results for amplitude and timing is probably due to several factors. They use a different measure and scale for SWB—life satisfaction, ranging in value from 0 to 11. Also, their sample comprises relatively healthy men from around age 40 onward (Mroczek and Spiro 2005, p. 192). It is likely that the peak for males as a whole occurs later than for females (Easterlin 2003b), and for healthier males, later than for all males.

The inverted U-shaped pattern here and in the Mroczek and Spiro (2005) study is the opposite of that reported by Blanchflower and Oswald (2004) and other economists. This difference results from the economists' studies including controls for circumstances that change over the life course such as work, marital, and economic status. In an alternative analysis similar to that given here, Blanchflower and Oswald regress happiness on age, controlling only for gender and race, and report an inverted U consistent with the present results (2004, Table 2a, col. 1).

Other longitudinal studies have heretofore usually reported constancy in happiness over the life cycle. Whether from a panel study or one using the demographic technique of cohort analysis, this pattern has been inferred from observations limited to segments of the life cycle—usually only a few years and at most about 25 years—for a small number of fairly sizable (10-year) birth cohorts. These are time spans and cohort sizes in which the small swing in happiness found here for the population as a whole over 71 years of the life cycle is unlikely to be detected.

All panels, synthetic or not, lose members of a cohort through mortality. (A synthetic panel, however, does not have the additional problem of attrition due to inability to locate the original panel members.) Over the life cycle, selection occurs in favor of happier persons, because persons in poor health are both less happy and more likely to die (Idler and Benyamini 1997; Mehnert et al. 1990; Smith, Taylor, and Sloan 2001). Such selection is not very great up to age 70, when three-fourths of the cohort alive at age 18 are still living. By age 80, however, the proportion surviving drops to one-half and by 89, to little more than a fifth.[10]

Mortality causes an upward bias at older ages of the curve in Figure 2.1, because the average is increasingly based on persons in better health. Mroczek and Spiro's thoughtful analysis (2005, pp. 194–5 and Table 4) gives an idea of the magnitude of this bias, because their estimates give separate life satisfaction trajectories for those who died and those who remained alive, an analysis possible only with data following the same individuals as they age. Their statistical results imply that at age 85 the mean life satisfaction of those who died would have been about 8 percent less than those who remained in the sample. Those who died comprise about one-third of the original sample; hence in the absence of attrition due to mortality mean satisfaction would have been about 3 percent less ($\frac{1}{3} \times .08$). In the synthetic panel analyzed here attrition due to mortality reaches one-third when people are in their mid-seventies. If the Mroczek–Spiro estimates are applicable here, then the bias due to mortality in Figure 2.1 is quite small at least through about age 75.

On the face of it, the life cycle pattern for overall happiness in Figure 2.1 appears largely to support the strong set point model—that happiness is highly stable and unaffected by life circumstances. True, there is some evidence of

[10] Survival rates are from the 2001 United States life table available at <http://www.ssa.gov/OACT/STATS/table4c6.html>.

change, but it is so small as hardly to contradict the model seriously. The domain patterns, however, are a different story.

The Overall Trends in Domain Satisfaction

In contrast to happiness, there is a sizeable amount of change in the individual domains over the life cycle (Figure 2.2; for the underlying equations, see Appendix C, columns 2–5). Satisfaction with family life rises slightly to about age 40, after which it drops quite a bit. Satisfaction with one's financial situation declines very slightly through age 36, but thereafter rises considerably, with the biggest increase in older age. Satisfaction with health declines throughout the life course. Satisfaction with one's work rises to age 58, and then drops.

The size of the changes in satisfaction with particular aspects of life are, on average, considerably greater than for happiness, even after allowing for the fact that, except for financial satisfaction, the number of response categories for the domain variables is greater than for happiness. The scales for domain satisfaction in Figure 2.2 are adjusted for differences in number of response categories; for example, health and family situation, which have a response range of 6 compared with a range of 2 for happiness, are drawn to a scale one-third as great as that for happiness. As can be seen, even after adjustment, the amplitude of life cycle change for each of the domain satisfaction variables is considerably greater than that for happiness. Clearly all four of the domain satisfaction patterns are counter to what one would expect if adaptation were rapid and complete within domains. (The possibility of adaptation across domains is taken up subsequently.)

Explaining Domain Satisfaction: Subjective Perceptions versus Objective Circumstances——The explanation of each of the domain satisfaction variables is a study in itself. But the patterns here do convey certain impressions about the dominant conditions determining domain satisfaction. The impact of actual life circumstances on domain satisfaction is most apparent in the life cycle patterns for family life, health, and work. As unions are formed and families built, satisfaction with family life rises; then, as children leave home, and divorce and widowhood take their toll on marital unions, satisfaction turns downward—a pattern roughly parallel to life cycle trends in objective circumstances in the family domain (Waite 1995; Delbes and Gaymu 2002). Satisfaction with health declines steadily as the actual incidence of disability and disease rises throughout the life course (Reynolds, Crimmins, and Saito 1998). Satisfaction with work rises as people move up the career ladder, but then drops off. If in each domain people were adapting rapidly and completely

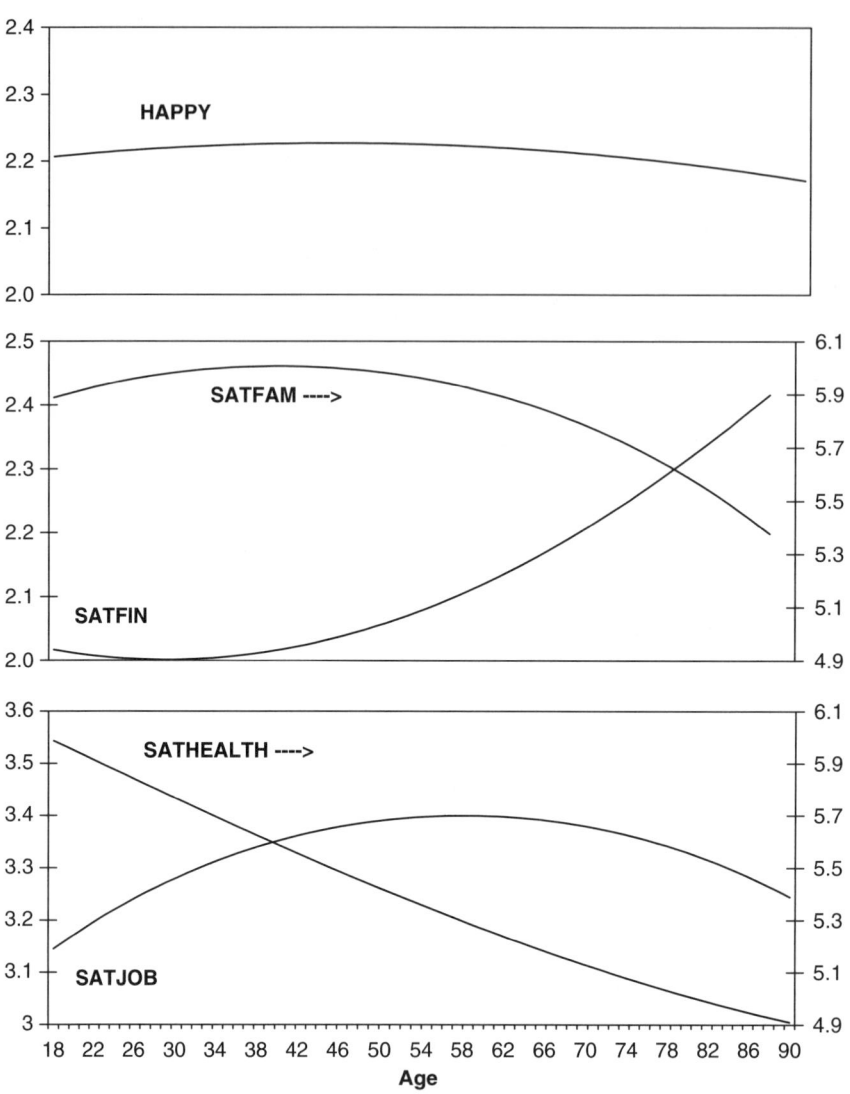

Figure 2.2. Overall trends in life cycle happiness and domain satisfaction

Source: Appendix C, columns 1–5.

to changing life circumstances, then satisfaction would not move with the pattern of actual events. This is not to say that no adaptation occurs, but clearly adaptation is not enough to maintain an unchanging level of satisfaction in each domain, as might be expected from the strong set point model.

In contrast to the other domains, satisfaction with one's financial situation does not move with the course of actual economic circumstances. Income rises throughout most of the working years and then levels off and declines, but satisfaction with one's financial situation moves almost inversely, starting to rise after age 40, and increasing most in late life when income, if anything, is typically declining. The upswing in satisfaction with one's financial situation in midlife and beyond demonstrates how economists' exclusive reliance on objective circumstances as a determinant of well-being is mistaken. The upturn clearly cannot be due to rising incomes; it is most likely due to a decrease in emotional strains arising from financial pressures, as perceptions of material needs diminish in the later stages of life. The pattern speaks eloquently of the need to consider the mediating influence on judgments of well-being of changes in subjective goals, as emphasized by psychologists.

Causality——Closely allied to the strong set point model is the "top down" view of causation as compared with the "bottom up" approach (Diener 1984; Diener et al. 1999; Headey, Veenhoven, and Wearing 1991). The "top down" view sees one's global happiness as a personality trait that leaves a corresponding imprint on the domain responses; the "bottom up" approach sees overall happiness as the outcome of satisfaction in the various domains. A "top down" advocate, who sees happiness as a reflection of one's personality and genetic make-up, would expect that the quite stable life cycle pattern of happiness would be replicated in each of the various domains. But this does not happen: the domain patterns differ markedly from the happiness pattern and also among themselves. The considerable variability in the domain patterns thus contradicts the "top down" view. The next two sections present evidence supporting the "bottom up" view, that causation runs primarily from satisfaction in the individual domains to global happiness.

The positive association between family formation and increasing satisfaction with family life runs counter to the argument that selection based on personality is sufficient to explain the positive cross sectional association between marriage and life satisfaction. If selection were all that is happening, that is, only people initially more satisfied were the ones getting married and forming families, then a rise in the satisfaction of those studied here—all persons, married and unmarried, taken together—would not occur. This is not to say that there is no selection at all, but the present evidence suggests that there is a real positive impact on happiness of the formations of unions.

Domain Satisfaction and Happiness

Do the domains studied here play an important role in shaping the life cycle pattern of overall happiness? To answer this, the relation of happiness to satisfaction in each of the individual domains is first examined. The subsequent section considers whether life cycle patterns for the four domains taken together predict the overall trend in life cycle happiness.

One would expect that if satisfaction in a particular domain had an important effect on happiness, then overall happiness would increase if satisfaction in that domain rises and no change takes place in any other domain. Is this, in fact, the case? The answer is yes. On average, happiness varies directly and significantly with each dimension of people's lives included here: with one's financial situation, family life, health, and work (Table 1, column 4). Thus, the greater is satisfaction with each of these life situations, the greater, on average, is overall happiness.

The domain satisfaction variables array as follows from high to low with regard to magnitude of effect on happiness: family life, financial situation, job, and health. When the effect on happiness of each domain variable is considered singly, family satisfaction has the highest likelihood ratio. After family satisfaction, the likelihood ratio increases most with the addition of financial situation, then with job satisfaction, and finally with health satisfaction (Table 2.1, columns 1–4).

Explaining Happiness: Subjective Perceptions versus Objective Variables——As measured by the pseudo-R^2, the four domain variables account for about one-seventh of the variance in happiness among individuals. Similar analyses of the explanation of happiness in terms of domain satisfaction (but with somewhat different life domains) have yielded even higher levels of

Table 2.1 Happiness on specified domain satisfaction variables: Ordered logit regression statistics (for all coefficients $P > |z| = 0.000$) Model

Independent variable	(1)	(2)	(3)	(4)
Satfam	.557	.524	.493	.430
Satfin	—	.737	.624	.595
Satjob	—	—	.529	.503
Sathealth	—	—	—	.252
Cut1	1.003	2.186	3.435	4.267
Cut2	4.084	5.432	6.792	7.691
n	18,457	18,457	18,457	18,457
Chi^2	2219	3499	4237	4698
Log likelihood	−16,177	−15,537	−15,168	−14,937
Pseudo R^2	.064	.101	.123	.136

explanation (e.g. Rojas 2005; Salvatore and Muñoz Sastre 2001; van Praag and Ferrer-i-Carbonell 2004).

The domain satisfaction variables derive from psychological theory and are typically taken as reflecting the extent to which objective circumstances match aspirations in each domain (Campbell 1981). Economists, as has been mentioned, typically set aside aspirations in seeking to explain happiness, and focus on objective conditions alone, running multivariate regressions of happiness on a variety of life circumstances. The relative merits of these two conceptions of the determinants of happiness may tentatively be assessed by considering how the statistical explanation of happiness provided by the psychologists' domain variables used here compares with the economists' explanation in terms of objective variables alone. To answer this, an economist-type regression was run—happiness on age, gender, race, education, income, health status, marital status, household size, and work status for comparison with the domain model in Table 2.1. The explanatory power of the economists' objective variables alone, as measured by the pseudo-R^2, is only slightly more than half of that of the four domain variables (.077 vs. .133). Indeed, the statistical explanation of happiness provided by any two domain variables together is as good as or better than that of the economist-type multivariate analysis.

An analysis of the domain and economists' models similar to the present one is done for Germany and the United Kingdom by van Praag and Ferrer-i-Carbonell (2004, chapter 4) although they do not go so far as to compare the statistical explanation provided by the two approaches. Their procedure adjusts the statistical explanation provided by the domain satisfaction model for a possible upward bias due to positive correlation between responses on the dependent variable (happiness) and independent variables (domain satisfaction) arising from a common unobserved influence on individual responses, such as personality. Their results are very much the same as those here with the domain approach superior to the economic model.

These findings further underline the importance of the psychologists' conception of SWB determinants versus one emphasizing purely objective variables. It is not that objective circumstances are of "negligible importance", but the results for the domain variables make clear that the mediating influence of psychological processes on judgments of well-being needs to be brought into models of SWB.

Causality Revisited——The evidence so far is that the domains studied here are important to individual happiness, and that domain satisfaction provides a better statistical explanation of happiness than the purely "objective" conditions emphasized by economists. But the statistical results also leave plenty of room for other influences, including personality and genetics, as indicated by the fact that in total only about one-seventh of individual differences in happiness is accounted for by satisfaction with financial situation, family life, health, and work. The relatively small role of life circumstances in accounting for individual differences in happiness is a standard finding in the literature.

The factors that are most important in determining *individual differences* in happiness, however, are not necessarily the same as those most important in explaining the *overall trend* in life cycle happiness. This is a distinction not generally recognized in the psychological literature where the role of a factor in explaining individual differences is invariably taken as the sole criterion of a variable's importance, perhaps because psychology focuses so much on understanding the individual. However, a variable that is important in explaining differences among persons is not necessarily equally important in accounting for changes common to these persons as a group.

To see how the importance of a variable may differ depending on the problem under study, consider the marked upswing and subsequent collapse in the United States rate of childbearing in the three decades after World War II—the great baby boom and bust. Among the various factors explaining individual differences in childbearing behavior at that time, both religion and economic circumstances are important. In explaining the temporal baby boom and bust, however, economic considerations are of overriding significance, and religion, which changes very little over time, is unimportant (Easterlin 1987). Similarly, it is possible that in explaining the overall trend of life cycle happiness, the relative importance of life circumstances is greater than it is in explaining differences among persons, because life circumstances change more over the life cycle than do factors that play a sizable role in accounting for individual differences such as personality and genetic heritage.

Predicting Life Cycle Happiness from the Domain Patterns

The critical question thus becomes whether the life cycle patterns for the domain satisfaction variables taken together can actually account for the observed life cycle pattern of happiness. In fact, the four domain satisfaction variables do predict very closely the actual change in happiness over the life course (Figure 2.3). Predicted life cycle happiness at each year of age from 18 to 89 is estimated here by substituting in the regression equation in column 4 of Table 2.1 the value for each domain satisfaction variable for each year of age shown in Figure 2.2.

The close correspondence between predicted and actual life cycle happiness supports the "bottom-up" view of the determinants of happiness, and implies that the high degree of stability observed in overall happiness is due, not to rapid and complete adaptation to life events within domains, but to offsetting changes in people's satisfaction with different domains of life. The slight rise in happiness

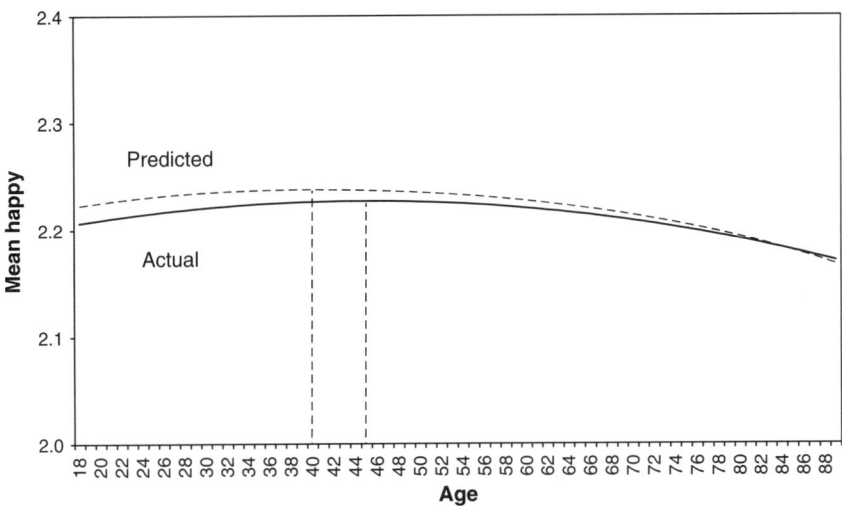

Figure 2.3. The overall trend in life cycle happiness, actual and predicted

Source: Actual, same as Figure 2.1. Predicted, Figure 2.2 values for each age entered in regression of Table 2.1, column 4.

through midlife that occurs in the population as a whole is due, on average, chiefly to growing satisfaction with family life and work, which in combination more than counteract diminishing satisfaction with health. Beyond midlife happiness decreases, because the continuing decline in satisfaction with health is joined by diminishing satisfaction with family life and work. However, these negative influences on happiness beyond midlife are offset somewhat by a progressive improvement in people's satisfaction with their financial situation.

Adaptation across domains——So far adaptation has been discussed as though it takes place within a domain through habituation to changing circumstances within that domain. A conceptual alternative is that adaptation may occur through a shift in the relative importance of domains. It is this type of adaptation that Parducci (1995, p. 161) prescribes when he speaks of "letting go" and "tuning out" unhappy domains and trying "to increase the relative frequency of what is already at the top of the contextual range".[11] This type of adaptation would imply that over the life cycle individuals might compensate for deteriorating circumstances within one domain, such as health, by decreasing the importance attached to that domain in determining happiness and increasing the importance of others.

---

[11] Parducci actually gives a mechanical illustration (1995, p.160, Fig 10.1) in terms of shifting weights. It should be noted that his discussion is not intended as a description of actual behavior, but as a suggested psychological strategy for improving well-being.

Is there evidence of across-domain adaptation? In the present analysis of the relation of domain satisfaction to happiness the relative weights of domains are kept constant over the life cycle, and thus across-domain adaptation is precluded. The fact that an analysis with constant domain weights predicts closely the actual trend in life cycle happiness suggests that across-domain adaptation is not an important adjustment mechanism in the population as a whole so far as these broad realms of life are concerned. However, as an additional check a regression of happiness on the domain satisfaction variables was run separately for young persons (ages 18–39), those in midlife (40–59), and the older population (60 +). A Chow test indicates no significant difference between any of the models estimated for the individual age groups and that for the population as a whole. Thus, the evidence suggests that the weights of the different domains do not change systematically by age, as might be expected if across-domain adaptation were occurring. Perhaps most notable is the result for the health domain. As has been seen, satisfaction with health declines throughout the life course. If people adjusted to this decline by "letting go" and "tuning out" to health, then the relative weight of the health domain should be less for older people. In fact, the coefficient on satisfaction with health for those aged 60 and over is almost exactly the same as for those aged 18 to 39 (Appendix D, cf. columns 1 and 3).

Implications for the "Pure" Effect of Age

The overall trend in life cycle happiness is predicted quite closely by life cycle changes in four domains—satisfaction with family, finances, health, and work. But where does that leave one with regard to the effect on happiness of aging itself—the "pure" effect of age? To answer this, one needs to eliminate the effect on happiness of the various changes in domain satisfaction considered here, and identify the relation of happiness to age, controlling not only for year of birth, gender, race, and education, but also satisfaction in the individual domains. Thus, one is, in effect, asking, if satisfaction were the same for young and old with regard to financial circumstances, family life, health, and work, what is the effect on the happiness of older versus younger persons of the sheer effect of aging itself?

The resulting (ordered logit) regression reveals a slight but significant positive relation of happiness to age, equivalent over the 71-year age span to an upward shift by one response category of 10 percent of the population (Figure 2.4). As in the regressions reported in Appendix C, various linear and quadratic combinations of age and cohort were tried; the best fit, on which Figure 2.4 is based, is linear for both the age and cohort variables, and is given in Appendix E.

The positive linear relation of happiness to age is consistent with Carstensen's socioemotional selectivity theory. It is counter to the economists' finding that

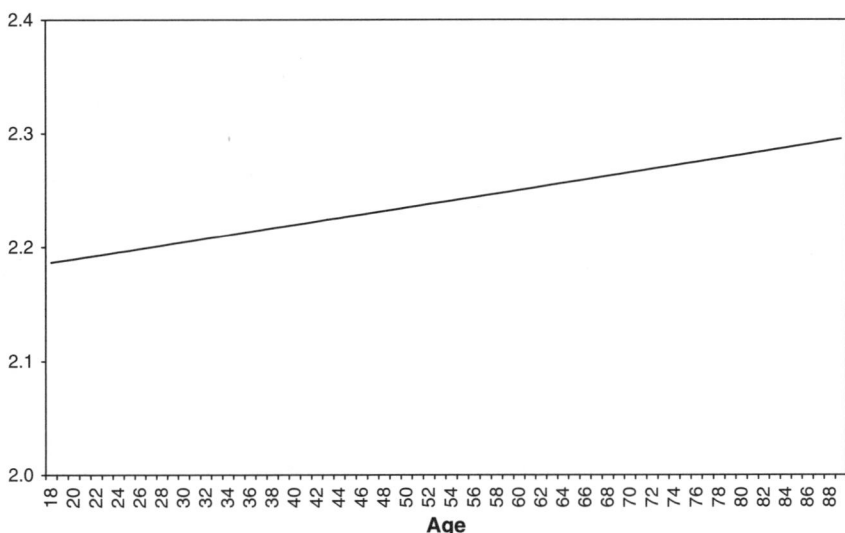

Figure 2.4. The pure effect of aging

Source: Appendix E.

the pure effect of age is U-shaped. As has been seen, however, the economists' model based on objective conditions alone provides a much less satisfactory statistical explanation of happiness than the psychologists' domain satisfaction model. The superiority of the domain model implies that it provides better controls for the factors other than age that are influencing happiness. For example, if, as has been suggested, perceptions of material needs change over the life cycle, and these changing perceptions are reflected in domain reports on satisfaction with financial life, then the domain variable captures better the circumstances affecting material well-being than does the economists' income variable. Hence, the present positive linear relation of happiness to age obtained when controlling for domain satisfaction is a better approximation to the pure effect of age than the economists' U-shaped pattern estimated by controlling for objective conditions alone.

Summary and Implications

If it is borne in mind that one is dealing here with averages for the total population and that no study can pretend to be definitive, the following tentative impressions may be pulled together from the analysis as a whole.

What We Have Learned

(1) In the population as a whole the tendency on average is for the happiness of a birth cohort to rise slightly from age 18 to age 45, and then decline mildly throughout the rest of the life course.

(2) The inverted U-shaped curvature of the overall trend in life cycle happiness is the result of various factors operating in offsetting ways. The pure effect of aging itself is to raise happiness slightly but steadily throughout the life course. The net effect of life circumstances through midlife is to reinforce slightly the pure effect of aging; thereafter, the net balance of life circumstances overrides the pure effect of aging and produces a decline in happiness with age.

(3) Life cycle changes in satisfaction within major life domains—the family, financial, work, and health realms—are in disparate directions and considerably larger in amplitude than the overall trend in life cycle happiness.

(4) If life circumstances are taken as a whole, and the pure effect of aging set aside, until people are in their forties increased satisfaction with family life and work outweigh diminished satisfaction with health and contribute, on average, to a slight rise in happiness. From midlife onward, decreasing satisfaction with family life and work join that in health in causing a decline in happiness. This negative impact is considerably offset, however, by increasing satisfaction of people with their financial situation.

(5) The overall trends in satisfaction with family life, work, and health appears to reflect the dominance, on balance, of objective changes in these domains, although some adaptation is doubtless occurring. This is consistent with economists' emphasis on the importance of objective conditions in determining well-being, but not necessarily with the strong economic model in which no adaptation occurs.

(6) The movement in people's satisfaction with their financial situation runs counter to the economists' emphasis on objective conditions, and underscores the importance in determining happiness that psychologists place on the mediating influence on well-being of perceptions, in this case, of material needs.

(7) The strong set point model in which objective life circumstances have a negligible role to play in determining life satisfaction is not supported by the evidence. The disparate directions and sizable amplitudes of the movements in satisfaction within individual domains is not consistent with the notion of rapid and complete adaptation to changing circumstances within individual domains. Nor does the evidence support the view that adaptation takes place by shifts in the emphasis accorded to individual domains, for example, that as satisfaction with health steadily lessens over the life course, people "tune out" the health domain and place more weight on other domains as sources of happiness.

(8) The bottom-up model of causation fits the evidence better than the top-down theory. On the basis of the top down approach, one might expect the individual domain life cycle patterns to parallel that of global happiness. In fact the domain patterns differ markedly from that of happiness and from each other. Moreover, the domain patterns taken together predict quite closely the overall trend in life cycle happiness.

(9) The importance of a variable in explaining individual differences in happiness is not necessarily a reliable guide to its importance in explaining the life cycle trend. Although the four domain satisfaction variables studied here account for only one-seventh of individual differences, they predict very closely the overall trend in life cycle happiness.

(10) Overall, the statistical explanation of happiness provided by the psychologists' domain variables, taken by themselves, is about twice as great as that given by the economists' purely objective conditions, again suggesting that the psychologists' conceptual framework with its emphasis on the mediating effect of perceptions is preferable to one focusing exclusively on objective conditions.

Research Needs

(1) There is need to study individual and group variability around the overall trends. For groups it is possible to make some progress with synthetic panel data of the type used here—to establish differences in overall trends between men and women, blacks and non-blacks, less and more educated persons. To follow individuals over the life cycle, however, requires true panel data, longitudinal studies of the same persons.

(2) There is need to develop models to explain life satisfaction in individual domains that encompass both objective circumstances and psychological processes. Although the results here for individual domains are suggestive with regard to adaptation, there is need to quantify the extent to which adaptation occurs. The pattern of, say, satisfaction with family life may, on average, follow roughly the course of actual life circumstances, but considerable adaptation may nevertheless occur. There is need too to clarify whether the degree of adaptation may vary by domain, for example, whether adaptation is greater for the pecuniary than nonpecuniary domains.

(3) Nothing has been said here about the psychological mechanisms underlying the empirical patterns. Does family life, for example, satisfy certain psychological needs such as relatedness or competence (Ryan and Deci 2000; cf. also Ryff 1995; Ryff and Keyes 1995)? Is the positive effect on happiness of aging itself found here due to the mechanism suggested in the theory of socioemotional selectivity (Carstensen et al. 2000)?

The fundamental importance of such questions needs hardly to be stressed.

Why Psychology and Economics Need Each Other

(1) Economics tends to generalize about group behavior; psychologists, about individuals. Both are important.
(2) Economics tends to focus on objective circumstances, psychology on subjective psychological mechanisms. Both are important.
(3) Economists tend to look only at the economics literature; psychologists, at the psychological literature. Both are important.

QUESTIONS AND RESPONSE CATEGORIES FOR HAPPINESS AND SATISFACTION VARIABLES

HAPPY: Taken all together, how would you say things are these days—would you say that you are very happy, pretty happy, or not too happy? (Coded 3, 2, 1 respectively.)

SATFIN: We are interested in how people are getting along financially these days. So far as you and your family are concerned, would you say that you are pretty well satisfied with your present financial situation, more or less satisfied, or not satisfied at all? (Coded 3, 2, 1 respectively.)

SATJOB: (Asked of persons currently working, temporarily not at work, or keeping house.) On the whole, how satisfied are you with the work you do—would you say you are very satisfied, moderately satisfied, a little dissatisfied, or very dissatisfied? (Coded from 4 down to 1.)

SATFAM: For each area of life I am going to name, tell me the number that shows how much satisfaction you get from that area.

   Your family life

1. A very great deal
2. A great deal
3. Quite a bit
4. A fair amount
5. Some
6. A little
7. None

(Reverse coded here.)

SATHEALTH: Same as SATFAM, except "Your family life" is replaced by "Your health and physical condition".

DESCRIPTIVE STATISTICS

Variable	Number of observations	Mean	Standard deviation	Minimum	Maximum
Happy	41,174	2.20	0.63	1	3
Age	41,174	45.35	17.73	18	89
Birth cohort (1890=0)	41,174	51.61	19.66	− 7	94
Male	41,174	0.44	0.50	0	1
Black	41,174	0.12	0.32	0	1
Educ ≤ 12 yrs	41,174	0.58	0.49	0	1
Satfin	29,710	2.04	0.74	1	3
Satjob	23,816	3.29	0.82	1	4
Satfam	23,189	5.91	1.36	1	7
Sathealth	23,235	5.43	1.49	1	7

HAPPINESS AND EACH DOMAIN SATISFACTION VARIABLE ON SPECIFIED INDEPENDENT VARIABLES: ORDERED LOGIT REGRESSION STATISTICS

Independent variable	Dependent variable (in parentheses, $P > \mid z \mid$)				
	Happy (1)	Satfin (2)	Satjob (3)	Satfam (4)	Sathealth (5)
Age	.008002	−.026918	.04546	.029533	−.034841
	(0.011)	(0.000)	(0.000)	(0.000)	(0.000)
Age^2	−.000090	.000375	−.000395	−.000365	.000139
	(0.002)	(0.000)	(0.000)	(0.000)	(0.028)
Cohort	−.005916	−.013026	−.025895	−.004026	.024266
	(0.0000)	(0.000)	(0.000)	(0.041)	(0.000)
$Cohort^2$	—	—	.000139	—	−.000327
	—	—	(0.031)	—	(0.000)
Male	−.057443	.050159	.030240	−.205047	.106025
	(0.003)	(0.023)	(0.234)	(0.000)	(0.000)
Black	−.673972	−.686270	−.449089	−.475853	−.263866
	(0.000)	(0.000)	(0.000)	(0.000)	(0.000)
Educ ≤ 12	−.285580	−.407715	−.221237	−.070838	−.251980
	(0.000)	(0.000)	(0.000)	(0.006)	(0.000)
Cut1	−2.45388	−2.39196	−3.14577	−3.96060	−5.00275
Cut2	.332442	−.366436	−1.81305	−3.13664	−3.91395
Cut3	—	—	.118279	−2.54034	−3.27805
Cut4	—	—	—	−1.74330	−2.17604
Cut5	—	—	—	−1.03424	−1.45935
Cut6	—	—	—	0.42733	−0.01585
N	41,174	29,710	23,816	23,189	23,235
Chi^2	805.8	1977.0	912.8	314.5	969.2
LR	−38465	−30799	−25481	−32582	−37419
Pseudo R^2	.0104	.0311	.0176	.0048	.0128

APPENDIX D

HAPPINESS ON SPECIFIED DOMAIN SATISFACTION VARIABLES BY AGE GROUP: ORDERED LOGIT REGRESSION STATISTICS

Independent variable	Age Group (for all coeffs $P > |z| = 0.000$)		
	(1) 18–39	(2) 40–59	(3) 60+
Satfam	.425	.478	.354
Satfin	.662	.560	.410
Satjob	.481	.520	.570
Sathealth	.237	.275	.238
Cut1	4.122	4.702	3.831
Cut2	7.684	8.101	6.833
N	9,644	6,250	2,550
Chi^2	2,360	1,765	567
Log likelihood	−7,689	−5,035	−2,172
Pseudo R^2	.133	.149	.115

THE PURE EFFECT OF AGE: HAPPY ON SPECIFIED INDEPENDENT VARIABLES ORDERED LOGIT REGRESSION STATISTICS

Independent variable	(1) (in paren, $P > |z|$)	Independent variable	(2) (in paren, $P > |z|$)
Age	.0055662	Satfam	.4251872
	(0.040)		(0.000)
Cohort	.0042324	Satfin	.5721769
	(0.090)		(0.000)
Male	−.1236323	Satjob	.4934133
	(0.000)		(0.000)
Black	−.5021257	Sathealth	.2558096
	(0.000)		(0.000)
Educ ≤ 12	−.1219073	Cut1	4.391715
	(0.000)	Cut2	7.838154
n	18,425		
Chi^2	4,832.6		
Log likelihood	−14,838		
Pseudo R^2	.1400		

References

Argyle, M. (1999). Causes and Correlates of Happiness. In D. Kahneman, E. Diener & N. Schwarz (Eds.). *Well-Being: The Foundations of Hedonic Psychology* (pp. 353–73). New York: Russell Sage.

—— (2001). *The Psychology of Happiness*. 2nd edn. New York: Routledge.

Blanchflower, G. & Oswald, A. (2004). Well-Being Over Time in Britain and the USA. *Journal of Public Economics*, 88, 1359–86.

Brickman, P. & Campbell, D.T. (1971). Hedonic Relativism and Planning the Good Society. In M.H. Appley (Ed.). *Adaptation Level Theory: A Symposium* (pp. 287–302). New York: Academic Press.

Campbell, A. (1972). Aspiration, Satisfaction, and Fulfillment. In A. Campbell & P. E. Converse (Eds.). *The Human Meaning of Social Change* (pp. 441–66). New York: Russell Sage Foundation.

—— (1981). *The Sense of Well-Being in America*. New York: McGraw-Hill.

—— Converse, P.E. & Rodgers, W.L. (1976). *The Quality of American Life*. New York: Russell Sage Foundation.

Cantril, H. (1965). *The Pattern of Human Concerns*. New Brunswick, N.J.: Rutgers University Press.

Carstensen, L.L., Pasupathi, M., Mayr, U. & Nesselroade, J.R. (2000). Emotional Experience in Everyday Life Across the Adult Life Span. *Journal of Personality and Social Psychology*, 79(4), 644–55.

Costa, P.T. Jr., Zonderman, A.B., McCrae, R.R., Cornoni-Huntley, J., Locke, B.Z. & Barbano, H E. (1987). Longitudinal Analyses of Psychological Well-Being in a National Sample: Stability of Mean Levels. *Journal of Gerontology*, 42, 50–5.

Csikszentmihalyi, M. & Hunter, J. (2003). Happiness in Everyday Life: The Uses of Experience Sampling. *Journal of Happiness Studies*, 4, 185–99.

Cummins, R.A. (1996). The Domains of Life Satisfaction: An Attempt to Order Chaos. *Social Indicators Research*, 38, 303–28.

Davis, J.A. & Smith, T.W. (2002). General Social Surveys, 1972–2002. University of Connecticut, Storrs: The Roper Center for Public Opinion Research. [Machine-readable data file] Principal Investigator, James A. Davis; Director and Co-Principal Investigator, Tom W. Smith; Co-Principal Investigator, Peter Marsden, NORC ed. Chicago: National Opinion Research Center, producer. Storrs, CT: The Roper Center for Public Opinion Research, University of Connecticut, distributor. 1 data file (43,698 logical records and 1 codebook (1,769 pp)).

Delbes, C. & Gaymu, J. (2002). The Shock of Widowhood on the Eve of Old Age: Male and Female Experiences. *Population-E*, 57, 885–914.

Diener, E. (1984). Subjective Well-Being. *Psychological Bulletin*, 95, 542–75.

—— (1996). Traits Can Be Powerful, but Are Not Enough: Lessons from Subjective Well-Being. *Journal of Research in Personality*, 30, 389–99.

—— & Seligman, M.E.P. (2004). Beyond Money: Toward an Economy of Well-Being. *Psychological Science in the Public Interest*, 5(1), 1–31.

—— Suh, E.M., Lucas, R.E. & Smith, H.L. (1999). Subjective Well-Being: Three Decades of Progress. *Psychological Bulletin*, 125, 302–76.

Duesenberry, J.S. (1949), *Income, Savings, and the Theory of Consumer Behavior*. Cambridge, Mass.: Harvard University Press.

Easterlin, R.A. (1987). *Birth and Fortune: The Impact of Numbers on Personal Welfare*, 2nd edn. Chicago: University of Chicago Press.

—— (1995). Will Raising the Incomes of All Increase the Happiness of All? *Journal of Economic Behavior and Organization*, 27, 1–34.

—— (2001a). Income and Happiness: Towards a Unified Theory. *The Economic Journal*, 111:473, 465–84.

—— (2001b). Life Cycle Welfare: Trends and Differences. *Journal of Happiness Studies*, 2, 1–12.

—— (2003a). Happiness of Men and Women in Later Life: Nature, Determinants, and Prospects. In M. J. Sirgy, D. Rahtz & A.Coskin Samli (Eds.). *Advances in Quality-of-Life Theory and Research* (pp. 13–26). Dordrecht, The Netherlands: Kluwer Academic Publishers.

—— (2003b). Explaining Happiness. *Proceedings of the National Academy of Sciences*, 100 (19), 11176–83.

—— & Schaeffer, C.M. (1999). Income and Subjective Well-Being over the Life Cycle. In C.D. Ryff & V.W. Marshall (Eds.). *The Self and Society in Aging Processes* (pp. 279–302). New York: Springer.

Frey, B.S. & Stutzer, A. (2002a). *Happiness and Economics*. Princeton: Princeton University Press.

—— —— (2002b). What Can Economists Learn from Happiness Research? *Journal of Economic Literature*, XL, 402–35.

Fujita, F. & Diener, E. (2005). Life Satisfaction Setpoint: Stability and Change. *Journal of Personality and Social Psychology*, 88(1), 158–64.

Gertner, J. (2003). The Futile Pursuit of Happiness. *New York Times Magazine*, September 7, 45ff.

Headey, B., Holmström, E. & Wearing, A. (1984). The Impact of Life Events and Changes in Domain Satisfaction on Well-being. *Social Indicators Research*, 15, 203–27.

—— Veenhoven, R. & Wearing, A. (1991). Top-down versus Bottom-up Theories of Subjective Well-being. *Social Indicators Research*, 24, 81–100.

—— & Wearing, A. (1989). Personality, Life Events, and Subjective Well-being: Toward a Dynamic Equilibrium Model. *Journal of Personality and Social Psychology*, 57, 731–9.

Herzog, A.R., Rodgers, W.L. & Woodworth, J. (1982). *Subjective Well-being among Different Age Groups*. Ann Arbor, Michigan: The University of Michigan, Institute for Social Research.

Idler, E.L. & Benyamini, Y. (1997). Self-Rated Health and Mortality: A Review of Twenty-Seven Community Studies. *Journal of Health and Social Behavior*, 38(1), 21–37.

Kahneman, D. (1999). Objective Happiness. In D. Kahneman, E. Diener & N. Schwarz (Eds.). *Well-Being: The Foundations of Hedonic Psychology* (pp. 3–27). New York: Russell Sage.

—— Krueger, A.B., Schkade, D.A., Schwarz, N. & Stone, A.A. (2004). A Survey Method for Characterizing Daily Life Experience: The Day Reconstruction Method (DRM). *Science*, 306, 1776–80.

Kammann, R. (1983). Objective Circumstances, Life Satisfactions, and Sense of Well-being: Consistencies across Time and Place. *New Zealand Journal of Psychology*. 12, 14–22.

Layard, R. (2005). *Happiness: Lessons from a New Science*. New York: Penguin Press.

Lucas, R.E., Clark, A.E., Georgellis, Y. & Diener, E. (2003). Reexamining Adaptation and the Set Point Model of Happiness: Reactions to Changes in Marital Status. *Journal of Personality and Social Psychology*, 84, 527–39.

—— —— —— —— (2004). Unemployment Alters the Set Point for Life Satisfaction. *Psychological Science*, 15(1), 8–13.

Lykken, D. & Tellegen, A. (1996). Happiness Is a Stochastic Phenomenon. *Psychological Science*, 7, 186–9.

Lyubomirsky, S. (2001). Why Are Some People Happier than Others? The Role of Cognitive and Motivational Processes on Well-Being. *American Psychologist*, 56(3), 239–49.

Mehnert, T., Krauss, H.H., Nadler, R. & Boyd, M. (1990). Correlates of Life Satisfaction in Those with Disabling Conditions. *Rehabilitation Psychology*, 35, 3–17.

Michalos, A.C. (1986). Job Satisfaction, Marital Satisfaction and the Quality of Life. In F.M. Andrews (Ed.), *Research on the Quality of Life* (pp. 57–83). University of Michigan, Ann Arbor: Survey Research Center, Institute for Social Research.

—— (1991). *Global Report on Student Well-Being: Vol. I: Life Satisfactions and Happiness*. New York: Springer-Verlag.

Modigliani, F. (1949). Fluctuations in the Savings–Income Ratio: A Problem in Economic Forecasting. In Conference on Research in Income and Wealth, *Studies in Income and Wealth, XI*. New York: National Bureau of Economic Research, 371–443.

Mroczek, D.K. & Kolarz, C.M. (1998). The Effect of Age on Positive and Negative Affect: A Developmental Perspective on Happiness. *Journal of Personality and Social Psychology*, 75, 1333–49.

—— & Spiro, A., III (2005). Changes in Life Satisfaction during Adulthood: Findings from the Veterans Affairs Normative Aging Study. *Journal of Personality and Social Psychology*, 88(1), 189–202.

Myers D.G. (1992). *The Pursuit of Happiness*. New York: Avon.

—— (2000). The Funds, Friends, and Faith of Happy People. *American Psychologist*, 55(1), 56–67.

Parducci, A. (1995). *Happiness, Pleasure, and Judgment: The Contextual Theory and Its Applications*. Mahwah, NJ: Erlbaum.

Pollak, R.A. (1970). Habit Formation and Dynamic Demand Functions. *Journal of Political Economy*, 78:4, 745–63.

—— (1976). Interdependent Preferences. *American Economic Review*, 66:3, 309–20.

Praag, B.M.S. van & Ferrer-i-Carbonell, A. (2004). *Happiness Quantified: A Satisfaction Calculus Approach* (chapter 3). Oxford: Oxford University Press.

—— & Frijters, P. (1999). The Measurement of Welfare and Well-Being: The Leyden Approach. In D. Kahneman, E. Diener & N. Schwarz (Eds.). *Well-Being: The Foundations of Hedonic Psychology* (pp. 413–33). New York: Russell Sage.

—— —— & Ferrer-i-Carbonell, A. (2003). The Anatomy of Subjective Well-Being. *Journal of Economic Behavior and Organization*, 51, 29–49.

Reynolds, S.L., Crimmins, E.M. & Saito, Y. (1998). Cohort Differences in Disability and Disease. *The Gerontologist*, 38, 576–90.

Robinson, J.P. & Godbey, G. (1997). *Time for Life: The Surprising Ways Americans Use their Time*, 2nd edn. University Park, PA: Pennsylvania State University Press.

Rojas, M. (2005). The Complexity of Well-Being: A Life Satisfaction Conception and Domains-of-Life Approach. In I. Gough & A. McGregor (Eds.). *Researching Well-Being in Developing Countries*. New York: Cambridge University Press.

Ryan, R.M. & Deci, E.L. (2000). Self-Determination Theory and the Facilitation of Intrinsic Motivation, Social Development, and Well-Being. *American Psychologist*, 55(1), 68–78.

Ryff, C.D. (1995). Psychological Well-being in Adult Life. *Current Directions in Psychological Science*, 4, 99–104.

—— & Keyes, C.L. (1995). The Structure of Psychological Well-being Revisited. *Journal of Personality and Social Psychology*, 69, 719–27.

Salvatore, N. & Muñoz Sastre, M.T. (2001). Appraisal of Life: "Area" Versus "Dimension" Conceptualizations. *Social Indicators Research*, 53, 229–55.

Saris, W.E., Veenhoven, R., Scherpenzeel, A.C., Bunting, B. (Eds.)(1995). *A Comparative Study of Satisfaction with Life in Europe*. Budapest: Eötvös University Press.

Seligman, M.E.P. (2002). *Authentic Happiness: Using the New Positive Psychology to Realize Your Potential for Lasting Fulfillment*. New York: Free Press.

Smith, V.K., Taylor, D.H. Jr. & Sloan, F.A. (2001). Longevity Expectations and Death: Can People Predict Their Own Demise? *American Economic Review*, 91(4), 1126–34.

Solberg, E.C., Diener, E., Wirtz, D., Lucas, R.E. & Oishi, S. (2002). Wanting, Having, and Satisfaction: Examining the Role of Desire Discrepancies in Satisfaction with Income. *Journal of Personality and Social Psychology*, 83, 725–34.

Stutzer, A. (2003). The Role of Income Aspirations in Individual Happiness. *Journal of Economic Behavior and Organization*, 54, 89–109.

Time (2005). The Science of Happiness, 165 (3, January 17), A1–A68.

Waite, L.J. (1995). Does Marriage Matter? *Demography*, 32, 483–507.

3

In Defense of Happiness: Why Policymakers Should Care about Subjective Well-Being

Pelin Kesebir and Ed Diener

James Madison, the statesman regarded as the father of the United States Constitution, writes in Federalist 51 that a good government implies two things: first, fidelity to the object of government, which is the happiness of the people; and second, a knowledge of the means by which that object can be attained. For a long time, policymakers have assumed that continuous economic progress embodies the primary means by which that object could be attained, which in turn, led economic indicators such as GDP and its various proxies to acquire immense stature. It is a fairly recent development that voices have been raised against the almost total emphasis placed on economic outcomes, and alternative methods to define and measure human welfare have been proposed.

We share with the capabilities approach, as well as with similar alternative paradigms, the conviction that there is more to progress than economic growth, and that economic indices alone are not sufficient in guiding welfare policies. It is difficult, if not outright impossible, to gauge progression towards "the good life" for any individual or towards a desirable society solely by employing the prevailing economic and social indicators of the day. Our aim in this chapter is to demonstrate the merit of using subjective well-being as an additional measure that should inform public policy, and the possibility of doing so without compromising on scientific validity and reliability issues. We will start with a critique of the indicators currently favored by policymakers, and then proceed to an elaboration on what is meant by "subjective well-being." A discussion on why subjective well-being measures should be incorporated into policymaking processes will be followed by evidence supporting the scientific adequacy of such measures.

Limitations of the Prevalent Economic and Social Indicators

Economic Indicators

The unchallenged reign of economic indicators in current policymaking may obscure one important point, namely that economic performance is not interesting or valuable in itself, but only as an instrument in the service of human welfare. As Oswald (1997) succinctly observed, "The relevance of economic performance is that it may be a means to an end. That end is not the consumption of beefburgers, nor the accumulation of television sets, nor the vanquishing of some high level of interest rates, but rather the enrichment of mankind's feeling of well-being. Economic things matter only in so far as they make people happier" (p. 1815).

Indeed, if the ultimate aspiration of all policymaking is—or should be—the advancement of human well-being, economic indicators certainly fall short of tracing the extent to which this end is being served by economic activity. Increased material wealth, as captured by GDP for instance, does not necessarily lead to increased happiness and life fulfillment. Below we list the main reasons why we believe economic well-being cannot automatically be equated with human well-being, just as it cannot be equated with societal well-being.

RISING NATIONAL INCOME DOES NOT INVARIABLY INCREASE LIFE SATISFACTION

The fact that economic indicators have traditionally been singled out in guiding and assessing policymaking can be at least partly explained by the assumption that they are a good approximation to well-being on the individual and societal levels. Such an assumption was probably more accurate in the late eighteenth century, when economic hardship and poverty were much more widespread and the modern academic field of economics was first conceived. However, in today's world, and particularly for developed countries, it simply is not true that money is a good proxy of happiness, and that increased affluence will automatically translate into increased subjective well-being.

Studies reveal a sizeable correlation (around .60) between average well-being and average per capita income across nations (Diener & Biswas-Diener, 2002), which still evidently leaves substantial unaccounted variance. The fact that people in Mexico and Venezuela report significantly higher average happiness levels compared to people in the United States or Japan (Inglehart et al., 2004) attests to the ambiguous nature of the role of affluence on well-being.

A more striking illustration of this imperfect relationship has been called the "progress paradox" (Easterbrook, 2003), and it refers to the finding that enormous increases in affluence across developed nations in recent decades have not been accompanied by any substantial increases in well-being in these nations (Diener et al., 2002; Oswald, 1997; Myers, 2000). In Japan for example, income per capita between the years 1958 and 1991 rose by a factor of six, yet in 1991 the average life satisfaction was exactly what it was in 1958, 2.7 on a four-point scale. This curious state of affairs is not unique to Japan, but is comparable to what happened in the United States and in many European nations over the same period of time (Frey & Stutzer, 2002a). In an article entitled "If we are so rich, why aren't we happy?" Csikszentmihalyi (1999) sums up the problem concisely:

> Inhabitants of the wealthiest industrialized Western nations are living in a period of unprecedented riches, in conditions that previous generations would have considered luxuriously comfortable, in relative peace and security, and they are living on the average close to twice as long as their great-grandparents did. Yet, despite all these improvements in material conditions, it does not seem that people are so much more satisfied with their lives than they were before. (p. 822)

Scholars have advanced various explanations for the Easterlin paradox, one of which is that people swiftly adapt to existing comforts and by engaging in temporal and interpersonal comparisons, set ever-higher aspirations for themselves. According to this account, happiness is a function of the gap between aspirations and achievements, and thus, the pleasure obtained by additional material goods and services is transitory. Another hypothesis has been that the current capitalist system and the accompanying monopoly of materialistic values has brought about an erosion of social capital, a point to which we will return later.

INCOME HAS DIMINISHING RETURNS ON LIFE SATISFACTION

Research demonstrates that the effects of income on happiness are not only small, but also diminishing. Frey and Stutzer (2002b) have established that across nations, increasing wealth above US$10,000 per capita income has diminishing returns. In other words, increased income contributes significantly to happiness at low levels of development, yet once the threshold of around US$10,000 has been passed, there is not a strong association between wealth and satisfaction with life. This relation holds both at the national and individual levels. In line with this, Diener, Horowitz, and Emmons (1985) reported that very wealthy people, selected from the *Forbes* list of the wealthiest Americans, were only modestly happier than a control group, and that 37 percent of the wealthiest Americans queried in the study were less happy than the average American.

STANDARD MEASUREMENTS OF ECONOMIC ACTIVITY
DO NOT CAPTURE HUMAN WELFARE

British critic John Ruskin wrote in the nineteenth century that not everything that an economy produces contributes to welfare, and, coining a neologism, he referred to this kind of wealth, which perhaps puts more money in circulation or creates new jobs, yet does not increase well-being, as "illth" (Cobb, Halstead & Rowe, 1995). Ruskin believed that conventional economic indicators lumped wealth and illth together and his analysis is as valid today as it was then. An economy that has an escalating GDP is promoted as an unmitigated good towards which all nations should strive. Yet, blindly and unreservedly aiming at economic progress without an understanding of its implications for the nation at large is "growth for the sake of growth," which has been likened to "the ideology of the cancer cell" (Abbey, 1988, p. 15).

GDP as the chief gauge of economic success and the main criterion to inform expert opinion is especially problematic in light of its obvious limits. GDP is a gross measure of market activity (i.e. production and consumption) that can only keep track of monetized exchange, and is only concerned with quantity, and not quality. It does not make any distinction between desirable and undesirable kinds of economic activity, or between "wealth and illth". Cobb, Halstead, & Rowe (1995) refer to the perverse logic of the cult of the GDP when they say that "It treats everything that happens in the market as a gain for humanity, while ignoring everything that happens outside the realm of monetized exchange, regardless of the importance of well-being" (p. 53). Again, in their apt language "by the curious standard of the GDP, the nation's economic hero is a terminal cancer patient who is going through a costly divorce," and "the happiest event is an earthquake or a hurricane" (p. 65). Similarly, the whole private security industry (e.g. home security systems for robbery prevention, car alarms) thrives on the prevalence of crime in a society, which doubtlessly does not increase social well-being; yet, an expanding security industry still raises the GDP.

As mentioned, GDP can only reckon with monetary transactions, meaning that anything that individuals provide each other for free has to be excluded. Care for children and the elderly, homework, and voluntary service for the community are only some examples of activities that are ignored by the GDP, even though they contribute significantly to individual well-being and social coherence. GDP does not account for family time or leisure time either, just as it does not discount for environmental pollution, depletion of nonrenewable natural resources, and other adverse effects of economic activity.

GDP and the other regnant economic indicators unquestionably have their strengths, nonetheless, they oftentimes prove incapable of fully capturing individual and aggregate well-being. Another case in point is the finding that people who work fewer hours have higher life satisfaction (Alesina, Glaeser, & Sacerdote, 2006). Higher levels of output due to longer hours of work increase GDP while apparently lowering life satisfaction. This is a finding of great significance; however, no economic indicator can address a question about life satisfaction, and—partly because of that—such questions are completely omitted from political discussions and the lawmakers' agenda.

MATERIALISM CAN BE TOXIC

Economic progress and affluence are the primary focus of policymakers today, and perhaps most disconcerting is the fact that such an overemphasis on materialism can be detrimental to well-being. Indeed, several investigators have documented that the more importance people place on money and on material possessions, the less satisfied are they with their lives and the more they act in ways that damage the social fabric (Kasser & Kanner, 2004). Materialistic values appear to be associated with pervasive problems in personal well-being, among which are depression, anxiety, narcissism, substance abuse, less positive affect, and more negative affect. Perkins (1991) demonstrated, for instance, that individuals who prefer wealth, professional success, and prestige over intimacy in marriage and with friends report being fairly or very unhappy twice as often as others who don't hold such preferences. People who believe that it is important to strive for possessions also report worse physiological health, such as more headaches, backaches, and sore muscles. The undermining effects of being disproportionately invested in materialistic pursuits are observed in children as well as elderly people, in poor as well as wealthy samples, and in a variety of cultures, including in Britain, Romania, Russia, India, and South Korea (Kasser, 2006).

Resonant, as well as alarming, are studies showing that the affluent youth, a population typically regarded as psychologically low risk, is experiencing adjustment problems, in the form of depression, anxiety, and substance abuse (Luthar, 2003). In a longitudinal study in which they followed more than 800 American adolescents through high school and beyond, Csikszentmihalyi and Schneider (2000) found a slight inverse correlation between socioeconomic status and psychological well-being, with youth from affluent suburbs manifesting lower average happiness and self-esteem levels than those in lower socio-economic status groups. These findings have been attributed by scholars to an overemphasis on achievement and to an isolation from one's parents.

It can be costly on many levels when materialistic wants become predominant over other goals, such as close interpersonal relations, personal growth, or betterment of one's community. Csikszentmihalyi (1999) has argued that "to the extent that most of one's psychic energy becomes invested in material goals, it is typical for sensitivity to other rewards to atrophy. Friendships, art, literature, natural beauty, religion and philosophy become less and less interesting" (p. 823). Relatedly, Robert Putnam in his influential book *Bowling Alone* (2000) reasons that in today's economy individuals rely heavily on the use of market-based services, which until a recent time were provided by their family and community. This leads to a decline in civic engagement outside the marketplace, to diminished levels of interpersonal trust and connectedness, and to an erosion of social capital, which have all empirically been related to low levels of well-being.

Our brief review suggests that economic progress cannot always be equated with individual and societal well-being, and economic indicators by themselves fall short of telling the whole story. A policymaking system that places the highest emphasis on economic outcomes may unintentionally lead to a less than optimal level of societal happiness.

Social Indicators

The growing awareness of the limitations of economic indicators has generated an interest in looking into social indicators by policymakers in the last few decades. Social indicators attempt to estimate the quality of life in a given cultural or geographic unit by considering the quality in various societal domains such as health, education, environment, and human rights. Infant mortality, life expectancy, crime, and literacy rates are examples of the most common social indicators in use today. That such indicators rely on objective, measurable statistics renders them convenient and sometimes methodologically reliable.

One potential objection to social indicators is that wealth accounts for such colossal variance in them that they may just be redundant (Diener & Suh, 1997). Diener and Diener (1995) report, for example, that in a survey across 101 countries, wealth of nations correlates .82 with number of books published per capita, .73 with income equality within nations, and .70 with the percentage of the population attending universities. Similarly, the composite Advanced Quality of Life Index of Diener, which consists of variables such as physicians per capita, income equality, and environmental treaties signed, correlates an astounding .91 ($p<0.001$) with per capita purchasing power of nations (Diener & Suh, 1997). Nevertheless, the same studies that reveal such strong correlations also reveal that social and economic indicators are not identical, and that there is more to quality of life than simply living in a wealthy country. Two nations can be similar in purchasing power and one can still enjoy a higher quality of life, as Spain does vis-à-vis Mauritius; or two nations can report similar quality of life levels, when one nation is significantly more affluent than the other, as is the case with Israel vis-à-vis Tunisia (Diener & Suh, 1997). Social indicators provide policymakers with a myriad of consequential information beyond what is captured by economic indicators and it would doubtlessly be misguided and foolish to dismiss them as useless.

A more serious limitation of social indicators is their potential failure to live up to the claims of objectivity and infallibility put forth by their proponents. Social indicators are not immune to measurement problems. For instance, we know that rape is one of the most underreported crimes and that this may compromise the usefulness of rape statistics, especially when this underreporting occurs systematically more frequently in certain kinds of societies and in certain groups. Similarly, in nations where a sizable portion of births occurs at home, it is difficult to determine actual infant mortality rates.

65

Another obvious problem with social indicators is that subjective judgments unavoidably affect the process of selecting, measuring, and interpreting social indicator variables. Diener and Suh (1997) give the example of the index of deforestation, and discuss how the index is dependent on idiosyncratic decisions about what kinds of cutting of trees and what kinds of planting of trees are counted.

Even if variables are measured as objectively and accurately as possible, there still looms large the question of what level of a social indicator embodies the most desirable state for a society. Should the government invest its limited resources in increasing longevity, even if this means that the elderly will spend their final years in a condition of severe mental and/or physical incapacitation? If infant mortality can only be reduced with enormous medical expense and if the infants saved are likely to be handicapped or retarded, is this a desirable policy goal? Such questions inevitably call for value judgments and cast doubt on the complete objectivity of social indicators.

And finally, the critical problem we observe with social indicators is their inadequacy in reflecting people's experiences of well-being. As we will elaborate later, correlations between objective life circumstances and individuals' reported levels of subjective well-being are only modest. Schneider (1976) was one of the earliest critics of this aspect of social indicators, and he demonstrated that objective social conditions of cities show no relation to the subjective life quality of their citizens. It seems clear that the complex and multiply determined nature of subjective well-being cannot be adequately gauged by aggregated social indicators, and that additional measures are necessary.

We are aware that, despite their limitations, social indicators convey information beyond that which is contained in economic measures, and constitute a valuable source in guiding policymakers. Yet we also believe that relying exclusively on a combination of economic and social indicators would still fall short of informing policymaking processes in an optimum way. Both economic and social indicators are only inexact approximations of the welfare of a society and the well-being of its citizens. Now we will turn our attention to the concept of subjective well-being and endeavor to substantiate our claim that subjective well-being indicators should be granted a place on a par with economic and social indicators.

Defining Subjective Well-Being

The term "subjective well-being" (SWB) refers to people's evaluations of their lives, and comprises both cognitive judgments of satisfaction and affective appraisals of moods and emotions. It would be accurate to conceptualize subjective well-being as an umbrella term, consisting of a number of interrelated yet separable components, such as life satisfaction (global judgments of one's life), satisfaction with important life domains (e.g. marriage or work satisfaction), positive affect (prevalence of positive emotions and moods), and low levels of negative affect (prevalence of unpleasant emotions and moods).

One point that bears emphasis is that subjective well-being is not an expression of frivolous hedonism or a ceaseless state of empty-headed merriness. Rather, a sense of satisfaction with one's life and positive affective experiences emanate primarily from the context of one's goals and values. What decades of research reveal is that individuals are most likely to experience high levels of subjective well-being when they strive for and make progress towards personal goals derived from their cherished values. Feelings of meaning, purpose, and fulfillment as well as a sense of self-efficacy are thus necessary ingredients of subjective well-being. In other words, for most people happiness is not only feeling good, but feeling good for the right reasons. As a demonstration of this, when asked whether they would be willing to have their brains put in a jar and hooked up to electrodes which would make them super-happy for the rest of their lives, an overwhelming majority of people say that this mode of existence does not appeal to them.

The things that make a movie great and timeless are not only the many enjoyable moments or the continuing fascination it offers, but also a strong overall meaning and the deep associations it presents. We believe that, just like a great movie, consummate happiness is much more than the sum of many pleasurable moments. Thus, having meaning and purpose in one's life, and acting in ways that benefit not only the individual but also the society and the world are integral parts of our definition of happiness.

Another point we wish to emphasize is the increasingly accepted view that people do not adapt to everything, much less to dire life conditions. Ever since Brickman and Campbell (1971) introduced the theory of the "hedonic treadmill," namely that our emotional systems adjust to just about anything that happens in our lives, good or bad, just as our noses quickly adapt to any kind of scent, it has been accepted almost as a truism and has even been called the "first principle" of happiness research (Myers, 1992). Closely affiliated with the hedonic treadmill model is the set point theory, according to which major life events, such as debilitating disease, birth of a child, or death of a partner, affect a person's happiness only temporarily, after which the person's happiness level reverts to a default determined by personality and genetic traits.

The implications of the "hedonic treadmill" and "set point" assertions for public policy are dispiriting at best and dangerous at worst. Taken literally, they indicate that objective life conditions have no bearing on one's subjective well-being, and that, at the end of the day, all individual and societal endeavors to increase happiness will prove to be hopeless and ineffectual. Indeed, some scholars have concluded that trying to be happier may be "as futile as trying to be taller and is therefore counterproductive" (Lykken & Tellegen, 1996, p. 189).

Studies, however, fail to support such drastic inferences, and accumulating evidence reveals the need to revise the hedonic adaptation theories of well-being (Diener, Lucas, & Scollon, 2006; Easterlin, 2005). A problem with such theories is that objective life circumstances do matter, as exhibited by national differences in well-being. If people automatically and inevitably adapted to just about anything that life put in their way, we would anticipate that differences in objective life conditions across nations would not lead to significant differences in national well-being levels. However, this does not seem to be the case. Survey data convincingly demonstrate that factors such as wealth, human rights, and societal equality do a good job of predicting average national well-being levels (Diener, Diener, & Diener, 1995).

Data from longitudinal studies dovetail with cross-sectional studies in showing that people do not show quick and/or complete adaptation to everything, and that long-term levels of happiness can change substantially. Fujita and Diener (2005) have observed in a large and nationally representative German sample that, over a seventeen-year period, average life satisfaction in the first five years correlated only .51 with average life satisfaction during the last five years and that almost 9 percent of the sample changed an average of 3 or more points on a 10-point scale from the first five to the last five years of the study. In a similar vein, Lucas et al. (2004) have demonstrated, in a longitudinal study, that individuals who experienced unemployment in the past, on average, did not fully recover and return to their initial life satisfaction levels, even after they found new employment.

Finally, findings from intervention studies corroborate the notion that people are not stuck with a happiness set point determined by their temperament. On the contrary, since Fordyce (1977) published one of the first and most comprehensive studies on increasing happiness, researchers have reported various intervention methods that succeed in elevating individuals' happiness level for extended periods of time (Lichter, Haye, & Kammann, 1980; King, 2001; Sheldon et al., 2002; Lyubomirsky, Sheldon, & Schkade, 2005). Emmons and McCullough (2003), for example, provided evidence that inducing feelings of gratitude about their lives leads participants to report higher life-satisfaction, increased positive affect, and decreased negative affect. Furthermore, these positive changes in well-being were also confirmed by the participants' romantic partners. Likewise, Seligman et al., (2005) recently demonstrated in a random-assignment, placebo-controlled Internet study, that simple happiness-building exercises, such as writing about three good things that happened each day and why they happened, increased happiness and decreased depressive symptoms up to six months later.

It follows from this body of findings that the endeavors to make people lastingly happier are not doomed to failure. If the fatalistic outlook encouraged by treadmill and set point theories has been a reason for policymakers to neglect happiness as an important policy goal in the past, we wish to make it clear that such an excuse is of little merit.

Defending Subjective Well-Being

Having delineated the problems with today's reigning economic and social indicators, and having established the meaning and basic features of subjective well-being, let us now proceed with a reasoned justification of our conviction that subjective well-being deserves the particular attention of policymakers.

Subjective Well-Being Is Important

The consummate significance of well-being in one's life and the central place it occupies in human strivings was elegantly expressed more than two millennia ago by Aristotle when he stated that "happiness is the meaning and purpose of life, the whole aim and end of human existence." Indeed, surveys conducted in forty-one nations echo Aristotle's words today by revealing that almost all people rate happiness as very important or extremely important. Similarly, King and Napa (1998) reported that Americans see happiness as more relevant to the judgment of a good life than wealth, moral goodness, and the likelihood of going to heaven. In the words of Goodwin Watson, one of the earliest happiness researchers, "no quest can claim a larger following than happiness" (1930, p. 79).

It is difficult to behold as desirable a life devoid of happiness, just as it is difficult to imagine a good society in which people are all unhappy and dissatisfied. This means that subjective well-being is one of the *sine qua nons* of a good society. This does not necessarily dictate that happiness in and of itself would be sufficient to produce such a society, yet it renders it imperative that policymakers regard happiness as an indispensable policy concern.

Subjective Well-Being Is Democratic

A most attractive feature of subjective well-being is that it captures individuals' own internal appreciation of well-being. Rather than depending on what policymakers, philosophers, or other elites deem important, SWB considers people to be the most reliable experts on the topic of their own happiness, and inquires about whether their life is going well, according to the standards they themselves have set for their lives. If life is experienced subjectively, it is only natural to ask people to evaluate their lives subjectively. This quality of directness renders well-being measures the most democratic ones among various economic and social indicators, and makes them resonate with some of the most cherished ideals in democracies, such as democratic participation and giving a voice to the people.

Subjective Well-Being Has Indisputable Benefits

A crucial discovery of happiness research in the last few years has been that happiness is not just an epiphenomenon, but plays a causal role in bringing about various benefits. In other words, subjective well-being is important not only because it feels good and people value it above anything else, but also because it is associated with a plethora of positive outcomes on individual, organizational, and societal levels. Better social relationships, higher income, more frequent organizational citizenship behaviors, and better health are only a few illustrative examples of these outcomes.

Barbara Fredrickson's influential work on the benefits of positive emotions and her "broaden-and-build theory" provide us with a convincing explanation of this phenomenon. According to Fredrickson (1998, 2001), positive emotions are not only symptomatic of flourishing, but they also produce flourishing, by allowing individuals to broaden their thought–action repertoires and building their intellectual, psychological, social, and physical resources over time. Whereas negative emotions, such as fear, anxiety, or anger, appropriately narrow the array of thoughts and actions that occur to a person's mind, and make the individual focus on the immediate threat or problem, positive emotions and general well-being engender an urge to explore the environment and approach new goals, thereby building enduring personal resources.

In this section we will summarize the accumulated evidence supporting the broaden-and-build theory and demonstrate that happiness not only correlates with success in various life domains, but it also precedes and causes it. For the most authoritative review of this literature to date, we refer the reader to Lyubomirsky, King, and Diener (2005).

ACHIEVEMENT AND WELL-BEING

Marcel Proust, French writer and one of the great romanticizers of unhappiness in literary history, expressed a fairly popular opinion when he wrote in *Remembrance of Things Past* that happiness is salutary to the body, yet it is unhappiness that develops the forces of the mind. Whereas Proust seems to have got it right in terms of the salutary effects of happiness on the body (see the section on *Health and Well-Being*), current research fails to substantiate the second part of this claim and, in fact, indicates that it is not unhappiness but rather happiness that leads to the development and better use of intellectual skills and resources.

In a test of this "sadder-but-wiser vs. happier-and-smarter" hypothesis, Staw and Barsade (1993) assessed the positive affect levels of first-year MBA students and made them complete a battery of diverse manager assessment tasks. Positive affect in their study was described as "being cheerful, enthusiastic, optimistic, accentuates the positive, versus pessimistic, discouraged, and emphasizes the negative" (p. 311). Their results revealed that positive affect significantly predicted decision-making accuracy, mastery of information, leadership, and ratings of managerial performance, after controlling for the effects of graduate management admission test (GMAT), age, gender, and years of experience. These findings are further supported by data showing that individuals experimentally put in a pleasant mood outperform others in a variety of tasks such as efficient decision-making (Forgas, 1989), clerical error-checking (Jundt & Hinsz, 2001), or anagram solving (Erez & Isen, 2002), and they also persist longer at tasks that require perseverance (Kavanagh, 1987). Beyond its positive effect on performance in complex mental tasks, positive affect, which is the hallmark of happiness, has also been found to heighten creativity. Induced happy mood seems to prompt more original and flexible thinking in laboratory studies (Isen, 1993), and field studies concur with this conclusion (e.g. Staw, Sutton & Pelled, 1994). Positive affect has also been shown to make people more active, energetic, and lively (Diener & Fujita, 1995).

It is perhaps not surprising in light of the evidence we just reviewed, but nevertheless interesting and significant, that studies show that happy individuals have a higher chance of succeeding in work life. Specifically, they are more likely to graduate from college, more likely to secure a job, more likely to receive favorable evaluations from their supervisors, more likely to find their job more meaningful, less likely to lose their job, quicker to be re-employed if they do, more likely to show organizational citizenship behaviors, and finally more likely to earn higher incomes (Frisch et al., 2004; Verkley & Stolk, 1989; Staw, Sutton, & Pelled, 1994; Borman et al., 2001; Marks & Fleming, 1999).

A few of these studies are particularly illuminating because of their longitudinal design and thus their ability to suggest the direction of causality. Roberts, Caspi, and Moffitt (2003), for example, found that positive affect at age 18 predicted financial independence and occupational attainment at age 26. In another study, Diener et al. (2002) used archival data from the "The American Freshman" survey database and demonstrated that greater self-rated cheerfulness in the first year of college predicted higher income and more job satisfaction nineteen or so years later, after controlling for the parents' income.

These and similar results provide powerful evidence that happiness is not only a product of achievement, but at the same time a producer of it, implying that individuals, organizations, and governments should value human happiness not only as an end in itself but also as a means to positive outcomes related to performance and success.

SOCIAL RELATIONSHIPS AND WELL-BEING

A robust finding of happiness research has been the strong association be-tween good social relationships and subjective well-being. That humans need to belong and to have intimate relationships has an axiomatic quality in social psychology, and hence it is not unexpected to find that well-being depends to a great extent on the fulfillment of this fundamental need. In keeping with this, Diener and Seligman (2002) found in their study of very happy people that every single one of them had satisfying social relationships. Quantity and, more significantly, quality of friendships correlate positively with subjective well-being, and perceived loneliness is strongly associated with depression. The benefits of having a close and long-term companion are probably most apparent in the case of marriage: study after study shows that married people are happier than people who are single, divorced, or widowed (Diener et al., 1999).

Whereas healthy social relationships certainly lead to increased well-being, there is also reason to suspect that the reverse is also true. Several studies have, for example, confirmed that individuals who are likely to get married and to stay married are happier, long before the marriage, than individuals who remain single, implying a selection effect (Lucas et al., 2003; Stutzer & Frey, 2003; Harker & Keltner, 2001).

Chronically happy people have a more positive attitude towards others in general. For example, people with naturally high or experimentally increased positive affect rate persons they have just met in more favorable terms (Berry & Hansen, 1996), and make more positive inferences and attributions about social targets (Mayer, Mamberg, & Volanth, 1988). Similarly, experimental studies show that when put in a pleasant mood, people become more inter-ested in social interaction and more prone to self-disclosure (Cunningham, 1988), pointing to the causative role of happiness in leading to better social relationships.

Now we turn to a review of the literature on prosocial behavior and well-being, which corroborates and extends the above in revealing subjective well-being as an important cultivator of healthy, desirable social relations.

PROSOCIAL BEHAVIOR AND WELL-BEING

British philosopher Bertrand Russell is reputed to have said, "The good life, as I conceive it, is a happy life. I do not mean that if you are good you will be happy; I mean that if you are happy you will be good." Indeed, his view that as people become happier, they also become better people is affirmed by empir-ical evidence. There appears to exist a virtuous cycle between well-being and socially desirable outcomes such as volunteering, ethical behavior, and inter-personal trust. Research shows for example, that it is not only the case that volunteering increases well-being, but also that people high in life satisfaction and happiness are the ones more likely to be community volunteers and to invest more hours in volunteer work (Thoits & Hewitt, 2001). Relatedly, Brehm and Rahn (1997) established that those who are more satisfied with their lives show more generalized trust in others. As is widely acknowledged, trust is the glue of any society, and a strong predictor of social stability and quality of life (Helliwell, 2003).

Happiness has also been found to be bicausally related to morality. It is not only true that ethical judgment and behavior leads to happiness, but also accurate to assert the reverse, namely that happiness leads to more ethical judgments and behaviors. As a demonstration of this, James and Chymis (2004) reported that when asked how justifiable they find some hypothetical ethical scenarios, such as cheating on taxes if you have a chance or buying something you know to be stolen, participants with higher subjective well-being responded in more ethical ways. A one-unit increase in the participant's answer to the question of how satisfied they are with life, on a scale from 1 to 10, increased the probability of ethical judgment by between 3 and 4 percent, after controlling for factors like income, gender, and age, that might influence the relationship between happiness and ethics. The authors concluded that improving subjective well-being may play a significant role in reducing the burden of improbity of all kinds (e.g. corruption, criminality) nationally and worldwide. Similarly, Inglehart and Klingemann's (2000) argument that general well-being is a harbinger of democratic governance, and that major decreases in well-being constitute a threat to democratic institutions implies that governments should care about their citizens' happiness, for selfish reasons, if for nothing else.

HEALTH AND WELL-BEING

Strong correlations between health as reported by the individual and subjective well-being have been consistently documented in the literature (Okun et al., 1984). Correlations between objective health as assessed by medical personnel and subjective well-being, on the other hand, have typically been weaker, for a variety of reasons. Still, it is a well-established finding that life-threatening illnesses, as well as illnesses that interfere with one's daily life and cause pain, do substantially lower one's well-being. Physical health thus inarguably affects well-being. What is more surprising is the discovery that the arrow of causality also runs in the opposite direction, so that well-being affects physical health and longevity.

As early as 1978, Larson showed that for Americans over 60, self-reported well-being seemed to be the factor most strongly linked to health, followed by socioeconomic factors. In recent years more evidence has surfaced to substantiate the notion that positive states of well-being and absence of negative affect lead to better physical health. For instance, Danner, Snowdon, and Friesen

(2001) remarkably demonstrated strong association between positive emotional content in handwritten autobiographies of Catholic sisters, composed when they were at the mean age of 22 years, and their longevity six decades later. In this study, the nuns in the highest quartile regarding the number of positive emotion words included in their autobiographical sketch lived on average 9.4 years longer than the nuns in the lowest quartile. In a similar vein, Pressman (2006) demonstrated that the frequent use of positive affective words (e.g. happy, good, fun) in the autobiographies of deceased psychologists was associated with longevity, after controlling for sex, age at writing, and date of birth.

In another study, researchers experimentally infected participants with a cold virus and then monitored them daily in quarantine. The findings were consistent with the causative role of well-being on health: people who reported experiencing high levels of positive emotions (i.e. those that were happy, pleased, relaxed) were much less vulnerable to the common cold (Cohen et al., 2003) than those who reported experiencing low levels of positive emotions. Of similar interest are studies showing that people put into a pleasant mood exhibit greater pain tolerance compared to control subjects (Zelman et al. 1991).

Finally, Vázquez, Hernangómez, and Hervás (2004) found that longevity of nations is predicted by their citizens' well-being, even after statistically controlling for national income and infant mortality (cited in Diener & Seligman, 2004). In light of such compelling evidence, and given that public health and health care policies are of major concern to governments, it seems fundamentally important that policymakers start allocating the time and resources to well-being that it deserves.

In this section, we have put forth and reviewed the evidence indicating that happiness is desirable because it is a reward in itself, but also because happy people function on a higher level in major life domains such as work, social relationships, and health. We do not mean to suggest that happiness is a cure-all in itself, a magic potion able to bring an end to all existing problems in the world. Yet when we take into account how all-important being happy is to any individual and how beneficial it proves to be for society as a whole to have happy members, the necessity of introducing measures of subjective well-being policymaking processes becomes unmistakable.

Adequacy of Subjective Well-Being Measures

Among the reasons why subjective well-being indicators have been little sought after in the policymaking arena have been the belief that happiness is an unscientific concept and the concomitant mistrust in the validity of SWB measures. Economists traditionally focus on concepts that can actually be observed; hence any attempt to put a number on a subjectively experienced feeling, such as SWB, leaves much to be desired according to their objectivist standards. We submit that measures of happiness will unavoidably be imperfect, yet this is not an acceptable pretext to ignore them. As Daniel Gilbert tells us in jest, "Any carpenter could tell you: Imperfect tools are a real pain, but they sure beat pounding nails with your teeth" (2006, p. 65).

Single-occasion self-report measures are among the most commonly used measures of subjective well-being. As reviewed by Schwarz and Strack (1999), contextual factors can influence individual responses, as is expected in any self-evaluative judgment; yet, SWB measures still possess adequate validity and reliability. Diener and Suh (1997) state that response biases are not as strong as some claim for self-reports of well-being, and that temporal stabilities in the range of .5 to .7 have been found over a number of years. Other methods to capture well-being include informant reports, daily moods ratings, and memory recall for positive versus negative events, and different measures of SWB have been demonstrated to converge with each other (Pavot et al., 1991; Seidlitz & Diener, 1993). Similarly, Sandvik, Diener and Seidlitz (1993) compared self-reports of SWB with non-self-reports and found that a single unitary construct underlies these measures, confirming their validity.

Another indicator of the validity of SWB measures is that they correlate with a host of behavioral observations. For example, people who report to be happy smile more often during social interactions, need less psychological counseling, and are less likely to attempt to commit suicide over the following five years (Frey & Stutzer, 2002a). In addition to that, a vast body of studies that investigate brain activity in relation to emotions can contribute to a better understanding and better measuring of well-being. It is well documented by now, for example, that experience or expression of positive emotions is correlated with greater relative left frontal activation in the brain (Tomarken, Davidson, & Henriques, 1990). Also, higher left rather than right baseline levels of prefrontal activation are associated with the experience of well-being (Tomarken et al., 1992).

There is unmistakably room for improvement in SWB measures, and their current limitations suggest that multi-method assessments of SWB should be preferred whenever possible. Yet, they still possess adequate validity and reliability to inform expert opinion about a very important topic.

Conclusion

In this chapter we have tried to justify and communicate our belief that policymakers should afford more consideration to subjective well-being measures than they currently do. Media attention and political discourse obsessively revolve around what economic indices have to tell; the fact that economic welfare is not an end itself but only a means to achieve happiness seems to be forgotten along the way. We endeavored to highlight some of the reasons why economic progress cannot be equated with subjective well-being, and why reigning economic and social indicators can only provide an incomplete picture of individual and societal well-being.

Happiness is most likely the ultimate aim of human existence, and perhaps even "the criterion of excellence in the art of living" (Fromm, 1947, p. 189). As our review has revealed, however, it is not a hollow dream that leaves people giddy and foolish, but rather has incontestable benefits in various life domains such as work, interpersonal relationships, and health. Apparently, a healthy society and a better future can only be built on the shoulders of happy people.

That SWB measures, by and large, display necessary metric features to allow valid and reliable observations renders it not only desirable but also possible that subjective well-being should be tracked and incorporated into policymaking processes. Naturally, we do not mean to suggest that happiness is the most important outcome that policymakers should value. We propose subjective well-being measures as complementary to current approaches to capture human welfare, believing that they will be a unique source of valuable information.

This chapter is also motivated by our faith in the psychological Heisenberg principle, namely the idea that "human systems grow in the direction of what they persistently ask questions about" (Cooperrider and Whitney, 2005, p. 9). It would not be inaccurate to say that the study of happiness has gone through a painfully long dark age since ancient Greek philosophers. The revival of interest in the topic on the part of psychologists and economists in the last few decades, and particularly in the last few years, is very encouraging and strengthens our hope that the day that policymakers begin to care about subjective well-being measures might not lie in a distant future.

References

Abbey, E. (1988). *One Life at a Time, Please*. New York: Henry Holt and Company.
Alesina, A., Glaeser, E. L., & Sacerdote, B. (2006). Work and leisure in the U.S. and Europe: Why so different? In M. Gertler & K. Rogoff (Eds.), *NBER Macroeconomics Annual 2005* (pp. 1–64). Cambridge: MIT Press.
Berry, D. S., & Hansen, J. S. (1996). Positive affect, negative affect, and social interaction. *Journal of Personality and Social Psychology, 71*, 796–809.
Borman, W. C., Penner, L. A., Allen, T. D., & Motowildo, S. J. (2001). Personality predictors of citizenship performance. *International Journal of Selection and Assessment, 9*, 52–69.

Brehm, J., & Rahn, W. (1997). Individual-level evidence for the causes and consequences of social capital. *American Journal of Political Science, 41*(3), 999–1024.

Brickman, P., & Campbell, D. T. (1971). Hedonic relativism and planning the good society. In M. H. Appley (Ed.), *Adaptation Level Theory: A Symposium* (pp. 287–302). New York: Academic Press.

Cobb, C., Halstead, T., & Rowe, J. (1995, October). If the GDP is up, why is America down? *The Atlantic Monthly,* 55–77.

Cohen, S., Doyle, W. J., Turner, R. B., Alper, C. M., & Skoner, D. P. (2003). Emotional style and susceptibility to the common cold. *Psychosomatic Medicine, 65,* 652–7.

Cooperrider, D., & Whitney, D. (2005). *Appreciative Inquiry: A Positive Revolution in Change.* San Francisco: Berrett-Koehler Publishers.

Csikszentmihalyi, M. (1999). If we are so rich, why aren't we happy? *American Psychologist, 54,* 821–7.

—— & Schneider, B. (2000). *Becoming Adult: How Teenagers Prepare for the World of Work.* New York: Basic Books.

Cunningham, M. R. (1988). Does happiness mean friendliness? Induced mood and heterosexual self-disclosure. *Personality and Social Psychology Bulletin, 14,* 283–97.

Danner, D., Snowdon D., & Friesen, W. (2001). Positive emotions in early life and longevity: Findings from the nun study. *Journal of Personality and Social Psychology, 80* (5), 804–13.

Diener, E., & Biswas-Diener, R. (2002). Will money increase subjective well-being? *Social Indicators Research, 57,* 119–69.

—— & Diener, C. (1995). The wealth of nations revisited: Income and quality of life. *Social Indicators Research, 36,* 275–86.

—— Diener, M., & Diener, C. (1995). Factors predicting the subjective well-being of nations. *Journal of Personality and Social Psychology, 69,* 851–64.

—— & Fujita, F. (1995). Resources, personal strivings, and subjective well-being: A nomothetic and idiographic approach. *Journal of Personality and Social Psychology, 68,* 926–35.

—— Horowitz, J., & Emmons, R. A. (1985). Happiness of the very wealthy. *Social Indicators Research, 16,* 263–74.

—— Lucas, R. E., & Scollon, C. N. (2006). Beyond the hedonic treadmill: Revising the adaptation theory of well-being. *American Psychologist, 61,* 305–14.

—— Nickerson, C., Lucas, R. E., & Sandvik, E. (2002). Dispositional affect and job outcomes. *Social Indicators Research, 59,* 229–59.

—— & Seligman, M. E. P. (2002). Very happy people. *Psychological Science, 13,* 81–4.

—— —— (2004). Beyond money: Toward an economy of well-being. *Psychological Science in the Public Interest, 5*(1), 1–31.

—— & Suh, E. (1997), Measuring quality of life: Economic, social, and subjective indicators. *Social Indicators Research, 40,* 189–216.

—— —— Lucas, R. E., & Smith, H. L. (1999). Subjective well-being: Three decades of progress. *Psychological Bulletin, 125,* 276–302.

Easterbrook, G. (2003). *The Progress Paradox: How Life Gets Better while People Feel Worse.* New York: Random House.

Easterlin, R. A. (2005). Is There an "Iron Law of Happiness"? *IEPR Working paper No 05.8,* retrieved June 21, 2006, from <http://www.finanzacomportamentale.it/files/Easterlin001.pdf>.

Emmons, R. A., & McCullough, M. E. (2003). Counting blessings *versus* burdens: An experimental investigation of gratitude and subjective well-being in daily life. *Journal of Personality and Social Psychology, 84,* 377–89.

Erez, A., & Isen, A. M. (2002). The influence of positive affect on the components of expectancy motivation. *Journal of Applied Psychology, 87,* 1055–67.

Fordyce, M. W. (1977). Development of a program to increase happiness. *Journal of Counseling Psychology, 24,* 511–21.

Forgas, J. P. (1989). Mood effects on decision making strategies. *Australian Journal of Psychology, 41,* 197–214.

Fredrickson, B. L. (1998). What good are positive emotions? *Review of General Psychology, 2,* 300–19.

—— (2001) The role of positive emotions in positive psychology: The broaden-and-build theory of positive emotions. *American Psychologist, 56,* 218–26.

Frey, B. S., & Stutzer, A. (2002a). What can economists learn from happiness research? *Journal of Economic Literature, 40,* 402–35.

—— —— (2002b). *Happiness and Economics: How the Economy and Institutions Affect Human Well-Being.* Princeton, NJ: Princeton University Press.

Frisch, M. B., Clark, M. P., Rouse, S. V., Rudd, M. D., Paweleck, J. K., Greenstone, A., & Kopplin, D. A. (2004). Predictive and treatment validity of life satisfaction and the Quality of Life Inventory. *Assessment, 10,* 1–13.

Fromm, E. (1947). *Man for Himself: An Inquiry into the Psychology of Ethics.* New York: Holt, Rinehart & Winston.

Fujita, F., & Diener, E. (2005) Life satisfaction set point: Stability and change. *Journal of Personality and Social Psychology, 88*(1), 158–64.

Gilbert, D. (2006). *Stumbling on Happiness.* New York: Alfred A. Knopf.

Harker, L., & Keltner, D. (2001). Expressions of positive emotions in women's college yearbook pictures and their relationship to personality and life outcomes across adulthood. *Journal of Personality and Social Psychology, 80,* 112–24.

Helliwell, J. F. (2003). How's life? Combining individual and national variables to explain subjective well-being. *Economic Modelling, 20,* 331–60.

Inglehart, R., & Klingemann, H.-D. (2000). Genes, culture, democracy, and happiness. In E. Diener & E. M. Suh (Eds.), *Culture and Subjective Well-Being* (pp. 165–84). Cambridge, MA: MIT Press.

—— Basañez, M., Diez-Medrano, J., Halman, L., & Luijkx, R. (Eds.). (2004). *Human Beliefs and Values: A Cross-Cultural Sourcebook Based on the 1999–2002 Values Surveys.* Mexico City: Siglo XXI.

Isen, A. M. (1993). Positive affect and decision making. In M. Lewis & J. M. Haviland-Jones (Eds.), *Handbook of Emotions* (1st edn, pp. 261–77). New York: Guilford Press.

James, H. S., & Chymis, A. (2004). Are happy people ethical people? Evidence from North America and Europe. University of Missouri Agricultural Economics Working Paper No. AEWP 2004–8.

Jundt, D., & Hinsz, V. B. (2001, May). *Are happier workers more productive workers? The impact of mood on self-set goals, self-efficacy, and task performance.* Paper presented at the annual meeting of the Midwestern Psychological Association, Chicago.

Kasser, T. (2006). Materialism and its alternatives. In M. Csikszentmihalyi (Ed.), *A Life Worth Living: Contributions to Positive Psychology.* Oxford: Oxford University Press.

—— & Kanner, A.D. (Eds.). (2004). *Psychology and Consumer Culture: The Struggle for a Good Life in a Materialistic World*. Washington, DC: American Psychological Association.

Kavanagh, D. J. (1987). Mood, persistence, and success. *Australian Journal of Psychology, 39*, 307–18.

King, L. A. (2001). The health benefits of writing about life goals. *Personality and Social Psychology Bulletin, 27*, 798–807.

—— & Napa, C. K. (1998). What makes a life good? *Journal of Personality and Social Psychology, 75*, 156–65.

Larson, R. (1978). Thirty years of research on the subjective well-being of older Americans. *Journal of Gerontology, 33*, 109–25.

Lichter, S., Haye, K., & Kammann, R. (1980). Increasing happiness through cognitive retraining. *New Zealand Psychologist, 9*, 57–64.

Lucas, R. E., Clark, A. E., Georgellis, Y., & Diener, E. (2003). Reexamining adaptation and the set point model of happiness: Reactions to changes in marital status. *Journal of Personality and Social Psychology, 84*, 527–39.

—— —— —— —— (2004). Unemployment alters the set point for life satisfaction. *Psychological Science, 15*(1), 8–13.

Luthar, S. S. (2003). The culture of affluence: Psychological costs of material wealth. *Child Development, 74*, 1581–93.

Lykken D., & Tellegen A. (1996). Happiness is a stochastic phenomenon. *Psychological Science, 7*, 186–9.

Lyubomirsky, S., King, L., & Diener, E. (2005). The benefits of frequent positive affect: Does happiness lead to success? *Psychological Bulletin, 131*, 803–55.

—— Sheldon, K. M., & Schkade, D. (2005). Pursuing happiness: The architecture of sustainable change. *Review of General Psychology, 9*, 111–31.

Marks, G. N., & Fleming, N. (1999). Influences and consequences of well-being among Australian young people: 1980–95. *Social Indicators Research, 46*, 301–23.

Mayer, J. D., Mamberg, M. H., & Volanth, A. J. (1988). Cognitive domains of the mood system. *Journal of Personality, 56*, 453–86.

Myers, D. G. (1992). *The Pursuit of Happiness*. New York: William Morrow and Company.

—— (2000). *The American Paradox: Spiritual Hunger in an Age of Plenty*. New Haven, CT: Yale University Press.

Okun, M. A., Stock, W. A., Haring, M. J., & Witter, R.A. (1984). Health and subjective well-being: A meta-analysis. *International Journal of Aging and Human Development, 19*, 111–31.

Oswald, A. J. (1997). Happiness and economic performance. *Economic Journal, 107*, 1815–31.

Pavot, W., Diener, E., Colvin, C. R., & Sandvik, E. (1991). Further validation of the Satisfaction with Life Scale: Evidence for the cross-method convergence of well-being measures. *Journal of Personality Assessment, 57*, 149–61.

Perkins, H. W. (1991). Religious commitment, Yuppie values, and well-being in post-collegiate life. *Review of Religious Research, 32*, 244–51.

Pressman, S.D. (2006). The impact of emotional and social word use in autobiography on longevity (Doctoral dissertation, Carnegie Mellon University, 2006).

Putnam, R. D. (2000). *Bowling Alone: The Collapse and Revival of American Community*. New York: Simon & Schuster.

Roberts, B. W., Caspi, A., & Moffitt, T. E. (2003). Work experiences and personality development in young adulthood. *Journal of Personality and Social Psychology, 84,* 582–93.

Sandvik, E., Diener, E., & Seidlitz, L. (1993). Subjective well-being: The convergence and stability of self-report and non-self-report measures. *Journal of Personality, 61,* 317–42.

Schneider, M. (1976). The quality of life and social indicators research. *Public Administration Review, 36,* 297–305.

Schwarz, N., & Strack, F. (1999). Reports of subjective well-being: Judgmental processes and their methodological implications. In D. Kahneman, E. Diener, & N. Schwarz (Eds.), *Well-Being: The Foundations of Hedonic Psychology* (pp. 61–84). New York: Russell Sage Foundation.

Seidlitz, L., & Diener, E. (1993). Memory for positive versus negative life events: Theories for the differences between happy and unhappy persons. *Journal of Personality and Social Psychology, 64,* 654–64.

Seligman, M. E. P., Steen, T. A., Park, N., & Peterson, C. (2005). Positive psychology progress. *American Psychologist, 60,* 410–21.

Sheldon, K. M., Kasser, T., Smith, K., & Share, T. (2002). Personal goals and psychological growth: Testing an intervention to enhance goal-attainment and personality integration. *Journal of Personality, 70,* 5–31.

Staw, B. M., & Barsade, S. G. (1993). Affect and managerial performance: A test of the sadder-but-wiser vs. happier-and-smarter hypotheses. *Administrative Science Quarterly, 38,* 304–31.

—— Sutton, R. I., & Pelled, L. H. (1994). Employee positive emotion and favorable outcomes at the workplace. *Organization Science, 5,* 51–71.

Stutzer, A., & Frey, B. (2003) Does marriage make people happy, or do happy people get married? Institute for Empirical Research in Economics, University of Zurich Working Paper Series, ISSN 1424-0459, No. 143.

Thoits, P. A., & Hewitt, L. N. (2001). Volunteer work and well-being. *Journal of Health and Social Behavior, 42,* 115–31.

Tomarken, A. J., Davidson, R. J., & Henriques, J. B. (1990). Resting frontal brain asymmetry predicts affective responses to films. *Journal of Personality and Social Psychology, 59,* 791–801.

—— —— Wheeler, R. E., & Doss, R. C. (1992). Individual differences in anterior brain asymmetry and fundamental dimensions of emotion. *Journal of Personality and Social Psychology, 62,* 676–87.

Vázquez, C., Hernangómez, L., & Hervás, G. (2004). Longevidad y emociones positivas [Longevity and positive emotions]. In L. Salvador, A. Cano, & J. R. Cabo (Eds.), *Longevidad: Tratado integral sobre salud en la segunda mitad de la vida* (pp. 752–61). Madrid, Spain: Panamericana.

Verkley, H., & Stolk, J. (1989). Does happiness lead into idleness? In R. Veenhoven (Ed.), *How Harmful is Happiness?* (pp. 79–93). Rotterdam, Holland: University of Rotterdam.

Watson, G. (1930). Happiness among adult students of education. *Journal of Educational Psychology, 21,* 79–109.

Zelman, D. C., Howland, E. W., Nichols, S. N., & Cleeland, C. S. (1991). The effects of induced mood on laboratory pain. *Pain, 46,* 105–11.

4

Some Insights on Development from the Economics of Happiness*

Carol Graham

Central to the findings of much of the happiness literature in the developed economies are numerous discrepancies between reported measures of well-being and income measures. Richard Easterlin pioneered the economics of happiness in the mid-1970s.[1] He found that across countries and cultures, the way that most people spend their time is similar: working and trying to provide for their families. Thus the concerns that they express when asked about happiness are similar. His finding—that wealthy people tend to be happier than poorer ones within countries, but that there is no such relationship among countries or over time—has since been supported by a number of subsequent studies, and is known as the "Easterlin paradox".[2]

More recently, Stefano Pettinato and I developed data for seventeen countries in Latin America. We found similar results in that there is no obvious relationship between income and happiness among our sample of developing

* The author is Senior Fellow and Charles Robinson Chair at the Brookings Institution and College Park Professor at the University of Maryland. She would like to thank Nancy Birdsall, Gary Burtless, Angus Deaton, Andrew Eggers, Michael Kremer, Margaret MacLeod, Andrew Oswald, and three anonymous reviewers for helpful comments. A companion paper, with a special emphasis on globalization, was presented at a WIDER conference on globalization and inequality in October 2004, benefited greatly from comments from participants there, and will be published as part of the conference proceedings. This paper was previously published in *World Bank Research Observer* 2005 20(2): 201–31. The paper has been reproduced with the kind permission of Oxford University Press on behalf of the International Bank for Reconstruction and Development/The World Bank.

[1] Easterlin used thirty surveys from nineteen countries, including some developing countries. See Easterlin (1974); (1995); (2001a); (2003). He also finds that health is a demographic variable with clear effects on happiness in all societies, a finding that other studies corroborate. For an excellent summary of many of these studies, see the October 4, 2002 issue of the *New Scientist* magazine.

[2] Easterlin (1974); and Blanchflower and Oswald (2004). They find that well-being in the US has trended slightly downwards, while in the UK it has trended slightly upwards. See also Diener (1984); and Frey and Stutzer (2000).

economies. Yet for the most part, average happiness levels are higher in the advanced economies than they are in the developing ones (Figure 4.1).

The objective of this chapter is to explore how the paradox that Easterlin originally highlighted—and the study of happiness more generally—provides insights into the way in which individuals in developing countries assess their own welfare, and how those assessments diverge from those based on traditional measures. Better understanding those divergences—particularly if they are significant and related to factors that can be influenced by policy—may help development economists and practitioners improve their benchmarks for measuring progress. My own research in Latin America and Russia, conducted jointly with several colleagues and discussed below, suggests that happiness surveys can tell us much about how the dynamics of poverty and inequality affect well-being, as well as about many other elements of well-being which are not captured by income measures alone.

In particular, they may help us understand public frustration in contexts where income measures alone provide insufficient explanation and/or they may help shed light on issues where a revealed preferences approach is limited. One example of the latter is the effect of inequality on well-being. It is difficult to imagine how a poor Bolivian, for example, who is made unhappy by nationwide inequality, can reveal his/her preferences and move to a context where there is less inequality (short of emigrating). Nor can he or she do much to alter the distribution of income by voting, given that progressive taxation is not on the policy agenda in much of the region. In such contexts, surveys of well-being may provide useful information.

It is important, though, to think of happiness surveys as complements to rather than substitutes for income-based measures of progress. While happiness surveys can provide us with novel information and suggest new analytical approaches, they can also pose challenges when translated into direct policy recommendations. For example, at the same time that countries have grown wealthier over time, they have also made major improvements in other indicators, such as morbidity, mortality, and literacy rates.[3] Yet if the direct policy conclusion from the Easterlin paradox is that more money does not make people happier, then a related conclusion could be that long-term gains in health and education also do not make people happier. Most development economists would find this extremely problematic.

Related to this, a prominent explanation for the Easterlin paradox is that norms and expectations adapt upwards at about the same rate as income increases, and thus after basic needs are met, more income does not make people happier. An additional—and in some cases plausible—explanation for the paradox is that happiness questions—which are usually based on a four- or

---

[3] For an excellent review of the relationship between health and development (and the links or lack thereof to inequality) see Deaton (2003).

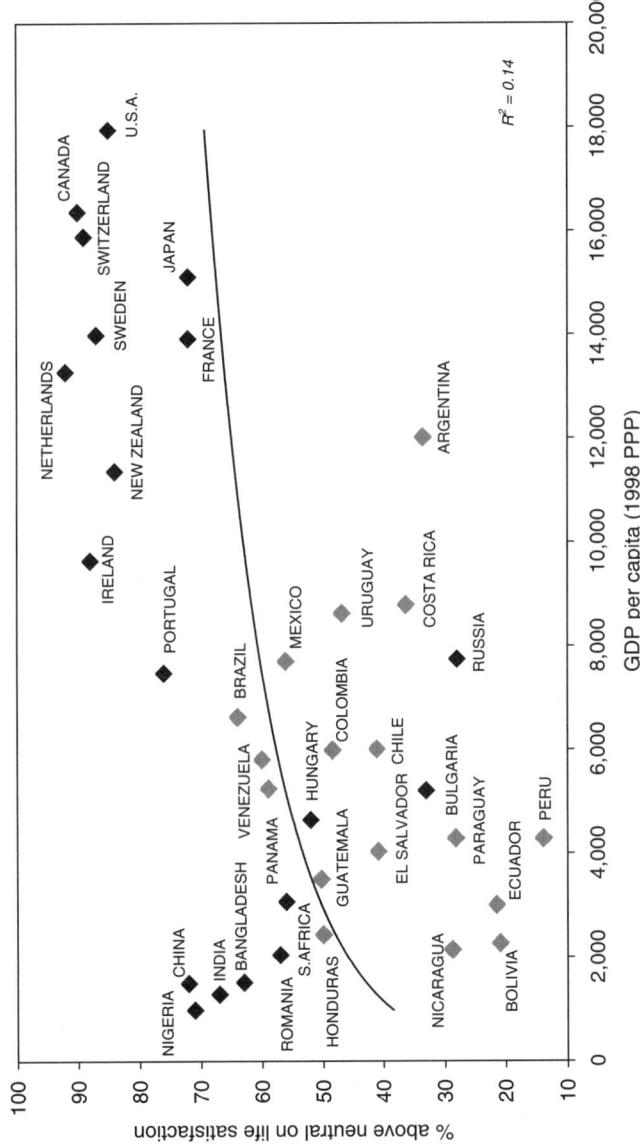

Figure 4.1. Happiness and income per captia, 1990s

Source: Graham and Pettinato, 2002.

seven-point scale—have an upper bound, while progress does not. This may help explain some of the cross-country conundrum, but does not explain why happiness levels have fallen after forty years of economic progress in Japan, for example. The extreme view of adaptation is the psychologists' "set point" theory, which posits that all individuals have a set point of happiness, which they adapt back to even after major events like winning a lottery or getting divorced.

Others, though, such as Easterlin (2003), cite research that shows that there are some events—such as unemployment and being widowed—that individuals do not adapt to, or take a tremendous time to adapt to. A recent study of monozygotic and dizygotic twins in Denmark, meanwhile, finds that reported happiness has some genetic components, but is also shaped importantly by experiences with partners and children (Kohler, Behrman, and Skythe, 2005).

A strict interpretation of the set point theory suggests that there is nothing much that policy can do to make people happier, and that happiness surveys cannot be usefully applied to development questions. That is, of course, unless one is willing to accept that extremely poor and destitute people who report they are happy, most likely because of psychological attributes, are as well off as much wealthier, healthier, and more educated respondents. Few policy-makers—or social scientists—would be comfortable with this, not least because decades of research—and economic progress—demonstrate that people live longer, healthier, and more fulfilling lives when they are not destitute, regardless of how they report their well-being. Easterbrook (2003), for example, discusses the paradoxical case of the United States, where virtually all of these indicators—health, wealth, and education—have improved over time, but reported well-being has gone down.

Yet the set point interpretation is an extreme one. There is no doubt that there is a tremendous amount of adaptation to all kinds of change, and the evidence suggests that people often do return to or near to their set point, particularly in the case of income changes. Yet there is also evidence that some things seem to have more lasting effects on people's happiness. Certainly people adapt over time to events such as divorce or serious illness, but the evidence is much less conclusive on whether they ever adapt fully. Easterlin (2003) posits that people adapt and recuperate much faster from pecuniary changes or shocks (upwards or downwards) than they do to changes in non-pecuniary areas such as marriage or health. His data shows that individuals never adapt fully to significant marital or health shocks. In contrast, evidence from panel data for Germany suggests that people eventually adapt fully from the negative effects of divorce.

Even if norms and adaptation play a major role in determining subjective well-being, there is ample evidence that objective conditions—and changes in objective conditions—matter. Within virtually all countries where such surveys are conducted, cross section data show that wealthier people are happier than poor ones. Healthier people are also happier, as are more educated people, employed people, and married people (Clark and Oswald, 1994; Blanchflower and Oswald, 2004). Conversely, economic and other forms of insecurity, such as high levels of crime, seem to have negative effects on people's happiness (Graham and Pettinato, 2002a; Powdthavee, forthcoming).

The extreme set point interpretation suggests that progress does not matter to happiness at all, an interpretation that this author is not comfortable with. A more nuanced view, however, posits that happiness surveys can tell us things that purely income-based measures of progress do not, and this may shed light on how the *direction* and *nature* of progress affects well-being. Having sufficient income seems to matter to people's happiness—and is essential to poverty reduction, but other non-income factors, such as stable employment, marital status, and good health, also matter a great deal to well-being (and, with the exception of marriage, also matter to poverty reduction).

While across nations there are diminishing returns to increasing income, other things that correlate with national income, such as health, quality of government, and human rights, are correlated with higher happiness levels (Frey and Stutzer, 2000; Diener and Seligman, 2004; Donovan and Halpern, 2002). In a recent cross-country study, for example, John Helliwell (2004) concludes that people with the highest well-being "are not those who live in the richest countries, but those who live where social and political institutions are effective, where mutual trust is high, and corruption is low". In addition, Stefano Pettinato and I (2002) find that happiness levels are still, on average, lower in most developing economies than they are in the advanced ones, suggesting that if there is a threshold beyond which more money does not enhance average levels of reported well-being, most developing economies have not yet crossed it.

The discrepancy between cross section and over-time country-level findings, meanwhile, is a paradox on its own. After minimum basic needs are met, respondents do not seem to factor in long-term, aggregate improvements in per capita income levels or in basic health and literacy standards as they assess their well-being. At the same time, at any point in time within individual countries, wealthier and healthier people are happier than are poorer and less healthy people; responses are also influenced by *changes* in both income and health status. And even if over time gains do not affect people's answers to happiness surveys, if life expectancy is longer and disease incidence is lower, then these temporarily happier, wealthier, and healthier people within countries will have more years to enjoy their lives.

One example of well-being surveys informing unresolved questions is the evidence that they provide, albeit mixed, that distributional outcomes matter to welfare. Experimental, firm- and region-level studies find that inequities in rank or in the distribution of particular rewards can erode the positive gains accrued from income.[4] Blanchflower and Oswald, on the basis of US data from the General Social Survey, find that relative income differences matter to happiness even when absolute income is held constant.[5] Andrew Felton and I (2005) find that relative income differences (as well as perceived income differences) make the rich in Latin America happier than average and the poor less happy. We posit that while inequality can signal mobility and opportunity as much as injustice in the advanced economies, in Latin America it seems to be a signal of persistent advantages for the rich and disadvantages for the poor.

Happiness surveys also suggest that macroeconomic conditions matter to well-being. Studies in the developed economies find that higher inflation and unemployment rates make respondents less happy, all else being equal (DiTella, MacCulloch, and Oswald, 2001). Our own research corroborates these findings for Latin America, with high inflation being bad for happiness, and with unemployment rates having a negative effect (Graham and Pettinato, 2002a; Eggers and Graham, 2004). Most economists and policymakers would be quite comfortable with the logical conclusion from these results: high inflation and unemployment are bad for well-being.

Yet caution is also necessary. In a more recent study of the costs of regional unemployment rates in Russia, we find that respondents that live in regions with higher unemployment rates are, all else held equal, happier than their counterparts in regions with lower rates (Eggers, Gaddy, and Graham, forthcoming). These results reflect the unusual nature of the Russian economy and its uneven transition to the market; a detailed interpretation is beyond the scope of this chapter. The point is that the policy implications, taken at face value, are that high unemployment rates are good for well-being in Russia. Few analysts would find that useful or conscionable.

While it is accepted that caution is necessary when drawing policy prescriptions, the point of this chapter is to demonstrate how happiness research can provide new *insights* into the development process and how individuals

---

[4] Experimental studies, such as the Ultimatum game, find that people are willing to turn down fairly large amounts of "reward" money rather than accept a reward that is unfairly divided between two people. Blanchflower and Oswald (2004) find that workers place a higher value on rank in a firm—and how their salary compares with that of other co-workers—than to the actual amount of salary. Hagerty (1999) finds, after controlling for personal income, that individuals living in higher-income areas in the US were lower in happiness than those living in lower-income areas.

[5] They use two specifications as proxies for relative income. The first is the ratio of individual income to state income per capita (controlling for regional housing prices) and the second is a series of variables which measure income relative to the average level of income in each of the different quintiles of income within the person's state. In both instances, greater relative differences make people less happy, and in the latter instance, the greatest effects come from the ratio of individual income to income in the top quintile. See Blanchflower and Oswald (2004).

fare—and/or perceive they fare—during that process. These insights complement but cannot replace the valuable information and benchmarks of progress provided by income-based measures. But they may be useful in helping to explain policy puzzles such as differences among societies' tolerance for inequality; divergent assessments of the benefits of the globalization process; and unexpected interruptions in social and political stability.

What Are Standard Measures Missing?

An obvious question is what are our traditional measures missing? Or what are our standard measures missing? Respondents assessments of their own welfare often highlight factors which are not adequately captured by income measures. Examples of these are real and perceived insecurity as rewards and incentives systems adapt to structural changes; the state of essential public services, such as education, health, and crime prevention; and norms of fairness and justice. Even the trends that can be measured in income terms, such as poverty and inequality, have broader dimensions—as well as dynamic elements—which are not captured by traditional income-based measures, such as poverty headcounts and Gini coefficients.

Gini coefficients, for example, are static, aggregate measures that do not change very much over time, and usually do not reflect distributional shifts among regions or skill cohorts. Poverty head-count studies based on cross section studies conducted every few years often miss short-term movements in and out of poverty.[6] Such movements are common in developing countries and create widespread insecurity among the middle class as well as the poor (Birdsall, Graham, and Pettinato, 2001). Panel data which measure income mobility are better suited to capturing such changes. Yet these data are rare and only exist for a few developing countries, and even then are usually for short time periods and small samples. Fixed international poverty lines, such as the $1 or $2 per day lines, meanwhile, while useful for inter-country comparisons, often have very little to do with public conceptions of poverty within particular countries and regions, which is why they are rarely used for these purposes.

An example of the incomplete picture provided by income-based measures is the gap between economists' assessments of the effects of globalization based on traditional measures and the more negative assessments typical from the average citizen experiencing the process. While this gap may be

---

[6] In the first three years of the financial crisis in Indonesia of the late 1990s, 20% of the population was below the poverty line at any given point in time. Yet 50% of the population was in poverty at some point during the three-year period. See Pritchett, Suryahadi, and Sumarto (2000).

exaggerated by the vocal opponents or proponents of globalization, it may also reflect trends—and broader dimensions of welfare—that standard income measures are not capturing. Few development economists dispute the notion that growth is a necessary but insufficient condition for poverty reduction. It should come as little surprise, then, that measures of poverty and inequality which only capture income and expenditure trends do not provide a complete picture of the many and broader dimensions of poverty and inequality, much less fully depict how they are affected by the complex process of globalization in the developing world.

Another example where income measures provide an incomplete picture is the seeming puzzle that civil unrest and social protest is more likely to occur in societies that are developing and growing than in those that are stagnant. Ted Robert Gurr (1970), in an oft-cited cross-country study, cites relative deprivation as "the basic, instigating condition for participants in collective violence.... Societal conditions that increase the average level or intensity of expectations without increasing capabilities increase the intensity of discontent." Despite many subsequent studies, there is still vast disagreement over the relationships between GDP growth, inequality, and civil violence (Collier et al., 2003; and Sambanis, forthcoming). Using broader measures may help shed insights.

A related example is public tolerance of inequality. Years ago, in a classic article, Albert Hirschman (1973) compared public tolerance of inequality in the development process to a traffic jam in a tunnel. He noted that when one lane moves forward, it gives those in the stalled lanes hope, as it provides a signal or information about where they might be going in the future. But if only one lane continues to move and the others remain stalled for a long period of time, then those in the stalled lanes become frustrated and are tempted to revert to radical behavior such as jumping the median strip. Note that the frustration and radical behavior comes after a period of growth and development (albeit unevenly shared), not at a time of overall stagnation. There is nothing in our standard measures of growth or inequality that allows us to gauge the timing of such frustration and how the tolerance threshold differs among societies.

The more important question, however, is whether this gap between economists' assessments and broader measures of well-being matters to *outcomes* in poor countries. Surely the bottom line or minimum requirement for economic development is economic growth. Will understanding broader and surely more difficult to measure dimensions of welfare contribute anything to the already complex challenges of development? And if there is merit in pursuing these broader concepts, how can we better measure what traditional tools do not capture? Can the economics of happiness provide some new tools to help answer these questions?

The Economics of Happiness

The study of happiness, or subjective well-being (terms which are used interchangeably), is a fairly new area for economists, although psychologists have been studying happiness for years. Some of the earliest economists, such as Jeremy Bentham, were concerned with the pursuit of individual happiness. As the field became more rigorous and quantitative, however, much narrower definitions of individual welfare, or utility, became the norm. In addition, economists have traditionally shied away from the use of survey data because of justifiable concerns that answers to surveys of individual preferences—and reported well-being—are subject to bias from factors such as the respondents' moods at the time of the survey and minor changes in the phrasing of survey questions, which can produce large biases in results (Bertrand and Mullainathan (2001). Thus traditional economic analysis focuses on actual behavior, such as revealed preferences in consumption, savings, and labor market participation, under the assumption that individuals rationally process all the information at their disposal to maximize their utility.

In recent years, however, the strictly rational vision of economic decision making has come under increasing scrutiny. One important innovation is the concept of bounded rationality, in which individuals are assumed to have access to limited or local information and to make decisions according to simple heuristic rules rather than complex optimization calculations (Conlisk, 1996; Simon, 1978). A more recent trend has been the increased influence of behavioral economics, which supplements the methods and questions of economists with those more common to psychologists. A notable recognition of the behavioralist approach was the awarding of the 2002 Nobel Prize in Economics to Daniel Kahneman, a psychologist.

Economists who work in the area broadly define happiness and/or subjective well-being as satisfaction with life in general. Indeed, the three sets of terms are used interchangeably in most studies. Most studies are based on a very simple set of survey questions that typically ask respondents, "How satisfied are you with your life?" or "How happy are you with your life?" Critics used to defining welfare or utility in material or income terms bemoan the lack of precise definition in these questions. Yet the economists who use these surveys emphasize their advantages in making comparisons across cohorts of individuals—in which they find a surprising consistency in the patterns of responses both within and across countries—rather than in evaluating the actual happiness levels of specific individuals. Psychologists, meanwhile, find a significant degree of "validation" in subjective well-being surveys, wherein individuals who report higher levels of happiness actually smile more, as well as meet several other psychological measures of well-being (Diener and Biswas-Diener, 2000; Diener and Seligman, 2004).

Economists that work in the area have devoted a fair amount of attention to trying to explain the paradox that improvements in living standards over time were not reflected in people's answers to happiness surveys. Easterlin explained the anomaly by suggesting that absolute income levels matter up to a certain point—particularly when basic needs are unmet—but after that, relative income differences matter more. Decades earlier, Pigou (1920) reasoned that because the rich derive much of their satisfaction from their relative, rather than absolute, income, satisfaction would not be reduced if the incomes of all the rich were diminished at the same time, justifying redistributive taxation.

Psychologist Ed Diener and his colleagues (1993) find a stronger relationship between income and happiness at the lower end of the income scale, and a flatter one at higher incomes that are well above subsistence levels. Across countries, they found a moderate relationship between affluence and life satisfaction. They based their analysis on a cross section of 18,000 college students in thirty-nine countries (primarily developed economies), and on a ten-year (1971–81) longitudinal study of 4,942 adults in the United States.

Norms and expectations also adapt upward with economic progress. Thus the expected gains of income on happiness are mediated by the rising aspirations that accompany the income gains. Empirical studies support this proposition, showing a much stronger relation between income and happiness at the lower end of the income scale (Veenhoven, 1991). Some scholars also find an additional effect at the top of the scale, which might be explained by greed or changing preferences resulting from high degrees of wealth (Argyle, 1999).

Easterlin's proposition about changing reference norms is supported by the well-known sociological work of James Merton (1957), based on Stouffer's analysis of the effects of promotions among US military men. Stouffer found that infantry men, for whom promotion was quite rare, were much more satisfied with promotions when they occurred than were air force men, for whom upward mobility was the norm rather than the exception.[7]

At about the same time that Merton wrote his book, James Duesenberry (1949) explored the relationship between income aspirations and social status. His specific interest was in ascertaining how this relationship influences savings behavior, but the empirical work on which he based his analysis was remarkably similar to Merton's work. He relied on sociological research based on public opinion polls in the United States in the 1940s. He found that those in the highest income group surveyed stated that they needed a higher percentage increase in income to make their family live comfortably than did those in many lower-income groups. In a much later study, Kapteyn (1999) finds that residents of higher-income neighborhoods in The Netherlands save

---

[7] I thank George Akerlof for pointing me in the direction of Stouffer's work.

less than residents with similar income levels that live in lower-income neighborhoods.

The importance placed on relative income and reference groups can lead to an ever-rising bar of perceived needs. In a classic work, Thorstein Veblen (1899) posits that in affluent societies, spending—and in particular conspicuous consumption—becomes the vehicle through which people establish social position. Almost a century later, Juliet Schor (1998) cites repeated surveys showing that more than half of the population of the United States, the richest population in the world, say they cannot afford everything they really need.

The importance of relative income differences to perceived well-being depends in part on social norms, which vary among societies. Under some norms, some societies, such as the United States, are more willing to tolerate higher levels of inequality in exchange for benefits (real or perceived) such as greater freedom or opportunity (Esping-Andersen, 1990; McMurrer and Sawhill, 1998; Graham and Young, 2003).

The concept of changing reference norms and aspirations is also relevant to the economic development process in poor countries. An anecdotal example comes from Peru in the 1960s. Richard Webb (1965) of the Instituto Cuanto interviewed a random sample of urban workers. Respondents of many different income levels were asked how much more income than they currently earned would they need to "live well". The vast majority of respondents—across all income levels—responded that they would need twice as much as they currently earned.

Increasing income levels and economic growth are necessary if not sufficient conditions for development. And the process can be quite uneven. Thus aspirations and reference norms may adapt upwards well before significant sectors of society see the benefits. The integration of global markets, meanwhile, has been accompanied by a marked increase in the availability of global information regarding living standards within poor countries and beyond their borders. Many developing countries, particularly in Latin America, have large gaps between the very wealthy and the rest of society, gaps which are often exacerbated by integration into global markets. If skilled labor benefits disproportionately from the process, as has been the case in Latin America, narrowing the gaps, which requires expanding the pool of skilled labor, is likely to take an order of magnitude longer than it does to increase awareness about them (Behrman, Birdsall, and Szekely, 2000).

The concepts of rising aspirations and relative deprivation are not at all new to the study of development economics. They are highlighted in Hirschman's work, for example. Yet these concepts are not well incorporated into our existing measures of progress, even though they may have significant effects on individuals' assessments of their welfare.

The broader question posed by the Easterlin paradox—why countries do not get happier as they get wealthier—is also very relevant to this discussion.

At minimum it introduces a rather different element into the discussion of the tradeoffs involved for developing countries when they opt to pursue objectives other than growth, such as more equitable distribution and better social welfare systems. Our research on happiness in the developing countries of course cannot answer these widely debated questions. Yet perhaps it can provide some new insights into them.

The Economics of Happiness in Developing Countries: An Initial Exploration

There are very few studies of happiness in the developing economies, and to the extent that they exist, they tend to cover individual countries. As far as we know, our study of reported well-being in Latin America and Russia is the first such study in a large sample of developing countries (Graham and Pettinato, 2002, 2001). While there have been some smaller studies in particular countries, such as Namafie and Sanfey (1998) in Kyrgystan, Rojas (2003) in Mexico, and Ravallion and Lokshin (1999) in Russia, as far as we know, there are no other region-wide studies in the developing countries. Our results strongly support the important role played by relative income differences, reference norms, and other non-income factors highlighted above. Indeed, we found that for the most part, the determinants of happiness were very similar in the developing economies to those in the advanced economies.

Our work began as an attempt to understand better the determinants of income mobility (as a proxy for the distribution of opportunities) in developing countries that are in the process of opening their economies. The challenge in answering this questions lies in a paucity of data. Baulch and Hoddinot (2000) provide an excellent summary of the few mobility studies that exist for the developing countries (prior to ours).

We also expanded our approach to examine the role of perceptions of past and future mobility, linking data on subjective well-being to detailed over-time data on income mobility for the same respondents. We introduced this approach to data collection in Peru, and were subsequently able to apply it to data from Russia. Unfortunately, we did not have similar mobility data for the larger Latin America-wide sample, which is a large cross section survey of respondents in seventeen countries.[8] In Peru, we re-interviewed a sub-sample (500) of respondents in a large, nationally representative panel for 1991–2000, and asked a number of questions about their perceptions of their past progress

---

[8] The Latinobarometro survey consists of approximately 1,000 interviews in 17 countries in Latin America, providing 17,000 observations for statistical analysis. The samples are conducted annually by a prestigious research firm in each country, and are nationally representative except for Brazil and Paraguay. The survey is produced by the NGO Latinobarometro, a non-profit organization based in Santiago, Chile, and directed by Marta Lagos

and for their future prospects. We repeated this perceptions survey three years in a row. A more detailed discussion of our methods can be found in Graham and Pettinato (2002a) and Graham (2003a).

Measurement Error and Other Concerns

Before reviewing our results, it is necessary to mention possible sources of measurement error in both our panel and perceptions data. Panel data on income mobility are rare, as they require following individuals over a prolonged period of time. And the most obvious drawback of panel data is its scarcity. There is a paucity of such data, in large part due to the expense of generating it. There are only a small number of nationally representative panels for developing countries. Even then, the data is rarely without flaws. Respondents move, leading to attrition and possible bias. Attrition tends to be greatest at the tails of the distribution, as the wealthiest respondents tend to move to better neighborhoods, and the poorest ones move in with others or return to their places of origin. In addition, as respondents in the panel age, they also become less representative of the population as a whole. In our studies, we had a 38 percent attrition rate over a five-year period in Russia, and a 25 percent attrition rate for the three-year period covered by our perceptions survey in Peru (and a lower rate for the 1991–2000 expenditures survey).

Another problem with longitudinal data is accounting for error in reporting income, a problem that is gravely aggravated by policy shocks such as devaluations and/or high levels of inflation. People who are self-employed or employed in the informal sector have a difficult time estimating any sort of monthly or annual salary, in part because their income fluctuates a great deal. Thus expenditure data is more accurate than income data for samples with large numbers of self-employed and/or informal sector workers and agricultural workers. It is also more difficult to under- or mis-report expenditures. Yet expenditure data miss part of the story, particularly at the upper end of the distribution, and do not capture volatility in income flows, as people tend to smooth their consumption where possible by saving and dissaving.

Adding perceptions data to longitudinal data has benefits, but creates its own set of methodological problems. While happiness questions are not very useful in measuring the well-being of particular individuals, there is surprising consistency in the patterns of responses both within and across countries. Psychologists find that a number of well-being indicators validate how most

<http://www.latinobarometro.org>. The first survey was carried out in 1995 and covered 8 countries. Funding began with a grant from the European Community and is now from multiple sources. Access to the data is by purchase, with a 4-year lag in public release. I have worked with the survey team for years and assisted with fundraising, and therefore have access to the data.

individuals respond to happiness or life satisfaction surveys. The correlation coefficient between happiness and life satisfaction questions, meanwhile, is approximately .50, and the micro-econometric equations have almost identical forms.[9]

The data are most useful in the aggregate, as an individual's answer to a question on happiness can be biased by day-to-day events, and the same person's answer could be quite different from day to day or year to year. The simple correlation from a regression of happiness in year two on happiness in year one was .2734 for our Russian sample, suggesting a significant amount of fluctuation in happiness levels. (Given the highly volatile economic context in Russia during the period, this correlation is probably lower than the average for other countries.)

Accuracy in reporting is another major issue. Responses can be biased by the phrasing or the placement of questions in the survey. Another problem is bias introduced by different or changing reference norms. If you ask people how much income they would need to make ends meet, and/or to be happy, they usually base their answers on their existing income and increase it by some proportion, regardless of the absolute level. Alternatively, people base their answers on others in their community or others "like themselves". When we asked people in our Peruvian survey to compare themselves with others in their community and then with others in their country, we found much more consistency in how respondents compared themselves with those in their community than with those in their country, as the latter is a much vaguer reference point.

There is clearly a large margin for error in both kinds of data. The most important, from the perspective of our analysis, is that income gains could be mis-measured. Thus what we are recording as respondents' positive or negative perceptions of those gains could instead be a more realistic assessment than what our measures report. While this may account for some of our findings, the positive correlation that we find between our reported perceptions and other contextual variables gives us some confidence that our results are not solely artifacts of error. Accepting that some error is likely and that caution is necessary in interpreting the results, we feel that they provide useful information that static income data alone would not.

Results

Our most significant and surprising finding in Peru was that almost half of the respondents with the most upward mobility reported that their economic

[9] Blanchflower and Oswald (2004) get a correlation coefficient of .56 for British data for 1975–92 where both questions are available; Graham and Pettinato (2002a) get a correlation coefficient of .50 for Latin American data for 2000–2001, in which alternative phrasing was used in different years.

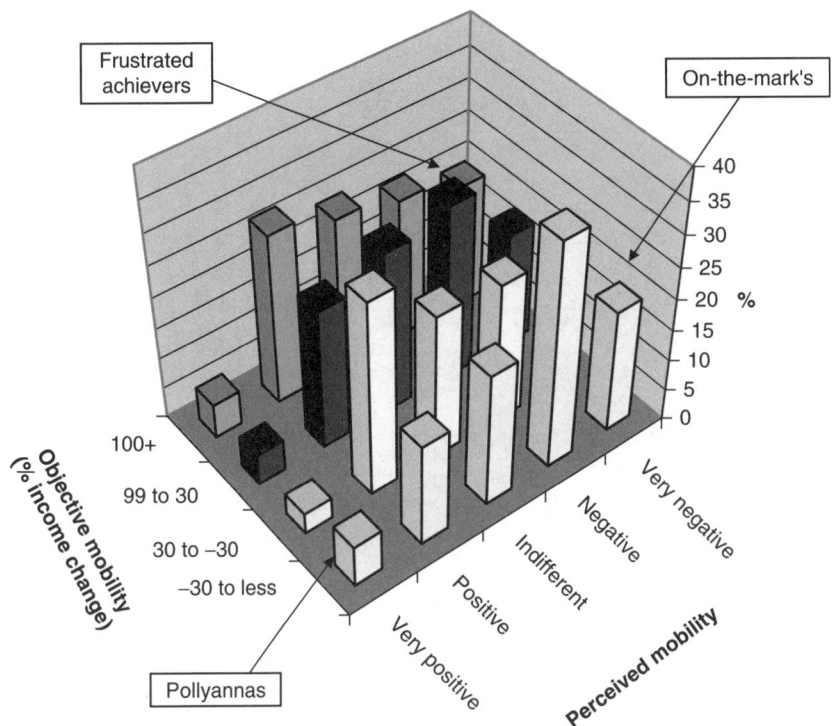

Figure 4.2. Long-term perceived mobility vs. 1991–2000 income mobility, Peru 2000
Source: Graham and Pettinato, 2002a.

situation was negative or very negative compared to ten years prior (Figure 4.2). We conducted a similar analysis based on comparable data for Russia, and found an even higher percentage of frustrated respondents—or "frustrated achievers" as we now call them.[10] These results are consistent with the existence of measurement error in the data (Figure 4.3).

A closer look at these frustrated achievers (FAs) shows that they are at or near average income (and therefore not the poorest in the sample), and that they are more urban and slightly older on average than non-frustrated respondents with upward mobility. There are no significant gender or educational differences (Graham and Pettinato, 2002a). Our frustrated achievers scored lower on

---

[10] The Peruvian data are in expenditures and the Russian data are in income. The uncertain economic context in Russia and the income data makes potential error an even larger problem. In one attempt to correct for error, we eliminated the roughly 60 zero-income respondents from our Russia panel, as many of them also reported that they were employed.

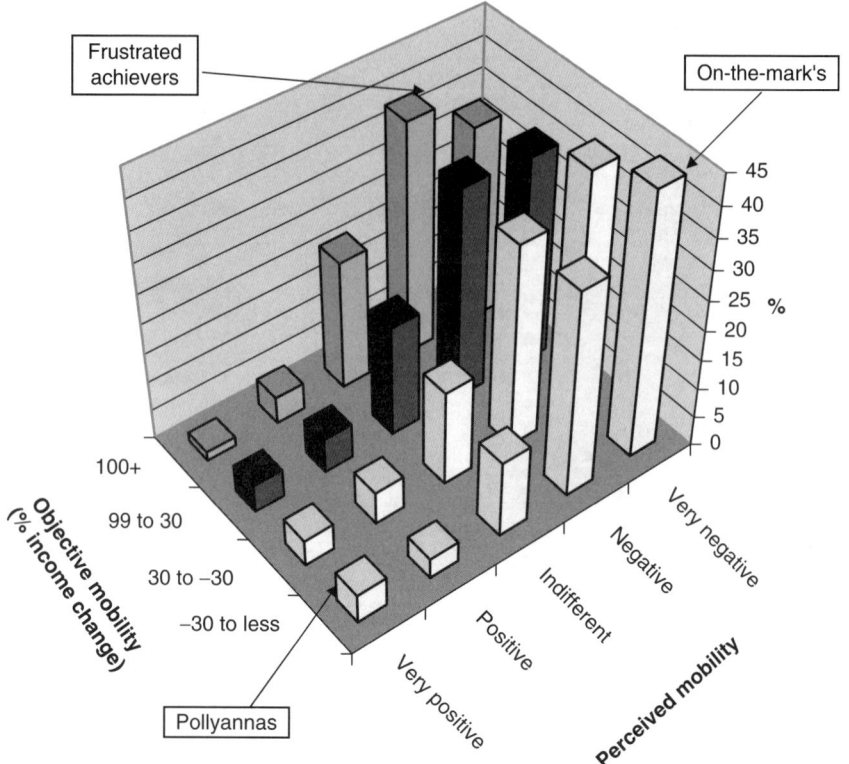

Figure 4.3. Perceived past mobility vs. 1995–99 income mobility, Russia 1999
Source: Graham and Pettinato, 2002a.

a whole host of perceptions questions, such as their perceived prospects of upward mobility, and their positions on a notional economic ladder. In keeping with the direction of these findings, the FAs also had a higher fear of being unemployed in the future. In addition, the Russian FAs were more likely to want to restrict the incomes of the rich, and were less satisfied with the market process and with democracy (we did not have the same questions in the original survey for Peru).

In Peru the likelihood of having upward mobility and being frustrated (an FA) is negatively related to initial income levels (Table 4.1). In other words, the frustrated achievers started from lower income levels, on average, even though they were not the very poorest in the sample at the time they answered our survey. This is not surprising, as thus even large percentage increases in their incomes will seem insufficient to reach the levels of wealthier groups. The FAs were also more likely to be urban, and therefore more informed about

Table 4.1. Frustrated Achievers in Peru, 1991–2000
(Dependent variable: Frustrated Achiever = 1; not = 0)*

Independent variables	Equation 1		Equation 2	
	Coef	Z	Coef	Z
Age	0.025	3.30	0.025	3.29
Male	−0.012	−0.05	−0.005	−0.02
Years of education	0.042	1.61	0.051	1.93
Married	−0.207	−0.89	−0.209	−0.89
Urban	1.495	3.58	1.349	3.35
Log equiv expend. 1991	−1.229	−6.04	—	—
Equivalent expend. 1991	—	—	0.000	−5.70
Constant	6.437	4.13	−2.471	−4.23
Observations	*500*		*500*	
Pseudo R²	*0.0968*		*0.1093*	

* Logit estimation
Source: Graham and Pettinato, 2002a.

the lifestyles of others, including those of the very wealthy. It is possible that in rural areas more aspects of life—perhaps particularly some that contribute to happiness—fall outside the monetary economy, and so money income is less important. There is, of course, also the strong possibility that initial income was mis-measured, which would overstate the gains that the FAs made.

Assuming that all our findings are not caused by error, what explains these frustrations? Relative income differences could certainly be a plausible explanation. Both Peru and Russia have high degrees of inequality. The FAs were more likely to score lower on the notional economic ladder in both surveys, as well as to compare their situations negatively to others in their community and their country in Peru (this latter question was not in the Russian survey).

A lack of adequate social insurance and insecurity could be another explanation. The FAs had a higher fear of unemployment than non-frustrated achievers. Thus even though the FAs are doing well by objective income measures, they perceive that there is no guarantee of stability in their earnings levels. This is not surprising, given that both surveys were conducted in very volatile economic contexts, and the objective mobility data reveal a remarkable degree of vulnerability. A higher percentage of respondents went from "rags to riches"—or from the bottom to the top quintile in a ten-year period in Peru (5%) than in a similar period in the United States (1%), for example. Yet a surprising 11 percent of respondents in the middle of the distribution (quintile 4 in Peru) fell back all the way to the bottom quintile, which is analogous to falling from the middle class into extreme poverty. In both these cases, some of the mobility that we find could be driven by newly educated individuals entering the labor force. Yet as neither study is able to control for this, the rates are, at least, comparable.

We explored whether the frustrated achievers suffered more from this volatility, which in turn might drive some of their frustrations. Yet in Peru, the FAs have less volatility in their income trajectory, as measured by the coefficient of variation, a puzzling result if uncertainty or volatility is an explanation for the frustrations. In Russia the coefficient of variation is higher, which at first glance seems a more intuitive finding.

Andrew Clark (2003) finds that respondents with greater income variance (controlling for levels) are more tolerant of inequality in Britain, presumably because the variance signals that great gains or opportunities are possible. This is the opposite of our initial intuition, in which volatility produces insecurity and reduces well-being. It may be that some combination of both interpretations is at play: while our frustrated achievers may be concerned about inequality and unemployment, they may also view income variance as a reflection of new opportunities, at least in Peru. Tolerance of inequality varies across societies. There may be similar differences in tolerance of volatility related to inequality.

The fact that most of the FAs were at mean levels of education is probably relevant to the discussion of volatility versus opportunity. In Latin America, with the opening of trade and capital markets in the 1990s, those with higher levels of education are gaining high marginal returns compared with the rest of society, while those with secondary education are seeing decreasing marginal returns compared with those with primary education (Behrman, Birdsall, and Szekely, 2000).

Lastly, it is quite plausible that some of the frustrations that we find are driven by individual character traits rather than by economic and other variables. There is probably some percentage of every sample that will always be negative or unhappy, regardless of objective conditions. That led us to ask if our population samples were significantly different from others. Unfortunately, we do not, at this point, have similar income mobility and perceptions data for a broader sample of countries, which would allow us to compare the percentage of frustrated achievers across countries. We were able to re-interview an urban sub-sample of our panel in 2003, and found that there are still frustrated achievers, although a slightly lower percentage of the (fewer) upwardly mobile respondents were frustrated (27% of our urban respondents were frustrated achievers in the 1991–2000 period, 18% were in the 2000–2003 period). The economy was contracting from 2000 to 2003, in contrast to the previous, rapid growth period. This suggests that frustrations decrease somewhat with aspirations, but that some percentage of our sample may be frustrated regardless of conditions (Graham and MacLeod, 2004).

We were able to explore the broader question of whether the determinants of happiness differ in the developing economies from those in the advanced industrial economies. We compared the determinants of happiness in Latin America and in Russia with those of the United States. For the US, we used the pooled data for 1973–98 from the General Social Survey (GSS). For Russia, we used the most recent available survey (2000) from the Russian Longitudinal

Table 4.2. Happiness in Latin America, 2001
(Dependent variable: Happiness)*

Independent variables	Coef.	Z
Age	−0.025	−4.21
Age squared	0.000	4.72
Male	−0.002	−0.07
Married	0.056	1.63
Log wealth index	0.395	10.56
Years of education	−0.003	−0.64
Minority	−0.083	−2.49
Student	0.066	1.01
Retired	−0.005	−0.06
Homemaker	−0.053	−1.04
Unemployed	−0.485	−7.54
Self employed	−0.098	−2.33
Health (self-reported)	0.468	24.58
Pseudo R^2	0.062	
Observations	15209	

* Ordered logit estimation; country dummies included but not shown
Source: Latinobarometro, 2001. Author's calculations.

Monitoring Survey (RLMS). For Latin America, we relied on the 2001 Latino-barometro survey because it is the one year for which we have variables for both self-reported health status and for being a member of a minority, which makes it comparable to the US and Russia surveys (Tables 4.2–4).

We find a remarkable degree of similarity in the effects of age, income, education, marriage, employment, and health. In all contexts, unemployed people are less happy than others. Self-employed people are happier in the US and in Russia on average, while in Latin America, they are less happy. While in the US self-employment is a choice, in Latin America the self-employed are often in the informal sector by default. Another difference is that women are happier than men in the US, while in Russia men are happier than women (due to disparities in status?). In Latin America there is no gender difference. Blacks are less happy than other races in the United States, and similarly, those that identify as members of a minority in Latin America are less happy. In contrast, members of a minority in Russia are happier than ethnic Russians.

We also find that, in both Latin America and Russia, happier people are more likely to support market policies, to be satisfied with how democracy is work-ing, and to prefer democracy to any other system of government. (Support for market policies was measured by an index based on several scaled questions about the private sector, foreign investment, free trade, and privatization.) A cross-canton study in Switzerland by Bruno Frey and Alois Stutzer (2000) finds that people who participate in direct democracy are happier than those who do not, all else being equal. While we do not have similar information on

Table 4.3. Happiness in Russia, 2000
(Dependent variable: Happiness)*

Independent variables	Coef.	Z
Age	−0.067	−7.42
Age squared	0.001	7.15
Male	0.152	2.80
Married	0.088	1.40
Log equivalent income	0.389	11.48
Education level	0.015	0.96
Minority	0.172	2.46
Student	0.199	1.59
Retired	−0.378	−3.97
Housewife	0.049	0.33
Unemployed	−0.657	−6.51
Self employed	0.537	2.23
Health index	0.446	3.82
Pseudo R²	0.033	
Observations	5134	

* Ordered logit estimation
Source: Graham, Eggers, Sukhtankar (2004).

Table 4.4. Happiness in the US, 1972–98
(Dependent variable: Happiness)*

Independent variables	Coef.	Z
Age	−0.025	−5.20
Age squared	0.038	7.53
Male	−0.199	−6.80
Married	0.775	25.32
Log income	0.163	9.48
Education	0.007	1.49
Black	−0.400	−10.02
Other race	0.049	0.59
Student	0.291	3.63
Retired	0.219	3.93
Housekeeper	0.065	1.66
Unemployed	−0.684	−8.72
Self employed	0.098	2.29
Health	0.623	35.91
Pseudo R²	0.075	
Observations	24128	

* Ordered logit estimation; year dummies included but not shown.
Source: GSS data. Author's calculations.

respondents' voting patterns, our results do suggest a virtuous circle of sorts, between happiness and support for democracy (even though we cannot establish the direction of causality).

Happier people, on average, have higher prospects for their own and their children's future mobility; are more likely to believe that the distribution of income in their country is fair; place themselves higher on a notional economic ladder (ELQ); and have lower fear of unemployment. (The ELQ question asked respondents to place themselves on a 9-step ladder representing their society, where the poor are on step 1 and the rich are on step 9.)

In contrast, the negative perceptions of our frustrated achievers in Peru and Russia are correlated with lower life satisfaction (happiness) scores; lower scores on a notional societal economic ladder (compared to non-frustrated respondents of comparable income levels); lower perceived prospects of upward mobility; higher fear of unemployment; and less satisfaction with market policies and a lower probability of preferring democracy as a system of government.

We are not aware of surveys in the OECD economies which take our approach and compare objective trends in income mobility with reported trends. However, there are some studies which link people's perceptions about mobility—such as perceived prospects of upward mobility—with voting behavior and views about redistribution. Most of these studies suggest that societies with widely held faith in prospects for upward mobility are more tolerant of income inequality than those where social mobility is more limited. Roland Benabou and Efe Ok (1998) develop a model which they apply to data from the panel study on income dynamics (PSID) that shows that even though the majority of Americans are well below mean income, they do not vote for redistribution. This is because they believe that they will be above the mean in the future (even though this is an unrealistic expectation for the median voter) (see also Piketty, 1995).

Alberto Alesina, Rafael di Tella, and Robert MacCulloch (2000) compare views about inequality in the United States and Europe. They find that inequality has a modest negative effect on all respondents in Europe, and it is strongest for the poor. In contrast in the US, the only group that is made less happy by inequality are left-leaning wealthy respondents! They posit that differences in views about the prospects of upward mobility between the two continents explain their results. This is something noted centuries ago by de Tocqueville in comparing the US and Europe. In our own analysis of GSS data, we find that US respondents that support redistribution are, on average, less happy than others (Graham, 2003).

Andrew Felton and I analyze inequality in Latin America, as noted above, and find that it makes the rich happier and the poor less happy, signaling persistent advantage for the former and disadvantage for the latter. Graham, Andrew Eggers, and Sandip Sukhtankar (2004) also examined responses to several questions related to redistribution. One asks respondents to place themselves on a 9-point scale, where 1 is preferring more freedom and money and 9 is preferring more rules and equality. Respondents that had higher perceived prospects of upward mobility were wealthier on average and were less likely to prefer equality and regulation.[11] This finding is similar to those for the US.

Rather surprisingly, wealthier people were more likely to support more taxation and social spending. While a surprising 67 percent of respondents said that taxes should be lower even if social welfare spending suffers, it was the wealthier respondents that tended to disagree. (We also split the sample into those respondents that were likely to pay taxes and those that were not, but did not get results that were significantly different.) At least some of these results reflect Latin Americans' mistrust of the state's ability to redistribute fairly rather than widely held beliefs about prospects for upward mobility (only 13% of Latin American respondents believe that the income distribution is fair or somewhat fair).[12] The limited support for redistribution seems to be among wealthier groups. A positive interpretation is that this reflects enlightened self interest. Yet a more realistic one may be that the poor typically receive fewer benefits from state spending than do wealthier groups in the region, and public faith in the state's capacity to redistribute fairly is quite minimal.

Rather surprisingly, we found that a remarkably similar percentage of respondents in the United States and Latin America thought that their children would live better than they (57% and 58% respectively). In contrast, far fewer Latin American respondents than US respondents felt that they lived better than their parents did (Graham, 2003a). There still seems to be a surprising amount of faith in the region in individual effort and prospects for getting ahead. Some of this faith is, no doubt, based on respondents' awareness that their children are likely to have, at the least, access to more and better quality education than they did. Some reflects hope and expectations as much as anything else. For our Peru sample, we found that some of the same respondents that assessed their own situation more negatively than was warranted by objective income measures still assessed their children's prospects in a positive light.

Those with higher prospects for upward mobility were also more likely to favor market policies, to support democracy over any other system of government, and to place themselves higher on the notional economic ladder. In

---

[11] In a regression with the variable EQUALSUP as the dependent variable, the coefficient on our prospects of upward mobility variable—POUM—was negative and significant. The coefficient on the wealth index was positive and significant. It even remained positive when we squared it to see if there were differences in the attitudes of the very wealthy. Results are available from the author.

[12] In an earlier study we found that support for redistribution was lower in poorer, more unequal countries in the region than in the wealthier ones, while within countries wealthy people were more likely to favor productivity over redistribution. This finding is based on a question in the 1998 Latinobarometro asking respondents if what their country needs most to get ahead is more redistribution or more productivity. For detail, see Graham and Pettinato 2002, chapter 3.

contrast, our frustrated achiever respondents in Peru and Russia, who on average had higher fear of unemployment and lower Prospects of Upward Mobility (POUM) scores, tended to be less supportive of market policies and of democracy. Our findings yield notable public frustration, frustration which is linked to concerns about income differentials and unemployment and with reduced support for markets and democracy (Graham and Pettinato, 2002a).

CAUSALITY CONUNDRUMS

While the frustrations and unhappiness that we find are indeed linked to policy-relevant questions, the direction of causality is not clear. We do not know whether policies and/or environments drive the frustrations, or whether underlying character traits (such as lower innate levels of happiness) drive negative assessments of policies and environments. In other words, it may well be that frustrated or unhappy people are more likely to be pessimistic about the future and concerned about relative income differences or insecurity.

At least some of the explanation for patterns in reported well-being lies in character traits. One of our studies in Russia finds that only 3 percent of the variation in happiness is explained by socio-economic and demographic variables; the rest is either behavioral or error driven (Graham, Eggers, and Sukhtankar, 2004). Yet there also seems to be an explanatory role for factors that policy can influence, such as inequality, macroeconomic volatility, and large gaps in rewards to different skill cohorts.

In a recent study, we tried to get a better understanding of the interaction between contextually driven attitudes and behaviorally driven ones. On the basis of Russian data for which we had observations on both happiness and income at two points in time, we found that behavioral traits had a role in explaining differences among individuals' performances and outcomes.

We found that happier people earn more income in later periods, on average, than less happy people (Graham, Eggers, and Sukhtankar, 2004) (Table 4.5). Our method of analysis entailed calculating the residual or unexplained happiness for each respondent in the first period—for example, the happiness that was not explained by the usual socio-economic and demographic variables, something that must be close to the behavioral component of reported happiness. We included that residual as an independent variable with second-period income as the dependent variable. Controlling for first-period income, we found that our residual had positive and significant effects on second-period income. We also found that happier people were healthier in future periods.

While it is accepted that there is a large margin for error and/or correlated error in this analysis, our results suggest that happier people seem to earn more income, perform better in the labor market, and are healthier. Psychologists attribute traits such as positive outlook and high self-esteem (so-called positive

Table 4.5. The effects of happiness on income in Russia, 1995–2000
(Dependent variable: Log equivalence income, 2000 (OLS))

Independent variables	a		b		c	
	Coef	t	Coef	t	Coef	t
Age	−0.013	−3.00	−0.013	−2.97	−0.015	−3.25
Age squared	0.000	3.18	0.000	3.15	0.000	3.52
Male	0.010	0.42	0.010	0.42	0.000	−0.02
Married	0.205	7.84	0.205	7.84	0.205	7.84
Education level	0.030	4.51	0.030	4.51	0.030	4.44
Minority	0.121	3.98	0.123	4.03	0.122	4.00
Student	−0.034	−0.34	−0.030	−0.31	−0.037	−0.38
Retired	−0.191	−4.85	−0.190	−4.83	−0.166	−4.18
Housewife	−0.249	−3.90	−0.249	−3.90	−0.239	−3.73
Unemployed	−0.345	−8.16	−0.344	−8.12	−0.343	−8.07
Self employed	0.142	1.46	0.141	1.46	0.128	1.33
Health index	0.060	1.11	0.059	1.09	0.056	1.04
Log equiv income 95	0.242	18.11	0.243	18.12	0.224	15.69
Log equiv income 95, poor[†]	*	*	*	*	0.009	2.60
Log equiv income 95, rich[†]	*	*	*	*	0.018	4.36
Unexplained happiness, 95[‡]	0.030	2.64	0.063	2.32	0.027	2.38
Unexp. happiness, 95[‡], 2nd quint	*	*	−0.044	−1.14	*	*
Unexp. happiness, 95[‡], 3nd quint	*	*	−0.036	−0.95	*	*
Unexp. happiness, 95[‡], 4th quint	*	*	−0.063	−1.71	*	*
Unexp. happiness, 95[‡], 5th quint	*	*	−0.023	−0.65	*	*
Constant	5.833	36.35	5.823	36.19	5.936	34.62
Observations	*4457*		*4457*		*4457*	
Adjusted R²	*0.134*		*0.133*		*0.152*	

* omitted
[†] "poor" is defined as bottom 40% of the income distribution in 1995; "rich" is the top 20%
[‡] the residual of basic happiness 1995 regression
Independent variables are from 2000 unless otherwise noted.
Regression a: no income quintile distinctions
Regression b: testing for a difference in the effect of unexplained happiness on 2000 income, by 1995 income quintile
Regression c: testing for a difference in the effect of 1995 income on 2000 income, by 1995 income quintile
Source: Graham, Eggers, and Sukhtankar (2004).

cognitive bias) to happier people. It is not surprising that these traits also contribute to productivity and health. A very tentative extension of these findings is that the frustrations of our achievers could be a signal of more negative future outcomes.

We also found that the correlation between happiness and future income was stronger for those at lower levels of income, while the role of first-period income was more important for future income for those at higher levels of income (Table 4.5). A positive outlook and high self-esteem may be valuable labor market assets for those with fewer assets or less income, particularly for those who provide services. These traits probably matter less for those who have sufficient income or assets to leverage in making future gains.

We found that related perceptions variables had a similar relationship with future income. Having a high POUM or placing oneself high on the notional economic ladder (ELQ) in the first period was positively correlated with higher

Table 4.6. Effect of perceptions variables on future income in Russia, 1995–2000 (Dependent variable: Log equivalence income in 2000 (OLS))

Independent variables	a		b	
	coef	t	coef	t
Age	−0.013	−3.00	−0.009	−0.78
Age squared	0.000	3.18	0.000	1.24
Male	0.010	0.42	−0.008	−0.23
Married	0.205	7.84	0.241	6.15
Education level	0.030	4.51	0.032	2.44
Minority	0.121	3.98	0.081	1.80
Student	−0.034	−0.34	0.427	1.07
Retired	−0.191	−4.85	−0.273	−4.60
Housewife	−0.249	−3.90	−0.166	−1.60
Unemployed	−0.345	−8.16	−0.373	−5.82
Self employed	0.142	1.46	0.094	0.72
Health index	0.060	1.11	0.061	0.84
Log equiv income 96	0.242	18.11	0.230	11.55
Unexplained happiness, 95[†]	0.030	2.64	−0.002	−0.11
Fear of unemployment, 95	*	*	−0.014	−1.22
Family better off next year, 95	*	*	0.041	2.27
Economic ladder question, 95	*	*	0.027	2.17
Constant	5.833	36.35	5.533	17.49
Observations	*4457*		*2296*	
Adjusted R^2	*0.134*		*0.126*	

* omitted
[†] the residual of basic happiness 1995 regression
Independent variables are from 2000 unless otherwise noted.
Regression a: no perceptions variables
Regression b: perceptions variables included

Source: Graham, Eggers, and Sukhtankar (2004).

levels of income in the second period. In contrast, having higher fear of unemployment was negatively correlated with future income (albeit only significant at the 10% level) (Table 4.6). Respondents' views or attitudes about their future prospects are correlated with their future outcomes and may play a role in determining those outcomes. It is likely that both happiness and perceptions variables are picking up similar character traits, such as optimism and self-esteem.

Indeed, it is plausible that some of what we find is explained by people's abilities to forecast or predict their future income, and thus first-period attitudes merely reflect people's knowledge of the future.[13] The highly unstable nature of the Russian context, however, renders this unlikely as the *entire* explanation. There is broader psychological evidence that character traits

---

[13] I would like to thank a number of participants at the Brookings Warwick Conference on "Why Inequality Matters: Lessons for Policy from the Economics of Happiness", June 2003, for discussing this insight, and in particular Gary Burtless for raising the point. It is also plausible, of course, that the results are also error driven, and that in the presence of measurement error, the effects of mis-measured variables are projected onto variables that are correlated with them. I thank Angus Deaton for raising this point.

have effects on individuals' labor market performance and on their health outcomes (Diener and Seligman, 2004; Cummins and Nistico, 2002). It may be that behavioral or attitudinal variables may be more important in extremely uncertain contexts such as in Russia, where it is more difficult to predict the future. Research based on comparable data for other countries is necessary to test such a proposition.

These results are suggestive and do not establish any direction of causality. It is possible that causality runs both from policy-relevant variables or factors such as economic performance to happiness, as well as in the other direction, or from third factors that influence both. What, then, are the implications?

At a minimum, it is clear that using longitudinal data on both mobility and subjective well-being gives a very different picture from looking at standard income data in isolation. While it is fairly standard to associate well-being or utility with income, our research and that of many others suggests that there are very important non-income determinants of well-being, a finding which is in keeping with the broader questions raised by the Easterlin paradox. These elements of well-being also seem to have a correlation with labor market performance and future earnings outcomes. An unanswered question, however, is how can we most usefully—and prudently—incorporate these novel approaches and new kinds of data into the analysis of developing economies and into the policies that stem from that analysis.

Relevance of Happiness Research to Development Theory and Policy

The fairly new research on reported well-being in both developed and now developing economies suggests that models based on rationally calculated, income-based utility may not capture all of what drives economic behavior and determines welfare. In addition, the research may provide us with new tools to help answer questions over which there is much debate among economists and other social scientists, such as the effects of inequality on well-being and the relationship between economic growth (or lack thereof) and social unrest.

Perhaps the most notable finding from this research is the notable gaps between measures of welfare as gauged in standard terms such as earned income or expenditures—and even other standard measures of development progress, such as gains in life expectancy, education, and reductions in infant mortality—and those reported in surveys of well-being. These complementary measures of welfare could inform our efforts to model and analyze economic behavior—and micro-level responses to policy incentives. Yet this poses a conceptual as well as an empirical challenge, not least because there are times when the policy implications of findings from reported well-being surveys run in the opposite direction to what most development experts would consider "sound" policies.

One problem is that it is difficult to separate cause from effect cleanly when assessing the importance of these gaps. In other words, the differences between measured and reported welfare may be driven by the effects of non-income variables which our income measures do not capture—such as job insecurity, relative income differences, and health and marital status. Yet it is also quite plausible that less happy people are more likely to attribute importance to these insecurities and differences, as well as less likely to be healthy and to get married.

Across countries, the Easterlin paradox suggests that there are limits to the extent that income growth alone—and even aggregate improvements in important areas such as health and education—can increase average levels of happiness, as individuals adapt their expectations upwards as societies progress. A strict interpretation of the "set point" theory would suggest that happiness surveys cannot offer any realistic insights for policy, as virtually nothing will make people happier for long.

There is some debate about the long-term consequences of events like serious illness, unemployment, and losing a spouse for people's happiness, with some studies suggesting that they are permanent, while others show that with sufficient time individuals adapt to virtually any event, including divorce or serious illness. Yet many studies find that many events have permanent effects on happiness. The findings on unemployment are the most consistent of these (Easterlin, 2003; Clark et al., 2004; Darity and Goldsmith, 1996).

Cross section studies of happiness within societies consistently conclude that individuals value things like health, stable employment, and marriage as much as, if not more than, income, and at the same time adapt less—or less quickly—to changes in these realms than to changes in income. Indeed, it may well be that changes in these variables, such as getting married or divorced—and related leads and lags—are the main drivers of these results, while the extent to which the effects last is less clear (and most likely varies across variables).[14] And even if happiness levels eventually adapt upwards to a longer-term equilibrium (after a negative shock like illness or divorce), mitigating or preventing the unhappiness and disruption that individuals experience for months, or even years, in the interim certainly seems like a worthwhile objective for policy.

---

[14] I would like to thank Angus Deaton for raising the point about the effects of changes. He cites evidence from the German GSEOP panel which shows that people adapt to the welfare losses of marriage or widowhood in about seven years. Our own work finds that during a five-year period in Russia, the most detrimental event for our sample of respondents was getting divorced. While our respondents may have adapted after the five-year period of study, they were significantly less happy than others during that period. See Graham, Eggers, and Sukhtankar (2004).

Across nations there are diminishing returns to increasing income. Yet there are other things that correlate with national income, such as health, quality of government, and respect for human rights, which seem to correlate with higher happiness levels. There is also some evidence that perceived equity in the distribution of income or rewards can matter as much to people's happiness as the rewards themselves. All of this suggests that happiness surveys—if used cautiously and with awareness that they do not well reflect long-term gains in income and health, which are important to the welfare of the poor—may broaden our understanding of a number of development questions.

Reported well-being seems to be correlated with economic outcomes. Reported happiness and many related perceptions, such as people's perceived prospects of upward mobility (which are highly correlated), are correlated with economic outcomes and with political views. No doubt some of what we might consider "effect" is individuals' abilities to predict or forecast their future outcomes. Yet there is also psychological evidence that character traits, such as high self-esteem and optimism, have effects on individuals' labor market performance and on their health outcomes. Thus a remaining challenge is how to account better for the role of subjective well-being and related perceptions in explaining individual economic and political behavior. Addressing such questions might enhance our understanding of development challenges such as persistent poverty traps, in which low expectations play a role in the willingness of the poor both to take risks and to make investments in their children's futures.

The same psychological factors that affect subjective evaluations of well-being also seem to explain individuals' abilities to adapt to tremendous adversity and/or negative shocks and often even to return to previous levels of happiness. A nuanced view of adaptation—to either negative shocks or to the disruptions and changes that often accompany economic progress and development—is that the process is very much moderated by people's norms about equity and perceptions of fairness. This helps to explain why there is often unexpected social stability in very poor societies, and, at the same time, unexpected outbreaks of violence and social unrest in societies where there is a great deal of economic progress—but differential rewards to different cohorts. Our upwardly mobile frustrated respondents are a case in point.

A remaining challenge is better understanding the interaction between norms about fairness and equity with economic progress and change—including integration into global markets and information systems. Norms about what is fair are endogenous to policy choices in the long run, and may explain, for example, the loss of unions' bargaining power over time (Atkinson, 1999). Tolerance of inequality seems higher in contexts where there are perceived (even if not real) prospects for upward mobility (Graham and Young, 2003). Downward mobility, meanwhile, or the threat thereof, is more likely to cause frustration and social unrest than is persistent poverty, as in the case of our frustrated achievers in Peru and Russia, or more generally as in Argentina in the late 1990s.

Our own research results suggest that we underestimate the effects of macro-economic volatility, unstable employment, and highly unequal income distributions on the well-being of individuals in the developing economies. One logical policy implication is the need for better social insurance and social policies in these countries. Not only the very poor but those in the middle of the distribution are often very vulnerable to falling into poverty, drops which can have lasting costs (Cline, 2002; Prasad et al., 2003). While such policy conclusions are hardly novel ones, what is novel is their strong backing in individual welfare assessments rather than in a more general political or public policy debate, as is usually the case.

The more fundamental point is that broader and/or novel measures of welfare can help us better understand development outcomes, both positive and negative. Surveys of reported well-being are a helpful tool, although alone are insufficient. Their potential contribution increases markedly when they can be matched with objective (and hopefully sound) income data for the same respondents. Yet caution is necessary when using this information as the basis for policy, particularly when surveys are conducted in unstable economic and political climates.

In the end, many of the results from surveys of reported well-being—or put more simply, from asking people what is important to their own welfare—drum home an old saw that seems to need constant reinforcing: growth is a necessary but not sufficient condition for poverty reduction. Other key factors—such as public investments in health; institutions that can ensure adherence to basic norms of equity and fairness; and collective investments in social insurance to protect workers from the volatility that often accompanies integration into global markets—are essential to sustaining the gains that growth and development bring about, and for increasing the chances that larger numbers of the world's poor can eventually lead happy and fulfilling lives.

References

Alesina, Alberto, Rafael di Tella, and Robert MacCulloch. 2000. "Inequality and Happiness: Are Europeans and Americans Different?" NBER Working Papers 8198. Cambridge, Mass.

Argyle, Michael. 1999. "Causes and Correlates of Happiness." In Daniel Kahneman, Ed Diener, and Norbert Schwarz, eds., *Well-Being: The Foundations of Hedonic Psychology*. New York: Russell Sage Foundation.

Atkinson, Anthony. 1999. "Equity Issues in a Globalising World: The Experience of OECD Countries." In Vito Tanzi, Ke-Young Chu, and Sanjeev Gupta, eds., *Economic Policy and Equity*. Washington, D.C.: International Monetary Fund.

Baulch, Bob, and John Hoddinot. 2000. "Economic Mobility and Poverty Dynamics in Developing Countries." *Journal of Development Studies* 36: 1–24.

Behrman, Jere, Nancy Birdsall, and Miguel Szekely. 2000. "Economic Reform and Wage Differentials in Latin America." IADB Research Working Paper No. 435. Washington, D.C.

Benabou, Roland, and Efe Ok. 1998. "Social Mobility and the Demand for Redistribution: The POUM Hypothesis." NBER Working Paper 6795. Cambridge, Mass.

Bertrand, Marianne, and Sendhil Mullainathan. 2001. "Do People Mean What they Say? Implications for Subjective Survey Data." MIT Economics Working Paper No. 01–04. Cambridge, Mass.

Birdsall, Nancy. Forthcoming. "Open Economy Social Contract." *Economica*.

—— Carol Graham, and Stefano Pettinato. 2001. "Stuck in the Tunnel: Has Globalization Muddled the Middle Class?" Center on Social and Economic Dynamics Working Papers No. 13. Washington, D.C.: The Brookings Institution.

Blanchflower, David, and Andrew Oswald. 2004. "Well-being in Britain and the USA." *Journal of Public Economics* 88: 1359–87.

Clark, Andrew. 2003. "Inequality-Aversion and Income Mobility: A Direct Test." Mimeo, DELTA, Paris.

—— and Andrew Oswald. 1994. "Unhappiness and Unemployment." *The Economic Journal* 104: 648–59.

—— Ed Diener, Yannis Georgellis, and Richard E. Lucas. 2004. "Unemployment Alters the Set Point for Life Satisfaction." Mimeo, University of Illinois.

Cline, William. 2002. "Financial Crises and Poverty in Emerging Market Economies." Center for Global Development Working Paper No. 8. Washington, D.C.

Collier, Paul, V. L. Elliott, Håvard Hegre, Anke Hoeffler, Marta Reynal-Querol, and Nicholas Sambanis. 2003. *Breaking the Conflict Trap: Civil War and Development Policy.* Washington, D.C.: The World Bank and Oxford University Press.

Conlisk, John. 1996. "Why Bounded Rationality?" *Journal of Economic Literature* 34: 669–700.

Cummins, Robert, and Helen Nistico. 2002. "Maintaining Life Satisfaction: The Role of Positive Cognitive Bias." *Journal of Happiness Studies* 3(1): 37–69.

Darity, William, Jr., and Arthur H. Goldsmith. 1996. "Social Psychology, Unemployment, and Macroeconomics." *Journal of Economic Perspectives* 10(1): 121–40.

Deaton, Angus. 2003. "Health, Inequality, and Development." *Journal of Economic Literature* 41: 113–58.

Diener, Ed. 1984 . "Subjective Well-Being." *Psychological Bulletin* 95(3): 542–75.

—— Ed Sandvik, Larry Seidlitz, and Marissa Diener. 1993. "The Relationship Between Income and Subjective Well-Being: Relative or Absolute?" *Social Indicators Research* 28: 195–223.

—— and Robert Biswas-Diener. 2000. "Income and Subjective Well-Being: Will Money Make Us Happy?" Mimeo, University of Illinois.

—— and Martin E. P. Seligman. 2004. "Beyond Money: Toward an Economy of Well-being." *Psychological Science in the Public Interest* 5(1): 1–31.

Di Tella, Rafael, Robert MacCulloch, and Andrew Oswald. 2001. "Preferences for Inflation and Unemployment: Some Evidence from Surveys of Happiness." *American Economic Review* 91(1): 335–41.

Donovan, Nick, and David Halpern. 2002. "Life Satisfaction: The State of Knowledge and Implications for Government." Mimeo, Strategy Unit, Office of the Prime Minister, United Kingdom.

Duesenberry, James. 1949. *Income, Saving, and the Theory of Consumer Behavior.* Cambridge: Harvard University Press.

Easterbrook, Gregg. 2003. *The Progress Paradox: How Life Gets Better While People Feel Worse.* New York: Random House.

Easterlin, Richard A. 1974. "Does Economic Growth Improve the Human Lot? Some Empirical Evidence." In Paul A. David and Melvin W. Reder, eds., *Nations and Households in Economic Growth.* New York: Academic Press.

—— 1995. "Will Raising the Incomes of All Increase the Happiness of All?" *Journal of Economic Behavior and Organization* 27: 35–48.

—— 2001a. "Life Cycle Welfare: Trends and Differences." *Journal of Happiness Studies* 2: 1–12.

—— 2001b. "Income and Happiness: Towards a Unified Theory." *The Economic Journal* 111(473).

—— 2003. "Explaining Happiness." *Proceedings of the National Academy of Sciences* 100 (19): 11176–83.

Eggers, Andrew, and Carol Graham. 2004. "The Costs of Unemployment in Latin America." Mimeo, The Brookings Institution. Washington, D.C.

—— Clifford Gaddy, and Carol Graham. Forthcoming. "Well-being and Unemployment in Russia in the 1990's: Can Society's Suffering Be Individuals' Solace?" *Journal of Socio-Economics.*

Esping-Andersen, Gosta. 1990. *Three Worlds of Welfare Capitalism.* Princeton: Princeton University Press.

Frey, Bruno, and Alois Stutzer. 2000. *Happiness and Economics.* Princeton: Princeton University Press.

Graham, Carol. 2002. "Crafting Sustainable Social Contracts in Latin America: Public Attitudes and Political Economy." Center on Social and Economic Dynamics Working Papers No. 29, The Brookings Institution. Washington, D.C.

—— 2003a. "The Role of Government in Enhancing Opportunities for the Poor: Economic Mobility, Public Attitudes, and Public Policy." In Gary Fields and Guy Pfeffermann, eds., *Pathways Out of Poverty: Private Firms and Economic Mobility in Developing Countries.* Boston, Mass.: Kluwer Academic Publishers.

—— 2003b. "Happiness and Hardship: Lessons from Panel Data on Mobility and Subjective Well-being in Peru and Russia." Paper presented to DFID–ODI–DPU Conference on Longitundinal Data, London.

Graham, Carol, and Stefano Pettinato. 2001. "Happiness, Markets, and Democracy: Latin America in Comparative Perspective." *Journal of Happiness Studies* 3: 237–68.

—— —— 2002a. "Frustrated Achievers: Winners, Losers, and Subjective Well-being in Emerging Market Economies." *Journal of Development Studies* 38(4): 100–40.

—— —— 2002b. "Happy Peasants and Frustrated Achievers: Mobility, Opportunity, and Perceptions in the Development Process." *Journal of Development Studies* 38(4).

—— and Peyton Young. 2003. "Ignorance Fills the Income Gulf." *The Boston Globe,* June 23.

—— and Margaret MacLeod. 2003. Mimeo, The Brookings Institution, Washington, D.C.

111

Graham, Carol, and Stefano Pettinato 2004. "Curmudgeons or Frustrated Achievers? Economic Adjustment, Mobility, and Unhappiness in Peru, 2000–2003." Mimeo, The Brookings Institution, Washington, D.C.

—— Andrew Eggers, and Sandip Sukhtankar. 2004. "Does Happiness Pay? An Exploration Based on Panel Data from Russia." *Journal of Economic Behavior and Organization* 55: 319–42.

—— and Andrew Felton. 2005 "Does Income Inequality Matter to Individual Welfare? An Initial Exploration Based on Happiness Surveys from Latin America." Center on Social and Economic Dynamics Working Paper Series No. 37, The Brookings Institution.

Gurr, Ted Robert. 1970. *Why Men Rebel.* Princeton: Princeton University Press.

Hagerty, M. 1999. "Social Comparisons of income in one's community: Evidence from National Surveys of Income and Happiness" (Mimeo).

Hayo, Berndt. 2003. "Happiness in Eastern Europe." Paper presented to the Fifth Conference of the International Society for Quality of Life Studies (ISQOLS), Frankfurt.

Helliwell, John. F. 2004. "Well-being and Social Capital: Does Suicide Pose a Puzzle?" NBER Working Paper 10896. Cambridge, Mass.

Hirschman, Albert O. 1973. "Changing Tolerance for Income Inequality in the Course of Economic Development." *Quarterly Journal of Economics* 87: 544–66.

Kapteyn, Arie. 1999. "Savings and Reference Groups." Paper presented for the MacArthur Network on Inequality and Social Interactions, The Brookings Institution, Center on Social and Economic Dynamics. Washington, D.C.

Kohler, Hans-Peter, Jere Behrman, and Axel Skythe. 2005. "Partner + Children = Happiness?: An Assessment of Fertility and Partnerships on Subjective Well Being." Mimeo, University of Pennsylvania.

McMurrer, Daniel, and Isabel Sawhill. 1998. *Getting Ahead: Economic and Social Mobility in America.* Washington, D.C.: Urban Institute Press.

Merton, Robert. 1957. *Social Theory and Social Structure.* Glencoe, Ill.: Free Press of Glencoe.

Namafie, Ceema, and Peter Sanfey. 1998. "Happiness in Transition: The Case of Kyrgyzstan." Discussion Paper 40, London School of Economics, Distributional Analysis Research Programme.

Pigou, A. C. 1920. *The Economics of Welfare.* London: Macmillan.

Piketty, Thomas. 1995. "Social Mobility and Redistributive Politics." *Quarterly Journal of Economics* 110: 551–84.

Powdthavee, Nattavudh. Forthcoming. "Happiness and the Standard of Living: The Case for South Africa." *Economica.*

Prasad, Eswar, Kenneth Rogoff, Shang-Jin Wei, and Ayhan Kose. 2003. "Effects of Financial Globalization on Developing Countries: Some Empirical Evidence." IMF Occasional Paper 220. Washington, D.C.

Pritchett, Lant, Asep Suryahadi, and Sudarno Sumarto. 2000. "Quantifying Vulnerability to Poverty: A Proposed Measure with Application to Indonesia." Development Economics Working Papers 83, East Asian Bureau of Economic Research.

Ravallion, Martin, and Misha Lokshin. 1999. "Subjective Economic Welfare." World Bank Policy Research Working Paper 2106. Washington, D.C.

Rojas, Mariano. 2003. "Happiness and Public Policy: Political Economy Considerations." Paper presented to the Fifth Conference of the International Society for Quality of Life Studies (ISQOLS), Frankfurt.

Sambanis, Nicholas. Forthcoming. "Poverty and the Organization of Political Violence: A Review and Some Conjectures." In Susan Collins and Carol Graham, eds., *Brookings Trade Forum 2004: Globalization, Poverty, and Inequality.* Washington, D.C.: The Brookings Institution Press.

Schor, Juliet. 1998. *The Overspent American: Why Want What We Don't Need.* New York: Basic Books.

Simon, Herbert. 1978. "Rationality as a Process and Product of Thought." *American Economic Review* 68: 1–16.

Veblen, Thorstein. 1899. *The Theory of the Leisure Class.* New York: Macmillan.

Veenhoven, Ruut. 1991. "Is Happiness Relative?" *Social Indicators Research* 24: 1–34.

Webb, Richard. 1965. "Reflexiones sobre los ingresos de los Informales", *Oiga*, Lima, Peru, 25 Julio.

5

Back to Aristotle? Happiness, Eudaimonia, and Relational Goods

Luigino Bruni

"It is clearly that wealth is not the good that we want: wealth is not more that one useful thing that is wanted for an other aim."

Aristotle

Contemporary economics is a badly equipped discipline for understanding the nexus between happiness and genuine, not instrumental, sociality. The intuition that inspired this chapter is the conviction that if economics accepts once again to consider non-instrumental interpersonal relations, that is, relational goods, it will profit by a rediscovery of its link with the Aristotelian tradition. In fact, mainstream political economy has considered genuine sociality as basically an extra-economic matter, or something to be taken into account in terms of externality. At the same time, one of the most meaningful tenets of the current debate on happiness is the evidence that genuine and not instrumental sociality is one of the heaviest components of people's subjective well-being.

In this chapter I intend to explore the nexus between happiness and relational goods, not empirically[1] but from a historical-methodological point of view, an issue deeply related to the subject of this volume.

Well-Being or Happiness?

The theme of happiness has begun to be among the interests of economists only recently,[2] trapped as they were by the "iron-curtain effect" of the

[1] An empirical analysis of this nexus is Bruni and Stanca (2008).
[2] The rediscovery of happiness started in the 1970s, although in the Latin tradition of Civil Economy happiness has been a key theme since the eighteenth century—on this cf. Bruni (2006) and Bruni and Zamagni (2007).

114

hypothesis of rationality. Other social scientists, however, in other fields, have been working on the theme for decades. Sociologists were perhaps the first to find "empirical" indicators of the *standard of living*, that went beyond the GDP per capita. Back in the 1920s William Ogburn launched a social research program on the "quality of life" which generated the important "movement of social indicators of the quality of life", that a few years later spread from the United States to Europe.[3]

The rise and diffusion of this movement were favored by the cultural climate of the 1960s which sought to overcome a pure economic conception of the process of economic growth. There were many "heterodox" economists (e.g. Myrdal, Galbraith, Hirschman) who were critics of the mainstream of neoclassical economics. Their works were sources of inspiration for sociologists and social scientists, and fostered research projects on the definition of social indicators. The aim was to find operational solutions capable of effectively quantifying the concept of "quality of life" in order to arrive at a sort of "social accountability".

This "quality of life movement" (Offer 2003) emphasizes mainly "objective" and normative (or ethical) ingredients of a good life, while the later "happiness movement" is characterized by a more "subjective" approach, being based on self-reported evaluations (basically questionnaires). In fact, mostly thanks to Sen and Nussbaum, the category of *quality of life* tends to encompass new indicators such as democracy, rights, health, working conditions, and fundamental capabilities. In the 1980s, a "list of fundamental human needs" was drawn up that was mainly based on the theory of capabilities, that has influenced the debate on the United Nation's *Human Development Indicators* (HDI).[4]

The quality of life approach, deeply linked with the capability approach, considers self-reported happiness as only *one* component of well-being, that, instead, has to be anchored on more *objective* bases. In this approach what counts in terms of happiness (here translated into "good life") is what people actually "do" and could do, and not what they "feel". The following very famous passage by Sen is enlightening:

Consider a very deprived person who is poor, exploited, overworked and ill, but who has been made satisfied with his lot by social conditioning (t[h]rough, say, religion, political propaganda, or cultural pressure). Can we possibly believe that he is doing well just because is happy and satisfied? Can the living standard of a person be high if the life that

---

[3] In 1954, the United Nations nominated a commission for the task of improving the studies on living standards by defining more precisely the contents which make up the *standard of living* concept as well as their indicators.

[4] The HDI turned out to be crucial in development policies. According to Sen (1999) it represents the most important example of putting into operation his *capabilities approach*, which measures individual well-being on the basis of what a person is capable of doing with his goods.

he or she leads is full of deprivation? The standard of life cannot be so detached from the nature of the life the person leads. (1979, p. 12)

The Economics and Happiness research project,[5] instead, is less concerned with this problem of preferences adaptation, and still thinks that what people feel and tell about the satisfaction of their own life is the most important indicator of personal well-being.

The aim of this chapter is to show that the category of "relational goods", being at the same time subjective (self-reported) and objective (in Aristotle's sense), can become an important link in the debate between capabilities and happiness.

Sociality and Happiness

In current economics a new season of interest for a genuine interpersonal dimension has to be registered.[6] Thanks also to the emergence of both experimental and behavioural economics, words typical of other traditions and disciplines (psychology, sociology, philosophy...) are brought back to economic theories and models. Reciprocity, trust, intentions, fairness, esteem, and similar concepts can be nowadays found even in the top economics journals, showing that something really new is going on.

Also the analysis of the specific connection between happiness and genuine sociality has been recently developing. Kahneman et al. (2004), for instance, found in an empirical research based on the Day Reconstruction Method (DRM), that in only 1 out of 15 activities of daily living (i.e. praying) was affect balance (positive minus negative emotions) greater when people were alone rather than with others. People enjoyed the other 14 activities (such as exercising, resting, commuting, and working around the house) more when others were present than when they were alone.[7]

In a similar line of inquiry (although with a more traditional econometric methodology), Meier and Stutzer (2004) find, using the German Socio-Economic Panel (GSOEP) for the period between 1985 and 1999,

[5] I am referring to the empirical studies along the line of Easterlin (1974): on this cf. Bruni and Porta (2005).

[6] Cf. among others, Akerlof and Kranton (2005) and Bowles (2004).

[7] This experiment, carried out by using the DRM (Day Reconstruction Method), is interesting also because it avoids the problem of causality. The DRM is an interesting methodological innovation in the debate on happiness: in fact, on the one hand it is still subjective and self-reported (the DRM is designed to collect data describing the experiences a person has on a given day, through a systematic reconstruction of the "experienced" or objective happiness, conducted on the following day); on the other, the aim of Kahneman and his colleagues is to arrive at an "objective" measurement of happiness, that, unlike the standard self-reported methodology based on "remembered happiness", is not subject to cognitive mistakes such as the "end-peak" bias.

robust evidence that volunteers are more satisfied with their life than non-volunteers.

More generally, psychological studies offer a large body of evidence on the importance of relationality on happiness and life satisfaction. There has been increasing appreciation within psychology of the fundamental import-ance of supportive interpersonal relationships for well-being and happiness. Especially within the "eudemonic" approach, many authors see a *universal* association between the quality of relationships and well-being: "Evidence supporting the link of relatedness to SWB is manifold. Studies suggest that, of all factors that influence happiness, relatedness is at or very near the top of the list . . . Furthermore, loneliness is consistently negatively related to positive affect and life satisfaction" (Deci and Ryan 2001, p. 154).

Similarly Ryff et al. (2001) reviewed evidence that positive relations predicted physiological functioning and health outcomes: "Central among the core criter-ial goods comprising optimal living is having quality ties to others. Across time and settings, people everywhere have subscribed to the view that close, mean-ingful ties to others is an essential feature of what it means to be fully human" (Ryff and Singer 2000, p. 30). In particular, Ryff and colleagues show empirical and theoretical evidence on the strict nexus between interpersonal relationships, health, and happiness (Ryff and Singer 2000). Furthermore, reduction of genuine interpersonal relationships "predicted incident cardiovascular disease, decline in physical function, and decline in cognitive function" (ibid. p. 38).

In economic theory, the new concept of relational goods is slowly but steadily emerging (Gui and Sugden 2005), as we'll see later.

In an empirical research based on the data of *World Values Survey* (Bruni and Stanca 2008), we found robust evidence of the nexus between happiness and genuine interpersonal relations. The analyses suggest that membership of a voluntary organization, and time spent with friends and parents—data used as proxy of relational goods—are associated with a statistically significant in-crease in life satisfaction. It is interesting to observe that the effect of volun-teering on life satisfaction is quantitatively the same as that of moving up by *one decile* on the income scale. These results suggest that the relational com-ponent of participation in voluntary organizations, represented by actual interaction with other people, has an independent positive effect on life satisfaction. Furthermore, time spent with the family has the largest effect on life satisfaction, and time spent with friends and with people from sport activities has positive and significant coefficients.

What Is Happiness? Eudemonic vs. Hedonic Happiness

Unlike economists, psychologists correctly acknowledge that "A widely pre-sumed component of the good life is happiness. Unfortunately, the nature of happiness has not been defined in a uniform way. Happiness can mean pleasure, life satisfaction, positive emotions, a meaningful life, or a feeling of contentment, among other concepts" (Diener et al. 2004, p. 188). Economists do not like even the question: "what is happiness?" To them happiness is not a concept clearly distinct from pleasure, satisfaction, or welfare. Ng (1997) defines happiness as "welfare", for Oswald happiness means "pleasure" or "satisfaction", and Easterlin is even too explicit: "I use the terms happiness, subjective well-being, satisfaction, utility, well-being, and welfare interchangeably" (2001, p. 465). To Frey and Stutzer (2005) "Happiness research in economics takes reported subjective well-being as a proxy measure for utility" (p. 2). The sociologist Ruut Veenhoven "use[s] the terms 'happiness' or 'life satisfaction' for the comprehensive judgment" (2005, p. 3). Happiness, by economists, is not generally *defined* but empirically *measured*, on the basis of the answers to questionnaires that ask people: "how much happy are you?" The questionnaires of the WVS (World Values Survey) ask people about both happiness ("how happy are you?") and life-satisfaction ("how much are you satisfied with your life?"), two data often used in the academic analyses about people's happiness. The Eurobarometer of the European Commission measures Europeans' self-evaluation of *life-satisfaction*, and these data are used as synonymous of self-reported happiness in economic analyses (see Oswald 1997). Inglehart, the coordinator of the World Values Survey, uses the Subjective Well-Being (SWB) Index which is a combination of the responses to "happiness" and the responses to "life-satisfaction" questions.[8]

Some economists (Frank 1997, 2005; Layard 2005) use the category of SWB as a synonym of happiness, relying on psychologists for the definition. Actually, in psychological studies the story is more complex. In psychology, in fact, experimental studies on happiness began in the 1950s; psychologists in general use the expression happiness with more precision than economists. Psychologists distinguish between a) "Life satisfaction", which is a cognitive element; b) "Affection", the affective component; c) SWB, defined as a "state of general well-being, synthetic, of long duration, which includes both the affective and cognitive component" (Ahuvia and Friedman 1998, p. 153).

Ed Diener, for example, a leading psychologist in the studies on happiness, proposes on the basis of abundant empirical evidence a hierarchical model of SWB where the four components are (1) pleasant emotions (joy, contentment, happiness, love, etc.), (2) unpleasant emotions (sadness, anger, worry, stress, etc.), (3) global life judgment (life evaluation, fulfillment, meaning,

---

[8] "The subjective well-being index reflects the average between (1) the percentage of the public in each country that describes itself as 'very happy' or 'happy' minus the percentage that describes itself 'not very happy' or 'unhappy' and (2) the percentage placing itself in the 7–10 range, minus the percentage placing itself in 1–4 range", on the 10-points scale of life-satisfaction (Inglehart 1996, p. 516).

success, etc.), and (4) domain satisfaction (marriage, work, health, leisure, etc.).[9] In this approach the SWB is made of all these components, and therefore, happiness is considered to be a narrower concept than SWB, and different from life satisfaction: life satisfaction and happiness are considered *components* of SWB—as in the Senian capability approach where happiness is just *a* component of a "good life". In particular, life satisfaction reflects individuals' perceived distance from their aspirations (Campbell et al. 1976). Happiness, instead, results from a balance between positive affect and negative affect (Bradburn 1969).[10]

SWB is instead defined as "a general evaluation of a person's life" (Diener et al. 2004, p. 191). In general, "the term subjective well-being emphasizes an individual's own assessment of his or her own life—not the judgment of 'experts'—and includes satisfaction (both in general and satisfaction with specific domains), pleasant affect, and low negative affect" (p. 189). For this reason, "SWB is not a unitary dimension, and there is no single index that can capture what it means to be happy" (p. 213).

In this approach to SWB is a concept close to the Aristotelian approach to happiness as eudaimonia. In fact, in psychological studies of happiness we find a tension between a "hedonic" idea of happiness and a "eudemonic" one. In the "hedonic" approach, happiness is the result of avoiding pain and seeking pleasure; according instead to the "eudemonic" approach, happiness arises as people function and interact within society, an approach that places emphasis on non-material pursuits such as relationality and intrinsic motivation (Deci and Ryan 2001; ch. 8). More precisely, "hedonism" (Kahneman et al. 1999, 2004) reflects the view that well-being consists of pleasure or happiness: "Hedonism, as a view of well-being, has thus been expressed in many forms and has varied from a relatively narrow focus on bodily pleasures to a broad focus on appetites and self-interests" (Deci and Ryan 2001, p. 144). In 1999 Kahneman et al. announced the existence of a new field of psychology. Its title, *Well-Being: The Foundations of Hedonic Psychology*, clearly suggests that, within this paradigm, the terms well-being and hedonism are essentially equivalent.[11]

The second view, both as ancient and as current, is instead that well-being consists of more than just hedonic or subjective happiness: "Despite the currency of the hedonic view, many philosophers, religious masters, and visionaries, from both the East and West, have denigrated happiness per se as a principal criterion of well-being" (Deci and Ryan 2001, p. 145). It lies instead

---

[9] Note the high role of marriage in this hierarchical model (Diener and Seligman 2003, pp. 192 ff.): in fact, marriage has been found to affect happiness in a significant and positive way (Diener 1984; Frey and Stutzer 2002).

[10] On SWB see also Diener and Lucas (1999), and Diener (1984).

[11] Kahneman's approach to happiness is nevertheless articulated: in some studies he follows explicitly a hedonist approach (Kahneman et al. 1997, 2004), but in other researches (such as that with Nickerson et al. 2003), he reaches conclusions in line with the Aristotelian approach.

in the actualization of human potentials. This view has been called *eudaimon-ism*, conveying the belief that "well-being consists of fulfilling or realizing one's *daimon* or true nature. The two traditions—hedonism and eudaimon-ism—are founded on distinct views of human nature and of what constitutes a good society. Accordingly, they ask different questions concerning how devel-opmental and social processes relate to well-being, and they implicitly or explicitly prescribe different approaches to the enterprise of living" (Deci and Ryan 2001, p. 143).[12] Ryff and Singer (1998, 2000), also drawing from Aristotle, describe well-being not in terms of attaining of pleasure, but as "the striving for perfection that represents the realization of one's true potential" (Ryff 1995, p. 100). Carol Ryff has even proposed to speak of Psychological Well-Being (PWB) as distinct from Subjective Well-Being (SWB): "Whereas the SWB tradition formulates well-being in terms of overall life satisfaction and happiness, the PWB tradition draws heavily on formulation of human devel-opment and existential challenges of life" (Keyes et al. 2002, p. 1008).[13] An-other, complementary, way of presenting this tension is to distinguish between an *ethical* approach to happiness (the Aristotelian) and a purely *subjectivist* one based on psychological experience (the hedonic). The philo-sophical reference point for the hedonistic approach is Bentham (or Epicurus), while Aristotle is the father of the eudemonic/ethical one. It is not by chance that one of Kahneman's seminal papers on happiness is entitled "Back to Bentham" (1997).

A similar tension, we'll see in the next sections, is present also in economics. On the one hand, the capabilities approach is in fact close to the Aristotelian eudaimonia (although Sen, as also restated in Chapter 1, is not happy with the literature on happiness in general), and Aristotelian is the approach of most economists (not all: see Sugden, for instance) working on "relational goods". On the other hand, the mainstream of economists of happiness today are close to the hedonic happiness, where happiness is actually declinated as pleasure, and sociality, where present, is considered basically as a sort of market failure, as we shall see in the next section, dedicated to the explanations of the East-erlin paradox based on relative consumption or, as I prefer to call it, the "social" treadmill.

---

[12] The meaning of the Aristotelian eudaimonia is far from the mythic idea of "good daimon": Aristotle, and the whole Greek philosophy, overcame the pre-philosophical idea of happiness=good daimon (or fortune) by linking happiness to virtues—the word remained the same, eudaimonia, but after Socrates, Plato, and especially Aristotle, the mean-ing is completely different. In the next section I will discuss more the Aristotelian idea of eudaimonia.

[13] Ryff and others presented a multidimensional approach to the measurement of PWB that taps six distinct aspects of human flourishing: autonomy, personal growth, self-acceptance, life purpose, mastery, and positive relatedness. These six constructs define PWB (Ryff and Singer 1998). See also Keyes et al. (2002).

The "Social Treadmill": Relative Consumption and Positional Competition

Explanations based on the relative consumption hypothesis can be rightly considered as a development of the "aspiration theory" (Frank 2005, Layard 2005). The "hedonic treadmill", based on adaptation, is essentially individual and a-social, whereas the satisfaction treadmill is associated with the social comparisons, although it can apply even in isolation: it can occur even on Robinson Crusoe's island when he tries to improve on his standards (in cultivation, fishing, etc.). In other words, the hedonic treadmill doesn't require society in order to work; the satisfaction occurs normally in society but neither the hedonic nor the satisfaction treadmill needs sociality by necessity. A pure social treadmill is instead the "positional" one.

Even the relative consumption hypothesis is not a new one. Duesenberry claimed that a person draws utility, or satisfaction, from his own level of consumption in relation to or in comparison with the level of other people's consumption (1949, p. 32).

In other words, he basically said that we are constantly comparing ourselves with some group of people and that what they buy influences the choices about what we buy. It is the old "keeping up with the Joneses" scenario, where the consumption function is constructed upon the hypothesis that our consumption choices are influenced by the difference between our level of income and the level of income of others, instead of the absolute level. Therefore, the utility of a person's level of consumption depends also on the *relative* level and not only on the *absolute* one.

We do not need to go back to classical authors for prominent considerations about the social dimensions of consumption (we shall consider later Smith and Genovesi). In more modern times, Veblen treated consuming as a social issue, because of the simple fact that the most significant acts of consumption are normally carried out in public, under others' gaze. In recent times, Scitovsky (1976, ch. 6) dealt with the relationship between consumption and status, and Fred Hirsch (1977) coined the term "positional good". The basic element of contemporary positional theory is the concept of *externality*: conspicuous commodities share some characteristics of the "demerit goods" (because private goods are generating negative externalities), with the typical consequence of Pareto inefficiency (for over-consumption):

That many purchases become more attractive to us when others make them means that consumption spending has much in common with a military arms race. A family can choose how much of its own money to spend, but it cannot choose how much others spend. Buying a smaller-than-average vehicle means greater risk of dying in an accident. Spending less on an interview suit means a greater risk of not landing the best job. Yet when all spend more on heavier cars or more finely tailored suits, the results tend to be mutually offsetting, just as when all nations spend more on armaments. Spending less— on bombs or on personal consumption—frees up money for other pressing uses, but only if everyone does it. (Frank 2005, pp. 83–4)[14]

In other words, there is a problem of self-deception: people consume an excessive amount of conspicuous goods, and, as a consequence, the amount of time devoted to "inconspicuous consumption" is inefficient (too little) (Easterlin 2005).

So, relative consumption theory can also be described by using the image of a treadmill: together with our income or consumption something else is running along, that is, the income of others.

The theories of "positional happiness", which are the main explanations of the paradox of happiness in current literature, take sociality into account mainly as a public-good problem: increases in aspirations or positional competition generate negative externalities in consumption that affect or "pollute" individual utility—from that consistently comes Layard's and Frank's recipe: Pigouvian taxes. In other words, these theories do not deal with the *direct* relationship between individual well-being and sociality-as-relationality. Coherently, the economic explanations of the "Easterlin paradox" do not refer to sociality as a source of happiness per se. Mainstream economic literature, in fact, finds it hard to do this kind of analysis: in the following pages I will try to show that maybe, although hard, it is not impossible.

To sum up. The sociality taken into consideration in studies of happiness is basically declinated as rivalry and envy. But, I would ask, is such a declination the only one possible or the one that better helps us to understand the Easterlin paradox? The final part of the chapter tries to answer this question. In order to do so, it will be necessary to say something about the original idea of happiness as is present in Aristotle's writings.

---

[14] Although the paradoxes of happiness are more relevant in high-income societies, affluent countries don't have the monopoly on positional or consumer competition. Anthropologists tell us that positional consumerism exists in all types of societies. Even the act of giving is often another way of showing off one's high consumer level in order to reinforce one's status. In the *Theory of the Leisure Class* (1899), Veblen blamed the depersonalization of social relations, typical of modern society, for the increase in conspicuous or positional consumption. While there are many ways to communicate one's social position in villages and small communities, consumerism is the only way to say who we are in today's anonymous society. The tribe's witch-doctor earned respect for his family for generations, the mighty warrior as well, as did the person who taught one's children to read. Now the big cars and homes tell the neighbors, whom we don't know, just who we are. Goods have become almost the only means to communicate status.

Civil Happiness

Aristotle's Eudaimonia

Most of the current philosophical debate on happiness, including the subjects of this chapter, is still centered on the classical tension surrounding the word *eudaimonia*.[15] Socrates, Plato, and Aristotle, as well as all the classical schools of philosophy (Epicureanism or Stoicism),[16] explored the diverse dimensions of happiness. The fundamental ideas they shared on happiness were

a) happiness is the final, or ultimate, end of life: is the "highest good" for the human being;
b) happiness is self-sufficient, because there is nothing that added to it would increase its value;
c) there is an inseparable bond between happiness and the practice of virtues;
d) because virtues bear fruits regardless of self-interest, happiness can be reached only as a by-product if it is sought in non-instrumental ways, seeking to be virtuous.

On the other hand, differences between Aristotle and the other classical Greek philosophers arose around such questions as the connection between the active and contemplative lives, and then over the role of sociality and civil virtues in order to reach the *good life*.

The Aristotelian meaning of *eudaimonia* is semantically impoverished when translated into the English word *happiness*: the Greek expression meant the highest end that a human person can realize: "what is the highest of all goods achievable by action" (Aristotle, *Nicomachean Ethics* (NE), I, 4, 1095a).

As a consequence, eudaimonia is an end "which is in itself worthy of pursuit more final than that which is worthy of pursuit for the sake of something else . . . for this we choose always for self and never for the sake of something else" (NE, I, 7, 1097a). That makes happiness "the best, noblest, and most pleasant thing in the world" (NE, I, 8, 1099a). All the other good things, including wealth, are only a means for reaching happiness. Happiness, therefore, *is never a means*; on the contrary, it is the only goal which is impossible to instrumentalize, because of its very nature. For this reason it is the "final" end:

---

[15] In Greek philosophy there are many words for expressing the concept of what we call nowadays happiness. In particular, the happy man is called *Makar, Eudaimon, Olbios*, or *Eutyches*. Nevertheless, in Plato, Aristotle, and also Epicurean and Stoic philosophers, eudaimonia was by far the most used term. On this cf. de Heer (1968).

[16] The fact that we find these essential ideas in other cultural universes makes us think of them as an emanation from an archetype lying at the wellspring of human history. For example, Hinduism and its sacred text, *The Bhagavadgita*, is built around the idea that happiness arrives from virtue only if it is sought as an end and not as a means. Also the epic poem *The Mahabharata* presents an idea of happiness as a by-product of non-instrumental and virtuous behavior.

being final, it cannot be an "instrument" for something else (there is nothing to be reached beyond it). Out of this comes the thesis that neither wealth, nor health can ever be ultimate ends. They can only be important means (instruments) for living a good life. As the philosopher Martha Nussbaum writes: "happiness is something like flourishing human living, a kind of living that is active, inclusive of all that has intrinsic value, and complete, meaning lacking in nothing that would make it richer or better" (2005, p. 171).

Furthermore, eudaimonia is a multidimensional and diverse reality. First, one of the primary objectives of Aristotle was to distinguish eudaimonia from the hedonism of Aristippus and his school: "To judge from the lives that men lead, most men, and men of the most vulgar type, seem (not without some ground) to identify the good, or happiness, with pleasure" (NE, I, 5, 1095b). Eudaimonia, then, cannot be identified with pleasure nor with honor or money.

This is why the neo-Aristotelian philosophers in the Anglo-Saxon world preferred to translate *eudaimonia* with "human flourishing" rather than happiness, because in common language today happiness also indicates momentary euphoria, carefree content, a pleasurable sensation or *tout court* pleasure.[17]

To Aristotle, pleasure is not the *end* of action, then, but only a *sign* that the action is intrinsically good. Pleasure, instead, can signal the value of an activity, not its scope; "virtuous actions must be in themselves pleasant" (I, 8, 1099a).[18]

Second, eudaimonia is the end of political activity. This idea can be rightly considered the synthesis of the fourth section of the first part of the *Nicomachean Ethics*: "what it is that we say political science aims at and what is the highest of all goods achievable by action ... for both the general run of men and people of superior refinement say that it is happiness" (I, 4, 1095a). The aim of politics is happiness because politics "gives utmost attention in forming citizens in a certain way, that is to make them good and committed to carrying out beautiful actions" (I, 9, 1099b). What is more, political life is the only place

---

[17] Elisabeth Anscombe (1958) was the first to translate eudaimonia into "human flourishing". There are some scholars who still maintain that "happiness", if qualified, renders the original meaning of eudaimonia more appropriately (Kenny 1999). In his *The Methods of Ethics*, Henri Sidgwick affirmed that "the English term Happiness is not free from a similar ambiguity". And adds, "It seems, indeed, to be commonly used in Bentham's way as convertible with pleasure" (1901[1874], p. 92). In a footnote (n. 2) he is even more explicit: "since by Stuart, as by most English writers, 'Happiness' is definitely conceived as consisting of 'pleasures' or 'Enjoyments' ". The ambiguity has not diminished recently, as the philosopher Hill says: "By common opinion now, one can be happy for a few moments, then unhappy, then happy again, and so on; but the same does not hold for *flourishing as a human being*" (Hill 1999, p. 145).

[18] Following the same line of thought, the "Aristotelian" Thomas Aquinas wrote that *dilectatio* (pleasure) is the very *accidens* of the virtuous life. The relationship between happiness and pleasure is conceived by Aristotelian theory in a substantially different way than by hedonism and utilitarianism. In certain situations, in fact, happiness requires pain and sacrifice (cf. Veenhoven 2005).

in which happiness can be fully experienced. "It is natural, then, that we call neither ox nor horse nor any other of the animals happy; for none of them is capable of sharing in such activity" (I, 9, 1099b).[19]

As a third (and very crucial) element, eudaimonia is the indirect result, a by-product, of the practice of virtues. Let us see why. The expression *eudaimonia*, in fact, originally derived from the word "good demon" (*eu daimon*), which meant that only a person who has a good demon or good fortune on his side can reach eudaimonia. So happiness and good fortune were used as synonymous words.[20] Socrates, but above all Plato and Aristotle, invested the word *eudaimonia* with new meanings. The idea that even a person with bad luck could *become* happy by means of virtuous actions began to enter onto the philosophical stage.

Aristotle defines *eudaimonia* as "a virtuous activity of soul" (NE, I, 9, 1099b). It also requires material goods such as health, beauty, contemplation (*theoria*), and "there are some things the lack of which takes the lustre from happiness" (I, 8, 1099b). And as has been sufficiently emphasized by many interpreters, happiness is tied to a right and balanced combination of various ingredients. Therefore, it is plural and multidimensional because it is composed of diverse things. While such things as beauty, friendship, and virtues are intrinsic, other things, like material goods, are merely instrumental. Then, Aristotle specifies, "happiness seems to need this sort of prosperity in addition; for which reason some identify happiness with good fortune" (I, 8, 1099b).[21]

Linked with the key connection between virtues and eudaimonia, we find a fundamental tension regarding the whole Aristotelian theory of happiness–eudaimonia: although the virtuous life is a way to happiness, virtues bear their fruit (happiness) only if sought *not instrumentally*, only if internalized as being *intrinsically good*. In fact, as soon as virtue is used as a means is ceases to be a virtue. So happiness is the indirect result of practicing virtues, which makes them, at the same time, means and ends, part of eudaimonia.

MacIntyre proposes an inspiring reading of this tension between virtues and happiness, between means and ends in Aristotle:

[19] Aristotle gives such essential importance to political life that he denies that children can be happy: "for this reason also a boy is not happy; for he is not yet capable of such acts, owing to his age; and boys who are called happy are being congratulated by reason of the hopes we have for them. For there is required, as we said, not only complete virtue but also a complete life" (NE, I, 9, 1099b). Furthermore, only the free adult male can be happy.

[20] Some modern Anglo-Saxon languages have kept the original meaning. In German, for instance, *"Glück"* means both happiness and good fortune, and, in English, "happiness" comes from "to happen".

[21] If happiness was not dependent on virtues but on good fortune (external events) then, Aristotle affirms, we could define a man as being happy only at the moment of his death, because, otherwise, events could turn against him at any second prior to that. Instead, if happiness is a life in conformity with virtue, then happiness can be dynamic yet permanent, because "we have assumed happiness to be something permanent and by no means easily changed" (NE, I,10,1100a).

The virtues are precisely those qualities the possession of which will enable an individual to achieve *eudaimonia* and the lack of which will frustrate his movement toward that *telos*. But although it would not be incorrect to describe the exercise of virtues as a mere means to the end of achieving the good for man, that description is ambiguous. Aristotle in his writings does not explicitly distinguish between two different types of means–end relationship. When we speak of any happening or state or activity as a means to some other, we may on the one hand mean that the world is as a matter of contingent fact so ordered that if you are able to bring about a happening or state or activity of the first kind, an event or state or activity of the second kind will ensue. . . . But the exercise of the virtues is not in this sense *a* means to the end of the good for man [eudaimonia]. For what constitutes the good for man is a complete human life lived at its best, and the exercise of virtues is a necessary and central part of such a life, not a mere preparatory exercise to secure such a life." (1984, pp. 148–9)

Virtues are paths to happiness only if they are *not only* a means: this represents the basic "Aristotle's happiness paradox", or "teleological paradox" (cf. Brennan and Pettit 2004), that leans toward the association of virtues with gratuitousness and genuineness.[22]

Only if we keep in mind this fundamental tension in Aristotle's vision of eudaimonia is it possible properly to understand the Aristotelian approach to the nexus between relationality and happiness. As we are about to see in the next section, interpersonal relations lead to happiness only if they are a genuine expression of the practice of virtues. To this key idea is also related every relational theory of happiness, ancient and modern. And, finally, we find this Aristotelian paradox any time we deal with a genuinely civil approach to happiness.

Eudaimonia, Happiness, and Sociality

The above analysis of Aristotle's eudaimonia has shown that his vision of happiness is basically *civil* happiness. Going ahead in this direction, in the *Nicomachean Ethics* there is a strong point of attraction, perhaps the strongest of the entire Aristotelian ethics. It is the *civil* or *political* nature of a good life, of happiness—notice that Aristotle, like all classical thinkers, did not distinguish between the *civil*, *social*, and *political* spheres; that is a typically modern distinction. This focus is one of Aristotle's most quoted passages:

Surely it is strange, too, to make the supremely happy man a solitary; for no one would choose the whole world on condition of being alone, since man is a political creature and one whose nature is to live with others. Therefore even the happy man lives with others; for he has the things that are by nature good. And plainly it is better to spend his

[22] This is the reason why a theory of happiness based on virtues is essentially an ethical theory.

days with friends and good men than with strangers or any chance persons. Therefore the happy man needs friends. (IX, 9, 1169b)

In its highest expression, friendship is a virtue, and for this reason having (virtue) friends, being part of eudaimonia, is more important than wealth, that is only a means to the end of the good life: "For without friends no one would choose to live, though he had all other goods; . . . for what is the use of such prosperity without the opportunity of beneficence, which is exercised chiefly and in its most laudable form towards friends? Or how can prosperity be guarded and preserved without friends? The greater it is, the more exposed is it to risk. And in poverty and in other misfortunes men think friends are the only refuge" (VIII, 1, 1155a).[23]

Like Aristotle, Plato advised the wise to be detached from external circumstances. Together with Epicurus, Pliny, and other classical philosophers, Plato put relationships-with-others in the category of external circumstances, because one's happiness is potentially dependent on other people's choices. Plato's aim, as Aristotle's, was to make happiness self-sufficient: coherently, Plato's suggestion was to be dependent as little as possible on external circumstances, interpersonal relationships included. In fact, if such an operation were possible, happiness would be separated from fortune, "goodness without fragility", as Nussbaum (1986) summarizes Plato's vision of the good life.

Aristotle, instead, thinks that the operation of separating happiness from fortune *is not possible*: "goodness without fragility" is not an achievable goal for the human life, perhaps, for a "god or a beast". This impossibility emerges clearly from his theory of the nexus between relationality and happiness.

For Aristotle, and in the whole Western civil tradition, there is an intrinsic value in relational and civil life, without which human life does not fully flourish. Though human life must be able to flourish autonomously, in the sense that it cannot be totally jeopardized by bad fortune, it is also true that in the Aristotelian line of thought some of the essential components of the good life are tied to interpersonal relationships. Participation in civil life, having friends, loving and being loved are essential parts of a happy life.[24]

Nussbaum calls "friendship, love and political commitment" the three basic *relational goods* in Aristotle's *Ethics*.[25] Therefore, from what we have said,

---

[23] As K. Polanyi (1957) has illustrated so well, commerce and exchange depend on the needs of the *philia* or better, on the maintenance of that reciprocal goodwill among its members, without which the community would cease to exist. We will find this theme at the heart of the medieval and humanistic reflection on civil life centered around the principle of reciprocity, in which also the principle of the contract is founded.

[24] We can't help but recall Raffaello's masterpiece *The School of Athens* as a splendid icon of these two souls of Greek philosophy. Plato, with *Timaeus* under his arm, pointing to the sky, expresses the contemplation of beauty in itself, while Aristotle, embracing the *Nicomachean Ethics* indicates the *polis*, the civil life, and its paradoxes.

[25] The expression "relational goods" is used by Nussbaum, in a sense that is different from the use by economists today: see Gui and Sugden (2005).

relational goods have intrinsic value and are part of eudaimonia. This has been a common point of agreement for many philosophers throughout history, and still is today, despite other differences between their schools of thought.[26]

The peculiarity of Aristotle's theory of the nexus between happiness and relationality emerges from his analysis of the diverse forms of friendships found in book VIII of the *Nicomachean Ethics*. Friendship, for Aristotle, "is besides most necessary with a view to living" (VIII, 1, 1155a). Thus, to him true friendship is virtue-friendship. It is that which remains in the virtuous and happy person even after he has reached contemplation. It is not friendship "For the sake of pleasure" or "For the sake of utility" (ibid.), but desired for the good of the friend: "Aristotle insists that virtue-friendship supplies the 'focal meaning' of friendship" (Brink 1999, p. 260).

Because they are *made of* relationships, "relational goods" can be enjoyed only in reciprocity. So, by affirming the importance of relational goods in a happy life ("The happy man needs friends"), Aristotle brings happiness back under the influence of fortune.[27]

This internal tension in the Aristotelian eudaimonia, that has to be at the same time the final end, self-sufficient,[28] *and* fragile (because it depends on others), marks the deepest difference between the two approaches to the happiness–sociality nexus (i.e. the Aristotelian and the Platonic) that have characterized the whole Western cultural trajectory until now.[29] Though Aristotle agrees with Plato that the contemplative life is superior to the active life,

[26] Neera Kapur claims that the most genuine idea of friendship cannot be instrumental but is an end in itself, because, she argues, a consequentialist's motivational structure is incompatible with a disposition to one kind of friendship (1991, p. 483). That is the reason why a consequentialist ethics (like the utilitarian) is not compatible with a theory of friendship, at least not in the classical sense. The entire Ciceronian theory of friendship, later appropriated by Medieval monastic ethics (cf. *The Spiritual Friendship* by Aelred of Rielvaulx in the twelfth century), was based on the conviction that friendship cannot exist except among virtuous persons (*summa amicitia proprie non est nisi inter bonos*). Thomas Aquinas called the virtue-friendship *amor amicitiae*.

[27] It is not by chance, as Nussbaum remarks, that Aristotle gives particular attention to the catastrophes which can happen because of the *philia*, when he writes about catastrophes. He tries to deal with the problem by defining eudaimonia as a self-sufficient reality that is, however, dependent on other people.

[28] In Aristotle's theory of eudaimonia, self-sufficiency, therefore, does not imply solitude.

[29] Nevertheless, it would be too simplistic to say that Plato was not aware of the importance of civil life or of friendship (it would be enough to think of his theory of *Eros*). He saw man as a political animal, mainly because of his inability to fend for himself alone and his need to unite with fellow creatures (*Republic*, 369b–c). Plato gives great importance to the *polis*, to which he dedicates the *Republic* and the *Laws*. He recognizes the importance of friendship and of love for reaching the truth (cf. *The Banquet* and *Letter VII*) as well as the importance of civil virtues, justice in particular. In any case, we can never fully understand Plato without recognizing the fact that he put the individual and his *journey to reach the truth* at the centre of his metaphysical and ethical system. The relationship with the other is above all a means by which the individual, especially the philosopher, can reach perfection. At a certain point in his journey, one must detach himself from his fellows, take flight in solitude, and dedicate himself entirely to the search for truth in a solo with the absolute beauty.

at the same time he affirms the necessity of friends *for every stage of life.* In an Aristotelian approach, happiness, the good life, is, *at the same time*, constitutionally civil and *therefore* fragile.[30] To renounce its fragility would mean to renounce the good life itself.

This is the basic stress on which the happiness–sociality nexus completely leans. The awareness of civic life's fragility accompanied the entire trajectory of Western thought up until modern times. Modern political philosophy wanted to resolve the paradox of civic life by renouncing, de facto, a fully civic life, hoping to avoid its fragility. In particular, the *invention* of the market economy is positioned at the centre of this trajectory and its tension. More than any other modern invention, the market emancipates us from *dependence* on other people's benevolence.[31] It frees us from the benevolence of our fellow citizens and from the wounds associated with the *communitas*. The market emancipates us from the need of non-instrumental sociality, but, in doing so, it may remove the locus of happiness itself. Can happiness be achieved without genuine sociality, without relational goods?

Relational Goods

The concept of "relational goods" is increasingly attracting the interest of economists. The concept was introduced within the theoretical debate almost at the same time by four different authors: philosopher Martha Nussbaum (1986), sociologist Pierpaolo Donati (1986), and economists Benedetto Gui (1987) and Carole Uhlaner (1989).

Gui defines relational goods as "immaterial goods, and yet not services that can be consumed individually, but connected to interpersonal relationships . . . goods that we may call 'relational'" (1987, p. 37).

Similarly, Uhlaner defines them as "goods that can only be 'possessed' by mutual agreement that they exist, after appropriate joint actions have been taken by a person and non-arbitrary others" (1989, p. 254). The two economists

---

[30] Plato does not have a *relational* vision of the political life and the state in either the *Republic* or the *Laws*. While in his *Politics*, Aristotle describes the origin of the state as the natural result of the single man associating himself into a family first, then with other families into a village, then with other villages into a state, Plato sees the State as a "enlargement" of the individual. He extended this vision to his theory of ethics. For example, justice has nothing to do with interpersonal relations, but is carried out when each individual, in one of the three classes, fulfills his office without interfering in that of the others. Just as the ultimate end of the individual is the good of the whole and not primarily the good of the single parts (which can be sacrificed if necessary for the good of the whole), the good of the State is the ultimate end of Plato's political vision. From here he gathers his idea of putting women and goods in common, which we read about in the *Republic*. It is an organicistic and holistic theory. It would be difficult to find a place for the relational and civic life in his *polis*. In today's words we would say that Plato had a *political* vision and lacked a vision of *civil* society.

[31] Cf. Schultz (2001).

call "relational goods" those dimensions of human relationships that cannot be produced or consumed by an individual alone, because they depend on the modalities of interactions with others and can be appreciated only when shared in reciprocity.

The economic approach to relational goods, however, leads to interpreting them as *distinct* from the relationship. Gui explicitly expresses this methodological position, in order to preserve a continuity within economics, which sees goods as a different instance from the act of consuming. For the same reason he tends to distinguish the relational good from the relationship. Therefore, in Gui's theory, which has been much further analytically developed, the relational good is distinct from the subjective characteristics (i.e. affective states and agents' motivations).[32] In particular, Gui (2002, 2005) proposes to examine every form of interaction as a particular productive process, which he calls an "encounter". He suggests that "between vendor and potential buyer, between doctor and patient, between two colleagues, and even between two clients of the same store" (2002, p. 27), in addition to traditional outputs (e.g. a transaction or a productive task carried out, a service provided) further intangible outputs are produced that have a relational nature: relational goods, in fact.

To sum up, according to Gui and Uhlaner, relational goods are not coincident with the relation: friendship cannot be defined as a relational good, but instead as a repeated interaction, a series of encounters and affective states of which the relational good *is just one component*.

Martha Nussbaum makes a different use of the expression "relational good", compared with that of Gui, because for her it is the relationship which constitutes the good: it comes into existence and expires with the relationship. According to the American philosopher, whose neo-Aristotelian background was also influenced by the thoughts of Sen and Mill, relational goods identify a class of human experiences in which the *relation itself constitutes the good*. All the definitions of relational goods that have so far been given ascribe a foundational role to the reciprocity dimension. Finally, it is worth pointing out that in the case of relational goods the motivation determining the other player's conduct is in fact an essential element (Aristotle already defended the idea that the highest friendship, which contributes to eudaimonia, can never be instrumental, because it is a virtue, as we will see).[33]

---

[32] In fact, in Gui's most recent works, the analysis has been further complicated by presenting preferences for affective states as a subjective aspect of the evaluation of relational goods, and affective states as an objective element of interaction. See Gui (2005).

[33] For this reason it seems little effective to ascribe relational goods to the class of "externalities". Gui—and I—would not do so both to preserve their nature as *goods* and because the lack of intentionality is usually considered an essential property of externalities, whereas it generally does not apply in the case of relational goods (often the particular atmosphere or a smile during an encounter are expressly chased, even at some cost).

Robert Sugden, similarly to Gui, maintains: "The affective and communicative components of interpersonal relations are relational goods (or 'bads'). I propose a theoretical strategy for analysing the affective component of interpersonal relations. The aim is to understand some of the mechanisms by which interpersonal relations generate affective states that are valued or disvalued by participants" (Sugden 2005, p. 53).[34]

Nussbaum also makes an important contribution on the theme of the "fragility" of relational goods: "These components of a good life are going to be minimally self-sufficient. And they will be vulnerable in an especially deep and dangerous way" (1986 [2001], p. 344).

In order to grasp the peculiarity of relational goods, the first thing we need to do is to get rid of the "public good–private good" grip. As a matter of fact, as long as we try to accommodate the notion of relational goods amongst private goods (goods that are rival in consumption and excludable, like a pair of shoes or a sandwich) or alternatively amongst public goods (non-rival and mostly non-excludable),[35] we still remain within a non-relational paradigm. Both the definitions of private and public good, in fact, do not imply any relation *amongst* the subjects involved: the only difference between the two types of goods consists in the existence of certain "interferences" in consumption. For this reason, the consumption of public goods is basically nothing more than an act of consumption that single individuals make independently from one another (as in the case of an unbusy road or two people contemporarily admiring the same painting in a museum, one's consumption not *interfering* with the other's), this according to the non-rivalry assumption. As a consequence, I consider misleading the attempts to accommodate relational goods among public goods, preferring to interpret relational goods as a third class, in addition to traditional "public" and "private" economic goods.

In the light of what has been discussed so far, and leaving unaltered the specificity of the different positions outlined, I would summarize the essential properties of relational goods as follows:

---

[34] Sugden (2005) proposes an analysis of the "technology" of relational goods in terms of emotions and affective states (that is, more than just the inputs and outputs of the encounter), extending beyond the reach of the classic theory of rational choice, which focused plainly on preferences and beliefs. Sugden shapes his theory by rethinking Smith's *Theory of Moral Sentiments* and fellow-feeling. According to Smith (and Sugden), the latter can be seen as a general anthropological tendency in human beings, something distinct from altruism (Sugden 2005): in fact, the fellow-feeling analysis developed by Smith is extremely different from modern theories on altruism. Fellow-feeling is "reciprocal sympathy": Smith maintained that the human being derives pleasure from all forms of fellow-feeling. Back to relational goods, Sugden claims that they arise, in this Smithian framework, from the perception of corresponding feelings, and that they can be enjoyed in any joint activity despite having an economic nature.

[35] Non-rivalry is in fact the assumption that changes a good into a public good, whereas non-excludability relates essentially to technology and costs: in principle, it could be possible to prevent those individuals who did not contribute from consuming any (produced) public good.

a) *Identity*: the identity of the persons involved is a fundamental ingredient. This is what Uhlaner means as she argues that "goods which arise in exchanges where anyone could anonymously supply one or both sides of the bargain are not relational" (1989, p. 255).[36]

b) *Reciprocity*: because they are *made of* relations, these goods can only be enjoyed within reciprocity; they are *reciprocity goods*. This concept is well expressed by Martha Nussbaum: "Mutual activity, feeling, and awareness are such a deep part of what love and friendship *are* that Aristotle is unwilling to say that there is anything worthy of the name of love or friendship left, when the shared activities and the forms of communication that express it are taken away. The other person enters in not just as an object who receives the good activities, but as an intrinsic part of the love itself. But if this is so, then the components of the good life are going to be minimally self-sufficient. And they will be vulnerable in an especially deep and dangerous way" (Nussbaum 1986, p. 344).

c) *Simultaneity*: contrary to normal market goods, be they private or public, whose production is technically and logistically separated from consumption, relational goods (like many persons' services) are produced and consumed simultaneously; goods are co-produced and co-consumed at the same time by the subjects involved. Even if contribution to the production of the encounter might be asymmetrical (like the organization of a party among friends or the management of a social cooperative), pure free riding is not possible in the consumption of relational goods because, in order to be enjoyed, they require the agents to be involved in a relationship with the characteristics we have been describing.[37]

d) *Motivations*: in genuine reciprocity relations, the motivation underlying behaviour is a substantial element. The "encounter" itself—a dinner, for example—can generate relational goods or only "standard" goods depending on the motivation that inspires the subjects. If the relationship is not conceived as an end in itself but only as a means to something else (e.g. negotiating business deals), then there is no relational good.[38]

e) *Emerging fact*: relational goods "emerge" within a relationship. Possibly, preferring the category of "emergence" rather than the economic category of "production" makes it easier to appreciate the very nature of relational goods. To say "emerging fact" is to stress the otherness of the relational good, its being a *third* component beyond the contributions made by the agents, and in

[36] Here, Carole Uhlaner's use of the term "relational" is attributive, not predicative.

[37] Let's consider for example three friends taking a short trip. The friends may put asymmetrical effort into the production of the encounter (i.e. the organization of the trip) and yet, if during the trip any of the friends makes no attempt to establish a genuine reciprocity relationship with the others, she will consume just a standard market good (the trip), but she won't be able to enjoy any relational goods.

[38] This is not equivalent to ruling out the possibility of relational goods in business relations, but for this to happen something new needs to *emerge*, something that does not entirely or primarily pertain to instrumentality (see also footnote 24).

many cases even beyond their original intentions. This is why a relational good can "emerge" even within a common market transaction, as, at some stage, and in the middle of an ordinary instrumental economic relationship, something happens that leads the agents to go beyond the initial motivation of their meeting and so the relational good emerges.[39]

f) *Gratuitousness*: we may well say that gratuitousness is a synthetic characteristic of relational goods, meaning that a relational good is such only as long as the relationship is not "used" for other purposes, that is, as long as the relationship is enjoyed as a *good in itself* and it arises from *intrinsic motivations*.[40] This is why, as Nussbaum says, the relational good is a kind of good whereas *the relation is the good*, a relation that is not a combination of interests but rather an encounter marked by gratuitousness.[41] Relational goods then demand intrinsic motivations towards that particular relation.

g) *Good*: finally, another synthetic account of relational goods arises from the substantive: they are *goods* but not *commodities* (in Marx's terms), that is to say, they have a *value* (because they respond to a need) but not a market price (because of the gratuitousness).[42]

Having listed these characteristics, we can't but acknowledge the difficulties experienced by economic theory in dealing with human relationships moved by complex motivations. As it is, economics looks at the world from the point of view of an *agent choosing goods*: it fails to grasp the relation (or regards it as a means or a constraint), just because the relational good is not a sum of goods or individual relations (that is a contradiction in terms!), and other agents are neither goods nor constraints.

---

[39] For example when a business meeting is being held and there is a phone call for one of the participants, the meeting is interrupted and the person concerned engages in a conversation about the kids or other private aspects, deviating from the order of the day. During those few minutes the participants can create and consume relational goods. Analogously we can imagine the occurrence of "relational bads".

[40] It should be clear by now that in this chapter I endorse the view of a profound connection between gratuitousness and intrinsic motivations. In it I see a much closer relation than the one between gratuitousness and altruism: in fact a gratuitous (intrinsically motivated) but non-altruistic act (like the acts of an athlete or a scientist) could be able to produce even more positive externalities than an altruistic act. I believe human beings possess a psychological mechanism that produces a feeling of pleasure every time we see someone (or even ourselves) accomplishing something led by intrinsic (and not instrumental) motivations, regardless of any direct benefit that might derive from it. This is the same psychological mechanism that makes us praise the missionary helping the lepers more than the company implementing cause-related marketing strategies, or makes us blame the athlete overly fond of monetary incentives.

[41] So defined, the relational good yields some characteristics that make it similar to a local public good (it is consumed together) or to an externality (it "emerges" and it can be unintentional), but it cannot be identified with any of those. For example, not only is the relational good different from a non-rival good, but it can even be defined *antirival* (borrowing this expression from Luca Zarri).

[42] Relational goods are produced in order to be consumed *only* by those who produce them.

A Clue for a Relational Explanation of the Happiness Paradox

Therefore, the lesson coming from "civil happiness" is also a general lesson addressed to economics *tout court* (not only, then, to the economics of happiness field): genuine sociality matters in the economic domain probably more than is held by contemporary economic theory.

The concept of relational goods can offer a hint for a different explanation of the Easterlin paradox. In fact, a relational theory of happiness would explain the income–happiness paradox by arguing that higher income levels are associated with a tendency to over-consume standard economic market goods and under-consume relational goods. Most literature in the social sciences offers many indications that the time devoted to interpersonal relations is falling, crowded out by the extension of markets (Lane 2000, Putnam 2000). In particular, the expansion of the market erodes "spaces" for interpersonal relations as by-products, creates greater mobility between jobs and areas, shifts the care of children and the old from family to market (cf. Gui and Sugden 2005).

Recent theoretical literature, such as Bartolini (2007), and Antoci et al. (2005), claims to explain the under-consumption of relational goods by focusing on relational goods as *public* goods: people in developed countries *intentionally* consume too little of relational goods, and this brings about a sub-optimal (non-Pareto) equilibrium.[43]

A possible "relational" explanation of the happiness–income paradox was originally put forward by Scitovsky in his *The Joyless Economy* (1976). According to Scitovsky, affluent societies' people consume too much of comfort goods and too little of stimulation goods because the economies of scale and the high investment in publicity by big corporations make it very difficult or extremely expensive to consume stimulation goods such as relational goods. In other words, the *relative price* of relational goods increases over time because the "technology" of interpersonal relationships has not improved whereas commodity technology has (it is a sort of "relational Baumol disease").

Furthermore, markets tend to substitute true stimulation goods with comfort goods *presented* as stimulation goods. We consume too much comfort also because it appears as *stimulation goods in disguise, but offered at a much lower price* than true stimulation goods.

Advanced markets tend more and more to offer relational goods in disguise. In Bruni and Stanca (2008), we show robust evidence that in all countries the number of hours spent watching TV are inversely correlated with the SWB index. People tend to consume "disguised" relational goods because they give

---

[43] Antoci et al. (2005), by a dynamic model, show the possibility of a social poverty trap.

more comfort, are less risky, and cheaper than true friendships, for which they are perceived as a substitute. The key element for an alternative and relational explanation of the Easterlin paradox is the different action of the treadmill effect (the hedonic, the satisfaction, and the positional) in the different kinds of goods. In the course of the thesis we have seen that positional studies of happiness show us a huge amount of data that consumption goods (in particular conspicuous consumption ones) are affected over time by several treadmill effects that tend to destroy almost totally the increase in SWB due to the increase in income. If we take into consideration the relational goods element, we can explain even better the empirical data about the happiness paradox: in fact, when we allocate our resources (time, effort) among the two kinds of goods, we underestimate (through a sort of myopia) the "relative treadmill effect", that is the simple evidence that relational goods are much less affected by adaptation, aspirations, and comparison than consumption goods, and even less so than conspicuous goods (Easterlin 2005).

We will never completely adapt to children, friends, and nephews, or at least much less so than to cars, houses, or mobile phones, because relational goods are not conspicuous. Psychologists have known that for decades. Maybe also economists and policy makers can learn something from this simple "relative treadmill effect" model—these issues, however, will be the subject of future work.[44]

Conclusion

In contemporary market societies, the idea of a sharp separation between market relations, conceived as pure instrumental dealings, and non-market ones, intended instead as the realm of reciprocity and genuine sociality, is not very useful in order to imagine and then carry on a good life. Markets, in fact, are occupying most of the social areas formerly covered by family, church, or community. The quality of life, our happiness, could improve if we began to conceive also market relations as a form of friendship, of mutual assistance (Bruni and Sugden 2008), and design civil institutions that could make this possible. Genuine or non-instrumental sociality, a relational good, therefore, seems to become an element more and more relevant in the explanations of happiness and its paradoxes.

It is from this perspective that the tradition of *civil happiness* can still have something important to say.

---

[44] A formal explanation of the happiness paradox on the basis of Scitovsky's theory is given by Pugno (2007).

References

Ahuvia, A. and Friedman, C. (1998), "Income, Consumption, and Subjective Well-Being: Toward a Composite Macromarketing Model", *Journal of Macromarketing*, 18, pp. 153–68.

Akerlof, G.A. and Kranton, R.E. (2005), "Identity and the Economics of Organizations", *Journal of Economic Perspectives*, 19(1), Winter, pp. 9–32.

Anscombe, G.E.M. (1958), "Modern moral philosophy", in The Collected Philosophical Papers of G.E.M. Anscombe, Vol. 3, *Ethics, Religion and Politics*, 1981, pp. 26–42, Basil Blackwell, Oxford.

Antoci, A., Sacco, P., and Vanin, P. (2005), "On the possible conflict between economic growth and social development", in Gui and Sugden (2005).

Aristotle (1980), *Nicomachean Ethics*, Oxford University Press, Oxford.

Bartolini, S. (2007), "Why are people so unhappy? Why do they strive so hard for money? Competing explanations of the broken promises of economic growth", in Bruni and Porta (2007), pp. 337–65.

Biavati, M., Sandri, M., and Zarri, L. (2002), "Preferenze endogene e dinamiche relazionali: un modello coevolutivo", in Sacco and Zamagni (2002), pp. 431–85.

Bowles, S. (2004), *Microeconomics: Behavior, Institutions, and Evolution*, Princeton University Press and Russell Sage Foundation, Princeton, NJ and New York.

Bradburn, N.M. (1969), *The Structure of the Psychological Well-Being*, Aldine, Chicago.

Brennan, G. and Petitt, P. (2004), *The Economics of Esteem: An Essay on Civil and Political Society*, Oxford University Press, Oxford.

Brink, D.O. (1999), "Eudaimonism, Love and Friendship, and Political Community", *Social Philosophy and Policy*, 16, pp. 252–89.

Bruni, L. (2006), *Civil Happiness: Economics and Human Flourishing in Historical Perspective*, Routledge, London.

—— and Porta, P.L. (eds) (2005), *Economics and Happiness: Framings of Analysis*, Oxford University Press, Oxford.

—— —— (eds) (2007), *Handbook on the Economics of Happiness*, E. Elgar, Cheltenham.

—— and Stanca, L. (2008), "Watching alone: Relational Goods, Television and Happiness", *Journal of Economic Behavior and Organization*, 65, pp. 506–28.

—— and Sugden, R. (2008), "Fraternity: Why the market need not be a morally free zone", *Economics and Philosophy*, 24, pp. 35–64.

—— and Zamagni, S. (2007), *Civil Economy*, Peter Lang, Oxford.

Campbell, A., Converse, P.E., and Rodgers, W.L. (1976), *The Quality of American Life: Perceptions, Evolutions, and Satisfactions*, Russell Sage Foundation, New York.

De Heer, C. (1968), Makar, Eudaimon, Olbios, Eutuches: *A Study of the Semantic Field Denoting Happiness in Ancient Greek to the End of the 5th Century B.C.*, Adolf M. Hakkert, Amsterdam.

Deci, R.M. and Ryan, E.L. (2001), "On Happiness And Human Potentials: A Review of Research on Hedonic and Eudaimonic Well-Being", *Annual Review of Psychology*, 52, pp. 141–66.

Diener, E. (1984), "Subjective Well-Being", *Psychological Bulletin*, 95(3), pp. 542–75.

—— and Lucas, R.E. (1999), "Personality and subjective well-being", in Kahneman et al. (1999), pp. 213–29.

—— and Seligman, M.P.E. (2003), "Beyond Money. Toward an Economy of Well-Being", *Psychological Science in the Public Interest*, 5(1), pp. 1–31.

—— Scollon, C.N., and Lucas, R.E. (2004), "The Evolving Concept of Subjective Well-Being: The Multifaceted Nature of Happiness", *Advances in Cell Aging and Gerontology*, 15, pp. 187–219.

Donati, P. (1986), *Introduzione alla sociologia relazionale*, Angeli, Milan.

Duesenberry, J. (1949), *Income, Saving and the Theory of Consumer Behaviour*, Harvard University Press, Cambridge, Mass.

Easterlin, R. (1974), "Does economic growth improve human lot? Some empirical evidence", in P.A. Davis and M.W. Reder (eds), *Nation and Households in Economic Growth: Essays in Honor of Moses Abromowitz*, Academic Press, New York and London.

—— (2001), "Income and Happiness: Towards a Unified Theory", *The Economic Journal*, 111, pp. 465–84.

—— (2005), "Towards a better theory of happiness", in Bruni and Porta (2005), pp. 29–64.

Frank, R. (1997), "The Frame of Reference as a Public Good", *The Economic Journal*, 107, pp. 1832–47.

—— (2005), "Does absolute income matter?", in Bruni and Porta (2005), pp. 65–90.

Frey, B.S. and Stutzer, A. (2002), *Happiness in Economics*, Princeton University Press, Princeton.

—— —— (2005), "Testing theories of happiness", in Bruni and Porta (2005), pp. 116–46.

Gui, B. (1987), "Eléments pour une définition d' 'économie communautaire' ", *Notes et Documents*, 19–20, pp. 32–42.

—— (2002), "Più che scambi incontri. La teoria economica alle prese con i fenomeni relazionali", in Sacco and Zamagni (2002), pp. 15–66.

—— (2005), "From transactions to encounters: The joint generation of relational goods and conventional values", in Gui and Sugden (2005), pp. 23–51.

—— and Sugden, R. (2005), *Economics and Social Interactions*, Cambridge University Press, Cambridge.

Hill, T.E. Jr. (1999), "Happiness and human flourishing in Kant's Ethics", in *Human Flourishing*, ed. E.F. Paul, F.D. Miller, J. Paul, Cambridge University Press, Cambridge, pp. 143–75.

Hirsch, F. (1977), *Social Limits to Growth*, Routledge, London.

Inglehart, R. (1996), "The Diminishing Utility of Economic Growth", *Critical Review*, 10, pp. 508–31.

Kahneman, D. (1999), "Objective happiness", in D. Kahneman, E. Diener, and N. Schwartz (eds), *Well-Being: The Foundations of Hedonic Psychology*, Russell Sage Foundation, New York.

—— Diener, E., and Schwartz, N. (eds) (1999), *Well-Being: The Foundations of Hedonic Psychology*, Russell Sage Foundation, New York.

—— Krueger, A., Schkade, D., Schwarz, N., and Stone, A. (2004), "A Survey Method for Characterizing Daily Life Experience: The Day Reconstruction Method (DRM)", *Science*, 306, pp. 1776–80.

—— Wakker, P.P. and Sarin, R. (1997), "Back to Bentham? Explorations of Experienced Utility", *Quarterly Journal of Economics*, 112, pp. 375–405.

Kapur, N.B. (1991), "Why It Is Wrong to Be Always Guided by the Best: Consequential-ism and Friendship", *Ethics*, 101, pp. 483–504.

Kenny, C. (1999), "Does Growth Cause Happiness, or Does Happiness Cause Growth?", *Kyklos*, 52(1), pp. 3–26.

Keyes, C.L.M., Shmotkin, D., and Ryff, C.D. (2002), "Optimizing Well-Being: The Empirical Encounter of Two Traditions", *Journal of Personality and Social Psychology*, 82(6), pp. 1007–22.

Lane, R. (2000), *The Loss of Happiness in the Market Democracies*, Yale University Press, Yale.

Layard, R. (2005), "Rethinking public economics: The implications of rivalry and habit", in Bruni and Porta (2005), pp. 147–69.

MacIntyre, A. (1984), *After Virtue*, University of Notre Dame Press, Notre Dame. Second edition.

Meier, S. and Stutzer, A. (2004), "Is Volunteering Rewarding in Itself?", IZA Discussion Papers 1045, Institute for the Study of Labor (IZA).

Ng, Y.K. (1997), "A Case for Happiness, Cardinalism, and Interpersonal Comparability", *The Economic Journal*, 107, pp. 1848–58.

Nickerson, C., Schwarz, N., Diener, E., and Kahneman, D. (2003), "Zeroing the Dark Side of the American Dream: A Closer Look at the Negative Consequences of the Goal for Financial Success", *Psychological Science*, 14, pp. 531–6.

Nussbaum, M.C. (1986), *The Fragility of Goodness: Luck and Ethics in Greek Tragedy and Philosophy*, Cambridge University Press, Cambridge. Second edition 2001.

—— (2000), *Woman and Human Development*, Cambridge University Press, Cambridge.

—— (2005), "Mill between Aristotle and Bentham", in Bruni and Porta (2005), pp. 170–83.

Offer, A. (2003), "Economic welfare measurements and human well-being", in *The Economic Future in Historical Perspective*, ed. P.A. David and M. Thomas, Oxford University Press, Oxford.

Oswald, A.J. (1997), "Happiness and Economic Performance", *The Economic Journal*, 107, pp. 1815–31.

Plato, (1997), *Complete Works*, ed. J.M. Cooper, associate ed. D.S. Hutchinson, Hackett Publishing Company Indianapolis, IN.

Polanyi, K. (1957), *Trade and Market in the Early Empires, Economics in History and Theory*, ed. with C.M. Arensberg and H.W. Pearson, The Free Press, Glencoe, Ill.

Pugno, M. (2007), "The subjective well-being paradox: A suggested solution based on relational goods", in Bruni and Porta (2007), pp. 263–89.

Putnam, R. (2000), *Bowling Alone*, Simon and Schuster, New York.

Ryff, C.D. (1995), "Psychological Well-Being in Adult Life", *Current Directions in Psychological Science*, 4, pp. 99–104.

—— and Singer, B. (1998), "The Contours of Positive Human Health", *Psychological Inquires*, 9, pp. 1–28.

—— —— (2000), "Interpersonal Flourishing: A Positive Health Agenda for the New Millennium", *Personality and Social Psychology Review*, 4, pp. 30–44.

—— —— Wing, E., and Love, G.D. (2001), "Elective affinities and uninvited agonies: Mapping emotion with significant others onto health", in *Emotion, Social Relationships, and Health: Third Annual Wisconsin Symposium on Emotion*, ed. C.D. Ryff and B.H. Singer, Oxford University Press, New York.

Sacco, P. and Zamagni, S. (2002), *Complessità relazionale e comportamento economico. Materiali per un nuovo paradigma di razionalità*, Il Mulino, Bologna.

Schultz, W.J. (2001), *The Moral Conditions of Economic Efficiency*, Cambridge University Press, Cambridge and New York.

Scitovsky, T. (1976), *The Joyless Economy: An Inquiry into Human Satisfaction and Consumer Dissatisfaction*, Oxford University Press, Oxford.

Sen, A.K. (1979), "Utilitarianism and Welfarism", *The Journal of Philosophy*, 76, pp. 463–89.

—— (1993), "Capability and well-being", in M. Nussbaum and A. Sen (eds), *The Quality of Life*, Clarendon Press, Oxford.

—— (1999), *Development as Freedom*, Oxford University Press, New York.

Sidgwick, H. (1901[1874]), *The Methods of Ethics*, Macmillan, London.

Sugden, R. (2005), "Fellow-feeling" in Gui and Sugden (2005), pp. 52–75.

Uhlaner, C.J. (1989), "Relational Goods and Participation: Incorporating Sociality into a Theory of Rational Action", *Public Choice*, 62, pp. 253–85.

Veblen, T. (1899[1998]), *The Theory of the Leisure Class*, Prometheus Books, New York.

Veenhoven, R. (2005), "Happiness in hardship", in Bruni and Porta (2005), pp. 243–66.

6

Capabilities and Happiness: Overcoming the Informational Apartheid in the Assessment of Human Well-Being

Flavio Comim

Introduction

Five years have passed, but I still remember well that day. The setting was one of the poorest neighborhoods of one of the largest Brazilian cities: Porto Alegre. He was very slim. His clothes were very dirty. He had few teeth. He seemed hungry. I asked him whether he would mind answering a few questions we had about the well-being of the population. He consented. It was a small list of questions. One of the questions was: "Are you happy?" I then explained the scale "0–10" and asked him to rank his current state of happiness. He replied: "Well, twenty!" "Twenty?"—I asked again. "Yes, twenty"—he confirmed. He was adamant about the reason: "I am very happy, because my church brothers have been treating me well recently." So, it seems, no measure of happiness would possibly have been able to capture his multiple deprivation story. But, and this is an important "but", it also seems fair to point out that we would be denying a fair assessment of his well-being if we dismissed the relevance of the social context that he was referring to.

Assessing human well-being (HWB) is a complex task not simply because it is difficult, but because it involves an understanding of human diversity in terms of context, motivation, reason, and circumstance. Universal criteria for assessing HWB are fallible, not as political principles, as argued by Nussbaum (2000, 2006), but as descriptively relevant to assessing concrete situations. For this purpose, universal criteria need further specification (we can call this, *multiple realizability*, as suggested by Nussbaum, 2000: 77). Think of some common lines: "It was a horrible illness, but he died happily," said the doctor. Or, "Yes, my husband hits me, but only when I annoy him," says the battered wife. Not much for happiness as a good criterion of assessing human well-being, one might think. But what about a different context? "What a virtuoso! But look how unhappy she seems," noted the porter when the violinist arrived for another painstaking afternoon of practice. Able to do, yes, but what for, one might wonder. So, interestingly, the diversity and complexity of life invites us to consider how many possible criteria one might use to assess human well-being (HWB) and whatever else matters for a good life. In the quest for the grail of normative assessment of human well-being we have seen, recently, the emergence of two powerful contestants, namely, the Capability Approach (or Capabilities Approach) (CA) and the Subjective Well-Being Approach (SWB), often known as "Happiness" theories (or the Life-Satisfaction Approach). To be precise, happiness is considered a narrower component of SWB (see Bruni and Porta, 2005, Introduction).

Quite intriguingly, despite the clear overlap in their subject of research, CA and SWB theories seem to turn their back on each other's contributions.[1] The more applied approach of SWB theories, that explores positive psychological features related to HWB and quantifies causes and processes underlying human happiness, seems simply to ignore the contribution of CA theorists. On the other hand, the more philosophically grounded CA, that puts emphasis on functionings and capabilities as ways of evaluating people's advantages, criticizes the usefulness and reliability of happiness measures.

It might seem prima facie that these two sets of criteria, happiness and capabilities, are inimical to each other, constituting an *informational apartheid* in the assessment of human well-being. By informational apartheid, I mean a total divide between the types of information accepted as valid by the different approaches. In fact, this applies not only to the types of information admitted by the approaches but to the types that they exclude. Whereas happiness theories focus their work on surveys based on people's subjective views about their own well-being, capability theories try to distance themselves from the biases implicit in these views, looking for objectively defined criteria of beings and doings, with their respective freedoms attached. The contextual reasons for this apartheid are multiple. Both approaches have been shaped by different contexts and agendas (CA by moral thought, political philosophy, and development economics, and SWB by psychology, neurology, and social studies); they focus on different research strategies (CA more qualitative, and SWB more quantitative[2]); and they interpret differently issues such as adaptation (CA sees

---

[1] There are few exceptions to this case. Beyond individual papers, such as Schokkaert's (2007), quoted here, it is worth mentioning the two conferences organized, first in Cambridge, St Edmund's College in March 2004, and then in Milan at the University of Milano-Bicocca in June 2005, as serious efforts towards thinking about the two approaches.

[2] As an illustration, we can mention Diener and Seligman's (2004: 1) claim that well-being's "rigorous measurement is a primary policy imperative"—a claim not supported by the CA. Sen, for instance, argues that (1999: 81) "Some capabilities are harder to measure than others, and attempts at putting them on a 'metric' may sometimes hide more than they reveal."

it as "resignation", "conformism", and "habituation" in face of adverse circumstances, and SWB as a positive feature).

Analyzing the differences and similarities between the two approaches is an important step towards exploring potential synergies between them (see, Comim, 2005 for an initial attempt to do so). However, a closer investigation of the origins of the CA reveals that the main justification of this approach lies in the possibility of carrying out normative assessments within *broader informational spaces*, which would include happiness, capabilities, resources, rights, other freedoms, and so on. Following this perspective means that no normative assessment should be based on a unique informational space. That should apply not only to happiness but also to capabilities, as informational spaces. Thus, an attempt at understanding "capabilities" as an approach, and not merely as an informational space, will take us necessarily, so I argue below, on the road of conciliation and harmonization between capabilities and happiness.

With the purpose of exploring conceptual and practical steps towards overcoming the informational apartheid between capabilities and happiness analyses, this chapter is divided into three parts. The first part investigates the main reasons why capability theories dismiss "happiness" as an informational space. The second part delves into the meaning of *informational analysis*, exploring its features and role. It argues that from an informational perspective, we have to go beyond the CA in order to understand how different informational spaces can be combined in assessing human well-being. Finally, the last part puts forward an empirical agenda based on a broader understanding of the role of informational analysis in providing more comprehensive views of human well-being. It argues that when analyzing HWB it is important to handle a multiplicity of informational spaces in a structured way, not only to respect the integrity of different informational spaces but to produce a coherent account of HWB.

The overall structure of the argument developed here is very simple. Written from a capability viewpoint, it first focuses on the main CA critiques of the SWB. It then argues that the CA is not merely about using capabilities but about operating within a variety of informational spaces. Within this perspective, bridging the gaps between the CA and the SWB is not only a step forward but a methodological necessity. The main critiques of SWB are then used constructively to propose an empirical route towards overcoming the current apartheid between the two approaches.

A word of caution. When reading Nussbaum's or Sen's arguments on the CA, one sometimes might be forgiven for getting confused about who is claiming what. This happens because it is not rare to find arguments in which they use the CA as the main subject of sentences.[3] Within this context, this is not much

[3] This appears, for instance, in Nussbaum (2006), when she argues that (p. 372) "The capabilities approach calls into question". Or, on the same page, "the capabilities approach

of a problem. The problem happens when one refers to the CA not meaning to address their particular views but to account for how capability theorists use their ideas. This happens with a certain frequency in what follows below. As such, it should be understood as a representation (a rational reconstruction, if you prefer) of the CA zeitgeist. It is therefore naturally open to particular inaccuracies. The next part starts with a sentence that suffers precisely from this limitation, but that somehow conveys an important idea.

If You're So Happy, Why Aren't You Well?

Most of the CA literature seems to be built on a straightforward rejection of happiness as a valid perspective to understand human well-being. There are four problems for the capability theorist in using happiness as an informational space. The first and most evident of all difficulties is related to the opportunity cost in using happiness as the general criterion to rank HWB. When using happiness other (important) considerations could be easily neglected. As Sen (1979d: 552 footnote 1) puts it: "The characterization of human behaviour as being based *exclusively* on the pursuit of one's own happiness (or one's own sense of well-being) irrespective of moral values, social conventions, or ties of class or community, produces a model of breathtaking simplicity." Here, happiness can be criticized for imposing a welfarist basis to normative analysis. Happiness, as Sen (1985a: 188) explains, refers to a "mental state" and for this reason leaves aside other aspects of a person's well-being. Furthermore, it ignores the role of other mental activities that may be important for human well-being, such as excitement or stimulation. The measure of happiness's narrowness as an informational space is given by the extent of all non-happiness information ignored by this perspective.

The fundamental question seems to be that the SWB perspective, by assuming (as a working assumption, not as an accurately descriptive hypothesis) that people's self-evaluation is a reliable criterion for producing well-being assessments, might pre-empty a serious investigation of the reflective exercise involved in the valuation of one's life. Thus, informational narrowness might be limiting because it avoids a proper characterization of those elements used by people in their particular evaluative exercises. It is like knowing the answer before asking the question: by "closing" the main criteria to be used to formulate the questions in advance, one might already know the sort of answers that one might get. The selection of criteria through which one

criticizes the approach to human rights". Ultimately, the reader knows that she is the one putting forward the critique, but importantly, she grounds her critique on particular features of the approach. There is nothing wrong with that. The problem, however, as explained above, is when one then refers to the CA, extending one's comment beyond Nussbaum's (in this case) particular argument.

would express one's answers should be a result of a proper evaluative exercise and not something to be decided a priori by the choice of a narrow informational space. In addition, if we acknowledge Sen's view (1985a, 1992) that well-being is not all that matters for the fulfillment of one's life, then the happiness perspective seems further limiting, once that it is restricted to an assessment of personal well-being, when dimensions other than well-being may be important for one's life. For instance, deontological reasons, or dimensions related to the exercise of one's autonomy or commitment can play an important role in defining actions, choices, and therefore, normative assessments, beyond well-being considerations.

But informational narrowness, although the most visible problem with happiness, at least as it is seen in the Utilitarian tradition, is not the most serious issue raised against this informational criterion in the CA literature. Rather, the problem known as "adaptive preferences" goes to the heart of the CA's critique of using subjective metrics and aspirations as reliable measures of HWB. The argument is: happiness metrics can be subject to distortions and biases[4] and therefore they should not be trusted in assessing human well-being. This critique, in its contemporary form, was first put forward by Berlin ([1958] 2002) in characterizing the effect of obstacles imposed on individuals on their own perceptions about their well-being. According to him, whenever lives are characterized by deprivation and obstacles, individuals tend to ignore their important desires, by "retreating to their inner citadel" (into themselves) because this might offer some psychological security to them. As Berlin notes (2002: 182):

I begin by desiring happiness, or power, or knowledge, or the attainment of some specific object. But I cannot command them. I choose to avoid defeat and waste, and therefore decide to strive for nothing that I cannot be sure to obtain. I determine myself not to desire what is unattainable. The tyrant threatens me with the destruction of my property, with imprisonment, with the exile of death of those I love. But I no longer feel attached to property, no longer care whether or not I am in prison, if I have killed within myself my natural affections, then he cannot bend me to his will, for all that is left of myself is no longer subject to empirical fears or desires. It is as if I had performed a strategic retreat into an inner citadel.

Berlin is concerned with freedom and individuals' use of critical reason. According to him, individual freedom cannot be justified on the basis of subjective

---

[4] In general lines, the SWB literature acknowledges two classes of biases in people's evaluation of well-being, namely, i) reporting (Schwarz and Strack, 1999) and ii) predicted utility. Diener (2000: 35) accepts that "SWB measures can be contaminated by biases" (of mood, ordering of items, situational factors, etc.) and that "Another potential problem is that people may respond to SWB scales in socially desirable ways." We should also include here substantive work done on the issues of "internalised reference standards" and "hedonic treadmill" (see Easterlin, 2003). Here, we explore the CA's critical assessments, but by no means should this be understood as lack of self-criticism and analysis within the SWB literature.

elements because there is no guarantee that they would be conducive to individuals' being capable of moral understanding and autonomy. Sen (1985a: 191) gives concrete meaning to this problem, when he notes that

The hopeless destitute desiring merely to survive, the landless labourer concentrating his efforts on securing the next meal, the round-the-clock domestic servant seeking a few hours of respite, the subjugated housewife struggling for a little individuality may all have learned to keep their desires in line with their respective predicaments. Their deprivations are gagged and muffled in the interpersonal metric of desire fulfilment. In some lives small mercies have to count big.

So, aspirations are shaped by reality, which is not the same to all people, and this diversity can distort the assessment of their views in ways that are difficult to understand. To adjust aspirations to what seems feasible might be a sensible strategy in most cases, but when this "what seems feasible" is below human dignity this adjustment process—that is the subject of the discussion of adaptive preferences—produces results that are not acceptable. So, what is at stake here is not a simple distortion in the scale of utilities, but the possibility that people's views of their own well-being can produce results against people's own interests, given that the chronically deprived learn to "celebrate" any minor achievements. Elster (1982) provides a broad investigation of this issue, arguing that individual want satisfaction could not be considered the criterion of justice and social choice. In the context of the CA, Nussbaum (2000, chapter 2) provides the most comprehensive discussion so far on the issue, highlighting different arguments, namely, the "argument from appropriate procedure", "the argument from adaptation", "the institutional argument", and "the argument from intrinsic worth", commonly used to discuss this problem. It is not the aim of the discussion here to provide a review or even throw new light on the issue of adaptive preferences (for more see Watts, 2008; Qizilbash, 2006, and Teschl and Comim, 2005), but to remark that this problem provides one of the main reasons for explaining the CA's rejection of SWB as a reliable information space for assessing human well-being.

Beyond the arguments of informational narrowness and biased metrics we find happiness being dismissed by the CA literature as part of its general critique of utilitarianism as a normative theory of well-being. The link between utility and happiness, or subjective well-being, seems evident from the literature. For instance, Sen (1979c: 463) defines that "Utility will be taken to stand for a person's conception of his own well-being, and although this would still permit alternative interpretations in terms of 'pleasure' and 'desire', there is no definitional link with the 'goodness of states of affairs'." He treats this link as an open moral issue when analyzing any equivalents of utility. What this means is that happiness, seen as utility, is criticized within a utilitarian structure, not only for its welfarism, as noted above, but also for its consequentialist and sum-ranking features[5] (for a further discussion of these issues see for instance, Sen, 1985a and 1987).

Finally, there are considerations of practical rationality that matter for understanding how happiness can count (or not) in defining—beyond individuals' theoretical conceptions of their own well-being—their concrete choices, and therefore, their normative reasoning. The tenets of theoretical rationality might be changed by the demands of practical rationality. Initial conceptions about one's own well-being can be modified by choice. That could happen for two interrelated reasons. First, individuals' choices can be strategic, in the sense of dependent on what other individuals would do. In this case, there is no clear translation between one's own conception of well-being into actions that may lead or not to desired outcomes (see Sen, 1974). But also, it might happen, as explained by Sen (1976b: 236) that "having a preference" and "wanting the preference to count" might be different according to certain social contexts. This clash between theoretical and practical tenets may force individuals to test and change their views. So, again, for a slightly different reason, the degree of reliability that one can have on the SWB metric is constrained by all these limitations. Someone can say that something is important but, not being prepared to suffer its practical consequences, change in practical terms his or her evaluations before choosing particular actions.

So, if SWB is informationally narrow, if it is vulnerable to biases of the sort raised by the adaptive preferences problem, if when used in a utilitarian framework it is often combined with consequentialism and sum-ranking, and if when people are choosing they might give a limited role to their SWB views, why should we bother about happiness as an informational space? In other words, to what extent are these criticisms raised by the CA literature insurmountable? Indeed, it might be tempting to the capability theorist to dismiss happiness on these grounds, and as a matter of fact many do. The task of using the CA is then reduced to an attempt at using capabilities as the only sovereign informational space. However, as argued in what follows, this might be the wrong way to consider capability as an *approach*.

Capabilities and Beyond: The Role of Informational Analysis

It is important to start with a conceptual distinction between capability as an "informational space" and capability as an "approach". Although capability

---

[5] Simply put, the problem with sum-ranking is that it is completely insensitive to distributional concerns, (between different persons and between different time periods in the life of the same person). For more see Sen (1979c: 468). The problem with consequentialism, understood as a requirement to evaluate states of affairs only on the basis on their consequences, is that it is indifferent to the *rightness* of actions. For more see Sen (1983a: 129).

theorists are more acquainted with the expression "capability approach", in fact, most of their work focuses on the use of capabilities as "an informational space" (involving a characterization of well-being in terms of "functionings", that is, "beings" and "doings"). Early definitions of "capability", in Sen's works, refer to "capability sets" (understood as sets of functionings, rather than as an approach). A good illustration is provided by Sen's (1981) discussion of a *Goal-Rights System* where "capabilities" are no more than one of the non-utility spaces used within a consequence-sensitive structure. Although he refers to it as an approach, in practice, it is through the operation of the *Goal-Rights Approach*, as he also names it, that the use of "basic capabilities" allows, as mentioned above i) the employment of non-utility information in addition to utility information and ii) the use of consequence-sensitive reasoning. Sen (1982) argues for the Goal-Rights System as an encompassing approach, allowing the formulation of some rights in terms of "capabilities". As he puts it (1982: 4), "Thus, goal rights, including capability rights, *and other goals* can be combined with deontological values (in the nonconstraint form), along with other agent relative considerations, in an integrated system" (emphasis added).

It is this search for an "integrated system" that characterizes most of Sen's work and the creation of many different approaches (in which the CA is the most renowned) to address normative assessments in social choice theory, moral philosophy, rational choice, and studies of actual behavior, among others. Indeed, Sen has also suggested the use of *Metarankings* as an approach (1974 and 1979e), *Named Goods Approach* (1979b), *The Vector View* (1980/1), *Capability Rights System* (1982), *Positional Approach* (1983b), and the *Intersection Approach* (1986). Despite serving different purposes, all these approaches have one element in common: they all share an "informational perspective" to normative assessments based on the characterization of broader informational set-ups. It seems relevant to take a closer look at this issue.

When Sen (1973) criticized the use of the revealed preference theory, in respect to the "prisoner's dilemma", arguing that it assumes only one type of rational behavior, he was already using an "informational perspective" in which other moral codes of behavior, in his view, should be considered in interpreting individual rationality. In the context of social welfare evaluation, Sen (1977: 1539) defined the concept of "informational analysis" as an examination of the types of information used by an approach. As such, its central idea is "informational admissibility", classifying the types of information into two groups, namely, the types it includes and the types it excludes. The information that it includes reflects the basic ends of that evaluative system. This means that these variables have intrinsic rather than merely instrumental importance. Beyond this classification—that points to the "invariance requirements"[6] used parametrically by different theories—he develops the concept of "informational extensions". According to it, informational constraints could be relaxed depending on its contextual relevance. Sen (1979e: 126) reinforces that "The usefulness of principles has to be judged in terms of the informational context."

He discusses what happens when principles conflict and how they can be combined. The context that he addresses is the conflict between the weak Pareto Principle and the libertarian principle, as put forward by Arrow in his "impossibility theorem" (for more see Sen, 1970 and 1979c). His solution is a defense of *pluralism* in using utility and non-utility information in defining moral judgments. More specifically, Sen (1985a: 176) suggests two different ways of defining pluralism. In his words, "One is in terms of plurality of principles (I shall call this *principle pluralism*), and the other in terms of plurality of informational variables (to be called *information pluralism*)." The main justification for introducing pluralism is based on a rejection of mechanical criteria and general formulae for assessing human well-being. Broader principles and informational variables should be considered in those assessments.

Emphasizing the need for information pluralism, Sen argues that (1996b: 61) "Modern welfare economics has to go more and more in these pluralist and heterodox directions, taking note of a variety of information in making the wide-ranging judgements that have to be made. Welfare economics is a major branch of 'practical reason'." Practical reason, as Sen (1996a) notes, involves both individual ("how should one live?") and public policy issues. Thus, the range of applicability of information pluralism is wide.

It seems logical to conclude that if the CA is informationally pluralist, it cannot be only about capabilities. In fact, the name "capability approach" seems to detract our attention away from its most important feature, namely, its emphasis on a comprehensive informational analysis.[7] Here is where any

[6] The criterion of "invariance" or "similarity" is relevant for informational analysis. As noted by Sen (1986: 29), "The philosophical foundations of informational analysis go back at least to Kant (1788) and to his discussion of the need for universalization in categorical imperatives. The need to make similar judgements in similar circumstances is a requirement that has been used in many different forms, and the domain and scope of such a requirement depend on the way 'similarity' of circumstances is interpreted and the way 'similarity' of judgements is required. But the 'bite' of such requirements of universalization lies in the constraint that excludes discriminations based on information *not* included in the relevant notion of similarity of circumstances."

[7] It is difficult to find a discussion about what Professor Sen means by "an approach". There are cases, when he refers to approaches in a very light way, simply as an attitude in seeing a problem, but there are others in which by an approach he means a certain theoretical structure. Indeed, his definition of "a structure", presented in his paper "Rational Fools", when explaining his *Metaranking* approach, seems to convey a clear idea (although incomplete) of what could be "an approach". In his words (1976a: 321), "A structure is not, of course, a theory, and alternative theories can be formulated using this structure. I should mention, however, that the structure demands much more information than is yielded by the observation of people's actual choices . . . It gives a role to introspection and communication."

capability theorist is likely to begin scratching her head (to use Nussbaum's 2000: 120 expression). "So, are you trying to say that the capability approach (or 'capabilities approach', if you prefer to use Nussbaum's terminology) is not simply about capabilities?" Most definitely! Apart from the slightly inaccurate remark that it is not "me" who is trying to say that, but Sen—if my reading of his seminal papers is correct—this is precisely the argument here. "What about his critiques of Rawls and utilitarianism?" A fair point—that should be addressed in what follows.

Sen has extensively criticized Rawls's concept of primary goods because, according to him, primary goods are resources and resources are "imperfect indicators of well-being" (Sen, 1985a, 1992, 1999). His emphasis is on the interpersonal variability of the relation between primary goods and people's achievements. In the traditional example of "consumption of food", Sen (1985a: 198–9) reminds us how factors such as metabolic rates, body size, age, sex, activity levels, climatic conditions, presence of parasitic diseases, access to medical services, and nutritional knowledge can all influence the conversion of food into the functioning of being well-nourished. But Sen also acknowledges that in addition to interindividual variations, there are also inter-ends variations that can be motivated by individuals' different conceptions of the good in the use of primary goods (for more see Sen, 1990: 120). As a result, resources (including Rawls's primary goods) are *imperfect* indicators of well-being. But being "imperfect" does not mean that they should not count at all. In fact, there are circumstances, in particular, those related to absolute deprivation of basic functionings, in which resource provision is essential. Resources should count depending on the context.

The same reasoning applies to Sen's critiques of utilitarianism. He has extensively criticized utilitarianism and welfarism for over 25 years and we cannot possibly do justice to the richness of his analyses within a couple of paragraphs. But it is worth stating that a large part of his discontent, in particular with welfarism, is related to the fact that it accommodates with great difficulty (if at all) values underlying the concepts of liberty, justice, exploitation, and rights, among others (see Sen, 1978). Consequently, its focus is unnecessarily narrow from an informational perspective. But this does not mean that utilitarianism does not have something to say. Sen (1978: 2–3) argues that

There is very little doubt that the basic principle of welfarism has considerable humanitarian appeal: the object of social choice should be the furtherance of personal welfares. . . . the focus of personal welfare clearly has the merit of ruling out arbitrary judgments based on taboos, dogmas and discriminations. In liberating policy discussions from the shackles of prejudice and blindness, utilitarianism undoubtedly had a creative role.

Similarly, when criticizing the use of Pareto optimality as a sufficient condition for a good society, Sen acknowledges that (1996b: 53) "If Pareto optimality is not sufficient (though necessary), we need some *further* criteria to make judgements about different distributions, and the question arises as to how that supplementation may be done." The issue of *supplementation* is very easy to be overlooked, but in fact, it is at the core of Sen's (and the CA's) contribution to contemporary analyses of human well-being. Capabilities are also not enough in themselves and need to be supplemented by other informational spaces in order to produce reliable assessments of HWB. As argued by Sen (1996b: 61),

It is true that the capabilities a person enjoys (depending as it does, both on personal features and social arrangements) give us considerable understanding of that person's real opportunities and the prospects of actual achievements. But that does not, in any way, "close" the issue of informational bases of social choice.

It is not simply the issue that the ranking of capability sets are often incomplete and partial, but that "liberty" as a principle should not be outweighed by over-specified considerations. So, if capability "as an approach" needs supplementation, we should look at (and for) other informational spaces, considered narrow on their own, but that when combined can provide an adequate foundation for assessing human well-being. There might be instances, as reminded by Nussbaum (2006: 371), in which "we may admit the wisdom in Utilitarianism".

Without trying to over-specify the CA, the question that remains to be answered is: how can we use informational analysis to provide guidelines (or some structure) for operating within a multiplicity of informational spaces?

Informational Analysis: An Empirical Agenda

If working with broader informational spaces in assessing HWB is a legitimate enterprise, as argued here, how can we work with those spaces? To begin with, following an informational analysis, we could subdivide information into i) utility (UI)[8] and ii) non-utility information (NUI). In "utility information" we can place much of the work done on happiness (but not all) and all those informational spaces that can be translated into utility, such as the space of resources (although these spaces have different characteristics). In the non-utility camp, we can include information traditionally excluded by utilitarianism, as mentioned by Sen (1979e: 116), such as: i) a description of social states; ii) other social states; iii) information going beyond personal welfares; iv) identity of persons; v) the welfare of someone who is indifferent between social states; vi) information about interpersonal comparisons of welfare

---

[8] Utility information can also be poor or rich. For instance, it can range from "ordinalism", going through "cardinal measures", "ratio-scale measures", towards "interpersonal comparisons". For more see Sen (1979d).

levels.[9] In addition to these elements defined within the context of social choice theory, other informational categories could be included, such as

- agency, autonomy
- commitment
- justice
- equality
- social responsibility
- obligations
- identity profiles
- freedom (liberty—opportunity aspect).

The main difference in allowing both UI and NUI in a broader informational structure consists in allowing priority to NUI over UI according to the circumstances (a possibility denied by utilitarian structures and ignored by happiness studies). The implications of using NUI have been widely discussed by Sen, but just to illustrate, we could mention his argument for supplementation of utility by rights, in particular liberty. In his words (1979a: 23),

Even nonlibertarian rights, e.g. those argued in favour of food, shelter, social security, or legal aid, need nonutility information for proper specification. The right of citizens not to go hungry, if accepted, would require discrimination between suffering arising from hunger as opposed to, say, having a morose temperament, and the requirement of nonutility information cannot really be met by utility data.

But the arrow does not always go in one direction, that is, from UI to NUI. It might also be the case, in specifying and comparing sets of capabilities, that preferences (understood here as an assessment of individuals' subjective well-being) need to be added to capability assessments. Comparing capabilities sets is not independent from preference evaluative processes. As explained by Sen (1991: 22), "The evaluation of the freedom I enjoy from a certain menu must depend to a crucial extent on how I value the elements included in that menu. Any plausible axiomatic structure in the comparison of the extent of freedom would have to take some note of the person's preference." SWB views should not be mechanically assumed to be translated into decisions, but they are important as a representation of individuals' normative reasoning. Deontological considerations can also compete with consequence-sensitive considerations and both can conflict with capability-based reasoning. If combined

---

[9] In a more specific setting, Sen (1974) shows how many alternative aggregation procedures in welfare economics differ in their informational bases, exploring the characterization of five "alternative informational set-ups", namely, i) individual orderings (i.e. without cardinality or interpersonal comparability), ii) non-comparable cardinal welfares, iii) extended orderings with interpersonal comparability, iv) interpersonally unit comparable cardinal welfare, and v) fully comparable cardinal welfare functions. As argued before, the problem would be not only the narrow informational space used, but also the chosen aggregation procedure that can hide distributional judgments.

with other elements, SWB does not pre-empty a proper evaluation of this assessment exercise. In contexts of broader characterizations of informational bases, SWB would still be important. Sen observes that (1991: 27)

If the informational foundation of welfarism is replaced by that of individual freedom as constitutive of a good social state, the need to use empirical information on individual *preferences* remains at least as strong.

So, capabilities and subjective well-being can and should be used together, but which one should we use first? We should elect the informational basis on which the judgment in question is directly dependent. At the same time, we should not forget the second difficulty discussed above against the SWB perspective.

Indeed, working with broader informational spaces is not all that matters. As mentioned above, the argument on informational narrowness in assessments of HWB is different from the argument about the distortion of preferences. How can SWB information be used when it is open to so many biases (as illustrated by the problem of adaptive preferences)? To answer this question, Sen's analysis on *positionality* and *agent relativity* should be seen side-by-side with new developments in the happiness literature, such as the empirical agenda put forward by Frey and Stutzer (2005a and 2005b).

Acknowledging that one of the dangers in assessing well-being is to indulge a pure subjectivist view, in terms of a mental-state metrics of utility, Sen (1985a) argues that it is possible to consider that moral evaluations do not vary with the person making the judgment, but with the position that one occupies when making the assessment. A positional interpretation of morality allows diversity in views without indulging into subjectivism. Rather, it emphasizes that evaluators differ among themselves because of the different positions that they occupy. In allowing for the existence of different points of view in assessing statements, Sen (1983a) distinguishes between the "objectivity" and "uniformity" issues. As he puts it (1983a: 103), "the question of objectivity does not turn only on the existence of relativity as such but also on what it is relative to." These relative positions depend also on the different *use-interests* expressed by individuals. Subjective statements can then be seen as "objectively conditional" on different individual features and values. Relativity can thus be compatible with objectivity. As argued by Sen (1985a: 184),

Moral valuation can be position-relative in the same way as such statements as "The sun is setting". The truth of that statement varies with the position of the person, but it cannot vary from person to person among those standing in the same position.

In other words, evaluations can be built parametrically as an objective function of individuals' features and use-interests. Emphasis is directed towards a selection of focal characteristics and the determination whether individuals' agency was part of the state to be evaluated. So, by combining SWB (with objectively conditional qualifications) with capabilities under a broader informational structure, none is epistemologically useless. The perspective of chosen positions, supported by SWB, can be complemented by the perspective of opportunities, defended by the CA. To a certain extent, Sen's positional interpretation of normative assessments is already taken on board by the happiness literature, for instance, in Frey and Stutzer's analysis of "the issue of causality", where a detailed investigation of individual features is used to picture subjective statements as "objectively conditioned" on the positions of the individuals. The absence of NUI in their analysis should provide new opportunities for enriching their discussion rather than a reason for closing the debate based on a priori theoretical preference for a particular informational space. Similarly, Schokkaert's (2007) modeling exercises also provide, as he puts it, (p. 428) "a whole domain of research", exploring the synergies between the two approaches. In particular, his distinction between "legitimate" and "illegitimate" sources of information (when discussing inequality in well-being), allows for a correction of the "undesirable side-effects" of the SWB approach, keeping its relevant insights. His approach appears to be coherent with positional objectivity.

To conclude this discussion, we should now return to the main question raised above, namely, how can we operate within a multiplicity of information spaces? And, how can they be "structured" in order to produce a coherent account of HWB? At the risk of not handling carefully Sen's warning about the importance of avoiding over-specifying informational structures, we could suggest, based on the discussion above, four *structuring principles* in order to harmonize the capabilities and happiness spaces.

Principle 1—Broad "Infobases" Working within a pluralist perspective cannot be reduced simply to a license to use all types of information. It is important to have an idea of what kinds of information are privileged by the different perspectives and relevant to different contexts. SWB is not simply about self-assessment or subjective views. Many insights from this approach are built on a dynamic perspective about individuals' valuation of their lives over time. On the other hand, the CA brings a whole range of NUI on board, including commitment, justice, equality, and so on. Informational analysis seems to provide a useful starting point for bringing together these different informational spaces as suggestions of dimensions that should be considered. In this sense, Nussbaum's list of *central human capabilities* (see, for instance, 2006: 76–7) can also be seen as an entry point for "asking the questions" rather than "giving the answers" (although a complete separation of these two stages is never possible).

Principle 2—Selection and Supplementation Context matters. But context is hard to define. Can we ignore it? Should we ignore it? Unfortunately, the selection of information spaces and the nature of judgments that follow depend very much on particular features of contexts. Ignoring them would lead to biases.

But part of these contexts can be understood as particular features of "use-interests" (related to ends) or "agent relativity" (related to positionality). When starting from the CA perspective, it seems that the rich empirical agenda of SWB can provide not only some guidance related to positionality features but also judgments that can be seen as part of the normative assessment proposed by the CA. When starting from SWB, it seems that an emphasis on "cleaning the happiness measures", as Schokkaert (2007) would put it, through any of the factors discussed above (including the use of positional interpretations as suggested by the CA), would provide a more solid structure to SWB. Of course, the need for working with broad "infobases" goes without saying for both approaches.

Principle 3—Calculation of Conversion Rates Operating within a diversity of informational spaces might be like shopping with different currencies. Conversion rates are needed to explore the equivalence between informational spaces. In the CA literature, Sen has advanced the discussion of conversion rates between resources and functionings (see, for instance, Sen, 1985b). In doing so, he was calling attention to people's ability to use resources in addition to their mere availability. In this perspective, human development would focus on individuals' ability to have and *use* resources (understood here not simply as "income" or "wealth" but as "primary goods" in Rawls's sense). Extrapolating this particular discussion, it is possible to see that what "conversion rates" do is construct a bridge between different informational spaces. From this perspective, why not have conversion rates between different capabilities and SWB measures? Why not relate them to other informational spaces, such as rights and resources? Discussing the equivalences between "different qualities" is an important area of research for assessing human well-being.

Principle 4—Look for Eudaimonia and Autonomous Behaviour An overlap between the two approaches is their recognition of autonomy and self-determination in the constitution of HWB. The CA attaches great importance to issues of autonomy and agency (see Sen, 1985a). This is less the case with the SWB, but we can also find there important work dedicated to eudaimonia. So, it is relevant to keep in mind Bruni and Porta's (2005: 9) observation that "With few exceptions, happiness is not intended as eudaimonia and is not distinct from individualistic pleasure." But this does not mean that we are not able to find views, such as that in Diener et al. (1999: 284), according to which "Commitment to a set of goals provides a sense of personal agency and a sense of structure and meaning to daily life." Thus, looking for "eudaimonic informational spaces" can provide a clear guidance in terms of what both approaches can additionally offer.

These principles should be seen as an attempt to produce a simple "structure" to operate within these two informational spaces (and others considered relevant). Keeping all informational categories open is a tenet of informational analysis, as proposed by Sen. When seen in this broader perspective, many of the critiques against SWB can provide, in fact, new opportunities for exploring a more consistent use of subjective information. As justified above, this "integrated view" is part of the structure attributed to capabilities as an approach.

Conclusion: So What?

To conclude, instead of simply repeating here the arguments that have already been presented above, I would like to propose a "tougher test" to this conclusion, by thinking about the well-being of that person that I met five years ago in light of what has been argued. The original survey applied to him was meant to assess how people convert resources into functionings. Using the categories and questions put forward by the survey, which followed a capability perspective, the conclusion was that he presented multiple capability deprivations. He was unable to answer successfully the questions about "basic knowledge" (we tried to assess education by the *use* that people make of knowledge, rather than simply by considering attendance or enrolment years). From his replies, we also verified the presence of many health problems and considerable difficulties in achieving a proper nutrition. He was a solitary man. He did not seem to be in command of his own life. On the basis of the "capability questions" that we asked (which naturally could be criticized for not capturing what we meant to capture—but this is a different issue), we would be confident in stating that he had very few valuable choices open to him and that therefore his well-being (and agency) were indicative of great multiple deprivations (both in incidence and depth). In view of this verdict, his reply about how happy he was could be seen as an aberration.

Conversely, interpreted from the SWB approach (and here, the particular question asked about "how happy he was" could be criticized on its own for not capturing what we meant to capture), he would appear simply as an "above the happiness benchmark" person. I have no doubts whatsoever that he was very happy during that day because an important dimension of his life, according to him, was being fulfilled. On the basis of the "happiness question" that we asked, we would then conclude that he had a very high level of subjective well-being, and therefore, *well-being*. Following this perspective, the fact that all other capability deprivations would seem less important could be looked at with a certain suspicion.

But is this *informational apartheid* appropriate when considering cases like this one? And if not, as argued above, what sort of further insights can we obtain in trying to overcome it? Can the *structuring principles*, as presented here, provide any help whatsoever, and most importantly, would they make any difference in assessing his situation?

When considering broader "infobases" for evaluating his case, we can quickly see that the informational space of "resources" would not be sufficient to characterize his well-being and that many different dimensions would be needed to assess his situation. He was indeed "health-poor", "education-poor", "dignity-poor", "autonomy-poor", among other forms of poverty that he was suffering. But he was also legitimately happy and this information was important for him. An appreciation of this situation in its plurality would allow an establishment of this apparent contradiction. As argued above, a considerable part of the *informational apartheid* carried out by much of the CA and SWB literature starts here, at the beginning, by dismissing a priori other informational spaces in the characterization of concrete situations. But overcoming this apartheid (however important) means more than merely allowing the use of these informational spaces as a question of principle. Rather, it means effectively using them.

We could start by noting that he had the right not to go hungry, not to be humiliated when he needed medical treatment, to have his dignity respected, and so on. The rights, or "basic entitlements" or "basic capabilities" spaces, as described by Nussbaum (2006), should command, in a consequence-sensitive way as explained by Sen (1983b), a certain priority in assessing HWB. In fact, whenever there are violations of basic human rights and justice, it is difficult to see how we can detach the assessment of a situation from these most obvious violations. Does it mean that the assessment will always be lexicographic (that is, hierarchical)? Not really. Those violations can provide the starting point for a consequence-sensitive analysis of their implications and should be supplemented by other criteria.

In our case, paying close attention to his preference evaluative process (not simply as empirical information on his individual preferences, but as a relevant characterization of his situation) is central to a proper specification of his situation. In fact, from a positional view, it is possible to see how some sorts of deprivation (in his particular case related to his social isolation) may push individuals towards assessing their own well-being in areas that become strategically crucial for their survival. A close attention to the issue of eudaimonia and autonomous behavior suggests that in his situation, "the frame effects of poverty" may give a sense of urgency to his needs that are related to a fundamental cry for human dignity. Being hungry did not seem to matter to his happiness ranking. Neither did his low schooling. He also did not refer to any chronic personal deprivation. He was happy about "the possibility of being happy", provided by that recent change of behavior among his friends. Thus, the search for hedonic forms of happiness could be seen as an endogenous element, resulting from his search for autonomy within hardship.

I would like to emphasize that the particular merits of these considerations are far less important than the acknowledgement that they are facilitated by respecting both capabilities and happiness spaces. In doing so, considerations seem less "mechanical" and more "empirical" (not "descriptively" empirical, but "analytically" empirical') in the sense of helping with the formulation of "hypotheses" for assessing HWB.

For assessing states-of-affairs beyond individual positions, conversion rates could be calculated between the suggested variables. They would be able to contribute to a better understanding between different forms of capability deprivation and the overall sense of self-satisfaction. More importantly, perhaps, these conversion rates could help in characterizing which informational spaces are more relevant for assessing particular problems. Here, measurement must be seen in a very broad sense (for more see Comim, 2008), involving quantitative or qualitative scales.

Overcoming informational apartheid in assessing human well-being is a project that started with the seminal contributions of Professor Sen, written mostly in the late 1970s and early 1980s. This project is bigger than simply understanding capabilities "as informational spaces". Rather, it tries to use capabilities "as an approach". The approach, in fact, is based on "informational analysis". But not any informational analysis would do here. The idea, as we presented above, is to look for a broad informational structure, exploring synergies, discussing differences and peculiarities between different informational spaces. Without pre-empting individuals' normative assessments, we should allow for deontological and consequence-based reasoning. Within this context, the main capability critiques of happiness should be seen as a step towards a broader understanding of HWB, instead of a reaffirmation of one particular informational space (even considering that one can go a long way with capabilities).

References

Berlin, I. (1958) "Two Concepts of Liberty". In Berlin, I. (2002) *Liberty*. Oxford: Oxford University Press.

Bruni, L. and Porta, P.L. (eds) (2005) *Economics and Happiness: framing of analysis*. Oxford: Oxford University Press.

Comim, F. (2008) "Measuring Capabilities". In Comim, F., Qizilbash, M., and Alkire, S. *The Capability Approach: concepts, measures and applications*. Cambridge: Cambridge University Press.

—— (2005) "Capabilities and Happiness: Potential Synergies". *Review of Social Economy*, Vol. LXIII, no. 2, June, pp. 161–76.

Diener, E. (2000) "Subjective Well-Being: the science of happiness and a proposal for a national index". *American Psychologist*, 55(1): 34–43.

—— and Seligman, M.E.P. (2004). "Beyond Money: toward an economy of well-being". *Psychological Science in the Public Interest*. 5(1): 1–31.

—— Suh, E., Lucas, R., and Smith, H. (1999) "Subjective Well-Being: three decades of progress". *Psychological Bulletin*, 125(2): 276–302.

Easterlin, R. (2003) "Building a Better Theory of Well-Being". *Discussion Paper Series* IZA, 742, March, mimeo.

Elster, J. (1982) "Sour Grapes—Utilitarianism and the Genesis of Wants". In Sen, A. and Williams, B. (eds) *Utilitarianism and Beyond*. Cambridge: Cambridge University Press.

Frey, B. and Stutzer, A. (2005a) "Testing Theories of Happiness". In Bruni, L. and Porta, P.L. (eds) *Economics and Happiness: framing of analysis*. Oxford: Oxford University Press.

—— —— (2005b) "Happiness Research: state and prospects". *Review of Social Economy*, Vol. LXII, no. 2, June, pp. 207–28.

Nussbaum, M. (2006) *Frontiers of Justice: disability, nationality, species membership*. Cambridge: The Belknap Press, Harvard University Press.

—— (2000) *Women and Human Development: the capabilities approach*. Cambridge: Cambridge University Press.

Qizilbash, M. (2006) "Well-Being, Adaptation and Human Limitations". In Olsaretti, S. (ed.) *Preferences and Well-Being*. Cambridge: Cambridge University Press, pp. 83–110.

Schokkaert, E. (2007) "Capabilities and Satisfaction with Life". *Journal of Human Development*, 8(3): 415–30.

Schwarz, N. and Strack, F. (1999) "Reports of Subjective Well-Being: judgmental processes and their methodological implications". In Kahneman, D., Diener, E., and Schwart, N. (eds) *Well-Being: the foundations of hedonic psychology*. New York: Russell Sage Foundation, pp. 61–84.

Sen, A. (1999) *Development as Freedom*. Oxford: Oxford University Press.

—— (1996a) "Rationality, Joy and Freedom". *Critical Review*, 10(4): 481–94.

—— (1996b) "On the Foundations of Welfare Economics: utility, capability, and practical reason". In Farina, F., Hahn, F., and Vannucci, S. (eds) *Ethics, Rationality, and Economic Behaviour*. Oxford: Clarendon Press.

—— (1992) *Inequality Re-examined*. Oxford: Oxford University Press.

—— (1991) "Welfare, Preference and Freedom". *Journal of Econometrics*, 50: 15–29.

—— (1990) "Justice: Means versus Freedoms". *Philosophy and Public Affairs*, 19(2): 111–21.

—— (1987) *On Ethics and Economics*. Oxford: Oxford University Press.

—— (1986) "Information and Invariance in Normative Choice". In Heller, W., Starr, R., and Starrett, D. (eds) *Social Choice and Public Decision Making: essays in honor of Kenneth Arrow*, vol. 1., pp. 29–55.

—— (1985a) "Well-Being, Agency and Freedom: the Dewey Lectures 1984". *Journal of Philosophy*, Vol. LXXXII, no. 4, April, pp. 169–221.

—— (1985b) *Commodities and Capabilities*. Oxford: Oxford University Press.

—— (1983a) "Accounts, Actions and Values: objectivity in social science". In Lloyd, C. (ed.) *Social Theory and Political Practice*. Oxford: Clarendon Press.

—— (1983b) "Evaluator Relativity and Consequential Evaluation". *Philosophy and Public Affairs*, 12(2): 113–32.

—— (1982) "Rights and Agency". *Philosophy and Public Affairs*, 11(1): 3–39.

—— (1981) "A Positive Concept of Negative Freedom". In Morscher, E. and Stanzinger, R. (eds) *Ethics: foundations, problems and applications*. Vienna: Holder-Pichler-Tempsky, pp. 43–56.

—— (1980/1) "Plural Utility". *Proceedings of the Aristotelian* Society, 80: 193–215.

Sen, A. (1979a) "Strategies and Revelation: informational constraints in public decisions". In Laffont, J.J. (ed.) *Aggregation and Revelation of Preferences*. Amsterdam: New Holland, pp. 13–28.

—— (1979b) "The Welfare Basis of Real Income Comparisons: a survey". *Journal of Economic Literature*, Vol. XVII, March, pp. 1–45.

—— (1979c) "Utilitarianism and Welfarism". *Journal of Philosophy*. Vol. LXXVI, no. 9, September, pp. 463–89.

—— (1979d) "Personal Utilities and Public Judgements: or what's wrong with welfare economics?" *Economic Journal*, 89 (September): 537–58.

—— (1979e) "Informational Analysis of Moral Principles". In Harrison, R. (ed.) *Rational Action: studies in philosophy and social science*. Cambridge: Cambridge University Press.

—— (1978) "The Poverty of Welfarism". *Intermountain Economic Review*, VIII(1): 1–13.

—— (1977) "On Weights and Measures. Informational Constraints in Social Welfare Analysis". *Econometrica*, 45(7): 1539–72.

—— (1976a) "Rational Fools: a critique of the behavioural foundations of economic theory". *Philosophy and Public Affairs*, 6(4) (Summer 1977): 317–44.

—— (1976b) "Liberty, Unanimity and Rights". *Economica*, 43 (August): 217–45.

—— (1974) "Choice, Orderings and Morality". In Korner, S. (ed.) *Practical Reason*. Oxford: Basil Blackwell.

—— (1973) *Behaviour and the Concept of Preference*. London: The London School of Economics and Political Science.

—— (1970) *Collective Choice and Social Welfare*. San Francisco: Holden-Day.

Teschl, M. and Comim, F (2005) "Adaptive Preferences and Capabilities: Some Preliminary Conceptual Explorations". *Review of Social Economy*, Vol. LXIII, no. 2, June, pp. 229–47.

Watts, M. (2008) "Vulpine psychology and viniculture: the fox, the grapes and adaptive preferences in higher education". Proceedings of the 'Cultures in Resistance: Discourse, Power, Resistance 7' Conference, Manchester Metropolitan University, March 2008.

7

The Division of Labor between the Capability and the Happiness Perspectives*

Johannes Hirata

1 Introduction

The capability and the happiness perspectives have both won lots of sympa-thies among development scholars and practitioners. They are generally wel-comed as more pertinent than conventional perspectives with respect to what development should be about and to what really matters for development to become *good* development. Despite this and some more common features, however, both perspectives differ quite fundamentally with respect to their specific normative status and interest.

In this chapter it will be argued that the two perspectives focus on two different aspects, or dimensions, of a comprehensive conception of good development, and that they are largely complementary, not rival. Their con-ceptual relationship is best understood as a division of labor, even though they do not, separately or jointly, provide for a comprehensive concept of develop-ment ethics unless they are complemented by a concept of legitimacy.

The next section will point out the common ethical ambitions of the two perspectives and will clarify the appropriate addressees of these endeavors to reconstruct the thinking about development. Section 3 will then briefly expli-cate the two-dimensional ethical conception of good development that will serve as the framework of reference throughout this chapter. Since the happi-ness perspective is, as of now, much more heterogeneous and conceptually less elaborate than the capability perspective, Section 4 will specify the conception of happiness adopted here. The subsequent section will mark and discuss two

* I am grateful for valuable discussions with Eduardo Giannetti and Ulrich Thielemann, and for the comments of the latter on a first draft of this paper. I gratefully acknowledge financial support from the Swiss National Science Foundation and the excellent working conditions granted by the Ibmec, São Paulo.

specific major differences between the two perspectives. Section 6 will point out the striking convergence of the two perspectives on some issues, and Section 7 proposes an understanding of a division of labor between the capability and the happiness perspectives while arguing that this division of labor is to be complemented by a comprehensive ethical framework. Section 8 draws a short conclusion.

2 The Common Ambition of the Capability and the Happiness Perspectives

It will be of help for the following considerations to reflect briefly on the common ambition or, perhaps better, on the underlying interest of the capability and the happiness perspectives. Both perspectives are clearly not, at least not primarily, concerned with factual, positive questions of the kind of "what happens when...?", "why did this happen?", and so on, but with normative questions of the kind of "what ought to be done?" and "why should this or that be done?" Being scientific endeavors, they do not, and should not, give specific prescriptions on which particular development decisions should be taken (a task reserved for the polity as discussed below), but rather clarify the appropriate point of view from which to make ethical judgments and from which to justify, or criticize, such decisions. In other words, they should evaluate the argumentative forcefulness of ethical principles and decision rationales, but not evaluate the specific judgments and decisions that are the *object* of such principles and rationales.

This ethical-reflective stance is characteristic of, and common to, all ethical cross-disciplines, such as bio-ethics, business ethics, and the like. It also identifies the capability and the happiness perspectives as fundamentally ethical approaches. What sets them apart from bio-ethics and business ethics, however, is their heuristic orientation towards what is perhaps best labeled *good development*. Both perspectives are guided by an ultimate concern for good development. This concern guides most methodological choices, the selection of worthwhile research questions, and the discrimination between more and less appropriate conceptual distinctions. By good development is meant the regulative idea (Ulrich 1998:11) of advancing justice and well-being, including a temporally and spatially universal scope (intergenerational and international justice, respectively). Put simply, good development is about doing the right and the good, in private as well as in political affairs, with respect to societal development. It is a regulative idea (similar to justice) that everybody must necessarily, in fact, as a matter of tautology, recognize as desirable, even though everybody may fill this idea with different (though not arbitrary) substantive content (just as in the case of competing conceptions of justice). In other words, the idea of good development is no utopia or political program, but rather a terminological container that can be filled with different content but that nevertheless occupies a clearly defined space within the terminological grid that orientates ethical judgments.

As ethical endeavors with a societal scope, the addressees of the two perspectives are not limited to specialists, but comprise the entire public, including—to propose some basic distinctions—all citizens, the scientific community, influential multipliers, and political decision makers. Even though these different addressees have different degrees of factual power, of legitimate authority, and of moral responsibility, ethical insights must not, under normal circumstances, bypass the democratic decision process and be simply "applied" by decision makers. The insights from the capability and from the happiness perspective should therefore not be understood as policy recommendations to be implemented by the "authorities" irrespective of the concerned people's reflected assessments (cf. Thomä 2003:155), but rather as argued hypotheses on the conditions or characteristics that the citizenry's reflected assessments must satisfy. These hypotheses themselves are to be critically evaluated by the public and should, ideally, be adopted and transpire into policy-making through the democratic legitimizing processes if, and only if, they are found to be irrefutable.

3 A Two-Dimensional Conception of Ethics

The capability and the happiness perspectives are both, as explained above, concerned with ethical questions. Yet, to reflect on ethical questions, one needs a conception of ethics, however tentative or incomplete. The majority of contributions on these two perspectives that do not explicitly lay down a conception of ethics must implicitly adopt one in order to be able to make any normative pronouncements at all. Since, as will be argued below, the relationship between the capability and the happiness perspective is best understood as a division of labor within a particular conception of ethics, I will briefly outline the conception of ethics adopted here.

The basic two-dimensional architecture of the conception of ethics proposed here is far from original. In fact, it can be found, to varying degrees, in ancient Greek conceptions of ethics as well as in contemporary ethical schools. It consists of a teleological and a deontological dimension, the teleological dimension referring to the good life, basically to questions of prudence (what do I really want in my life? who do I want to be?), and the deontological dimension referring to the righteous life, basically to questions of rights and duties with respect to other human beings (what may I do? what am I obliged to do?).[1]

---

[1] I do not use the term "deontological" in opposition to "consequential", as Sen (e.g. Sen 1982) and much of the English speaking literature do, but in opposition to "teleological" as

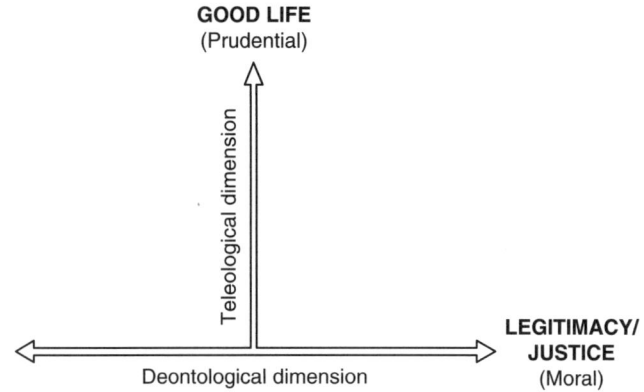

Figure 7.1. A two-dimensional conception of ethics

It is helpful to visualize this architecture, as is sometimes done (Habermas 1999:43, Ulrich 2001/1997:122), by considering the teleological dimension as a vertical perspective and the deontological dimension as a horizontal perspective, as in Figure 7.1.

The vertical perspective would then be concerned with evaluative questions of what makes a human life a good life. This is clearly not a moral question in the sense of the ascription of rights and duties since it is difficult to see how one can have rights or obligations towards oneself. Rather, it is largely a prudential question of how best to lead one's life by the criterion of one's own reflected self-interest. This self-interest is not necessarily egoistic in the pejorative sense. It simply refers to those things that a person evaluates positively as aspects of a good life for other than moral reasons. In other words, it is about the things that make a life meaningful, fulfilled, worth living, happy, or simply pleasurable, but that do so for other reasons than for being required as a moral duty. Repaying one's debts, for example, could be argued to be an aspect of a good life, but it would not qualify as a teleological value. Rather, it would be an aspect of a good life (if this could be convincingly argued) only for its being a moral duty. On the other hand, a mother certainly has a moral duty to care for her child, but since this will not usually be the dominating reason for her to care for her child, this may nevertheless qualify as a teleological content of a good life, despite *also* being a moral duty. In Harsanyi's (1955) terminology, the good life would consist in meeting one's subjective rather than ethical preferences.

described in the following. My (and much of the German language literature's) understanding of the deontological dimension includes consequential considerations and therefore comes close to what Sen (ibid.: 15) calls a "goals rights system" or "consequence-sensitivity in an otherwise deontological perspective" (Sen 1984b:314). I will sometimes substitute "moral" for deontological, whereas I will use "ethical" to refer to both dimensions jointly.

The horizontal perspective would be concerned with questions of how to live together in a potentially conflicting world, and in particular how to solve conflicts of interest by the judicial balancing of rights and duties, that is, by reason rather than by the principle of "might is right" (cf. Ulrich 2001/ 1997:235). The primary virtue of the horizontal perspective would be legitimacy. Legitimacy does not mean selflessness or charity (as the terms "ethical" or "moral" are sometimes, problematically, used), but the condition that an act can in principle be justified before all those potentially concerned (as in discourse ethics; cf. Habermas 1983:103). More loosely put, it means not being indifferent to anybody's moral rights; being prepared to listen to arguments brought forward against one's interests; impartially appraising their moral forcefulness; and being prepared to revise one's interests whenever one finds them to be unjustifiable from an impartial point of view. This impartial point of view, probably most aptly analyzed by Adam Smith as the "impartial spectator" in his *The Theory of Moral Sentiments* (1976/1759:24, 69ff), can also be described by the idea of universalizability which can be found in a large number of philosophical traditions and religious texts and which means, very roughly, that an act is right when its rationale can be justified from an inter-subjective point of view in an exercise of "ideal role taking" (Habermas).

It should be clear that the vertical and the horizontal dimensions cannot be neatly separated and stand each for itself. To the contrary, they are inherently dependent on each other. A life can hardly be considered good without any genuinely human communication and interaction, that is, interaction in which the other person is not treated purely instrumentally but as a moral subject, not (only) as a means, but (also) as an end (Kant 1977/1785:61). Human interaction, therefore, requires the capacity to take "the moral point of view" (Baier 1958), even though a person must not be perfectly moral all of the time to lead a good life (Seel 1999/1995:205)—otherwise, only saints could lead good lives. If this capacity is lacking, or not realized, altogether, however, a life would be deprived of one fundamental and distinguishing aspect of a good human life. A life without this capacity can still be human (as in the case of a person with a particular brain damage), but it cannot be called a *good* human life. In short, a (vertically) good human life cannot be conceived without (horizontal) morality.

Conversely, in order to make sense of legitimacy, one must have a prior notion of a good life and of well-being. This does not require having an exhaustive list of the specific aspects of a good life, but at least to reserve a conceptual space for a substantive idea of a good life. After all, the point of morality is to respect others' moral rights, and the *raison d'être* of rights is obviously to protect (the access to) the good life (cf. Seel 1999/1995:229). It is always *with respect to* (but not as a function of) the substantive idea of a good life that morality must clarify specific persons' rights and duties. Without any notion of what is valuable, therefore, we cannot understand the systematic status of rights. The (horizontal) imperative of legitimacy follows necessarily from the coexistence of moral and dignified beings who have potentially conflicting (vertical) conceptions of a good life. Teleology and deontology, value and legitimacy are inextricably related like two faces of the same coin, bound together by the idea of practical reason.[2]

When it comes to taking decisions and acting, the horizontal dimension is lexically prior to the vertical one. Affirming that a given action is valuable to a specific person is not in itself sufficient to derive a right to this action. An act must first of all be legitimate; only in the selection among legitimate alternatives is it admissible to give preference to the action one considers more valuable.[3] It is for this reason that Kant (and not only he) talks of the condition of legitimacy as a *categorical imperative*. It is therefore impossible to say "Doing *A* would be illegitimate, but since it is so important for *N*'s good life, *N* is right to do it anyway." Either the benefit to *N*'s life (or lives, if *N* stands for a group of people and *A* for a political decision) justifies doing *A*, which is another way of saying that doing *A* would be legitimate, or it does not justify it, in which case doing *A* would be illegitimate, or simply wrong.

Thus, to relate this conception of ethics to development, development ethics must be concerned with both the prudential question of what characterizes a good life (where the answer can take the form of meta-conditions rather than of a list of values), and with the moral question of how conflicting moral rights are to be appraised. This last question is altogether inevitable once conflicts of interest need to be settled. For example, in deciding whether or not to build a hydropower dam, it is not sufficient to establish that more electricity would improve most people's lives, or, for reasons that cannot be discussed here, to force moral considerations into terms of utility (costs and benefits), sum them up, and check whether the outcome is positive or negative. Rather, to judge whether it is right or wrong to build the dam, one has to assess, from the moral point of view, all potentially affected people's interests and moral rights in an impartial way and with respect to the idea of the good life, and judge which decision can be justified.[4]

This mental exercise may often not be conclusive in the sense of yielding a definite judgment, an absolute certainty as to what is right and what wrong. However, this indeterminacy is not a weakness of this specific conception of morality, but rather a reflection of the indeterminate nature of ethics itself (where indeterminacy is of course not the same as arbitrariness). Sen put this succinctly:

---

[2] I owe this metaphor to Ulrich Thielemann (personal communication).

[3] This is not the same as a lexical priority of consequence-independent rights before consequential considerations, since legitimacy already is consequence-sensitive.

[4] This is of course the description of a moral *judgment*, not of the just political *decision process* that should precede the decision whether or not to build the dam.

An approach that can...compare inequalities without any room for ambiguity or in-completeness, may well be at odds with the nature of these ideas....if an underlying idea has an essential ambiguity, a *precise* formulation of that idea must try to *capture* that ambiguity rather than lose it. (Sen 1995:48–9, emphasis orig.)

Judgment and indeterminacy should not only be characterizing features of any conception of ethics, but also of happiness, as will be argued in the following section.

4 A Self-Transcendent Conception of Happiness as a Judgment

Since the happiness perspective is still much more heterogeneous and concep-tually immature than the capability perspective, this section will clarify the concept of happiness adopted here, without, however, attempting to provide an iron-clad definition. My concern here is with the "political" strand of the happiness perspective rather than with the psychological one.[5] The two hall-marks of the conception of happiness proposed here are already expounded in the section heading: happiness is a self-transcendent phenomenon, and it is to a large extent a judgment. Both of these aspects imply a free will and, as a corollary, indeterminacy. For the sake of a more tractable argument and assuming some basic familiarity with economic theory, I will outline my conception of happiness in opposition to the standard utilitarian-hedonistic conception of utility and the related conception of the *homo oeconomicus*.

The *homo oeconomicus* is a utility maximizer. He maximizes his discounted expected net utility which is a function of preference fulfillment. His prefer-ences, in turn, are given. He simply has them as a consequence of genetic heredity, socialization, and so on. They may well change over time, but then the change itself is again an exercise of utility maximization which must rely on given preferences. The origin of change will therefore always be external causes (including new information, specific experiences, etc.) and not a free decision of the person. All observed behavior is nothing else but the manifestation of preferences. A murderer, in this perspective, must have such a set of preferences that killing is the way he maximizes his (discounted expected) utility, just as taking drugs maximizes the drug addict's utility (Becker & Murphy 1988) or as helping the poor maximized Mother Teresa's utility (cf. Hirata 2001), simply because these people happen to have such preferences. Whenever a person does something good to others, it is supposed

---

[5] As major contributors to the political strand may be considered Easterlin (1974), Frank (1999), Frey & Stutzer (2002), Lane (2000), Layard (1980), and Oswald (1997); the psycho-logical strand is associated mainly with the work of, among others, Diener (1994), Kahneman & Schwarz (Kahneman, Diener, & Schwarz 1999), Myers & Diener (1996), Ryan & Deci (2001), Ryff (1995), and Veenhoven (1996). The "political" strand of course relies to a large extent on psychological research.

that such an act is motivated solely by the benefits accruing to the actor, including the "psychic income" (Becker 1976/1960:172) expected from acts of altruism (including the utility derived from a clear conscience). Utility, in turn, is closely related to happiness, historically as well as implicitly in its current use, especially in welfare economics (cf. Edgeworth 1881).

This economic conception of behavior is solipsistic. It portrays man as being ultimately concerned with his own utility alone, and his actions as motivated solely by the prospect of maximizing his utility. Other people's well-being and rights enter his "felicific calculus" (ascribed to Bentham) only if and to the extent they have an impact on his own happiness.

In a self-transcendent conception, by contrast, the horizon of human intentions extends beyond one's own psyche. In this perspective, too, the well-being of others will be important for my own happiness, but now for what it *is*, not—or at least not primarily—for what it *does to me*. For example, when a couple makes savings to leave as an inheritance to their children, they usually do this out of a concern for their children's well-being, not in order to maximize their own happiness by means of some mental payoff (even though some "mental payoff" may be an unintended consequence). The same holds, in this self-transcendent perspective, for more trivial acts. Whether I help a blind person across the street; visit a sick friend; or go all the way to the ballot box to cast my insignificant vote; in all these cases my motives are transcending the limited horizon of my own psyche.[6]

Regarding happiness, the perspective is now turned upside down: what I ultimately care about is not the *experience* of happiness, but the *things* that lead to this experience. Helping a blind person across the street, visiting a sick friend, and even casting my vote; all this may contribute to making me happy, but my resulting happiness is not usually the underlying intention. It is a largely incidental side effect. The very fact of intending happiness can even obstruct it, as Epicurus already pointed out (without, however, realizing the paradox this created within his own theory): a friendship is not a friendship when I use my (so-called) friend merely as a means for my own happiness. In other words, a friendship is worthy to be called a friendship and will bring happiness only when the resulting happiness is not the underlying intention (Spaemann 1989:59). This self-transcendent view of the person and of happiness is also taken by the utilitarian philosopher Sidgwick (1907/1874:I/IV/2 and II/III/2), as Sen (1984/1983:98) himself points out (and agrees). It is particularly aptly defended by Frankl (1992) and adopted by Singer (1995:213, who explicitly refers to Frankl).

I would not go as far as saying that "happiness cannot be pursued" at all and that "it must ensue" (Frankl 1978:20). To some limited degree, happiness can be pursued. When I exercise in order to feel better physically, for example, I do not

---

[6] For a more elaborate justification of this view see Hirata (2004, 2006).

do this for the sake of any self-transcendent purpose, I suppose, but simply for my own happiness. But the more fundamental and enduring sources of happiness indeed seem to be those that are intended primarily for their own sake and not as a means to my personal happiness—such as friendship. This is also the reason why we do not want to substitute genuine happiness as derived from friendships and the like by the mere *feeling* of happiness based on an illusion (i.e. pleasure) brought about by a happiness drug (Giannetti 2002) or a happiness machine (Nozick 1989). If a drug could make us feel happy in the face of the loss of a dear friend, we would, I suppose, not want to take it because what we ultimately care about is being true to what is actually the case out there (ibid.) rather than our hedonic experience as such. In other words, we care primarily about *having reason* for *being* happy, not so much about *feeling* happy; about the reasons for happiness, not about the experience of pleasure. This is not to say that I do not *also* care about *feeling* happy and about pleasure in a purely psychological sense, but it does mean that this is not the overriding concern. In fact, both are constitutive of a good life. A life full of pleasure but without any self-transcendent reasons for being happy can hardly be called a good life, but a life full of reasons for being happy but without any subjective experience of happiness (due to, for example, a clinical depression) is certainly not a good life either.

As a crucial distinction, then, I will propose that between pleasure and happiness. Pleasure is the pre-reflective feeling that something good is happening to oneself (adapted from Wierzbicka 1999:52). A cool drink on a hot day, for example, makes me experience pleasure without involving any reflection. Happiness, by contrast, is a result of the reflection on a certain state of affairs, including, but not limited to, pleasure. A tasty meal, for example, will immediately instill pleasure. But whether it instills happiness depends on whether or not I can also approve of it ethically. If I am a vegetarian but it contains meat, I will not be happy about it, nor if I am breaking in that instant a solemn promise to fast. Happiness does not necessarily involve reflectedly approved pleasures, however. For example, I can experience happiness about a friend's recovery from her illness without any pleasure being involved.

It should now be clear that happiness is always also a judgment. Even though pleasure need not, but can, be involved, reflection and approval *must* precede happiness[7]. In contrast to purely physical pleasures or neural reflexes, happiness is not a neural stimulus-response program, but largely a cognitive judgment. This is illustrated by the finding that student-aged people tend to experience above-average levels of SWB (Blanchflower & Oswald 2004) despite their very low incomes (Easterlin 2001) apparently because young people simply find it OK to be poor by adult standards and because they do not think they are treated unfairly. This interpretation is consistent with a study

[7] This appears not to be the case with *unhappiness*—a person can be unhappy even before reflecting on the reasons for her unhappiness.

of US data which found that the most powerful predictor of satisfaction with one's salary were equity considerations (Berkowitz, Fraser, et al. 1987, reported in Argyle & Martin 1991:81).[8]

This conception of happiness as a judgment made by a person with self-transcendent intentions must admit to ultimate indeterminacy. Contrary to the *homo oeconomicus*, the person underlying this conception does not *have* his preferences; he *chooses* them in an indeterminate way. The *homo oeconomicus* is a determined being, deprived of the free will that is constitutive of the person (Frankfurt 1971), a mere "bundle of preferences that happen to coexist inside a single skin" (Schwartz 2000:81). It is sometimes said that the *homo oeconomicus* may "choose" to change his preferences, but then this "choice" is again understood as an exercise of utility maximization which must, as a matter of logical necessity, be based on given preferences (cf. Hirata 2006). Choice, however, involves free judgment. A person chooses when she could also do something else than she is choosing to do, an option not open to the utility maximizer whose "choice" is predetermined by the constellation of his preferences and the constraints he faces. A person can not only choose *against* her preferences, but also *choose* her preferences (within limits, of course—I cannot make myself dislike sugar and like crank oil instead). A person can change her mind. A passionate safari hunter, for example, can—but does not have to—judge that there are good reasons to derive happiness from watching, rather than killing, endangered animals. In other words, there is no complete utility function to begin with, and hence there is nothing that could possibly be maximized.[9] Human beings are not pushed around by deterministic causes, they rather have reasons for choosing as much as they have reasons for being happy.

The point I am trying to make is not that a causal model of choice and of happiness is always inadequate. For statistical inquiries, imputing causality *in lieu* of free judgment is often a fruitful heuristic strategy. Rather, my point is that conceptualizing happiness as a judgment appreciates the intricate relationship between happiness and ethics. What is ultimately desirable is not the net balance of hedonic experiences but the reflected approval of states of affairs that, incidentally, also tend to trigger happiness. In other words, we do not care about the pleasure that we can get from feel-good pills, but about the just realization (horizontal dimension) of things we deem valuable for a good life (vertical dimension; note the similarity with Sen's "valuable functionings") and which, more or less incidentally, tend to make us happy. As far as policy is concerned, the happiness perspective does therefore not prescribe

---

[8] This concept of happiness is evidently not equivalent to the empirical concept of subjective well-being (SWB), but it seems plausible that the two concepts will generally move together.

[9] This analytical argument complements, rather than substitutes, the forceful *ethical* criticism of the utility maximization view of man (e.g. Ulrich 1998, Thielemann 2000, Sen 1983b).

utilitarian-style happiness maximization. What it does recommend will become clearer in the remainder of this chapter.

5 Conceptual Differences between the Two Perspectives

It has been argued above that the capability and the happiness perspectives share a concern for good development as their guiding criterion. This still leaves a lot of room for differences between the two perspectives, however, which will be discussed in this section. The major underlying difference, it will be argued, is one of ethical focus.

The capability perspective as developed by Sen has, according to himself (Sen 1993:30, 49), its origin in Sen's Tanner Lecture "Equality of What?" (Sen 1983/1979) in which he argues that equality should be evaluated not primarily with respect to marginal happiness (sum-total utilitarianism), nor with respect to total happiness (egalitarian utilitarianism), nor with respect to basic goods (Rawls), but above all with respect to basic capabilities. The focus of the capability perspective is thus on social justice (of which distributional equality is but one aspect), more precisely on the informational basis of social justice. Sen does not claim that capabilities should be the only measure of equality, nor that equality is all that matters with respect to morality (Sen 1983/1979:219), though over time he seems to have become more assertive about the domain of the capability perspective.[10] What the capability perspective says is rather that capabilities, that is, the real freedoms to realize functionings one has reason to value, represent a vital category in matters of social justice.

The happiness perspective in its modern form was initiated by Easterlin's 1974 article in which he argued that differences in happiness (more precisely, in subjective well-being, SWB) between rich and poor countries were much smaller than one would expect on the basis of within-country variation, and that, based on time-series evidence (which was very limited by the time of his study), it is not obvious that income and happiness go together over time. Easterlin thus gave empirical backing to already existent doubts about whether consumption (as measured by GDP) is an adequate measure of human betterment (cf. also Boulding 1972, Galbraith 1958). Since the publication of Easterlin's original article, the political strand of happiness research has focused on this question of human betterment. While the focus has been on happiness, most authors acknowledge that happiness (or at least subjective well-being) is not the only aspect of a good life. The happiness perspective can therefore be

---

[10] e.g. Sen (1999) defines development in terms of capabilities alone, as "the removal of shortfalls of substantive freedoms from what they can potentially achieve" (in endnote no. 5 on p. 350). He continues to acknowledge, however, that "the capability perspective [does not] exhaust ... all relevant concerns for evaluative purposes" (ibid.:77).

considered to be a particular perspective on the conditions of a good life and on how to realize it. It does not, however, endeavor to establish principles of social justice, even though it can of course contribute some insights to the clarification of such questions.

The difference between the capability and the happiness perspectives can thus be expressed, somewhat boldly, in the following way: While the capability perspective says that judgments of social justice should be based on the freedom to realize valued functionings, the happiness perspective is concerned with (some of) the conditions that distinguish valuable functionings from less valuable ones. In other words, while the capability perspective is concerned with deontological questions, the happiness perspective is concerned with teleological ones (even though neither perspective provides an exhaustive concept of the respective dimension).

The difference between the two approaches will be further described and illustrated in the remainder of this section. I will discuss two conceptual differences—teleological content and the role of the person—and illustrate them by the example of addictive behavior.

5.1 Conceptual Differences

5.1.1 TELEOLOGICAL CONTENT

With respect to the teleological ("vertical") dimension of good development, the capability perspective (in Sen's specification, unlike most others) is rigidly formal and, as a consequence, almost agnostic with respect to specific questions of valuation. It does not identify any specific possible contents of a life as valuable, except for one—freedom. Freedom is explicitly acknowledged as an intrinsic value, and as a central one at that. "The overriding value of freedom as the organizing principle of this work has this feature of a strong universalist presumption" (Sen 1999:244). It is to be noted, however, that freedom is understood by Sen as "substantive freedom" to actually do things (ibid.: 5), not merely as non-interference. Beyond freedom, however, Sen's capability perspective remains largely mute as to which functionings are more and which are less valuable (though he sometimes, almost casually, advocates some basic functionings of uncontroversial value).

This openness is of course not accidental, nor is it a shortcoming. It is a conscious choice in favor of an incomplete but general theory that can expect a large intercultural and interpersonal consensus and against a complete but culture-specific and person-specific theory of the good (Sen 1993:48). It is not that listing valuable functionings as such would be illegitimate, but that any such list would at least risk being particularistic and more controversial than the incomplete capability perspective. What would be illegitimate, in the eyes of Sen, would be to erect "a grand mausoleum to one fixed and final list of capabilities"(Sen 2004:80).

The happiness perspective, by contrast, goes much further in its teleological content than does the capability perspective. It stipulates happiness as a substantive and universal value without, in the large majority of contributions, justifying that claim. Usually, the universal desirability of happiness is simply declared, hoping that it intuitively appeals across cultures, and sometimes referring to authoritative statements to this effect (including the "unalienable Right" of the "pursuit of Happiness" in the Declaration of Independence—which, interestingly, holds "liberty" to be an equally unalienable right). The happiness perspective can still be very open, however, as long as two distinct conditions are met: The *contents* of a happy life should not be specified too narrowly and happiness should not be elevated to the ultimate and single *summum bonum*.

Consistent with the concept of happiness proposed above, it is claimed here that happiness is universally valued, even though it may rank differently in the value systems of different cultures and individuals. Yet, its universal value does not derive from an alleged observation that "pain and pleasure . . . govern us in all we do, in all we say, in all we think" (Bentham 1970/1789: I.1), which, even if true, would mean committing the natural fallacy of deriving norms from (supposed) facts, but rather from its quality as a symptom, or indicator, of the presence of valued states of affairs as well as from its intrinsic desirability. If happiness indeed has the tendency to result from the presence of valued states of affairs, as argued above, then it makes for an excellent substantive indicator (albeit not necessarily a quantifiable one) for the goodness of people's lives. Happiness should therefore be valued primarily because of its role as an indicator in this sense, but also as an intrinsically valuable constituent of a good life.

5.1.2 THE ROLE OF THE PERSON

As the second conceptual difference, the role of the person differs significantly between the capability perspective and the happiness perspective as specified here. The capability perspective is exclusively concerned with living *conditions* (focusing on the particular space of capabilities), not with what people make out of these conditions. Sen expressly denies, or at least qualifies, the ethical relevance of the way people transform their capabilities into happiness (or into utility, for that matter). A "grumbling rich man" (Sen 1983a:160), for example, is considered to have a high standard of living despite not being happy and, we may infer, may very well have a large capabilities set. As a corollary, the capability perspective is not concerned with whether people actually seize their freedoms in a way that would be in their best reflected interest (with interest not being limited to self-directed concerns).

The happiness perspective, however, does include this concern for how living conditions are transformed into happiness, in addition to a concern for living conditions themselves (even though different formulations of the happiness perspective may differ on this point). It acknowledges that there is an active task left to human beings to make wise use of whatever capabilities they have. Even, or perhaps especially, a person with a maximum of freedoms must actively reflect on how she really wants to use them, who she really wants to be, and what she really wants to do in her life. What the happiness perspective, at least this particular conception of the happiness perspective, suggests is that each individual, and ultimately societies, will benefit immensely from taking happiness as an orientating concept in this inescapable task. Specifically, the orientation towards happiness may unmask distorted ideologies, self-defeating desires, excessively myopic preferences, and so on (cf. Hirata 2003). Human beings are not seen, in this perspective, as merely having a right to living conditions that would allow them to lead happy lives, but also as having some role to play in transforming these living conditions into happiness. It is not that they have the duty to be happy against their will (cf. Bruckner 2000, for a criticism of such a view), but happiness is recommended as an orientating concept—even if an individual decides upon reflection not to give much weight to being happy. *If* a person wants to be happy, however, then she has some responsibility to contribute to this outcome by, for example, resisting avarice or envy. In short, "happiness is not something that happens to people but something that they make happen" (Csikszentmihalyi 1999). The happiness perspective is thus not simply about building an agreeable world around people, but also about the ability of people to live happily in a world that is inevitably not always agreeable. This line of thinking can also be found in a number of philosophical traditions, notably in Stoic and in Buddhist philosophy. Interestingly, Buddhist philosophy in particular sometimes puts the virtue of controlling one's desires in terms of freedom from desires, creating a terminological bridge towards the capability perspective.[11]

5.2 The Case of Addictive Behavior

Let us consider the question of whether smoking should be banned in the light of the two perspectives under discussion. The argument along the lines of the capability perspective might go like the following: Since there are some people who have reason to value the functioning of smoking (whoever disagrees may kindly accept this proposition for the sake of the argument), and since making smoking legal does not force people to smoke and, hence, does not reduce anybody's capability set, smoking should be allowed. Making smoking legal

[11] This perspective of happiness as freedom from desire also plays an important role in Bhutan's policy of Gross National Happiness (Thinley 1999, Ura & Galay 2004).

would be seen as a pure enhancement of capabilities (assuming that possible encroachments on the capabilities of non-smokers are ruled out by bans on smoking in public places etc.).

In the happiness perspective, by contrast, smoking would probably be considered as generally undesirable because, even if some people genuinely benefit from smoking, it tends to deduct from happiness in a wider perspective, especially when health impacts are taken into account (again, my assumptions may not be beyond controversy but should be acceptable for the sake of the argument). Being a largely teleological concept without a built-in position on questions of social justice, the happiness perspective alone would not give any recommendation as to whether or not to ban smoking. After all, one has to distinguish between considering X prima facie undesirable, evaluating X as on the whole undesirable, and advocating X to be outlawed. The happiness perspective is limited to the first type of pronouncements. It identifies X as prima facie undesirable (i.e. as having adverse aspects with respect to happiness, whatever beneficial aspects it may also have) and challenges potential critique as to why it should not be suppressed, without making pronouncements as to what would be the right thing to do (more on this below in Section 7). Moreover, the happiness perspective would also say that people would fare better if they did not acquire the desire to smoke in the first place, or if they rid themselves of this desire once they have acquired it.

My suggestion of a possible argument by the capability perspective is certainly not the only possible position consistent with the capability perspective. What argument really follows from the capability perspective seems to depend on two particular issues. This dependence will come out clearer when the question is not that of banning smoking, but of banning hard drugs.

First, the concept of the person and in particular the extent of free will make a large difference. With respect to strongly addictive hard drugs, it would be difficult to consider the option to take them as an overall enhancement of one's capabilities set because once a person is addicted, her capabilities set will be reduced. She will no longer be able to *choose* to take or not to take the drugs, she will be psychologically *compelled* to take them (and *not* to make a number of alternative uses of her time). In a sense, capabilities are enhanced (or at least not reduced) when drugs become available, but when a person gets addicted, her capabilities are reduced. Yet, if this interpretation is plausible, it means that the capability perspective must make a distinction between, on the one hand, *choices* that are based on some "reason to value" the chosen functioning and, on the other hand, pre-reflective *behavior* that is the result of compulsion rather than reflected choice. In other words, pronouncements in terms of capabilities depend on the extent we ascribe to free will. Sen himself acknowledges the theoretical need for such a distinction when he says that:

Freedom, of course, is not an unproblematic concept. For example, if we do not have the courage to choose to live in a particular way, even though we could live that way if we so chose, can it be said that we do have the freedom to live that way, i.e. the corresponding capability? (Sen 1993:33)

Thus, a person who believes that a drug addict could overcome his addiction if he really wanted will consider the legal availability of drugs an enhancement of capabilities, while a person who sees drug addicts as victims of neural compulsion would consider the availability of drugs as a threat to people's capabilities.[12]

The second and related issue on which the interpretation of the capability perspective depends is the question of whether the goodness of a capabilities set is monotonous in the number of capabilities. In other words, is a capabilities set always improved when a valued functioning is added to the set of available functionings or when genuinely new choices are made possible? Some authors have argued that this is questionable. Thomas Schelling (1974:57), for example, argues that it would be a bad idea if we could choose the gender of our children or, one might add, their body size or musical talents.[13] Barry Schwartz (2000) reports that adding options sometimes makes choice situations less rather than more attractive to people, such as in the case of a supermarket's toothpaste assortment (some large manufacturers of household consumer items have actually reduced their product variety in response to consumer complaints, he reports), but perhaps also with respect to job and wedding decisions. A larger range of options apparently makes people more likely to feel regret afterwards because the chance of choosing a suboptimal option is greater. Moreover, the information problem becomes intractable beyond a certain limit. Schwartz even draws a connection between more clinical depression and more choice and control, mediated by a concomitant increase in expectations ("I can make my life perfect") and in causal self-attribution in the case of less-than-perfect outcomes ("I could have chosen differently"). He argues that "when self-determination is carried to extremes, it leads not to *freedom* of choice but to *tyranny* of choice" (Schwartz 2000:80–1).

One should not overdo this point, and I am not suggesting that this possibility of too many capabilities is a major impending threat to most societies. To my knowledge, however, the question of whether the goodness of a capabilities set is monotonous in the number of capabilities has not yet been dealt with. My suggestion would be that not only functionings can be more or less

---

[12] Consider also the case of the deliberate construction of casinos in black "homelands" by the South African apartheid regime that resulted in addictive gambling and (even more) deprivation among the black population (Gasper 2004:78). It seems difficult to object against this policy in the name of capabilities, but not in the name of happiness.

[13] In addition to the apparent private dilemmas such capabilities would bring about, Schelling points out social dilemmas that would result from such capabilities as control over the weather or the extension of life by one hundred years.

valuable, but also capabilities (even when they include *valued* functionings only), and that adding valuable functionings to a capabilities set does not necessarily constitute an improvement.

As one further example, and one that brings us closer to concrete questions of development, consider the interpretation of the fate of Australian Aboriginals as interpreted by Peter Singer. He argues that the nomadic Aboriginals, who traditionally reaped daily gratifications from the successful exercise of their subsistence skills, lost their sense of purpose in life after they were given the possibility of a life in modern civilization.

When food comes from a shop, bought with a government welfare cheque provided by a well-meaning social worker eager to see that all Australians get what they are legally entitled to receive, the [Aboriginals'] skills and knowledge acquired over a lifetime are immediately devalued. The result is deeply demoralizing. Almost everything... has lost its point. (Singer 1995:198)

Of course, the Aboriginals were not forced actually to make use of their cheques or even of supermarkets. The mere possibility to have free access to food, however, deprived their traditional lifestyle of much of its purpose. Adding capabilities, it seems, can sometimes disturb lives and do more harm than good.

6 Convergence of the Two Perspectives

In spite of the differences discussed above, the capability and the happiness perspectives converge on a number of issues, even though considerable differences remain. Two such issues of convergence will be discussed in this section: the role of functionings and positional competition (6.1) and a deontological deficit (6.2).

6.1 Functionings and Positional Competition

The role of functionings in the capability perspective hardly needs mentioning. Sen clearly describes the fundamental conceptual role of functionings in his capability perspective, but also explains why they are morally subordinate to capabilities. The architecture of the self-transcendent conception of happiness, as described above (cf. Section 4), also reserves a prominent place for functionings. The "reasons for happiness" that play a central role in that conception will naturally consist also of functionings. In other words, happiness depends very much on what I can actually do or be.

Interestingly, this recognition of the fundamental role of functionings as opposed to commodities is in both perspectives connected to the recognition of positional competition (Hirsch 1976:52) as a zero-sum process that often generates commodity opulence without bringing any increase in functionings on a social level (nor, therefore, in capabilities or happiness). Sen himself repeatedly (e.g. Sen 1983a:159, 1999:74) quotes Adam Smith's example of the "creditable day-labourer [who] would be ashamed to appear in publick without a linen shirt" in "present times" (i.e. in 1776) even though the Greeks and Romans managed to live "very comfortably" without linen (Smith 1979/ 1776:870). The functioning to appear in public without shame is therefore dependent on, among other things, the spending habits prevalent in society. If I increase my apparel budget simply in order to be able to continue to appear in public without shame, it will look, to the observing economist, as though my welfare is increased even though the only thing I do is *maintain* a given functioning at a higher price than in the past (cf. Hirsch 1976, Frank 1999).

In the happiness perspective, the role of positional competition has received much attention because it seems to account for much of the happiness paradox. This consists in the coexistence of a positive correlation between income and happiness in the cross section and an absence of such a correlation over time. Apparently, the richer people are happier than the poorer at any given point in time largely because they can afford positional goods (in particular, social status) that the relatively poor can never achieve. In other words, happiness seems to depend to a large extent precisely on such *(absolute)* functionings as "being able to take part in the life of the community and having self-respect" (Sen 1999:75) that are often obstructed by a low *(relative)* socio-economic rank.

The convergence, therefore, consists in the recognition of the central importance of functionings which reveals that the happiness paradox is a paradox only when one is blinded by "commodity fetishism" (Sen 1985a:28, borrowing an expression from Marx 1887).

6.2 Deontological Deficit

So far, the capability perspective has been classified as belonging to the deontological (horizontal) dimension of ethics and the happiness perspective as belonging to the teleological (vertical) dimension. However, this simple classification does of course not say that either perspective exhaustively specifies either the deontological or teleological dimension, as has been suggested already on some occasions in this chapter. In particular, neither perspective formulates deontological principles of how to deal with conflicts of interest or, equivalently, how to judge legitimacy, an indispensable requirement of any *comprehensive* concept of development ethics.

As for the capability perspective, even though it is concerned with deontological questions, it does not seem to contain any principles which might give guidance in conflicts of interest. What it does say is that it is capabilities that matter for questions of justice. It does not, however, specify which kind of reasoning, principles, or procedures can establish legitimacy. In other words, it is concerned solely with the *informational basis* of questions of justice, not with the way this information should be used in judgments of legitimacy or in the establishment of moral rights and duties. Arguably, its ethical "cutting power" (Sen 1993:48) is extended when the capability perspective is interpreted as a hermeneutical approach (as suggested by Conill 2005). Indeed, even the most uncontroversial value judgments made in the name of the capability perspective are intelligible only in a hermeneutical perspective. It remains, however, that out of itself, the capability approach does not provide any such principles.

The happiness perspective as a teleological perspective should not be expected to provide guidance in conflicts of interest to begin with. Yet, a particular happiness-based school of thought, to wit, utilitarianism, has provided not only guiding principles, but exact decision rules that are supposed to correctly solve conflicts of interest. Utilitarianism claims that correct judgment, that is, legitimacy, consists in whatever maximizes the sum-total of utility, that is, basically happiness, in society. This ethical principle does not only have some intuitive appeal, but also the nice properties of internal consistency and arithmetic precision which made it fit "hand in glove" (Little 1957:10) with quantitative economic theory.

It should be clear, however, that the happiness perspective does not by itself imply utilitarian ethical principles. It is only when the deontological deficit of the happiness perspective is "solved" by means of an ad hoc principle, such as happiness maximization, that it turns utilitarian. The happiness perspective as such, as conceptualized here, does by no means require that the informational basis for ethical judgments be restricted to happiness information, let alone that ethical judgments be equivalent to happiness maximization. It does not even suggest that happiness be of privileged informational significance in matters of justice at all. All it claims (I should perhaps say, *should* claim) is that happiness is an important constituent of any good life for the two reasons cited above (as an indicator of valuable states of affairs and as intrinsically valuable; Section 5.1.1).

This deontological deficit should not be seen as an embarrassment to either perspective. It only means that both perspectives are limited in the sense that neither of them provides a *complete* development ethical framework. Incompleteness with respect to some specific ambition is of course an inevitable property of any system and does not require any apologies as long as that ambition has not been claimed. In a larger development ethical framework, the relationship between these two perspectives emerges as one of a division of labor between individually (but also jointly) incomplete components, as the next section will argue.

7 The Division of Labor between the Capability and the Happiness Perspectives

Let us start from what we can now describe as the joint between the capability and the happiness perspectives, namely "valuable functionings". Valuable functionings are important as the substance of positive freedoms (i.e. capabilities) and as reasons for happiness. My suggestion is now that the two perspectives complement each other in understanding valuable functionings. The happiness perspective can provide the capability perspective with orientation in distinguishing between more and less valuable functionings and in deciding whether adding options improves a given choice situation. By itself, that is, without any substantial criterion such as happiness, the capability perspective seems unable to identify, say, a situation of excessive options. On the other hand, the capability perspective identifies freedom (in particular the freedom to choose between a range of valuable functionings) as valuable in itself above and beyond the value of the effectively chosen functioning and its contribution to happiness. This recognition in turn, if accepted as valid, directs the focus of the (self-transcendent) happiness perspective to capabilities as important, perhaps even paramount, reasons for happiness.

Yet, even in combination, these two perspectives do not provide a complete framework of development ethics. What is still missing is an account of how to deal with conflicts of interests or, more generally, a description of the principles by which to judge legitimacy. This deficit bears especially on Sen's objection against the reliance on happiness information. He argues on several occasions (e.g. Sen 1984b:309, 1985b:24, 1987:46, 1999:63) that happiness may be misleading as it may be present even when a person has a scandalously low endowment of capabilities. For example, when the capability-deprived "exploited landless labourer... taking pleasure in small mercies" reports to be happy, this would not be of evaluative significance because "the mental metric of happiness or desire-fulfillment can take a deeply biased form due to the fact that the mental reactions often reflect defeatist compromises with harsh reality induced by hopelessness" (Sen 1984a:512). No doubt, Sen's argument is very forceful indeed. But his criticism is directed not against the use of happiness information as such (as he clarifies on another occasion)[14] and therefore not against the happiness perspective itself as laid out here (cf. Section 6.2), but rather against the exclusive reliance on happiness information for judgments of justice. More specifically, what Sen appears to be criticizing is that the *exclusive* reliance on happiness makes it impossible to identify unacceptably, or rather illegitimately, low capability endowments.

---

[14] Cf. Sen (1985a:31), where he says that "strength of desire" (and other parameters) is rejected as a source of value, but not as an informational clue to value.

If this interpretation is correct, however, the capability perspective does not fare much better on this account. It is true that the capability perspective would be able to rank a generous capability endowment as better than that of an exploited landless laborer, but it would in itself be unable to distinguish unacceptable and acceptable, illegitimate and legitimate capability endowments for the apparent reason that it lacks a conception of legitimacy. If our interest is not the mere ranking of capability opulence but the ethical evaluation of societal development (including a distinction between legitimate and illegitimate capability sets), we need to have a perspective to discriminate between (vertically) good and bad and between (horizontally) justifiable and unjustifiable (distributional patterns of) capability sets. Specifically, we must be able to distinguish between justifiably and unjustifiably limited capability sets.

The examples Sen puts forward as unjustifiable capability deprivation ("exploited landless labourer", "subdued housewife", "overworked domestic servant", Sen 1985b:24) are actually not in the first instance cases of capability deprivation, but cases of injustice that happen to be also cases of capability deprivation. The capability perspective itself does not dispose of the conceptual distinctions that would be necessary to establish principles for moral judgments such as these. All it does is detect inequalities that are *morally relevant*, without specifying principles or criteria to judge whether they are *unjustifiably* unequal. Sen's examples owe their undeniable plausibility to quite uncontroversial moral judgments that are external to the capability perspective. Some of his examples are even by definition unjust ("exploited"), so that the diagnosis of injustice cannot possibly be challenged. Other examples appear self-evident, but the moral judgment comes in only through a prior moral stance of the capability theorist, not out of the capability theory itself. However, clearly not all cases of prima facie appalling inequalities are unjust, and the same degree of capability deprivation may be justifiable in one case and unjustifiable in another. A seriously indebted person, for example, may be described as capability-deprived, but when he is solely responsible for his indebtedness this would not be an unjustifiable case of capability deprivation.[15] Rather, whether he is justifiably or unjustifiably capability-deprived must be judged by reference to principles and norms that lie outside the domain of the capability perspective. Conversely, not all cases of injustice are also cases of capability deprivation (or even if they can be put in terms of capability deprivation, that is

---

[15] I am not advocating a purely meritocratic ethic here. My point is simply that such cases do exist (as in the case of a justly imprisoned murderer). Still, I would concede that there are basic capabilities to which every person has an unconditional right (as in the basic needs perspective), but such a view would equally require deontological justification that the capability perspective does not provide. Its domain would also be much more limited than that of the capability perspective.

not what makes them unjust) and can therefore not be diagnosed as such in the capability perspective. For example, if a policeman refrains from fining a driver for speeding because the driver is a friend of his, this injustice would not be detected on the radar screen of the capability perspective.[16]

The same obviously holds for the happiness perspective. Unhappiness itself is obviously not necessarily a reason for moral indignation. A person's unhappiness may, for example, be simply due to jealousy with respect to people who are deservedly better off, but it may also be due to unfair treatment.

Both perspectives, therefore, need to be complemented by a third perspective that provides a basis for moral judgments. Even though this is not the place to go too deep into this third perspective, I would suggest that discourse ethics (as developed by Habermas, 1983, and Apel, 1973, and refined by Ulrich 1998, 2001/1997) is not only particularly convincing as an ethical theory, but also strikingly compatible with the capability perspective. Sen's insistence that moral norms must ultimately be founded on public reasoning, and that political decisions must be based on critically *reflected* tastes and opinions brings him very close to the discourse ethical (regulative) idea of a public moral discourse (cf. Habermas 1983). His proximity to discourse ethical ideas transpires on several occasions:

The problem is not with listing important capabilities, but with insisting on one predetermined canonical list of capabilities, chosen by theorists without any general social discussion or public reasoning. To have such a fixed list, emanating entirely from pure theory, is to deny the possibility of fruitful public participation on what should be included and why. (Sen 2004:77)

An attempt to choke off participatory freedom on grounds of traditional values (such as religious fundamentalism, or political custom, or the so-called Asian values) simply misses the issue of legitimacy and the need for the people affected to participate in deciding what they want and what they have reason to accept. (Sen 1999:32)

Sen seems to borrow directly from the terminology of discourse ethics when he says that:

This issue [the procedural priority of liberty] is particularly important in the context of the constitutive role of liberty and political and civil rights in making it possible to have

---

[16] Sen himself professes that the capability perspective is not designed to capture all possible kinds of injustice: "since it is not claimed that the capability perspective exhausts all relevant concerns for evaluative purposes (we might, for example, attach importance to rules and procedures and not just to freedoms and outcomes), there is the underlying issue of how much weight should be placed on the capabilities, compared with any other relevant consideration" (Sen 1999:77, similarly Sen 1983/1979:219). However, in criticizing the metric of happiness for its blindness to certain forms of injustices, he implicitly claims that the capability perspective cannot be accused of the same blindness. Again, what Sen should be criticizing is not, as he states, the metric of happiness or utility, but a utilitarianism or a welfarism that claims to exhaust all relevant concerns for evaluative purposes.

public discourse and *communicative emergence of agreed norms* and social values. (Sen 1999:65, emphasis mine)

Even so, Sen fails to articulate the distinction between the regulative idea of a moral discourse as the counterfactual point of reference for any individual's moral *judgments* and the notion of a practical discourse as an (always imperfect) mechanism to arrive at political *decisions*.

Sen's position on the question of whether or not to draw up a list of capabilities (in the first of these three quotes) already hints at the division of labor that I would like to suggest if the objective is a development ethical conception that provides both substantive guidance with respect to meaningful objectives of development (vertical dimension) as well as an appropriate moral point of view (horizontal dimension). In such a conception, the capability perspective would indicate the space of capabilities as the major (though not exclusively) relevant informational base for judgments of justice. The way this information should enter a moral judgment would then be specified by discourse ethics.[17] The happiness perspective would provide "vertical" orientation to the participants of the discourse, aiding their reflection on what they really consider worth doing and being. To the extent that happiness is affirmed as an orientating concept for the reflection on private preferences, it would then naturally enter the public discourse as a legitimizing motive brought forward by the participants themselves, so that it would not need to be imposed as an objective by any authority. The actual political decision, however, cannot be conclusively evaluated by philosophical argument alone. Here the division of labor goes on, leaving the establishment of de facto justified, but always contestable, decisions to the practical use of reason (Kant) in the domain of the polity.

8 Conclusion

Rather than by summarizing the reasoning presented here, I shall conclude by relating these ideas on the capability and the happiness perspectives to their common political concern. Roughly speaking, the capability perspective has been developed in response to appalling and unjust living conditions in low-income countries (in particular in the example of famines), whereas the happiness perspective emerged in reaction to the observation that economic growth fails to increase subjective well-being (SWB) in the high-income coun-

---

[17] In fact, the identification of capabilities as the major informational base would not be, in this perspective, an analytical achievement injected into the discourse, but rather itself an intermediary result of the discourse. Each participant of the discourse could, in principle, reproduce Sen's argument in order to demonstrate that capabilities, and not commodities, matter in questions of justice.

tries. As different as these two problems are in some important respects, they both should be seen as development deficiencies when development is understood as "the removal of shortfalls of substantive freedoms from what they can potentially achieve" (Sen 1999:350). Moreover, both problems are present in both low- and high-income countries. There is no reason to delay the reflection on a country's (teleological) overall development objectives until all major injustices are rectified just as the affluent countries have to continue to reduce injustices while they are reflecting on the ultimate purpose of economic activity. In fact, Bhutan as a low-income country has embarked on a development path under the motto "Gross National Happiness" which combines happiness-oriented policies with a capability-oriented transition towards democracy.[18]

In fact, both concerns are often intimately related. The systematic disregard of certain groups' happiness (minorities, children, future generations, foreign residents) is a blatant injustice, and at the same time injustice is often an immediate reason for desperate unhappiness. Yet, neither is reducible to the other; each concern addresses ethically relevant aspects towards some of which the other is blind. In other words, neither perspective is sufficient, but both are necessary.

The convergence that emerges from interpreting the relationship between the capability and the happiness perspectives as a division of labor, then, is that good development consists in providing people with their fair share of freedom to do and be whatever gives them legitimate reasons for happiness. What constitutes a fair share and which reasons for happiness are legitimate has to be judged from the moral point of view described by discourse ethics and is to be decided through the practical use of reason in the polity.

References

Apel, K.-O. (1973). "Das Apriori der Kommunikationsgemeinschaft und die Grundlagen der Ethik: Zum Problem einer rationalen Begründung der Ethik im Zeitalter der Wissenschaft." In K.-O. Apel (Ed.), *Transformation der Philosophie*, Vol. 2: *Das Apriori der Kommunikationsgemeinschaft* (Engl.: *Towards a Transformation of Philosophy*, London: Routledge, 1980) (2nd edn). Frankfurt a.M.: Suhrkamp, pp. 358–435.

Argyle, M., & M. Martin. (1991). "The Psychological Causes of Happiness." In F. Strack, M. Argyle, & N. Schwarz (Eds.), *Subjective Well-Being: An Interdisciplinary Perspective* (Vol. 21). Oxford: Pergamon, pp. 77–100.

Baier, K. (1958). *The Moral Point of View: A Rational Basis of Ethics*. Ithaca: Cornell University Press.

Becker, G. S. (1976/1960). "An Economic Analysis of Fertility." In G. S. Becker, *The Economic Approach to Human Behavior*. Chicago: University of Chicago Press, pp. 171–94.

---

[18] Cf. (Ura & Galay 2004) and <http://www.constitution.bt>.

Becker, G. S., & K. M. Murphy. (1988). "A Theory of Rational Addiction." *Journal of Political Economy*, 96, 675–700.

Bentham, J. (1970/1789). *An Introduction to the Principles of Morals and Legislation*. London.

Berkowitz, L., C. Fraser, F. P. Treasure, & S. Cochran. (1987). "Pay Equity, Job Qualifications, and Comparison in Pay Satisfaction." *Journal of Applied Psychology*, 72, 544–51.

Blanchflower, D. G., & A. J. Oswald. (2004). "Well-Being Over Time in Britain and the USA." *Journal of Public Economics*, 88, 1359–86.

Boulding, K. E. (1972). "Human Betterment and the Quality of Life." In B. Strumpel, J. N. Morgan, & E. Zahn (Eds.), *Human Behavior in Economic Affairs: Essays in Honor of George Katona*. Amsterdam: Elsevier, pp. 455–70.

Bruckner, P. (2000). *L'euphorie perpétuelle: essai sur le devoir de bonheur*. Paris: Grasset.

Conill, J. (2005). "Ethische Grundlagen des Ansatzes der Fähigkeiten von Amartya Sen." In K. Homann, P. Koslowski, & C. Lütge (Eds.), *Wirtschaftsethik der Globalisierung*. Tübingen: Mohr Siebeck.

Csikszentmihalyi, M. (1999). "If We Are so Rich, Why Aren't We Happy?" *American Psychologist*, 54(10), 821–7.

Diener, E. (1994). "Assessing Subjective Well-Being: Progress and Opportunities." *Social Indicators Research*, 31, 103–57.

Easterlin, R. A. (1974). "Does Economic Growth Improve the Human Lot? Some Empirical Evidence." In P. A. David & M. W. Reder (Eds.), *Nations and Households in Economic Growth: Essays in Honor of Moses Abramowitz*. New York and London: Academic Press, pp. 89–125.

—— (2001). "Income and Happiness: Towards a Unified Theory." *The Economic Journal*, 111(473), 465–84.

Edgeworth, F. Y. (1881). *Mathematical Psychics: An Essay on the Application of Mathematics to the Moral Sciences*. London: Kegan Paul.

Frank, R. H. (1999). *Luxury Fever: Why Money Fails to Satisfy in an Era of Excess*. Princeton: Princeton University Press.

Frankfurt, H. G. (1971). "Freedom of the Will and the Concept of a Person." *Journal of Philosophy*, 68(1), 5–20.

Frankl, V. E. (1978). *Der Wille zum Sinn*. (2nd edn). Bern: Huber.

—— (1992). *Man's Search for Meaning: An Introduction to Logotherapy*. (4th edn). Boston: Beacon Press.

Frey, B. S., & A. Stutzer. (2002). *Happiness and Economics: How the Economy and Institutions Affect Human Well-being*. Princeton: Princeton University Press.

Galbraith, J. K. (1958). *The Affluent Society*. Boston: Houghton Mifflin.

Gasper, D. (2004). *The Ethics of Development: From Economism to Human Development*. Edinburgh: Edinburgh University Press.

Giannetti, E. (2002). *Felicidade: Diálogos sobre o bem-estar na civilização*. São Paulo: Companhia Das Letras.

Habermas, J. (1983). *Moralbewusstsein und kommunikatives Handeln*. (Engl.: *Moral Conciousness and Communicative Action*, Cambridge, MIT Press, 1992). Frankfurt a.M.: Suhrkamp.

—— (1999). *Die Einbeziehung des Anderen*. Frankfurt a.M.: Suhrkamp.

Harsanyi, J. C. (1955). "Cardinal Welfare, Individualistic Ethics, and Interpersonal Comparisons of Utility." *Journal of Political Economy*, 63, 309–21.

Hirata, J. (2001). "Was Mother Teresa an Egoist?" *Eloquent*, 8(1), 37–8.

—— (2003). "Putting Gross National Happiness in the Service of Good Development." *Journal of Bhutan Studies*, 9, 99–139.

—— (2004). "Happiness Research: Contributions to Economic Ethics." *Zeitschrift für Wirtschafts- und Unternehmensethik (zfwu)*, 5(2), 141–59.

—— (2006). *Happiness, Ethics, and Economics*. Unpublished doctoral thesis, University of St. Gallen, <http://www.johannes-hirata.de>.

Hirsch, F. (1976). *Social Limits to Growth*. Cambridge, MA: Harvard University Press.

Kahneman, D., E. Diener, & N. Schwarz (Eds.). (1999). *Well-Being: The Foundations of Hedonic Psychology*. New York: Russel Sage Foundation.

Kant, I. (1977/1785). *Grundlegung zur Metaphysik der Sitten*. Collected Writings Vol. VII, ed. W. Weischedel. Frankfurt a.M.: Suhrkamp.

Lane, R. E. (2000). *The Loss of Happiness in Market Democracies*. New Haven: Yale University Press.

Layard, R. (1980). "Human Satisfaction and Public Policy." *The Economic Journal*, 90, 737–50.

Little, I. M. D. (1957). *A Critique of Welfare Economics*. (2nd edn). Oxford: Oxford University Press.

Marx, K. (1887). *Capital: A Critical Analysis of Capitalist Production*. ed. F. Engels, trans. S. Moore & E. B. Aveling. London: Sonnenschein.

Myers, D. G., & E. Diener. (1996). "The Pursuit of Happiness." *Scientific American*, 272, 70–2.

Nozick, R. (1989). "Happiness." In R. Nozick, *The Examined Life: Philosophical Meditations*. New York: Simon & Schuster, pp. 99–117.

Oswald, A. J. (1997). "Happiness and Economic Performance." *The Economic Journal*, 107 (November), 1815–31.

Ryan, R. M., & E. L. Deci. (2001). "To Be Happy or to Be Self-fulfilled: A review of research on hedonic and eudaimonic well-being." *Annual Review of Psychology*, 52, 141–66.

Ryff, C. D. (1995). "Psychological Well-Being in Adult life." *Current Directions in Psychological Science*, 4, 99–104.

Schelling, T. C. (1974). "On the Ecology of Micromotives." In R. Marris (Ed.), *The Corporate Society*. London: Macmillan, pp. 19–64.

Schwartz, B. (2000). "Self-Determination: The Tyranny of Freedom." *American Psychologist*, 55(1), 79–88.

Seel, M. (1999/1995). *Versuch über die Form des Glücks*. Frankfurt a.M.: Suhrkamp.

Sen, A. K. (1982). "Rights and Agency." *Philosophy and Public Affairs*, 11(1), 3–39.

—— (1983a). "Poor, Relatively Speaking." *Oxford Economic Papers*, 35(July), 153–69.

—— (1983b). "Rational Fools: A Critique of the Behavioural Foundations of Economic Theory." In A. K. Sen (Ed.), *Choice, Welfare and Measurement*. Oxford: Basil Blackwell, pp. 84–106.

—— (1983/1979). "Equality of What?" In A. K. Sen, *Choice, Welfare and Measurement*. Oxford: Basil Blackwell, pp. 353–69.

—— (1984a). "Goods and People." In A. K. Sen, *Resources, Values and Development*. Cambridge, MA: Harvard University Press, pp. 509–32.

—— (1984b). "Rights and Capabilities." In A. K. Sen, *Resources, Values and Development*. Cambridge, MA: Harvard University Press, pp. 307–24.

Sen, A. K. (1984/1983). "The Profit Motive." In A. K. Sen, *Resources, Values and Development*. Cambridge, MA: Harvard University Press, pp. 90–110.

—— (1985a). *Commodities and Capabilities* (Vol. 7). Amsterdam: North-Holland.

—— (1985b). "Rights as Goals." In S. Guest & A. Milne (Eds.), *Equality and Discrimination: Essays in Freedom and Justice*. Stuttgart: Franz Steiner, pp. 11–25.

—— (1987). *On Ethics and Economics*. Oxford: Basil Blackwell.

—— (1993). "Capability and Well-Being." In M. C. Nussbaum & A. K. Sen (Eds.), *The Quality of Life*. Oxford: Oxford University Press, pp. 30–53.

—— (1995). *Inequality Reexamined*. Oxford: Oxford University Press.

—— (1999). *Development as Freedom*. Oxford: Oxford University Press.

—— (2004). "Capabilities, Lists, and Public Reason: Continuing the Conversation." *Feminist Economics*, 10(3), 77–80.

Sidgwick, H. (1907/1874). *The Methods of Ethics* (7th edn). London: Macmillan.

Singer, P. (1995). *How Are We to Live? Ethics in an Age of Self-interest*. Amherst: Prometheus Books.

Smith, A. (1976/1759). *The Theory of Moral Sentiments*. ed. D. D. Raphael. & A. L. Macfie. Oxford: Oxford University Press.

—— (1979/1776). *An Inquiry into the Nature and Causes of the Wealth of Nations*. edited by R. H. Campbell & A. S. Skinner. Oxford: Oxford University Press.

Spaemann, R. (1989). *Glück und Wohlwollen: Versuch über Ethik*. Stuttgart: Klett-Cotta.

Thielemann, U. (2000). "A Brief Theory of the Market—Ethically Focused." *International Journal of Social Economics*, 27(1), 6–31.

Thinley, J. Y. (1999). "Values and Development: Gross National Happiness." In S. Kinga, K. Galay, P. Rapten, & A. Pain (Eds.), *Gross National Happiness: A Set of Discussion Papers*. Thimphu: The Centre for Bhutan Studies, pp. 12–23.

Thomä, D. (2003). *Vom Glück in der Moderne*. Frankfurt a.M.: Suhrkamp.

Ulrich, P. (1998). *Integrative Economic Ethics: Towards a Conception of Socio-Economic Rationality* (discussion paper of the Institute for Business Ethics at the University of St. Gallen No. 82). St. Gallen.

—— (2001/1997). *Integrative Wirtschaftsethik: Grundlagen einer lebensdienlichen Ökonomie* (3rd edn). Berne: Haupt. (Engl.: *Integrative Economic Ethics: Foundations of a Civilized Market Economy*. Cambridge: Cambridge University Press (2008, forthcoming)).

Ura, K., & K. Galay (Eds.). (2004). *Gross National Happiness and Development: Proceedings of the First International Seminar on Operationalization of Gross National Happiness*. Thimphu: Centre for Bhutan Studies.

Veenhoven, R. (1996). "Developments in Satisfaction-Research." *Social Indicators Research*, 37, 1–46.

Wierzbicka, A. (1999). *Emotions Across Languages and Cultures: Diversity and Universals*. Cambridge: Cambridge University Press.

8

Self-Determination Theory and the Explanatory Role of Psychological Needs in Human Well-Being*

Maarten Vansteenkiste, Richard M. Ryan, and Edward L. Deci

Introduction

Human capabilities and happiness have received increasing attention from psychologists and economists over the past half-century. Implicit in such concepts are ideas such as thriving and flourishing—ideas that involve individuals having resources and opportunities to live healthy, full, and productive lives. At the same time, both economic and psychological theories have been limited by assumptions about the power of tangible rewards and incentives to drive behavior and about accumulation of wealth as *the* behavioral outcome, rather than taking a fuller view of both what people need to flourish and live well, and what goals, given adequate freedom, they would feel most fulfilled in pursuing. One result has been that the intrinsic motivations that underlie much of human functioning have tended to be neglected or peripheralized. Yet there is substantial evidence that intrinsic satisfactions can have great potency in fostering individual and collective motivation, optimal performance, productivity, and wellness.

Herein we review a rapidly growing theory in motivational psychology, the implications of which bear on prescriptions for both personal and economic development and human well-being. Specifically, we discuss self-determination theory (SDT) (Deci & Ryan, 2000a; Ryan & Deci, 2000b), which empirically addresses both the basic psychological needs associated with well-being across gender, development, and culture, and the motivational and social

* The first author's contributions were supported by a grant for scientific research from Flanders (FWO-Vlaanderen), and the second and third authors' contributions were supported by a grant from the National Cancer Institute (CA 106668).

conditions that allow for fulfillment of these needs. Further, SDT accounts for why rewards and material acquisitions so often fail to produce sustained motivation, performance, and well-being.

Psychology, Motivation, and Well-Being

For many decades the dominant view within psychology was that people are largely driven and shaped by reward contingencies in their external environment (e.g. Skinner, 1953). Moreover, even after behaviorism began to wane as a dominant view, the cognitive models that replaced this reinforcement view advocated a relatively content free "expectancy-valence" view (e.g. Vroom, 1964) that still underpins current social-cognitive models (e.g. Bandura, 1989). In these latter views, people thrive and do well whenever they feel efficacious with respect to their goals and have the capabilities to accomplish them. What is interesting about such views is how they focus mainly on the success of instrumentalities, but not at all on the contents of the goals underlying them or on the forces that initiate people's goal pursuits (Vansteenkiste et al., 2005). In the expectancy-valence view, it is presumed that as long as one feels effective at one's valued goals, well-being results, and, as such, all goals are "created equal" (see Ryan et al., 1996).

Research guided by SDT has made it increasingly apparent, however, that people's motivated actions, even when efficacious, are not all equally beneficial either to themselves or to others. People can be afforded capabilities, and even rewarded for reaching many goals, but SDT suggests that differences in both *what* goals are pursued and *why* individuals embrace them predict differences in the motivational, performance, and well-being outcomes that result.

With respect to the "why" of goals, evidence suggests that pursuing and attaining goals can be done through autonomous (or self-endorsed) versus heteronomous (or controlled) regulations. When people feel controlled by external forces, or lack a true inner endorsement of a pursued goal, efficacy and success at the goals do not yield the enhanced well-being that classic expectancy-valence models predict. Further, controlled regulation of behavior is linked to poor performance and lack of persistence when the contingencies are removed (Deci & Ryan, 2000).

As well, much research suggests that goal contents—the "what" of motivation—can be characterized as either intrinsic or extrinsic (Kasser & Ryan, 1996), a distinction that empirically holds up across diverse cultures (Grouzet et al., 2005). Investment in and success at *intrinsic goals* such as self-development, affiliation, and community contribution, which are said to be most directly related to satisfaction of basic psychological needs, reliably enhance well-being. In contrast, the pursuit of, and even success at, *extrinsic goals* such as materialism, appearance, and fame do not reliably enhance wellness, and can diminish it (e.g. Kasser, 2002; Ryan et al., 1999; Vansteenkiste, Simons, Lens,

Sheldon, & Deci, 2004), a position echoed by some consumer psychologists (e.g. Richins & Dawson,1992). The lynchpin in these findings is satisfaction of the basic psychological needs for autonomy, competence, and relatedness, which mediates these differential relations between goal contents and the outcomes they yield. Such findings, like those concerning the autonomy versus control distinction, have deep implications for understanding people's thriving, and what is entailed in living personally and collectively meaningful lives (Ryan, Huta, & Deci, 2008).

Economics, Development, and Human Freedom

Within economics, examination of human flourishing has taken some parallel pathways. Most mid-century economists held to a view of people as rational beings who function to maximize their own gains, and these economists assumed that people's pursuit of self-interests ultimately benefits the society as a whole. However, the concept of self-interest has often been viewed narrowly in terms of maximizing extrinsic outcomes, without due attention to intrinsic satisfactions that are key to human nature and critical for optimal performance and well-being.

Important contributions in economics over the past half-century have challenged the traditional assumptions that decision-making is wholly rational and that individuals' view self-interest primarily in terms of extrinsic incentives. Indeed, it has become increasingly clear that these assumptions lead to an unsatisfactory view of freedom, development, and well-being. Thus, as in psychology, it has been necessary to distinguish among types of benefits individuals' motivated action might yield if one is to understand the thriving of both individuals and the collective.

Among the earliest contributions that challenged traditional economic reasoning was Simon's (1955) theory of decision-making that involved people making choices that *satisfice* rather than optimize their interests and thus are not fully "rational" in the sense that some economists had used that term. Further, Tversky and Kahneman (1987) showed how various information-processing factors lead people to make choices that are often not rational, and Frey (1997), in line with psychological work by Deci and Ryan (2000), presented an economic examination of some negative consequences of monetary rewards in decision-making and behavior. Finally, over the past two decades, the work of Sen (1999) has emphasized that raw economic growth is only part of the story of promoting human well-being. Sen's work changed the focus from economic expansion as the sole outcome of economic development to freedom, which economic development can help promote but does not guarantee. Freedom entails provisions that allow people to actualize capabilities, and thus to thrive.

Psychological and Economic Contributions to Happiness and Human Capabilities

The simultaneous growing interest in the study of positive mental states and human freedom within psychology (e.g. Diener, 1984; Ryan & Deci, 2000b; Ryff & Singer, 1998) and economics (e.g. Frey & Stutzer, 2001; Sen, 1999) provided the foundation for the *International Workshop on Capabilities and Happiness* that was held in Milan, Italy in 2005 and spawned this collection. One of its central premises is that human capabilities too frequently remain under-actualized because social conditions interfere with the actualization. These conditions include not only material affordances, but also the social and economic conditions that allow individuals to freely engage their capabilities, which, we argue, they are intrinsically prone to pursue.

Self-Determination Theory

In this chapter, we lay out basic aspects of SDT (Ryan & Deci, 2000b) as they relate to concepts of development, autonomy, well-being, and freedom. SDT is a psychological theory that goes to the heart of the issues of happiness and human capabilities and deals directly with the ideas of human actualization and flourishing. The primary level of analysis of the theory is on individual psychological processes; however, the theory also addresses how social environments affect need satisfaction and motivation— whether the environments are experimentally induced (e.g. Vansteenkiste et al., 2004), are ongoing social contexts such as work groups or families (e.g. Deci, Connell, & Ryan, 1989; Grolnick & Ryan, 1989), or are cultural and macro-economic systems (e.g. Chirkov, Ryan, Kim, & Kaplan, 2003; Deci et al., 2001).

We turn now to a discussion of the basic psychological needs for competence, autonomy, and relatedness that are essential for human flourishing and wellness (Ryan, 1995) and then address both the regulatory processes involved in intrinsic and extrinsic motivation (the "why" of behavior) and the contents of people's goal pursuits (the "what" of behavior). Finally, we discuss some implications of SDT for social-economic systems.

Basic Psychological Needs in Motivation and Wellness

Self-determination theory (SDT) maintains that humans have three basic and universal psychological needs: *the need for competence—that is,* feeling effective in one's interactions with the social and physical environments (Deci, 1975; White, 1959); *the need for relatedness—*that is, caring for and feeling cared for by others (Baumeister & Leary, 1995; Ryan, 1995); and *the need for autonomy*—that is, feeling volitional and fully endorsing one's actions, (de Charms, 1968; Deci & Ryan, 1985). According to SDT, when social contexts allow satisfaction of these psychological needs, people thrive, but ill-being follows thwarted satisfaction.

Although the concept of psychological needs has been used by various psychologists over the years (e.g. McClelland, 1985; Ryan, 1995) and has received increasing empirical attention (e.g. La Guardia, Ryan, Couchman, & Deci, 2000; Reis et al., 2000), the construct of needs has been controversial concerning whether needs are innate or acquired; what criteria are necessary for naming a need; what distinguishes basic needs from need derivatives; and whether any psychological needs are universal (e.g. Baumeister & Leary, 1995; Chirkov et al., 2003; Markus, Kitayama, & Heiman, 1996; Ryan, 1995).

Psychological Needs: Basic and Universal

SDT takes a unique position on needs by maintaining that the concept specifies the nutriments essential for growth, integration, and wellness (Deci & Ryan, 2000). Whether or not need satisfaction is personally valued or culturally endorsed, SDT suggests that failure to satisfy a need will yield negative consequences across individuals and cultures. Thus, SDT's definition provides objective criteria for assessing the effectiveness of social contexts, organizations, and cultures—namely, whether or not they promote satisfaction of the basic human needs.

Using this definition, SDT identified the needs for competence, relatedness, and autonomy, and we have not yet found any compelling empirical evidence for adding others (see Deci & Ryan, 2000). By strictly defining the needs concept, SDT provides a means of parsimoniously accounting for a broad variety of phenotypically divergent phenomena with very few constructs. Such parsimony is very important from an applied perspective, because it provides socializing agents and policy makers in diverse contexts with a concise but comprehensive theoretical framework for structuring organizations (e.g. schools, companies, families) and optimally motivating other individuals (e.g. students, employees, children).

Supporting the claim that basic need satisfaction promotes thriving and optimal functioning, studies have shown that greater psychological need satisfaction promotes greater well-being, beyond personal income (e.g. Vansteenkiste, Neyrinck et al., 2007), as well as health and fewer physical complaints (e.g. Deci et al., 2001; La Guardia et al., 2000; Sheldon, Ryan, & Reis, 1996). Studies of within person variations in daily need satisfaction have indicated that satisfaction of each need independently predicts well-being, indexed by variables such as vitality and life satisfaction, and is negatively associated with ill-being, indexed by variables such as depression and negative affect (Reis et al., 2000). Supports for basic need satisfaction have also predicted thriving in the domains of work (e.g. Baard, Deci, & Ryan, 2004), physical exercise (e.g. Ntoumanis, 2001; Standage, Duda, & Ntoumanis, 2003), religion (Ryan, Rigby & King, 1993), and health care (e.g. Sénécal, Nouwen, & White, 2000; Williams et al., 2006).

Competence, Relatedness, and Autonomy

The *need for competence* (White, 1959) describes the natural propensity to explore, manipulate, and master the environment, and actively to seek challenges that extend physical and psychological functioning. The need for competence underlies people's exploratory nature, contributes to their growth, and helps them adapt to complex surrounds. When people are not afforded opportunities to master the environment or when they fail at their mastery attempts (e.g. they receive regular indicators of incompetence), they tend to become amotivated—that is, they display little motivation and tend to function poorly. The need for competence maps well onto theories of self-efficacy, perceived control, and expectancy value (e.g. Bandura, 1989; Rotter, 1966), even though they do not explicitly posit competence as a basic need. Still, because the concept of competence is so pervasive in contemporary psychology, the postulate of a need for competence has been non-controversial.

The psychological *need for relatedness* assumes people are naturally inclined to seek close and intimate relationships and to work toward a sense of belonging within social groups (Ryan, 1993; Baumeister & Leary, 1995). This goes beyond the idea of interdependence for physical maintenance and is satisfied only by the experience of supportive, caring relationships in which people feel significant and respected. The need for relatedness underlies the human propensity to engage in social-support systems (Ryan & Solky, 1996), form secure attachments (La Guardia et al., 2000), and transmit communal knowledge among individuals and between generations (Deci & Ryan, 2000). The construct of a relatedness need helps interpret findings from the study of close relationships in social psychology (Reis & Patrick, 1996) and with developmental perspectives such as attachment theory (Bretherton, 1987). This postulate of a relatedness need, like that for competence, has been relatively non-controversial.

The *need for autonomy*, SDT's third basic need, is manifest in striving to feel a sense of volition and choice in behavior. The idea that people are naturally inclined to experience themselves as origins of their behavior was emphasized by de Charms (1968), and we (e.g. Deci & Ryan, 1985) have argued that the need for autonomy stems from the general self-organizing tendencies of human development leading to actions that are integrated and self-endorsed.

Autonomy provides many adaptive advantages, including the ability to regulate actions and emotions better, to become more internally coherent, and to disengage from exogenous goals when necessary. Nonetheless, unlike the needs for competence and relatedness, specifying a need for autonomy has been highly controversial, with authors suggesting that it is primarily a Western, male value rather than a universal need (Jordan, 1997; Markus, Kitayama, & Heiman, 1996). One implication of these latter views is that people from collectivist cultures, or women, would not need autonomy, that they can flourish without a sense of volition or choice. Yet, the empirical evidence shows that autonomy is associated with enhanced well-being in Eastern as well as Western cultures (e.g. Chirkov et al., 2003; Vansteenkiste, Zhou, et al., 2005) and in women as well as men (Deci et al., 2006; Vallerand, 1997).

The Regulation of Behavior

We turn now to a discussion of *behavioral regulation* and its relation to need satisfaction. Regulation concerns the motivational processes that organize and direct behaviors and is reflected in people's reasons for engaging in the behaviors—for example, whether they act out of interest or because they would be punished for not acting. Much SDT research has focused on different types of behavioral regulation and their distinct consequences.

Intrinsic and Extrinsic Motivation

The differentiation of behavior regulation begins with the broad distinction between intrinsic and extrinsic motivation. To be intrinsically motivated means to engage in an activity because the activity itself is interesting and enjoyable. Intrinsically motivated behavior is spontaneously satisfying so it persists without reinforcement from operationally separable consequences (Deci, 1975; Ryan & Deci, 2000a). When intrinsically motivated people become absorbed in the activity and may experience what Csikszentmihalyi (1975) referred to as "flow," an intensely positive experience in which people's attention is highly focused on an activity and they lose a sense of time. For example, soccer players, at their best moments on the field, will be fully immersed in the game, feeling excited, engaged, and wholly focused on the play.

Intrinsic motivation is considered a prototype of autonomous or volitional motivation because people's interest is central to a self-catalyzing chain of activities. It is also the earliest expression of autonomy, as infants are intrinsically motivated actively to explore and learn. When pursuing interests, people's behavior emanates spontaneously from their sense of self. In the terminology of attribution theory, intrinsic motivation is characterized by an *internal perceived locus of causality* (I-PLOC) (de Charms, 1968; Ryan & Deci, 2000a).

In contrast to intrinsic motivation, *extrinsic motivation* entails doing an activity because it leads to some outcome that is operationally separable from the activity. Extrinsic motivation concerns activities enacted because they are instrumental rather than because one finds the actions satisfying in their own right (Deci & Ryan, 2000). The classic cases of extrinsic motivation are behaviors done to obtain externally administered rewards or to avoid punishments levied by others. Such extrinsic motivators are often brought to bear to prompt or sustain behavior. For example, when children show no interest in studying, parents may offer them rewards to do homework. Although such rewards may have a short-term impact, the contingencies have been found, typically, to diminish autonomy and intrinsic motivation (Deci, Koestner, & Ryan, 1999), and to be ineffective in longer-term maintenance of behavior. In attribution terms, the behavior has an *external perceived locus of causality* (E-PLOC).

An important question, however, is whether extrinsically motivated behavior always has an E-PLOC or can sometimes be autonomous. SDT maintains that some extrinsically motivated behavior is experienced as volitional and autonomous. SDT specifically argues that individuals can assimilate the personal value or social importance of an uninteresting behavior, in which case the behavior and its regulation would be experienced as autonomous rather than controlled. For instance, traffic laws are introduced by policy makers and have significant punishments associated with violations; but when people follow the laws because they accept their importance for preventing accidents and saving lives, they are likely to do them autonomously. Once accepting the value of traffic laws, people are also more likely to take responsibility for regulating corresponding behaviors (Deci & Ryan, 1985; Ryan & Deci, 2000b).

Internalization and Types of Regulation

The process of coming to value or endorse an extrinsically motivated action is described within SDT by the concepts of *internalization* and *integration*. On the basis of both their needs for relatedness and autonomy, SDT argues, people are prone towards attempting to adopt and integrate into their personal value system ambient social norms and practices. This tendency toward internalization is of vital importance for the effective functioning of our society because it is the crucial means through which individuals are socialized and thus adopt the regulations, mores, and values societies transmit (Maccoby, 1984; Ryan & Deci, 2003). In other words, internalization describes the active processes of taking in and integrating social norms.

When considering such behaviors as recycling, paying taxes, or voting, none of which are typically inherently enjoyable and thus not intrinsically motivated, SDT suggests that when people internalize and integrate a regulation, they more likely perform the behavior well and persist at it over the long term (e.g. Koestner et al., 1996). SDT proposes, further, that internalization can occur to varying degrees; in other words, people can internalize a value and regulation more or less fully. In fact, the theory distinguishes among four types of regulation that represent different degrees of internalization of extrinsically motivated behaviors, and predicts different outcomes for each of these regulatory types.

The least internalized form of motivated actions is depicted within SDT as *externally regulated*. Such behaviors are initiated and controlled by contingencies of reward and punishment that are wholly external to the person. The concept of external regulation relates to operant behaviorism (Skinner, 1953), which maintains that behaviors are controlled by reinforcement contingencies. Thus, external regulation is the only form of regulation well conceptualized within operant theory. Although external regulation is a powerful form of motivation, its downfall concerns the phenomena of maintenance and transfer (Deci & Ryan, 1985). Because externally regulated behaviors are dependent on the external contingencies, the behaviors will not be forthcoming when the contingencies are not active. For example, if a boy eats vegetables because his parents reward him with dessert for doing so, he is unlikely to eat them when his parents are away or there is no dessert (a lack of maintenance), or if he goes into a new situation such as summer camp (a lack of transfer). From the perspective of SDT, this failure of generalization occurs because the behavioral regulation has not been internalized.

A second form of extrinsic motivation within SDT is *introjected regulation*. Introjection derives, etymologically, from the Latin words "intro" and "jacere", which mean "into" and "to throw". Introjection is thus a process in which an external value or regulation is thrown into people. People then use these internalizations as a basis for regulating themselves. They thus engage in behaviors to meet intra-individual (instead of external) pressures, such as avoiding shame, aggrandizing themselves, or feeling social approval. As a result, introjected regulation is still experienced as nonautonomous because people feel pressured to do the activity (Deci & Ryan, 2000). To illustrate, a man who recycles because he imagines he will feel approval only if he does so would be displaying introjected regulation.

A behavior becomes more autonomous as people begin to identify with the value of the behavior for themselves. As they personally understand its importance, they accept the regulation and become more volitional in carrying it out. *Identified regulation* thus occurs as people find meaning in an activity and feel a sense of choice when performing it. Canceling a tennis match in order to stay home and care for a sick child would represent identified regulation if the person did it volitionally, recognizing that it was more important than playing the sport.

An even greater sense of self-determination will be experienced when people not only identify with the importance of an activity, but also bring that identification into coherence with other values, desires, and identifications. This is labeled *integrated regulation*. As people adopt various identifications, each needs to be integrated with other values and motives to establish psychological harmony and cohesiveness. Identifications that remain *compartmentalized* may feel volitional when enacted, but insofar as they are not fully integrated, they may be less stable and can conflict with other motives or values. For instance, a man who works continuously to accumulate wealth, but who simultaneously wants to spend time with his children may have difficulty integrating the two identifications. SDT posits that integrated regulation is the endpoint of the internalization process and is the highest degree of autonomy for extrinsic motivation.

From the perspective of SDT, intrinsic motivation and well-internalized forms of extrinsic motivation represent two different forms of autonomous motivation. When intrinsically motivated, people behave volitionally because the behavior is interesting and enjoyable; when autonomously extrinsically motivated, they act because they have accepted the value of the behavior as their own. The two types of autonomous motivation do, however, share the sense of volition, the feelings of willingness and choice, and the experience of an internal perceived locus of causality that characterize autonomous motivation (Reeve, Nix, & Hamm, 2003).

To summarize, although external, introjected, identified, and integrated regulation are all forms of extrinsic motivation, they differ considerably in their degree of autonomy. Research in the 1980s resulted in a conceptual shift away from intrinsic versus extrinsic motivation as the central motivational distinction to *autonomous versus controlled regulation* as the more important distinction for making predictions about health, persistence, performance, and relationship quality (Ryan & Deci, 2000b). In other words, whereas in early theories only one form of extrinsic motivation had been specified and was viewed as an antipode to intrinsic motivation and self-determination (e.g. de Charms, 1968), the recognition that some types of extrinsic motivation can be relatively autonomous led to the alignment of intrinsic motivation and well-internalized extrinsic motivation as positive forms of human mobilization.

Figure 1, derived from Ryan and Connell (1989), shows the basic taxonomy of motivation types, which fall along a continuum of relative autonomy or self-determination. At the far right is intrinsic motivation, representing a prototype of autonomy. To its left is extrinsic motivation with its four types of regulation shown on the line below. The types of regulation that are more autonomous are closer to intrinsic motivation on the continuum. On the left end of Figure 8.1 is *amotivation*. It refers to lacking either type of motivation. When people feel unable to do a behavior, when they do not value the behavior or the outcome it yields, or when they do not believe that their

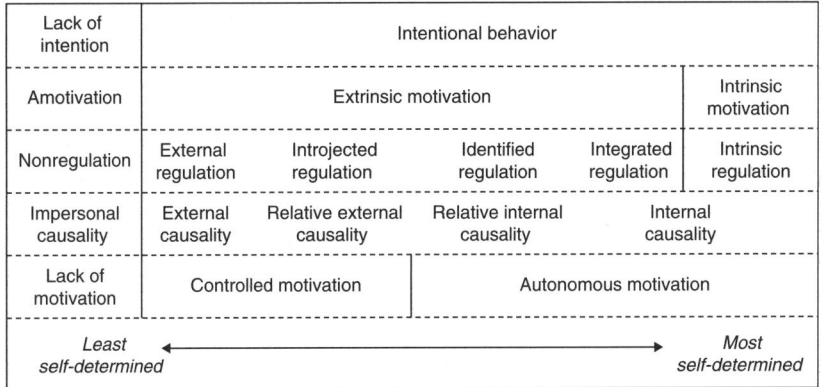

Lack of intention	Intentional behavior				
Amotivation	Extrinsic motivation				Intrinsic motivation
Nonregulation	External regulation	Introjected regulation	Identified regulation	Integrated regulation	Intrinsic regulation
Impersonal causality	External causality	Relative external causality	Relative internal causality	Internal causality	
Lack of motivation	Controlled motivation		Autonomous motivation		
Least self-determined ←					→ *Most self-determined*

Figure 8.1. Schematic representation of the types of motivation and regulation within Self-Determination Theory. Included are the intrinsic–extrinsic conceptualization of motivation; the autonomous-controlled conceptualization of motivation; the differentiation of extrinsic motivation into type of regulation; and the perceived locus of causality for each type of regulation. Shown at the bottom is the degree of relative self-determination for each type of motivation and regulation.

behavior is reliably related to outcomes they will not be motivated—that is, they will be amotivated. Amotivation stands in contrast to both extrinsic and intrinsic motivation because it represents a lack of motivation (i.e. a lack of intention to behave), whereas intrinsic and extrinsic motivation are the two important classes of motivated or intentional actions.

Independence, Conformity, and Agency: Their Relation with Autonomy

Although the concept and dynamics of autonomy have been examined empirically from the SDT perspective more than from any other perspective, various other psychologists have also discussed the concept of autonomy with respect to cross-cultural, developmental, and personality perspectives. Below, we discuss other views as they relate to SDT.

INDEPENDENCE AND AUTONOMY

Some perspectives within cross-cultural (e.g. Markus, Kitayama, & Heiman 1996) and developmental (e.g. Steinberg & Silverberg, 1986) psychology have equated autonomy and independence. This has led to considerable confusion in the literature, because although autonomy and independence are sometimes dynamically related to one another, they often are clearly distinct. In SDT, independence refers to not relying on others, whereas autonomy refers to experiencing volition and choice. As argued by Ryan and Solky (1996), it is possible to depend on others autonomously. Thus, the opposite of autonomy is not being dependent, but is being heteronomous or controlled. Relying on others for support can be done either autonomously or non-autonomously (Ryan & Lynch, 1989; Soenens et al., 2007). One can willingly accept guidance from others, but it is a very different matter when one feels coerced to accept the guidance. Simply put, autonomy does not necessarily imply lack of reliance on others, nor independence from them (Ryan et al., 2005).

Consistent with the view that autonomy and relatedness are highly compatible, Hodgins, Koestner, and Duncan (1996) demonstrated that autonomous regulation allows people to be more open and less defensive in their daily interpersonal experiences with parents and peers, presumably because the interactions are seen as a source for personal growth and satisfaction. Further, Soenens and Vansteenkiste (2005) showed that autonomy-supportive parenting predicted more autonomous regulation of adolescents' friendships, indicating that autonomy is indeed compatible with having close relationships with parents and peers.

Confusions persist however, when autonomy and independence are not conceptually or empirically distinguished. For example, Markus, Kitayama, & Heiman (1996) have argued that the concepts of autonomy and individuality (which they equate) do not enhance mental health within collectivist cultures and individuals with an interdependent (versus independent) self-construal. They thus criticized SDT, with its concept of autonomy, as being a Western theory in which the assumption that autonomy is universally important for well-being and optimal performance is inappropriate. The problem is that they defined autonomy as independence rather than volition so their criticism of SDT was irrelevant to the theory.

Autonomy involves volitionally regulating one's actions, experiencing a sense of choice, and concurring with one's actions when they are viewed from the highest or truest level of reflection (Friedman, 2003). There is no inconsistency between autonomy and either collectivism or interdependence. A person can fully internalize a collectivist value and thus be autonomous (i.e. volitional) in enacting it, just as one could fully internalize an individualist value and be autonomous in enacting it. Indeed, Chirkov et al. (2003) found that autonomy was an important predictor of psychological health in both Eastern cultures such as South Korea and Western cultures such as the United States, even though the specific practices that people experience as more or less autonomous can differ across cultures. Further, Vansteenkiste, Zhou, et al., (2005) found that Chinese students' autonomous reasons for studying positively predicted their self-regulated learning, performance, and well-being. Similar findings have been obtained in Germany (Levesque et al., 2004), Japan (Hayamizu, 1997), Russia (Chirkov & Ryan, 2001), Israel (Assor et al., 2005), Korea (Chirkov et al., 2003), and Belgium (Vansteenkiste, Lens, et al., 2004).

Just as some cross-cultural psychologists maintain that autonomy is not crucial for all cultural groups, some developmental psychologists argue that the development of autonomy involves breaking away from dependence rather than developing volition and self-regulation. Blos (1979) argued that adolescents must "individuate" from their parents, becoming what he describes as self-reliant and autonomous. In line with this, Steinberg and Silverberg (1986) argued that adolescents must move away from relying on parents to become healthy adults. As pointed out by Ryan and Lynch (1989), however, that view implies that establishing autonomy requires adolescents distancing themselves from parents, a view that SDT does not endorse.

SDT suggests that people can be autonomously dependent or autonomously independent (Ryan et al., 2005). Steinberg and Silverberg viewed autonomy as the pursuit of independence, implying that autonomy's positive effects on optimal functioning would necessarily undermine relatedness to others (particularly to parents). Ryan and Lynch (1989) showed in contrast that, when autonomy was understood as volition, autonomy was not antagonistic to relatedness; indeed, having a strong supportive relationship with parents facilitated adolescents' autonomy rather than diminished it, Further, Niemiec et al. (2006) found that autonomy support from parents predicted their adolescents' well-being.

CONFORMITY AND AUTONOMY

The concept of conformity, although it might seem similar to control (and thus antagonistic to autonomy), is, conceptually, largely orthogonal to autonomy, as also suggested by philosophical analyses of autonomy (e.g. Dworkin, 1988). This is premised on the definition of conformity as simply acting in accord with an external prompt, rule, or norm. SDT (Ryan, 1993) suggests people's adherence to external guidelines and influences may reflect mere obedience or coercion, in which case it would be controlled and thus not autonomous, or it might represent a reflective valuing of the direction or guidance that these inputs provide, in which case the people would be acting autonomously. For instance, students might follow a teacher's rules because they fear the teacher's reprimand or because they believe fully in the rules' importance. The former conforming would be heteronomous, the latter autonomous.

As such, SDT maintains that merely acting in accord with social norms is not a hallmark of "authentic" or preferred behavior, as suggested by some cross-cultural perspectives (Markus & Kitayama, 2003). Rather, it is the degree of subjective endorsement and ownership of these norms that determines whether the adherence to social obligations constitutes authentic willingness versus pressure and coercion (Ryan & Deci, 2003).

SELF-REGULATION AND AGENCY

Within the SDT framework, self-regulation refers to regulation by the self, that is, by one's personal interests that spontaneously emanate from the self (i.e. intrinsic motivation) or by one's personal values and commitments that have been accepted and integrated (i.e. fully internalized motivation). Introjected regulation, even though it is regulation by an aspect of the person, is not typically referred to as true self-regulation or autonomy because it is not regulation by well internalized aspects of the self.

In psychology, being agentic is typically equated with being motivated. As such, within many psychological perspectives (e.g. Bandura, 1989) agency does not distinguish between motivated actions that are autonomous versus controlled. Thus, the SDT approach goes beyond agency to emphasize the importance of autonomous action for the realization of capabilities.

SDT's view of self-regulation is largely compatible with Sen's (1999) capabilities approach. For Sen, "functionings" refer to a person's current way of behaving whereas capabilities refer to possible functionings. The distinction between functionings and capabilities is between what has been realized and what is possible, that is, between what people have actualized and the options and opportunities that are available to them and from which they can choose to live the lives they have reason to value. Agency within this approach is defined as the capacity to turn capabilities into effective functionings through action. Agentic behavior is the means for actualizing capabilities. Thus, we interpret Sen's position to suggest that it is through motivated actions that people realize their capabilities. Further, Sen placed *valuing* in a key position with respect to agency. In this regard there is overlap with the SDT position. Certainly the flavor of autonomy appears in Sen's writings, but the importance of specifying autonomy, and the conditions that support it, is in our view critical for appreciating the processes that transform capabilities into effective functionings and, as result, promote thriving.

The Benefits of Autonomous Functioning

Much of this research on the benefits of autonomous regulation is founded on the assessments of regulation introduced by Ryan and Connell (1989), who were examining correlates and consequences of autonomous versus controlled motivation. Subsequently, dozens of studies have applied the Ryan and Connell (1989) approach to the domains of relationships (Blais et al., 1990), religion (Ryan, Rigby, & King, 1993; Neyrinck, Lens, & Vansteenkiste, 2005), work (Gagné & Deci, 2005), education (Black & Deci, 2000), parenting (Grolnick, Ryan, & Deci, 1991), and health care (Williams et al., 1996). These studies have convincingly shown that regulating one's behavior more on the basis of autonomous than controlled motives is associated with greater persistence, more effective performance, higher quality relationships, and better social adjustment and well-being.

As an example, studies have shown that acting in a pro-ecological manner for more autonomous reasons (i.e. out of personal valuing) predicts engaging in a broad variety of such pro-ecological behaviors, including reusing old materials, using environmentally friendly transportation, and saving energy (Pelletier et al., 1998). The positive effects of more autonomous regulation are especially prevalent for difficult ecological behaviors—behaviors that require considerable effort and energy. Controlled regulation can yield initial pro-environment efforts, but they are unlikely to be maintained over time.

Promoting Self-Regulation through Autonomy Support and Need Satisfaction

SDT maintains that individuals have the natural tendencies to be intrinsically motivated and to internalize and integrate extrinsic motivation and thus to be autonomous and self-regulating. Nonetheless, these natural tendencies toward self-determination and growth require the support of the basic psychological needs. Numerous studies have shown that specific structures and events in the social environment as well as general interpersonal climates affect autonomous behavior and in turn performance and well-being outcomes. Many of the studies have compared interpersonal contexts that are *autonomy supportive* versus *controlling*.

An autonomy supportive context is one in which people are empowered as their feelings of volition and choice are supported. Structurally, this entails the minimal use of external regulators, the maximal provision of meaningful rationales when demands are forwarded, and the opportunity to choose when alternative strategies or goals are possible. In such contexts authority figures such as managers set policy and relate to others such as employees in ways that consider the others' perspective and are responsive to the others' needs. Concretely, this would involve allowing an optimal amount of choice, encouraging self-initiation, providing meaningful rationales and feedback, and using a style of communication that is encouraging (Deci et al., 1994). Autonomy support allows people to experience need satisfaction, because the authority is acknowledging them, conveying respect for their judgment, and supporting their initiative, which facilitates greater internalization and autonomous regulation.

In contrast to autonomy support, a controlling context is one that pressures people to think, feel, and behave in particular ways. Controlling contexts can be externally controlling or they can prompt people's introjects thus being "internally controlling" (Ryan, 1982). Externally controlling contexts created with rewards, punishments, and overtly controlling language pressure people and tend to prompt external regulation. Internally controlling contexts, which involve the use of contingent love and guilt induction (Assor, Roth, & Deci, 2004; Barber, 1996; Soenens et al., 2006), pressure people by stimulating introjected regulation. Regardless of whether the pressure is activated through internally or externally controlling means, SDT predicts that such controlling means of motivating others undermines autonomous motivation and, in turn, yields less effective performance and poorer well-being.

INTERPERSONAL CONTEXT

The concept of an interpersonal context refers to the general social climate that exists in a situation. For example, the language used and the attitudes conveyed by an authority figure in a particular situation (e.g. a teacher in a classroom) could convey a general sense of control—of things having to be done the way the authority wants them to be done. Other contexts, however, are more generally supportive and encouraging of people's initiative. The concept of autonomy-supportive versus controlling interpersonal contexts has been studied in both the laboratory and the field.

Deci et al. (1994) performed a laboratory experiment in which they created an autonomy-supportive context for individuals doing a signal-detection task, contrasting that context with a controlling one. Results indicated that those in the autonomy-supportive condition displayed greater internalization as reflected in greater subsequent behavior, and also that the internalized regulation they displayed was better integrated. In contrast, participants in the controlling condition were less likely to internalize the regulation of the activity and those who had internalized it merely introjected rather than integrated the regulation. A recent set of field experiments (Vansteenkiste, Simons, et al., 2004) replicated and extended these above findings by showing that using an autonomy-supportive (versus controlling) style to introduce a learning activity enhanced persistence at studying, and led to deeper-level processing and better performance.

Reeve and Jang (2006) identified specific autonomy-supportive teaching practices and found that these instructional behaviors, such as asking questions, being empathic, listening to students, being responsive to questions, encouraging students, providing positive feedback, and offering a meaningful rationale, were associated with students being more autonomously engaged in learning. In contrast, teachers who were directive, used controlling language, asked controlling questions, and gave solutions were experienced as autonomy thwarting. Such research sheds light on concrete instructional behaviors that support students' autonomy.

Many other studies have been done in which autonomy-supportive versus controlling climates were assessed with questionnaires or observations in field settings. For example, studies examined health-care climates and physicians' communication style and indicated that when health-care providers are autonomy supportive their patients become more personally motivated to behave in healthy ways (e.g. exercising regularly or taking prescribed medications), and their health improves. For example, when providers were more autonomy supportive, patients with diabetes were better able to regulate glucose levels in a healthy range (Williams, Freedman, & Deci, 1998), and patients who used tobacco were more able to quit (Williams et al., 2006).

Deci, Connell, and Ryan (1989) found that when managers in a multinational corporation were more autonomy supportive, their employees were more trusting of the organization and satisfied with their jobs. Similarly, Deci et al. (2001) found that when managers both in a U.S. corporation and in Bulgarian state-owned companies were more autonomy supportive, employees in both cultures reported greater satisfaction of psychological needs, were more engaged in their jobs, and experienced less anxiety. Baard, Deci, and Ryan (2004), who assessed U.S. workers, similarly found that employees of autonomy-supportive managers evidenced better performance and wellness.

Studies of parenting and education have shown comparable results, with autonomy supportive teaching and parenting promoting engagement and well-being in children and adolescents of varied cultures (Chirkov & Ryan, 2001; Niemiec et al., 2006). Supporting people's autonomy by using an encouraging communication style and creating a general autonomy-supportive climate appears to be relevant and desirable in all of life's domains.

EVENTS AND STRUCTURES

Within the SDT research tradition we have used the term "event" to refer to a specific environmental occurrence—for example, the offer of a reward for doing an activity, the opportunity to choose which activity to work on, the imposition of a deadline, or a piece of performance feedback. There has been an enormous amount of research examining the effects of specific events on autonomy, intrinsic motivation, and perceived competence. People can experience these events as being either supportive of autonomy or controlling of behavior, and such events can become enduring, structural components of dyadic relationships, groups, organizations, and societies. For example, as a motivational strategy, managers can create competitions and reward winners with bonuses. As another example, clinics for patients with eating disorders may make weekend family visits contingent upon gaining weight. State or federal governments similarly apply "high-stakes" to test scores as a strategy of motivating schools or students to improve performance. Each strategy in these examples relies on reward contingencies to motivate behavior, and these structures interact with general interpersonal climates to affect the motivation of people exposed to them.

To predict whether particular events or structures will positively or negatively affect people's intrinsic motivation and/or internalization, it is important to consider what is called the *functional significance* or psychological meaning of these events to people (e.g. Ryan, 1982). Any event—for example, a reward contingency, a piece of feedback, an imposed goal, or an opportunity to make a choice—has both an *informational* component and a *controlling* component, and these components are differentially salient in different events. It is the relative salience for a person of these two components that will determine the effect of the event on that person. The informational component signifies competence while affirming one's sense of autonomy, whereas the controlling component pressures people to behave. To the extent that an event is perceived as informational, it is likely to facilitate people's growth tendencies by satisfying their basic needs for autonomy and competence, whereas to the extent that it is perceived as controlling it is likely to undermine growth by frustrating these needs.

Frequently, in people's lives, authority figures and organizations will use tangible rewards, deadlines, or other such events as ways of getting the people to do things they would not otherwise do, so people come to experience these events as controls and thus as undermining of autonomy. On the other hand, positive feedback, which can also be controlling (Ryan, 1982), is typically used as a way of acknowledging good performance and is thus often competence enhancing. Events that are controlling are expected to decrease intrinsic motivation by thwarting the need for autonomy, whereas those that are not controlling are expected to increase intrinsic motivation by satisfying the need for competence and allowing autonomy.

A great deal of research has examined the effects of various events on people's intrinsic motivation, performance, and well-being, but the event that has received by far the most empirical attention is the offer of a tangible reward. In fact, more than 100 experiments have examined reward effects on intrinsic motivation. Deci, Koestner, and Ryan (1999) performed a meta-analysis of these studies and the results showed consistently that the use of tangible rewards to motivate behavior tended to leave people feeling controlled and to diminish their intrinsic motivation for the target activities. When participants were told they would get rewards (money, prizes, or symbolic awards) if they worked on a task, finished it, did well at it, or beat others at it, people found the task less interesting and persisted less long at it after the rewards were terminated than did participants who had not been offered rewards. It seems that working on a task for rewards shifts the focus from the task to the rewards and shifts the perceived locus of causality from internal to external. As well, it undermines people's sense of autonomy and intrinsic motivation.

Threats of punishment, imposition of deadlines, close surveillance, and competitions where participants tried to beat each other also tended to diminish people's sense of autonomy and undermined their intrinsic motivation. In fact, it seems that many of the ways people typically think of for motivating others tend to backfire, diminishing rather than enhancing the types of motivation that are associated with effective performance, creativity, positive affect, and well-being (e.g. Amabile, DeJong, & Lepper, 1976; Deci et al., 1981; Plant & Ryan, 1985). Findings also indicated that such external events result in poorer achievement and less conceptual integration of learning, presumably because such controlling factors all produce an external perceived locus of causality (see Deci & Ryan, 2000).

Structures and events can also serve to support autonomy and enhance intrinsic motivation when the informational component is highly salient. For instance, at some universities, students are given considerable flexibility in choosing elective courses that interest them. This allows more self-regulation and conveys a sense of competence and respect for the students. Further, positive feedback can provide people with information to use in self-regulating. When people make meaningful choices and receive competence-enhancing feedback, they tend to experience the feedback as informational, which leads to greater satisfaction and enjoyment (Levesque et al., 2004). For example, studies showed that when people were given choice about what activities to do or how to do them, they tended to feel more autonomous and interested, and they persisted longer at the activities (Deci et al., 1994; Ryan, 1982; Zuckerman et al., 1978). Similarly, positive feedback has been found to enhance intrinsic interest and persistent behavior (Deci, Koestner, and Ryan 1999; Vansteenkiste & Deci, 2003).

To summarize, experiments have studied the effects of various events on intrinsic motivation, and have shown that some events—tangible rewards, deadlines, surveillance—tend, on average, to have a controlling functional significance and thus undermine intrinsic motivation. Other events—choice and positive feedback—tend, on average, to be perceived as informational and thus are likely to enhance intrinsic motivation.

EVENTS AND INTERPERSONAL CONTEXTS

It is important to keep in mind that, although specific events (e.g. tangible rewards) tend to have a particular functional significance, the events interact with the general interpersonal climate within which they are administered. Thus, for example, although tangible rewards tend, on average, to undermine intrinsic motivation, if they are administered in an autonomy supportive context, they will be less detrimental and may even enhance intrinsic motivation (Ryan, Mims, & Koestner 1983). Similarly, although competition is often controlling, Reeve and Deci (1996) found that much of competition's detrimental effect comes from pressure to win applied by coaches or parents.

A condition in which people were competing in a more autonomy-supportive context did not affect intrinsic motivation. As another example of the interaction of events and interpersonal contexts, positive feedback has enhanced intrinsic motivation in many situations (Deci, 1971), but Ryan (1982) showed that when positive feedback was given in a controlling context, its effects on intrinsic motivation were more negative.

In sum, specific events such as reward structures tend to have either an informational or controlling functional significance, so they tend to affect autonomy, interest, and persistence accordingly. However, these events interact with the interpersonal climate, which can change the functional significance. Controlling events become less controlling if the interpersonal context is autonomy supportive, and informational events become more controlling if the interpersonal context is controlling. Simply stated, both events and interpersonal contexts affect intrinsic motivation, internalization, persistence, and performance in accord with the degree to which they support versus thwart satisfaction for the basic needs for autonomy, competence, and relatedness.

Goals and Aspirations

The previous section of this chapter focused on types of motivation and their corresponding styles of regulation, with the emphasis being on autonomous versus controlled motivation and the types of regulation associated with each. That focus on motives and regulations concerned the reasons people were doing a behavior (e.g. because I would feel guilty if I did not) and was thus said to address the "why" of behavior (Deci & Ryan, 2000). Another important question for the field of motivation concerns *what* it is that people are trying to achieve or attain. We turn now to the importance of distinguishing among the contents of people's goals.

Intrinsic and Extrinsic Goals as Individual Differences

Within the SDT tradition, goals researchers have worked primarily with the concept of *intrinsic versus extrinsic goals or aspirations* (Ryan et al., 1996). Intrinsic aspirations refer to goals that are satisfying in their own right because they are closely linked to satisfaction of the basic psychological needs. Empirical projects by Kasser and Ryan (1993, 1996) have shown that growing and developing as a person, becoming more physically healthy and fit, cultivating meaningful relationships, and being generative and contributing to the collective are all intrinsic goals. In contrast, extrinsic goals are ones that are less directly linked to need satisfaction and healthy development but are instead more compensatory and superficial, representing external signs of worth and success. They include amassing wealth, creating an attractive image, having power over others, and becoming famous. Kasser and Ryan (1996) showed that the two groups of goals are factor-analytically distinct across many diverse cultures (Grouzet et al., 2005).

GOAL PURSUITS

Many studies have shown that a strong emphasis on extrinsic aspirations is negatively associated with well-being and positively associated with ill-being. When people placed greater importance on attaining extrinsic goals than intrinsic goals, the individuals were lower on self-esteem, self-actualization, and life satisfaction, and higher on anxiety, depression, and physical symptoms (Kasser & Ryan, 1996; Sheldon et al., 2004). Of course, some wealth, appeal, and recognition is important for people, but when these goals become stronger for people than the intrinsic goals that provide deeper need satisfaction, there tends to be ill effects. Further, adolescents embracing extrinsic goals are more likely to engage in risky behaviors such as smoking tobacco, drinking alcohol, and starting sexual intercourse earlier in life (Williams et al., 2000). Strong extrinsic aspirations are also associated with poorer quality relationships and with greater social dominance and ethnic prejudice (Duriez et al., 2006; McHoskey, 1999). Bauer, McAdams, and Sakaeda (2005) studied life narratives and found that people whose stories emphasized the intrinsic goals of personal growth, relationships, and community displayed greater hedonic and eudaimonic well-being than did those whose stories emphasized the extrinsic goals of wealth, status, approval, and appearance.

Research in a work organization by Vansteenkiste et al. (2007) showed other negative consequences of strong extrinsic, relative to intrinsic, aspirations, including lower job satisfaction, more symptoms of burn-out, and greater tendency to leave the organization.

DEVELOPMENT OF LIFE GOALS

Kasser et al. (1995) found that teens who strongly valued the extrinsic aspiration for money had mothers who were low on democracy and warmth and high on controllingness, suggesting that parents who thwart their children's need satisfaction tend to promote development of extrinsic aspirations. Similarly, the Williams et al. (2000) study found that the teens who perceived their parents as low in autonomy support (i.e. as more controlling) had significantly stronger extrinsic aspirations than those who perceived their parents as high in autonomy support.

Kasser, Koestner, and Lekes (2002) analyzed data collected over a twenty-five-year period from 30-year-old adults whose mothers had first provided data when the children were 5 years old. The results showed that the adult children tended to have strong relative extrinsic goals when their mothers had been very restrictive many years earlier. In contrast, the adult children who displayed strong, relative intrinsic aspirations had mothers who had been less restrictive with the children when the children were young. It appears that parents who thwart their children's basic psychological needs lead their children to develop extrinsic aspirations.

MOTIVES AND GOALS: INDEPENDENT EFFECTS

Studies have indicated that when people are pursing intrinsic goals such as health or community contribution they tend to be autonomous in those pursuits, whereas when they are pursuing extrinsic goals such as wealth they tend to be controlled. This raises the interesting question of whether the effects of the content of people's goals such as wealth or community contribution can be reduced to the effects of the motivational style through which they are pursued. In fact, some psychologists have suggested that the effects of goal contents accrue not from the content per se, but from the fact that the contents are associated with particular motives (Carver & Baird, 1998; Srivastava, Locke, & Bartol, 2001).

In fact, the statistical relations between the "what" and "why" of behaviors is only modest because it is possible to pursue an intrinsic goal for either controlled or autonomous reasons. Sheldon et al. (2004) conducted a set of studies examining whether there are significant unique effects of goal contents (the "what") and goal motives (the "why"). They assessed the strength of people's intrinsic and extrinsic goals, as well as the motives people have for pursing each of the goals. Analyses indicated that the two concepts—intrinsic relative to extrinsic goals and autonomous relative to controlled motives—were correlated, as expected. However, analyses also showed that each concept contributed significant independent variance to psychological well-being. In other words, the content of people's goals has a direct relation to well-being even after controlling for the motives people had for pursuing those goals.

GOAL ATTAINMENT

The research about goal contents discussed thus far has concerned primarily the intrinsic versus extrinsic goals people are *pursuing*. We now turn to the question of what happens when people actually attain the intrinsic versus extrinsic goals they are pursuing.

Many goal-setting theories (e.g. Locke and Latham, 1990) argue that the attainment of valued goals, whatever type of goals they might be, is beneficial for well-being. In contrast, SDT maintains not only that the pursuit of extrinsic goals has negative correlates but that even the attainment of extrinsic goals is typically not beneficial, as these goals do not typically fulfill basic psychological needs. Studies (Kasser & Ryan, 2001; Ryan et al., 1999) have found that the degree of attainment of people's extrinsic aspirations was unrelated to their well-being after controlling for their degree of intrinsic goal attainment. Niemiec, Ryan, and Deci (2007) in a longitudinal study showed that the attainment of intrinsic goals had a positive effect on well-being and a negative effect on ill-being, whereas the attainment of extrinsic goals did not contribute to well-being but contributed to symptoms of anxiety and depression. The study also showed that the reason attainment of intrinsic aspirations was related to psychological well-being is that intrinsic attainment promoted need satisfaction. Specifically, change in attainment of intrinsic aspirations over a one-year period predicted change in psychological well-being over that period, and this relation was significantly mediated by change in need satisfaction. In contrast, change in attainment of extrinsic aspirations did not affect change in need satisfaction.

THE MATCH HYPOTHESIS: PERSONAL AND CONTEXTUAL GOALS

Although the negative relations between people valuing extrinsic life goals and their well-being seem to be quite strong, some people have argued that this effect is likely to be moderated by the type of goals prevalent in people's environment. For example, perhaps students studying in a business school where wealth is highly valued would not demonstrate the negative relations that appeared in past studies (e.g. Kasser & Ryan, 1993, 1996) because they might benefit from holding goals consistent with those endorsed by the social context within which they operate. Certainly, such match hypotheses have been advocated in areas such as social psychology (Sagiv & Schwartz, 2000) and organizational studies (Meglino, Ravlin, & Adkins, 1989).

Vansteenkiste, Duriez, Simons, and Soenens (2006) examined the relations between the relative importance of extrinsic goals and well-being among business school students and education students and found that extrinsic goals were negatively related to well-being among both student groups. Thus, it appears that the negative association between strong extrinsic life goals and psychological health holds whether or not the extrinsic goals are strongly valued in the social environment, thus disconfirming the match hypothesis.

ASPIRATIONS AND POLICY

Earlier we suggested that the thwarting of basic psychological needs leads people toward more extrinsic aspirations with their negative consequences. It is probable that deprivation of basic material goods would also promote strong materialistic goals. For example, Kasser et al. (1995) found that teenagers whose life circumstances were more disadvantaged in terms of low socio-economic status and crime-ridden neighborhoods placed stronger values on extrinsic, relative to intrinsic, aspirations and also displayed poorer psychological adjustment. This is consistent with Inglehart's (1990) argument that individuals and societies that hold strong materialistic values are likely to have developed these values from experiencing a sense of material deprivation and insecurity during formative periods. In contrast, individuals and societies that had experienced material security would be likely to have developed more of a focus on intrinsic, non-materialistic goals. More broadly, we suggest that individuals who had grown up in disadvantaged neighborhoods or societies are likely to have been deprived of basic psychological need satisfaction and that this psychological need deprivation is likely to promote the insecurity described by Inglehart. In terms of policy implications, this work seems quite consistent with the capabilities approach used by Sen (1999) and others, for it highlights not only the importance of opening economic opportunities for individuals and groups that have experienced deprivations but also providing other freedoms such as educational opportunities that provide basic psychological need satisfaction.

Intrinsic and Extrinsic Goals When Prompted by Others

The research on intrinsic versus extrinsic goals that we have examined until now used the concept of aspirations or life goals as individual differences that developed over time as a function of the satisfaction versus thwarting of the basic psychological needs. Further, the bulk of the research concerned the relations of the pursuit and attainment of the intrinsic versus extrinsic goals with well-being and ill-being outcomes.

Vansteenkiste and colleagues have extended this work by examining whether presenting and emphasizing intrinsic versus extrinsic goals in a particular situation such as a classroom will have direct effects on the optimal learning, persistence, performance, and well-being of people in that situation. As is the case for autonomy-supportive versus controlling environmental factors, the induction of intrinsic versus extrinsic goal orientations for particular activities can be examined at the level of events (e.g. the focusing of a particular learning activity on an intrinsic versus extrinsic goal) and more broadly as a structural or climate factor (e.g. a broad endorsement within, say, a school of a particular goal such as pro-environment actions). Thus far, the research has focused primarily on specific events using experimental paradigms in real life situations where people's goal orientations to an activity have been manipulated with instructions.

Vansteenkiste, Simons, et al. (2004) reported three experiments that examined differences in learning, persistence, and performance that resulted when students were given a rationale for their learning that represented either an intrinsic goal or an extrinsic goal. In the first study, college-level education students were given a text related to recycling and reusing materials. Some were told that learning about this topic was important because it could help save the environment (an intrinsic goal), whereas others were told it was important because it could help them save money (an extrinsic goal). Those who received intrinsic-goal framing subsequently reported having learned the material more deeply, and they performed better in testing sessions. Further, the students given the intrinsic rationale engaged in additional activities to learn about recycling. Another interesting aspect of this experiment is that half the participants in each goal condition were given the introduction to the learning task with an autonomy-supportive style and the other half were given it with a controlling style. Analyses showed that not only did goal framing have a significant main effect, but also the interpersonal style yielded a main effect, with the autonomy-supportive style leading to better learning, performance, and persistence than did the controlling style. Finally, the condition in which the intrinsic-goal framing was done in an autonomy-supportive way led to better outcomes than would be expected from two main effects. That is, the intrinsic-goal framing and autonomy-supportive style were positively synergistic.

In a second experiment, the effects were replicated with college-level business students who read about communication styles, because it would serve either the intrinsic goal of self-development or the extrinsic goal of making more money in business (Vansteenkiste, Simons, et al., 2004). Finally, in the third experiment, high school students from grades 10–11 learned a physical activity, Tai-bo. The goal induction portrayed the activity as being useful either for being healthier (intrinsic) or more attractive (extrinsic), and was done in either an autonomy-supportive or a controlling way. Results of this study replicated the first two studies of the series.

Other studies (e.g. Vansteenkiste, Simons, et al., 2005) extended the above results confirming that orienting people toward intrinsic versus extrinsic goals can impact people's learning and performance. For instance, framing a learning activity in terms of attaining both an intrinsic and an extrinsic goal was found to undermine performance and persistence compared to framing the learning activity in terms of just an intrinsic goal (Vansteenkiste, Simons, Lens, Soenens, et al., 2004). This finding could *not* be predicted on the basis of expectancy-valence models, which would suggest that adding value or utility to a learning activity should result in more optimal learning (Wigfield & Eccles, 2000).

Extrapolating the research on the specific event of framing task engagement with an intrinsic versus extrinsic goal prompt we see that goal prompts can be embedded in the structural components of organizations (e.g. companies, schools, sport clubs). Some companies, for example, provide employees with regular training opportunities, which relates to the intrinsic goal of self-development. Some health clubs place mirrors on the walls of their fitness areas, likely prompting exercisers to focus more on their looks (extrinsic) than their health (intrinsic).

Intrinsic versus extrinsic goals can also be studied as general aspects of the interpersonal context—that is, as goals endorsed by authority figures in a setting—and could thus affect the way people being supervised by the authority figures would orient in that situation. It seems likely that when people are supervised or taught by someone who is extrinsically oriented, the people will become more extrinsic, at least in that situation. Further, interacting with an authority who emphasizes intrinsic goals may lead people to become more intrinsic. Vansteenkiste, Duriez, et al. (2006) had parents rate the extent to which they promoted intrinsic and extrinsic goals in their family environment for their adolescent children who also participated in the research. Then, the adolescents completed questionnaires. The parents' general intrinsic versus extrinsic goal emphasis was found strongly to predict their children's ethnic prejudice. Although much more work is needed to confirm these initial findings, the study does indicate that the type of goals that are emphasized in individuals' interpersonal environments has ramifications for their own goals and their effective social functioning.

Both the specific and more general framing of activities in terms of intrinsic versus extrinsic goals have important relevance for social policy at the societal level. Cultures can be more oriented toward intrinsic versus extrinsic aspirations and goals, and they can form national policies that are in line with intrinsic versus extrinsic goals. For example, the Belgian minister of culture provided funding to sponsor local committees to organize festivals that were intended to bring people together and reinforce the importance of social relationships. Other policies such as the high-stakes tests that are currently widely prevalent in American schools focus people's attention on getting grades rather than on learning—that is, on extrinsic rather than intrinsic values and goals. As would be expected, on the basis of SDT, policy favoring high-stakes tests has had a range of negative consequences in classrooms, schools, and districts (Ryan & Brown, 2005).

Economic Systems

Thus far we have focused on how autonomy, motivation, performance, and well-being are affected by (1) specific events such as the offer of a reward; (2) immediate interpersonal contexts, such as managerial, classroom, or coaching climates; and (3) organizational or government policies such as competitive "pay-for-performance" systems or "high-stakes" tests. It is possible to extend this to a still more global level, considering how economic factors can affect people's basic psychological need satisfaction, motivation, and psychological health.

We suggest that macroeconomic systems can differentially impact human motivation, thus generating to differing degrees *human capital,* defined as the catalyzation of energy, talents, and positive effort. It would come as little surprise then that, from an SDT perspective, economic systems that depend largely upon external controls or threat-based motivations have, historically, been less productive than those that depend on well internalized values or meaningful incentives. For example, studies of Bulgarian workers in state-run organizations (Deci et. al, 2001) found that workers generally felt deprived of competence feedback and recognition of talents, as the system was prone to "level" all workers. Surprisingly, however, in day-to-day work, these employees often felt more autonomy than their American counterparts. Typically, they were not closely supervised so they felt freedom to act as they chose, and in some cases they were able to elect their own supervisors and have a voice in work strategies. Nonetheless, central planning economies generally lack provisions for macro-choices as to vocation and life goals, as well as opportunities to pursue one's unique competencies and talents. Thus, SDT pinpoints numerous faults in central planning economies, because they often fail to facilitate needs for autonomy and competence, and sometimes even the relatedness that is ideologically central to the system.

As well, SDT points to motivational hazards in capitalism, often touted as the most productive macro-economic system in history (Kasser et al., 2007). In saying this, we point out that capitalism is not a unitary system, that it varies, for example, from market economies constrained by social policies, as in the "socialist democracies", to "Anglo-American" corporate capitalism (AACC), which represents a relatively unchecked operation of market forces and is typically embedded within cultures that emphasize individualism, giving it its unique motivational flavor. For purposes of parsimony our comments are focused on AACC.

AACC advocates (e.g. Locke & Latham, 1990) often emphasize the association of capitalism with freedom, and yet, that term requires some deeper consideration. A person can be politically free, but still lack opportunities, so he or she may feel very much controlled by economic necessities. Indeed, the employment conditions and very low pay experienced by many workers within AACC leave them feeling anything but free both on the job and in their lives (Ehrenreich, 2001). The low pay level may lead them to take two jobs to try to make ends meet, resulting in work weeks that are longer and harder than those of "medieval peasants," as highlighted by de Graaf (2003) among others. Because there is only a minimal safety net within AACC, these workers are especially vulnerable to experiencing little freedom of movement, and thus to being alienated, lacking any sense of autonomy, intrinsic motivation, or commitment.

It is also worth noting that, while AACC entails strong instrumentalities connecting behaviors to outcomes, which are the means for people being controlled, many individuals, for example because they were raised in poor, high-crime neighborhoods, have not had the opportunities to develop competencies to benefit from these instrumentalities. Thus, they are likely to experience amotivation and disaffection. There is ongoing political debate about the degree to which the public sector is responsible for helping such individuals (Sen, 1999).

In short, AACC may have negative motivational effects on people at lower socio-economic levels with few skills either because they feel controlled in their pursuit of a meager living or because they fall out of the bottom of the system and into amotivation.

Even many high-level workers also feel controlled by their work situations and thus pay significant costs in terms of their performance and well-being. For example, they may feel little choice about their working hours or tasks, and even about changing jobs. Moreover, rewards, along with the materialistic outlook cultivated within the AACC, can insidiously control these workers, making them dependent on pursuing more and more rewards. This is likely to lead to the thwarting of relatedness as there is no time for family and friends, and to the thwarting of autonomy as the workers are likely to feel a lack of volition, freedom, and choice in relation to their work. In short, people in high-level jobs may feel controlled into overworking by work demands coupled with the desire to amass wealth, which is emphasized within AACC.

SDT makes clear, as the above discussion implies, that the simple fact of a person's pursuing a reward "agentically" does not mean he or she is autonomous or free. Rewards, as we noted, have both controlling and informational aspects, and the controlling aspect can be very potent. When economic rewards in the marketplace are structured to provide competence feedback through tangible incentives, as when they are distributed fairly in accord with effort, talent, and degree of responsibility, and when such structures are administered within an autonomy-supportive work climate, without emphasizing competition and using the rewards to pressure the workers, the rewards may well be experienced as informational, thus supporting the needs for both competence and autonomy. However, rewards can control worker's behavior, and indeed often do, as when they are used to motivate without addressing other needs for voice or choice in the workplace. In such cases, the controlling aspect of the rewards will be more salient, to the detriment of the workers' quality of engagement and health (Gagné & Deci, 2005).

There is another risk to the contingent rewards of the AACC system that have been isolated by SDT research. Specifically, pay-for-performance contingencies can encourage both organizational leaders and workers to take the shortest route to the desired outcomes (Shapira, 1976), often at great organizational, and sometimes societal (e.g. environmental), costs. During the past decade, revelations from the highest levels of numerous corporations have illustrated that outcome-focused contingencies such as huge bonuses and stock options for raising stock prices can lead managers not only to compromise the integrity of their companies, but even to engage in criminal behavior. It is not just at the top of organizations that such dynamics occur, as workers at any level may invest only in those aspects of their jobs that are rewarded and may cut various corners to get to the rewards. Similarly, in domains such as education where outcome-focused high-stakes tests are now prevalent, such deleterious results can accrue even when targeted outputs or test scores seemingly improve (e.g. Deci, Koestner, and Ryan, 1999; Ryan & Brown, 2005). Although the risks associated with outcome-focused rewards have not been deeply considered within performance-goal (e.g. Hidi & Harackiewicz, 2000) or operant (e.g. Eisenberger & Cameron, 1996) approaches, they are explicitly considered within SDT (Ryan & Brown, 2005).

Finally, as argued by Kasser et al. (2007), research on values and goals suggests that many of the values and aims traditionally associated with capitalism (such as materialism, self-interest, and competition) stand empirically in opposition to (i.e. are negatively correlated with) values and goals such as caring about the broader world, having close relationships, and, for many people, feeling competent and free (Grouzet et al., 2005; Schwartz, 1992). Given the current concerns with sustainability of our environment and the costs of massive accumulations of wealth by the few over the many, this clash of values, which is both psychological and cultural in nature, is an issue that accompanies the AACC relative to other forms of capitalism.

Every economic system has its strengths and weaknesses. Our aim is not to provide an evaluation of any system, but instead is to use empirically supported SDT principles to consider economic systems and cultures. The SDT principles include the idea that rewards and incentives are not only motivating, but can also be controlling and thus can crowd out or undermine important human propensities and the satisfaction of basic psychological needs. Moreover, when the goals of economic systems are extrinsic in nature they can stand opposed to intrinsic goals for caring, community, and sustainability that are critical to human well-being. In short, an economic system's success cannot be defined only by its total growth, or even the material security it provides, but must also be evaluated by its capacities to support satisfaction of people's inherent psychological needs.

Summary and Conclusions

Emerging research and interpretation based in self-determination theory provide an important and provocative basis for examining the actualization versus thwarting of human capabilities and wellness. SDT is based in the premise that all human beings have basic psychological needs for competence, relatedness, and autonomy that, in addition to basic physical needs, are required for human flourishing. The theory and accompanying research have shown that autonomous (versus controlled) motivation is associated with more effective behavioral regulation, enhanced performance, and greater psychological well-being, and the theory specifies the social contextual conditions that satisfy the basic needs and promote autonomous motivation and its positive consequences. Further, SDT addresses the content of goals, distinguishing between intrinsic life goals for growth, relationships, health, and community, and extrinsic life goals for wealth, fame, image, and power. Research has confirmed that the relative strength of intrinsic-goal pursuits is associated positively with well-being, whereas extrinsic-goal pursuits, because they typically fail to fulfill basic psychological needs, are not associated with these positive outcomes. The research has also uncovered many of the interpersonal and social conditions that promote internalization of extrinsic relative to intrinsic values and pursuits, including the relative deprivation of material necessities as well as the thwarting of basic psychological needs during socialization. Such findings make clear that researchers in both psychology and economics who are concerned with developing policies and programs that promote human thriving should consider more deeply the basic needs that define human nature as well as the social and economic conditions that support it.

References

Amabile, T. M., DeJong, W., & Lepper, M. (1976). Effects of externally imposed deadlines on subsequent intrinsic motivation. *Journal of Personality and Social Psychology, 34*, 92–8.

Assor, A., Kaplan, H., Kanat-Maymon, Y., & Roth, G. (2005). Directly controlling teacher behaviors as predictors of poor motivation and engagement in girls and boys: The role of anger and anxiety. *Learning and Instruction, 15*, 397–413.

—— Roth, G., & Deci, E. L. (2004). The emotional costs of parents' conditional regard: A self-determination theory analysis. *Journal of Personality, 72*, 47–88.

Baard, P. P., Deci, E. L., & Ryan, R. M. (2004). Intrinsic need satisfaction: A motivational basis of performance and well-being in two work settings. *Journal of Applied Social Psychology, 34*, 2045–68.

Bandura, A. (1989). Human agency in social cognitive theory. *American Psychologist, 44*, 1175–84.

Barber, B. K. (1996). Parental psychological control: Revisiting a neglected construct. *Child Development, 67*, 3296–3319.

Bauer, J. J., McAdams, D. P., & Sakaeda, A. R. (2005). Interpreting the good life: Growth memories in the lives of mature, happy people. *Journal of Personality and Social Psychology, 88*, 203–17.

Baumeister, R., & Leary, M. R. (1995). The need to belong: Desire for interpersonal attachments as a fundamental human motivation. *Psychological Bulletin, 117*, 497–529.

Black, A. E., & Deci, E. L. (2000). The effects of instructors' autonomy support and students' autonomous motivation on learning organic chemistry: A self-determination theory perspective. *Science Education, 84*, 740–56.

Blais, M. R., Sabourin S., Boucher, C., & Vallerand, R. (1990). Toward a motivational model of couple happiness. *Journal of Personality and Social Psychology, 59*, 1021–31.

Blos, P. (1979). *The adolescent passage*. New York: International Universities Press.

Bretherton, I. (1987). New perspectives on attachment relations: Security, communication and internal working models. In J. Osofsky (Ed.), *Handbook of infant development* (pp. 1061–100). New York: Wiley.

Carver, C. S., & Baird, E. (1998). The American dream revisited: Is it what you want or why you want it that matters? *Psychological Science, 9*, 289–92.

Charms, R. de (1968). *Personal causation*. New York: Academic Press.

Chirkov, V., & Ryan, R. M. (2001). Parent and teacher autonomy-support in Russian and U.S. adolescents: Common effects on well-being and academic motivation. *Journal of Cross Cultural Psychology, 32*, 618–35.

—— —— Kim, Y., & Kaplan, U. (2003). Differentiating autonomy from individualism and independence: A self-determination theory perspective on internalization of cultural orientations and well-being. *Journal of Personality and Social Psychology, 84*, 97–110.

Csikszentmihalyi, M. (1975). *Beyond boredom and anxiety*. San Francisco: Jossey-Bass.

Deci, E. L. (1971). Effects of externally mediated rewards on intrinsic motivation. *Journal of Personality and Social Psychology, 18*, 105–15.

—— (1975). *Intrinsic motivation*. New York: Plenum.

Deci, E. L., Betley, G., Kahle, J., Abrams, L., & Porac, J. (1981). When trying to win: Competition and intrinsic motivation. *Personality and Social Psychology Bulletin, 7*, 79–83.

—— Connell, J. P., & Ryan, R. M. (1989). Self-determination in a work organization. *Journal of Applied Psychology, 74*, 580–90.

—— Eghrari, H., Patrick, B. C., & Leone, D. (1994). Facilitating internalization: The self-determination theory perspective. *Journal of Personality, 62*, 119–42.

—— Koestner, R., & Ryan, R. M. (1999). A meta-analytic review of experiments examining the effects of extrinsic rewards on intrinsic motivation. *Psychological Bulletin, 125*, 627–68.

—— La Guardia, J. G., Moller, A. C., Scheiner, M. J., & Ryan, R. M. (2006). On the benefits of giving as well as receiving autonomy support: Mutuality in close friendships. *Personality and Social Psychology Bulletin, 32*, 313–27.

—— & Ryan, R. M. (1985). *Intrinsic motivation and self-determination in human behavior*. New York: Plenum.

—— —— (2000). The "what" and "why" of goal pursuits: Human needs and the self-determination of behavior. *Psychological Inquiry, 11*, 227–68.

—— —— Gagné, M., Leone, D. R., Usunov, J., & Kornazheva, B. P. (2001). Need satisfaction, motivation, and well-being in the work organizations of a former Eastern Bloc country. *Personality and Social Psychology Bulletin, 27*, 930–42.

Diener, E. (1984). Subjective well-being. *Psychological Bulletin, 95*, 542–75.

Duriez, B., Vansteenkiste, M., Soenens, B., & De Witte, H. (2006). Evidence for the social costs of extrinsic relative to intrinsic goal pursuits: Their relation with right-wing authoritarianism, social dominance, and ethnic prejudice. Unpublished manuscript, University of Leuven.

Dworkin, G. (1988). *The theory and practice of autonomy*. New York: Cambridge University Press.

Ehrenreich, B. (2001). *Nickel and dimed: On (not) getting by in America*. New York: Metropolitan Books.

Eisenberger, R., & Cameron, J. (1996). Detrimental effects of reward: Reality of myth? *American Psychologist, 51*, 1153–66.

Frey, B. S. (1997). *Not just for the money: An economic theory of human motivation.* Brookfield, VT: Edward Elgar.

—— & Stutzer, A. (2001). *Happiness and economics: How the economy and institutions affect human well-being.* Princeton, NJ: Princeton University Press.

Friedman, M. (2003). *Autonomy, gender, politics.* New York: Oxford University Press.

Gagné, M., & Deci, E. L. (2005). Self-determination theory and work motivation. *Journal of Organizational Behavior, 26*, 331–62.

Graaf, J. de (2003). (Ed.). *Take back your time: Fighting overwork and time poverty in America.* San Francisco, CA: Berrett-Koehler.

Grolnick, W. S., & Ryan, R. M. (1989). Parent styles associated with children's self-regulation and competence in school. *Journal of Educational Psychology, 81*, 143–54.

—— —— & Deci, E. L. (1991). The inner resources for school achievement: Motivational mediators of children's perceptions of their parents. *Journal of Educational Psychology, 83*, 508–17.

Grouzet, F. M., Kasser, T., Ahuvia, A., Dols, J. M., Kim, Y., Lau, S., Ryan, R. M., Saunders, S., Schmuck, P., & Sheldon, K. M. (2005). The structure of goals across 15 cultures. *Journal of Personality and Social Psychology, 89*, 800–16.

Hayamizu, T. (1997). Between intrinsic and extrinsic motivation: Examination of reasons for academic study based on the theory of internalization. *Japanese Psychological Research, 39*, 98–108.

Hidi, S., & Harackiewicz, J. M. (2000). Motivating the academically unmotivated: A critical issue for the 21st century. *Review of Educational Research, 70*, 151–79.

Hodgins, H. S., Koestner, R., & Duncan, N. (1996). On the compatibility of autonomy and relatedness. *Personality and Social Psychology Bulletin, 22*, 227–37.

Inglehart, R. (1990). *Culture shift in advanced industrial society.* Princeton, NJ: Princeton University Press.

Jordan, J. V. (1997). Do you believe that the concepts of self and autonomy are useful in understanding women? In J. V. Jordan (Ed.), *Women's growth in diversity: More writings from the Stone Center.* (pp. 29–32). New York: The Guilford Press.

Kasser, T. (2002). *The high price of materialism.* Cambridge, MA: MIT Press.

—— Cohn, S., Kanner, A. D., & Ryan, R. M. (2007). Some costs of American corporate capitalism: A psychological exploration of value and goal conflicts. *Psychological Inquiry, 18*, 1–22.

—— Koestner, R., & Lekes, N. (2002). Early family experiences and adult values: A 26-year, prospective longitudinal study. *Personality and Social Psychology Bulletin, 28*, 826–35.

—— & Ryan, R. M. (1993). A dark side of the American dream: Correlates of financial success as a central life aspiration. *Journal of Personality and Social Psychology, 65*, 410–22.

—— —— (1996). Further examining the American dream: Differential correlates of intrinsic and extrinsic goals. *Personality and Social Psychology Bulletin, 22*, 280–7.

—— —— (2001). Be careful what you wish for: Optimal functioning and the relative attainment of intrinsic and extrinsic goals. In P. Schmuck & K. M. Sheldon (Eds.), *Life goals and well-being: Towards a positive psychology of human striving* (pp. 115–29). Goettingen: Hogrefe & Huber.

—— —— Zax, M., & Sameroff, A. J. (1995). The relations of maternal and social environments to late adolescents' materialistic and prosocial values. *Developmental Psychology, 31*, 907–14.

Koestner, R., Losier, G. F., Vallerand, R. J., & Carducci. D. (1996). Identified and introjected forms of political internalization: Extending self-determination theory. *Journal of Personality and Social Psychology, 70*, 1025–36.

La Guardia, J. G., Ryan, R. M., Couchman, C. E., & Deci, E. L. (2000). Within-person variation in security of attachment: A self-determination theory perspective on attachment, need fulfillment, and well-being. *Journal of Personality and Social Psychology, 79*, 367–84.

Levesque, C., Zuehlke, N., Stanek, L., & Ryan, R. M. (2004). Autonomy and competence in German and U.S. university students: A comparative study based on self-determination theory. *Journal of Educational Psychology, 96*, 68–84.

Locke, E. A., & Latham, G. P. (1990). *A theory of goal setting and task performance.* Englewood Cliffs, NJ: Prentice-Hall.

McClelland, D. C. (1985). *Human motivation.* Glenview, IL: Scott, Foresman.

Maccoby, E. E. (1984). Socialization and developmental change. *Child Development, 55*, 317–28.

McHoskey, J. W. (1999). Machiavellianism, intrinsic versus extrinsic goals, and social interest: A self-determination theory analysis. *Motivation and Emotion, 23*, 267–83.

Markus, H. R., Kitayama, S., & Heiman, R. J. (1996). Culture and "basic" psychological principles. In E. T. Higgins & A. W. Kruglanski (Eds.), *Social psychology: Handbook of basic principles* (pp. 857–913). New York: Guilford Press.

—— —— (2003). Models of agency: Sociocultural diversity in the construction of action. In V. Murphy-Berman & J. J. Berman (Eds.), *Cross-cultural differences in perspectives on the self: Nebraska symposium on motivation* (Vol. 49, pp. 1–57). Lincoln, NE: University of Nebraska Press.

Meglino, B. M., Ravlin, E. C., & Adkins, C. L. (1989). A work values approach to corporate culture: A field test of the value congruence process and its relationship to individual outcomes. *Journal of Applied Psychology. 74*, 424–32.

Neyrinck, B., Lens, W., & Vansteenkiste, M. (2005). Goals and regulations of religiosity: A motivational analysis. In M. L. Maehr & S. Karabenick (Eds.), *Advances in motivation and achievement* (pp. 77–106). Greenwich, Conn.: JAI Press Inc.

Niemiec, C. P., Lynch, M. F., Vansteenkiste, M., Bernstein, J., Deci, E. L., & Ryan, R. M. (2006). The antecedents and consequences of autonomous self-regulation for college: A self-determination theory perspective on socialization. *Journal of Adolescence, 29*, 761–75.

—— Ryan, R. M., & Deci, E. L. (2007). The path taken: Consequences of attaining intrinsic and extrinsic aspirations in post-college life. Unpublished manuscript, University of Rochester.

Ntoumanis, N. (2001). A self-determination approach to the understanding of motivation in physical education. *British Journal of Educational Psychology, 71*, 225–42.

Pelletier, L. G., Tuson, K. M., Green-Demers, I., Noels, K., & Beaton, A. M. (1998). Why are you doing things for the environment?—The Motivation Toward the Environmental Scale (MTES). *Journal of Applied Social Psychology, 28*, 437–68.

Plant, R., & Ryan, R. M. (1985). Intrinsic motivation and the effects of self-consciousness, self-awareness, and ego-involvement: An investigation of internally controlling styles. *Journal of Personality, 53,* 435–49.

Reeve, J., & Deci, E. L. (1996). Elements within the competitive situation that affect intrinsic motivation. *Personality and Social Psychology Bulletin, 22,* 24–33.

—— & Jang, H. (2006). What teachers say and do to support students' autonomy during a learning activity. *Journal of Educational Psychology, 98,* 209–18.

—— Nix, G., & Hamm, D. (2003). Testing models of the experience of self-determination in intrinsic motivation and the conundrum of choice. *Journal of Educational Psychology, 95,* 375–92.

Reis, H. T., & Patrick, B. P. (1996). Attachment and intimacy: Component processes. In E. T. Higgins & A. W. Kruglanski (Eds.) *Social psychology: Handbook of basic principles* (pp. 523–63). New York; Guilford.

—— Sheldon, K. M., Gable, S. L., Roscoe, J., & Ryan, R. M. (2000). Daily well-being: The role of autonomy, competence, and relatedness. *Personality and Social Psychology Bulletin, 26,* 419–35.

Richins, M. L., & Dawson, S. (1992). A consumer values orientation for materialism and its measurement: Scale development and validation. *Journal of Consumer Research, 19,* 303–16.

Rotter, J. B. (1966). Generalized expectancies for internal versus external control of reinforcement. *Psychological Monographs, 80* (1, Whole No. 609), 1–28.

Ryan, R.M. (1982). Control and information in the intrapersonal sphere: An extension of cognitive evaluation theory. *Journal of Personality and Social Psychology, 43,* 450–61.

—— (1993). Agency and organization: Intrinsic motivation, autonomy and the self in psychological development. In J. Jacobs (Ed.), *Nebraska symposium on motivation: Developmental perspectives on motivation* (Vol. 40, pp. 1–56). Lincoln, NE: University of Nebraska Press.

—— (1995). Psychological needs and the facilitation of integrative processes. *Journal of Personality, 63,* 397–427.

—— & Brown, K. W. (2005). Legislating competence: The motivational impact of high stakes testing as an educational reform. In C. Dweck & A. E. Elliot (Eds.) *Handbook of Competence* (pp. 354–74). New York: Guilford Press.

—— Chirkov, V. I., Little, T. D., Sheldon, K. M., Timoshina, E., & Deci, E. L. (1999). The American dream in Russia: Extrinsic aspirations and well-being in two cultures. *Personality and Social Psychology Bulletin, 25,* 1509–24.

—— & Connell, J. P. (1989). Perceived locus of causality and internalization: Examining reasons for acting in two domains. *Journal of Personality and Social Psychology, 57,* 749–61.

—— & Deci, E. L. (2000a). Intrinsic and extrinsic motivation: Classic definitions and new directions. *Contemporary Educational Psychology, 25,* 54–67.

—— —— (2000b). Self-determination theory and the facilitation of intrinsic motivation, social development, and well-being. *American Psychologist, 55,* 68–78.

—— —— (2003). On assimilating identities to the self: A self-determination theory perspective on internalization and integrity within cultures. In M. R. Leary & J. P. Tangney (Eds.), *Handbook of self and identity* (pp. 255–73). New York: Guilford.

——— Huta, V., & Deci, E. L. (2008). Living well: A self-determination theory perspective on eudaimonia. *Journal of Happiness Studies, 9*, 139–70.

——— La Guardia, J. G., Solky-Butzel, J., Chirkov, V., & Kim, Y. (2005). On the interpersonal regulation of emotions: Emotional reliance across gender, relationships and cultures. *Personal Relationships, 12*, 145–63.

——— & Lynch, J. (1989). Emotional autonomy versus detachment: Revisiting the vicissitudes of adolescence and young adulthood. *Child Development, 60*, 340–56.

——— Mims, V., & Koestner, R. (1983). Relation of reward contingency and interpersonal context to intrinsic motivation: A review and test using cognitive evaluation theory. *Journal of Personality and Social Psychology, 45*, 736–50.

——— Rigby, S., & King, K. (1993). Two types of religious internalization and their relations to religious orientations and mental health. *Journal of Personality and Social Psychology, 65*, 586–96.

——— Sheldon, K. M., Kasser, T., & Deci, E. L. (1996). All goals are not created equal: An organismic perspective on the nature of goals and their regulation. In P. M. Gollwitzer & J. A. Bargh (Eds.), *The psychology of action: Linking cognition and motivation to behavior* (pp. 7–26). New York: Guilford.

——— & Solky, J. (1996). What is supportive about social-support? On the psychological needs for autonomy and relatedness. In G. R. Pierce, B. K. Sarason, & I. G. Sarason (Eds.), *Handbook of social support and the family* (pp. 249–67). New York: Plenum.

Ryff, C. D., & Singer, B. (1998), The contours of positive human health. *Psychological Inquiry 9*, 1–28.

Sagiv, L., & Schwartz, S. H. (2000). Value priorities and subjective well-being: Direct relations and congruity effects. *European Journal of Social Psychology, 30*, 177–98.

Schwartz, S. H. (1992). Universals in the content and structure of values: Theoretical advances and empirical tests in 20 countries. In M. P. Zanna (Ed.), *Advances in experimental social psychology* (Vol. 25, pp. 1–65). Orlando, FL: Academic Press.

Sen, A. (1999). *Development as freedom.* New York: Alfred A. Knopf.

Sénécal, C., Nouwen, A., & White, D. (2000). Motivation and dietary self-care in adults with diabetes: Are self-efficacy and autonomous self-regulation complementary or competing constructs? *Health Psychology, 19*, 452–7.

Shapira, Z. (1976). Expectancy determinants of intrinsically motivated behavior. *Journal of Personality and Social Psychology, 34*, 1235–44.

Sheldon, K. M., Ryan, R. M., Deci, E. L., & Kasser, T. (2004). The independent effects of goal contents and motives on well-being: It's both what you pursue and why you pursue it. *Personality and Social Psychology Bulletin, 30*, 475–86.

——— ——— & Reis, H. T. (1996). What makes for a good day? Competence and autonomy in the day and in the person. *Personality and Social Psychology Bulletin, 22*, 1270–9.

Simon, H. (1955). A behavioral model of rational choice. *Quarterly Journal of Economics, 69*, 99–118.

Skinner, B. F. (1953). *Science and human behavior.* New York: Macmillan.

Soenens, B., & Vansteenkiste, M. (2005). Antecedents and outcomes of self-determination in three life domains: The role of parents' and teachers' autonomy support. *Journal of Youth and Adolescence, 34*, 589–604.

Soenens, B., & Vansteenkiste, M., Duriez, B., & Goossens, L. (2006). Parental separation anxiety and psychological control: Psychological control as a mediator of links between parental separation anxiety and adolescent adjustment. *Journal of Research on Adolescence, 16*, 539–59.

—— —— Lens, W., Luyckx, K., Goossens, L., Beyers, W., & Ryan, R. M. (2007). Conceptualizing adolescent perceptions of parental autonomy support: Adolescent perceptions of promoting independence versus promoting volitional functioning. *Developmental Psychology, 43*, 633–46.

Srivastava, A., Locke, E. A., & Bartol, K. M. (2001). Money and subjective well-being: It's not the money, it's the motive. *Journal of Personality and Social Psychology, 80*, 959–71.

Standage, M., Duda, J. L., & Ntoumanis, N. (2003). A model of contextual motivation in physical education: Using constructs from self-determination theory and achievement goal theory to predict physical activity intentions. *Journal of Educational Psychology, 95*, 97–110.

Steinberg, L., & Silverberg, S. (1986). The vicissitudes of autonomy in adolescence. *Child Development, 57*, 841–51.

Tversky, A., & Kahneman, D. (1987). Rational choice and the framing of decisions. In M. Robin & M. W. Reder, (Eds.), *Rational choice: The contrast between economics and psychology* (pp. 67–94). Chicago, IL: University of Chicago Press.

Vallerand, R. J. (1997). Toward a hierarchical model of intrinsic and extrinsic motivation. In M. P. Zanna (Ed.), *Advances in experimental social psychology* (Vol. 29, pp. 271–360). San Diego: Academic Press.

Vansteenkiste, M., & Deci, E. L. (2003). Competitively-contingent rewards and intrinsic motivation: Can losers remain motivated? *Motivation and Emotion, 27*, 273–99.

—— Duriez, B., Simons, J., & Soenens, B. (2006). Materialistic values and well-being among business students: Further evidence for their detrimental effect. *Journal of Applied Social Psychology, 36*, 2892–908.

—— —— Soenens, B., & De Witte, H. (2006). *Understanding the effects of parental extrinsic versus intrinsic goal promotion and parental educational level on adolescent ethnic prejudice.* Unpublished manuscript, University of Leuven.

—— Lens, W., Dewitte, S., De Witte, H., & Deci, E. L. (2004). The "why" and "why not" of job search behavior: Their relation to searching, unemployment experience, and well-being. *European Journal of Social Psychology, 34*, 345–63.

—— —— De Witte, H., & Feather, N. T (2005). Understanding unemployed people's search behavior, unemployment experience and well-being: A comparison of expectancy-value theory and self-determination theory. *British Journal of Social Psychology, 44*, 1–20.

—— Neyrinck, B., Niemiec, C. P., Soenens, B., De Witte, H., & Van den Broeck, A. (2007). Examining the relations among extrinsic versus intrinsic work value orientations, basic need satisfaction, and job experience: A self-determination theory approach. *Journal of Occupational and Organizational Psychology, 80*, 251–77.

—— Simons, J., Lens, W., Sheldon, K. M., & Deci, E. L. (2004). Motivating learning, performance, and persistence: The synergistic effects of intrinsic goal contents and autonomy-supportive contexts. *Journal of Personality and Social Psychology, 87*, 246–60.

—— —— —— Soenens, B., & Matos, L. (2005). Examining the motivational impact of intrinsic versus extrinsic goal framing and autonomy-supportive versus internally controlling communication style on early adolescents' academic achievement. *Child Development, 2*, 483–501.

—— —— —— —— —— & Lacante, M. (2004). Less is sometimes more: Goal-content matters. *Journal of Educational Psychology, 96*, 755–64.

—— Zhou, M., Lens, W., & Soenens, B. (2005). Experiences of autonomy and control among Chinese learners: Vitalizing or immobilizing? *Journal of Educational Psychology, 96*, 755–64.

Vroom, V. H. (1964). *Work and motivation.* New York: Wiley.

White, R. W. (1959). Motivation reconsidered: The concept of competence. *Psychological Review, 66*, 297–333.

Wigfield, A., & Eccles, J. S. (2000). Expectancy-value theory of achievement motivation. *Contemporary Educational Psychology, 25*, 68–81.

Williams, G. C., Cox, E. M., Hedberg, V., & Deci, E. L. (2000). Extrinsic life goals and health risk behaviors in adolescents. *Journal of Applied Social Psychology, 30*, 1756–71.

—— —— —— —— McGregor, H. A. Sharp, D., Levesque, C., Kouides, R. W., Ryan, R. M., & Deci, E. L. (2006). Testing a self-determination theory intervention for motivating tobacco cessation: Supporting autonomy and competence in a clinical trial. *Health Psychology, 25*, 91–101.

—— Freedman, Z. R., & Deci, E. L. (1998). Supporting autonomy to motivate glucose control in patients with diabetes. *Diabetes Care, 21*, 1644–51.

—— Grow, V. M., Freedman, Z. R., Ryan, R. M., & Deci, E. L. (1996). Motivational predictors of weight loss and weight-loss maintenance. *Journal of Personality and Social Psychology, 70*, 115–26.

Zuckerman, M., Porac, J. F., Lathin, D., Smith, R., & Deci, E. L. (1978). On the importance of self-determination for intrinsically motivated behavior. *Personality and Social Psychology Bulletin, 4*, 443–6.

9

Capabilities, the Self, and Well-Being*

Maurizio Pugno

"Economic analysis based on... [such] variables as food availability per head, or GNP per head, can be very misleading in understanding starvation and hunger, and deprivation in general."

A. Sen, *Resources, Values and Development*, Oxford: Blackwell, 1984, p.528

"Mental illness is Europe's unseen killer. [It] is just as deadly as physical illnesses like cancer. More Europeans die from suicide each year than are killed in car accidents or as a result of murder."

M. Kyprianou, European Commissioner for Health, Jan. 2005

Introduction

The Capability Approach (CA), as is well known, originates in and is developed by Sen's numerous works (e.g. Sen 1985a, 1987, 1992, 1999a). Its main aim is twofold: to provide a method for the assessment and measurement of individual well-being, social arrangements, and designs of welfare policies; and to propose theoretical foundations for a paradigm of human development, where human beings form the "ends" of economic activity, rather than its means. The straightforward implication is that it provides the bases for urgent policy interventions.[1]

* A previous version of this chapter was presented at the Conference "Capabilities and Happiness" (Milan, Bicocca University, 16–18 June 2005), and at the Workshop "Capabilities and Identity" (Cambridge, UK, 21–23 June 2005). I wish to thank the discussants of these presentations, and especially the economists F. Comim, J. Davis, M. Teschl, and the psychologists R. Ryan and J. La Guardia, for comments and encouragement. The usual disclaimer applies. Miur and the University of Trento are acknowledged for their financial support.
[1] Nussbaum's (2000, 2003) *"capabilities* approach" is a slightly different variant of the CA, since it aims at contributing to the foundation of a theory of justice (Gasper 2007; Robeyns 2005). Her approach is more philosophical than economic.

The CA has elaborated path-breaking analytical concepts for normative theory, but it cannot be regarded as a positive theory. The CA has criticized traditional economic concepts like utility, rationality, and maximization, and it has been greatly effective in highlighting widespread and persistent socio-economic problems and malaise. However, its focus is not on the explanation of these problems, which would show further inadequacies of mainstream economic theory.

This weakness of the CA is made particularly evident by a puzzling fact. In rich countries, where both the usual standards of opulence and liberties point to high and rising levels, a significant and increasing part of the population suffers from a subtle malaise taking the form of depression, anxiety, eating disorders, and conflicts within the family and among adolescent peers. Epidemiologists find that in the US more than half of the adult population is moderately mentally healthy. The recent literature on happiness shows that self-reported well-being substantially lags behind economic growth (Easterlin 1974; Frey and Stutzer 2002; Clark et al. 2007).

It could be argued that in these cases some functionings and capabilities are impaired, but it must be recognized that these are special in character. In fact, the functionings and capabilities usually considered by the CA are clearly defined also when they are impaired, thus straightforwardly implying the need for policy intervention. For example, the functioning of the intestine to assimilate essential substances can be defined as impaired when infected by some bacteria, and this calls for health care. In this case, the individual's choice set is clearly constrained, and the policy implication is action for the removal of the constraint. However, in rich countries, where the apparent constraints are relaxed, at least for a great part of the population, there is a growing number of cases where the real constraint to individual choice is not clear. For example, the current ample possibility for couples to cohabit should have made the choice of marriage particularly informed and hence successful. However, the evidence shows that these marriages are less successful, and that the survivors of breakdowns are less happy than those of marriages without previous cohabitation. What has prevented couples from making the right choice?

In these cases the constraint affects a special type of functioning that can be called the *ability to choose* among different available goods or different possible lines of actions. This is "special" because it is observable in the effects but not in the cause of its impairment. Policy implications are thus lacking, and the need for a theory of the failure—at least for rich countries—to achieve widespread and rising well-being and advantage becomes evident.

This chapter thus attempts to develop the CA in an unexplored direction, which allows us to deal with the puzzling fact arising in the rich countries, and, more generally, to contribute to a positive theory of human development. Taking seriously the functioning of the ability to choose for individuals' well-being requires investigation into psychology and related disciplines, since it requires the study of the constraints on decision-making, and how they arise in individuals' minds. To this aim, it is useful to organize the investigation around the concept of the *self*, since this plays the key role in decision-making. In this regard, the chapter stresses the suggestions made in psychology and related disciplines that the self comprises both a conscious and a non-conscious component in decision-making, and that the self develops from infancy to adulthood.

This point of attack is a powerful one for a number of reasons. First, psychological malaise and unhappiness in rich countries can find an explanation; secondly, the bias in self-reported indices of well-being due to psychological adaptation can be evaluated; thirdly, some policy implications become possible. These results are also useful for the CA, because they can effectively extend its application to rich countries, provide evaluations for the reliability of subjective well-being as a further capability dimension, and suggest new policies.

Unfortunately, there is no theory of the self in economics, and there are different approaches to the self in other disciplines. Therefore, the research strategy of this chapter will be to take the problem arising from rich countries as the point of departure for an exploratory search for explanations in psychology, psychiatry, and neuroscience, and to draw useful conclusions for CA and for economics generally.

The chapter is organized as follows: Section 1 presents the problem of the diffusion of mental malaise in rich countries; Section 2 highlights why this problem challenges the CA as well as mainstream economic theory; Section 3 argues for the need to introduce the concept of the self into the CA; Section 4 reviews some contributions to the theory of the self in psychology and related disciplines; Section 5 attempts to extend and revise the CA by considering the role of the self; Section 6 concludes with some suggestions for policy implications.

1. The Diffusion of Mental Malaise in Rich Countries

One reason for the success of the Capability Approach (CA) in both interpreting facts and in challenging the utility theory is that wealth across nations, as usually measured by GDP per head, is not well correlated with individuals' capacity to access and enjoy that wealth, as measured by life expectancy, physical health, education, employment, housing, and so on (Kuklys and Robeyns 2005; UNDP 1990–2004). The CA appears to capture the well-being of a country's population better than the usual income or consumption measures.

Recently, an increasing body of evidence has challenged not only the usual measures of well-being, but also the CA measures. In the group of the richest countries, where also individuals have better and growing opportunities to access wealth, a substantial and increasing part of the population suffers from a special form of malaise which is deeply harmful in its effects but hard to explain and to cure. This is a deep dissatisfaction with the self and the relationship with the world, and it takes the forms of depression and anxiety, eating disorders and various other forms of addiction, violence within the family and among adolescents, and unhappiness in marriage.

A precise account of these forms of malaise is precluded by the unavailability of proper data, but the existing literature systematically points in the same worrying direction. Several studies show that depression has significantly increased through generations in the US and other major developed countries since WWII (Klerman 1988, 1993; Lavori et al. 1993; Olfson et al. 2002; Rutter and Smith 1995; Maughan et al. 2005). It was estimated in 1998 that the likelihood of US residents experiencing major depression episodes during their lifetimes decreased with age: from 15 percent of 10-year-olds to 1.5 percent of 70-year-olds (Joiner 2000).[2] The extreme form of malaise, that is, suicides, similarly increased for the US, the EU, and Japan from the mid-1960s until the 1980s in proportion to population (Levi et al. 2003; Lane 2000:23). Lester and Yang's (1997) survey of several studies shows that the correlation between income per head and suicide rates has been *positively* significant for the US since WWII, and for a cross-section of the European countries.[3] The picture appears less bleak since the 1980s, in that suicide rate has declined for the US, Japan, and for many European countries. However, it has risen for Ireland and Spain (Levi et al. 2003; Chishti et al. 2003:111), and the absolute number of suicides is still at an astonishingly high level for the whole EU: around 58,000 each year (Kyprianou 2005).[4]

Malaise in the young section of the population is especially worrying. The suicide rate among adolescents and young adults has also risen in the US, and in the four major European countries (Putnam 2000:262; Lane 2000:23; Cutler et al. 2000). Mental disorders among children and adolescents appear to be rising, as evidenced by the threefold increase in their psychotropic medication, and in particular in treatment of Attention Deficit Hyperactivity Disorder between 1987 and 1996 in the US.[5] The incidence of "pervasive developmental

---

[2] Although it cannot be ruled out that genetic factors contribute to depression, it is safe to say that genes are not deterministic, and are only expressed in response to environmental triggers (Huppert 2005).

[3] Similar findings have been obtained by Jungeilges and Kirchgaessner (2002), and Huang (1996). Moreover, according to Lester and Yang, if suicide rates are regressed against the unemployment rate and income per head for European countries, only the latter variable emerges as positively significant.

[4] The European Commission (2004) has also estimated the economic costs of mental health for the EU: 2% is the health care cost, but 3–4% is the cost also inclusive of the effects on personal income, and on ability to work.

[5] The possible objection that greater income means that people can afford more medication seems contradicted by the fact that ADHD is more frequently treated among poorer groups (Olfson et al. 2002, 2003).

disorder", depression, and suicides among young people is also increasing in the UK (Fombonne 1998; Fombonne et al. 2003). Homicides among adolescents are on the rise as well (Merrick et al. 2003). Putnam (2000:264) observes that the incidence of headaches, insomnia, and indigestion was roughly the same in the late 1970s across age groups, but thereafter it was more pronounced, the younger the group. A similar finding applies to anxiety and neuroticism (Twenge 2000).

Malaise within the family can be captured by various indices. The most dramatic of them is the infanticide rate, which, for babies aged 1 year or less, rose from 51 per million-population in 1974–8 to 84 in 1995–9 in the US (Pritchard and Butler 2003). Less dramatic but still disquieting is the evidence on marriages. Despite the increasing frequency of divorce, whose incidence shows no signs of diminishing even recently in the US (Glenn and Weaver 1998), the marriages that survive appear to be less satisfactory on the basis of self-ratings (Lane 2000:24), especially if marital interaction and time spent together are considered across generations (Duane et al. 2002; Rogers and Amato 1997; Amato et al. 2003; Glenn and Weaver 1998). Increasing cohabitation, from 10 percent to 50 percent during 1972–94 in the US, which would imply that getting married is a more informed choice, appears instead to have worsened the quality of marriage, and to have destabilized it (see Kamp Dush et al. 2003, for the US; and Halli and Zimmer 1991, for Canada).

One may observe that depression, suicides, and other similar problems do not affect the bulk of the population. However, recent epidemiological studies point out that the diffusion of many common diseases in the population is positively related to the population mean of the underlying risk factor. In the significant case of clinical mental disorder, it has been shown that its diffusion is positively related to the mean number of symptoms in the population (Huppert 2005). In the case of the US, it has been reported that, on the basis of diagnostic tests, 54 percent of adult population is moderately mentally healthy, and 11 percent is characterized by an "emptiness" whereby individuals are devoid of positive emotions toward life but are not mentally ill (Keyes 2003). Secondly, the data on self-reported well-being show that the proportion of those who rate themselves as "very happy" has been declining in the US, and has been stationary in Japan and the UK in recent decades. Therefore, although mental malaise affects populations very differently, all the various sections of the populations in rich countries appear to have worsened, or at least not improved, their mental health and well-being despite the fact that material quality of life has enormously increased.[6]

---

[6] The diffusion of mental malaise is not restricted to rich countries but is widespread throughout the world (WHO 2001). In poor countries the problem *adds* to material deprivations. Obviously, in rich countries not all the other functionings and capabilities are satisfactory for all people.

Consistent with this evidence is an ample body of empirical studies in psychology on the link between "materialism" and unhappiness. "Materialism" having been defined as the especial valuation given to material wealth in one's ranking of values, for example, in the aspiration for future well-being, these studies provide much evidence that those people more inclined toward materialism also rate themselves as less happy with their lives, and exhibit more depression, more anxiety, less vitality, and an even greater propensity for mental illness (Ryan and Deci 2001; Deci and Ryan 2000a; Nickerson et al. 2003). Unfortunately, this group of people is growing in rich countries, according to sociologists (Lane 2000:ch.8). For example, poll-surveys on the values expressed by successive cohorts of college freshmen in the US show a rise from about 40 percent in the late 1960s to 75 percent in the late 1990s of those who rated "being very well off financially" as a very important personal objective (Putnam 2000:260, 272–4).

In conclusion, in rich countries the evidence based on objective measures shows that ill-being is not a minor problem which will be automatically resolved by economic growth. The evidence based on subjective measures as recently provided by the economic literature on happiness (Frey and Stutzer 2002; Layard 2005; Blanchflower and Oswald 2004) is consistent with this finding, thus confirming that self-reported well-being contains valuable information.

2. The Challenge for the Capability Approach

The CA can be synthesized, as in Sen (1985a), as a chain of different concepts linking goods to utility, whereas the link is direct in the standard utility theory. First, the CA includes also non-market goods, like environmental ones, in the set of available goods for choice. Secondly, goods are transformed into characteristics as ultimate desirable properties, so that the same properties can be found in different goods. Thirdly, the *functioning* set is the individual's actual achievement in enjoying the characteristics of the chosen goods, like the body's functioning of absorbing nourishing substances from food. Fourthly, the *capability* set is the individual's potential achievement in enjoying the characteristics of available goods, like fasting for health or for religious reasons. Finally, evaluation is the ability to rank the capability sets. The concept of utility itself has been criticized in both its version of subjective desires and of subjective satisfaction (Sen 1985a), and it has been reformulated as substantive freedom and advantage (Sen 1999a).

The CA appears to open the black box of the standard utility function to include a broader set of goods and characteristics, and considers the act of choosing as a value in itself. However, Sen is generally skeptical of the direct self-rating of well-being, because—thus he argues—the psychological phenomenon of adaptation induces individuals to be content with their current material state (e.g. Sen 1985a). Since contemporary standards of evaluation are widely shared, the self-evaluation may be better proxied by the standard evaluation.

The above evidence on malaise in rich countries appears at first sight to challenge only the traditional approach to the well-being of people, whereas it appears to be well accommodated by the CA. In fact, the evidence shows that material wealth is not sufficient to warrant well-being, while the CA highlights that the individuals' functionings and capabilities to use and enjoy goods may account for the gap remaining in full explanation of people's actual well-being. Therefore, the challenge for the CA does not appear.

However, this evidence shows that some individuals' functionings and capabilities are special in character, since they pertain to the *human mind*. Deprivation is something special in the cases of mental illnesses, of non-clinical mental problems, and even of the distressful consequences of persistent conditions which appear to be freely chosen. In these cases the constraints to functionings arise from within, they do not lie in bacteria, low education, or social and economic injustice; instead, they lie in the mind. Even in many cases of mental illnesses, no bacterium, no physical injury or malformation, but functioning itself appears to be responsible from infancy and youth onwards. Whereas the appearance of mental ill-functionings can be observed, the constraints to these functionings are not observable. The CA is thus challenged because the consequences of mental ill-functionings cannot be ignored, but the unobservability of the constraints impedes the drawing of policy implications.[7]

The CA criticizes the use of income per head as the target for policy, since in many instances access to wealth is hindered by material and physical deprivations. However, the evidence on mental malaise in rich countries also makes material and physical deprivation an insufficient target for policy. Income and this kind of deprivation may even be misplaced targets, given that the rush to materialism seems to damage individual well-being.

Secondly, since the evidence based on objective measures of ill-being confirms the finding of economic literature on happiness, then self-reported well-being cannot be easily dismissed as "a flawed measure of wellbeing for public purposes" (Gasper 2007). Sen does not seem to draw such an extreme conclusion from his criticism on the bias of self-reported well-being (Schokkaert

---

[7] In Nussbaum's (2003) list of central human capabilities some items clearly pertain to the human mind, such as "being able to use the senses, to imagine, think and reason", "to love those who love and care for us", "to show concern for other human beings", "to laugh and play". Unfortunately, many people in the world are deprived of these capabilities by misery and a lack of civil and political liberty. In these cases, the constraints and the policy implications are obvious and observable. However, the evidence in the rich countries shows that the removal of these constraints does not suffice to warrant those capabilities.

2007). On the contrary, a contribution to the enrichment of the CA may derive from studying the origin and extent of the bias in self-reported measures as reliable additional evidence.

Thirdly, Sen's criticism of the bias of these measures has been applied when adaptation to material conditions may upwardly bias self-evaluation.[8] But in the case of rich countries, adaptation appears to work in the reverse direction, that is, well-being is self-rated less than what material indices would have predicted. This poses a new problem for policy. In fact, the possible error in taking action with welfare policies when objective evidence shows worse conditions in people's well-being than indicated by subjective measures would be a lesser error than in the opposite case, that is, ignoring worrying information yielded by subjective measures but not revealed by objective evidence.

3. The Self and the Capability Approach

The functioning of the human mind is not discussed in mainstream economic theory, since the assumption of substantive rationality implies a perfect functioning of the individual's mind, although this perfection in processing information is not typical of humans.[9] Individuals are represented with characterizations like preferences, constraints, endowments, and information, but not with specific functionings of the mind.

The CA attempts to give a human characterization to its representation of individuals in various ways. It broadens the set of goods subject to choice so that it includes non-market goods, and it introduces functionings and capabilities of enjoying goods. In particular, since the CA considers that the availability of potential functionings and of goods in the choice set contributes to well-being, provided that people have reason to value each option (Sen 1992), this makes the act of choosing a good in itself which is typically human. Furthermore, replacing substantive rationality with the evaluation of capability sets gives individuals a human characterization insofar as evaluation is not restricted to the efficiency aspect but is extended to the ends of choice.

Therefore, by characterizing individuals as humans the CA aims to provide theoretical foundations for a paradigm of human development, and thus depart from mainstream economic theory. However, as the previous section

[8] Sen (1984:512), for example, considers the case of the "exploited landless labourer", and then observes that "the mental metric of happiness . . . can take a deeply biased form due to the fact that the mental reactions often reflect defeatist compromises with harsh reality induced by hopelessness."

[9] Interesting different researches on rationality in economics are Simon's studies on procedural rationality (Simon 1976), and behavioral economics, which focuses on the "anomalies" in substantive rationality (Camerer et al. 2003).

231

has shown, the CA does not depart from this theory by neglecting the functioning itself of the human mind, that is, its decision-making capacity.

This chapter proposes to consider both the functionings of the mind and its human characterizations in order to explain and assess individuals' ability to choose in order to realize their life expectations and to experience well-being. The psychology literature suggests, as the next section will briefly discuss, that the mind's functionings which guide human behavior are organized by the *self*.

Sen appears to deal with the role of the self in the CA when he discusses the role of identity (Sen 1985b, 1999b, 2006). He distinguishes between personal and social identity, and discusses the problem of the extent to which the former identifies with the latter in relation to well-being.[10] Sen recognizes that the individual has some autonomy in choosing her/his own identity, possibly by identifying with some or other social group.[11] The individual cannot change her/his skin colour—Sen observes—but s/he can break away from her/his original community's legacy of traditions if he, but more probably she, finds it too constraining. More generally, Sen places much emphasis on the ability to commit oneself in pursuing some autonomous interest, which may be the interest of the group but not also necessarily self-serving, nor primarily self-centred.[12] Davis (2004:24–6) even proposes to "define personal identity for Sen as a special capability whereby individuals exercise a reflexive capacity to make commitments in social settings in a sustained way", so that "the entire capability-as-freedom framework depends on the one central freedom or capability of being able to sustain a personal identity." In this sense, Sen appears to consider individuals' ability to choose.

However, Sen's analysis of personal identity is not developed. As the title of his book states (*Reason before Identity*), he appeals to "reasoning and self-scrutiny" (Sen 2002:36) which allow individuals to recognize their specific personal identity, and effectively to choose among social identities, and more generally to doubt received rules and knowledge. But there is no discussion about the information set on options and beliefs for this rational thought. Individuals are usually informed in a very unbalanced way about their possible social identities. The "behavioural economics" literature has shown that, even for simple problems of decision-making, a variety of biases arise in the rational

---

[10] These considerations allow Sen (1999a) to justify the importance of taking a particular social group, like the community, the nation, the gender, etc., as the benchmark for evaluating individual well-being from an "impartial spectator's" point of view by using Adam Smith's concept.

[11] Akerlof and Kranton (2000) hypothesize that individuals maximizing their own utility function acquire personal identities by identifying themselves with a socially recognized ideal identity.

[12] Since individuals—in Sen's view—are more inclined to be identified with others in some particular groups than to be self-interested, he regards routinized behavior in compliance with the community's rules more important than maximizing behavior.

procedure of maximizing utility, including the bias in updating unbalanced information. One may expect even greater biases for the complex problem of choosing social identity. Even for groups of individuals who may debate this kind of problem, unbiased decision-making is not guaranteed.[13]

In conclusion, the problem of the ability to choose clearly emerges as crucial in Sen's analysis, especially in his discussion of identity and rationality. However, the literature in psychology and related disciplines reveals a discussion and results on these problems that are much richer, and particularly useful in finding a solution for the puzzle posed by the rich countries.

4. Contributions of Psychology and Related Disciplines to a Theory of Self

This chapter attempts to integrate the CA with a theory of self. No theory of this kind yet exists in economics, a fact which has recently been recognized as unfortunate (Davis 2003; Kirman and Teschl 2004). The evidence emerging from rich countries as discussed above suggests that research should be extended to psychology, and even to psychiatry, since these disciplines have studied the functioning of the mind and of the self, and since they share with economics a special attention paid to the empirical bases of the arguments. However, no mainstream theory of the self yet exists in these other disciplines either. Proposed here, therefore, is an exploratory integration of the CA with various contributions drawn from various studies in psychology, psychiatry, and neuroscience.

Mainstream economic theory considers individuals insofar as they adopt actual behaviors and choices, while assuming their underlying structure of preferences, and their ability to maximize utility. Social psychology, instead, as the authoritative and extensive survey by Baumeister (1998) shows,[14] goes deeper in its analysis of the individual by considering three roots of selfhood: the agentic self, the reflexive self, and the social self.[15] Each root will be discussed in a subsection by drawing on appropriate studies. It will be shown that studies on the agentic self can explain the dynamics of the self, and hence the formation of fundamental preferences, and the attainment of well-being (Subsection 4.1). Studies on the reflexive self can explain why the self may fail to learn from experience in order to achieve optimum dynamics and

---

[13] Nussbaum (2001) recognizes that emotions can bias rational thought, and that this bias may be due to how emotions develop during infancy, as discussed below.

[14] For other surveys on the self in psychology besides Baumeister (1998), see Banaji and Prentice (1994) and Leary and Tangney (2003).

[15] Kirman and Teschl (2005:61), on claiming that economics should extend analysis to identity, draw a similar distinction among the "*what* we consider as constitutive of a person's identity over time", the *who* we consider as the person's self-perception, and the *where* we consider as the person's social space.

maximum utility (4.2). Studies on the social self can explain the origin of the self and the initial conditions of its development (4.3). The analysis will be a preliminary exploration, rather than an exhaustive survey or even a formal presentation.[16]

4.1 The Agentic Self and Well-Being

Mainstream economics is interested in individuals' behavior within the domain of the market, while the CA attempts to consider also other domains relevant to the individual's well-being. The self is treated in psychology as a unit of specific behaviors in different domains.

In studying the self as agency, psychology considers the self to be the origin of the motivation to control, that is, to act effectively upon the environment and the self. More precisely, the self attempts to change the environment to suit itself, and to change itself to fit the environment (Baumeister 1998:714). This hypothesis gives individuals a typically human characterization. In fact, it implies that individuals project possibilities of change, and draw satisfaction from a potentiality which gives them freedom to choose and to conceive new options,[17] whereas the other animals are limited to attempts to exploit the environment as simple reactions to stimuli according to a pre-programmed pattern of behavior. Therefore, when the CA includes in its evaluation of well-being the extent of the set of choice possibilities, it captures an interesting aspect of the human self but disregards its very nature.

Deci and Ryan's (1985, 1991, 2000a) research, which develops the organismic approach begun by Goldstein (1934), is an attempt to define the nature of the self as agency, and the consequences for well-being (see also Vansteenkiste et al. in Ch. 8). They maintain that "self... is not a set of cognitive mechanisms and structures but rather a set of motivational processes with a variety of assimilatory and regulatory functions" (Deci and Ryan 1991:238). According to these authors, humans' organismic activity is inherently oriented to developing their own interests and capacities by drawing energy from *motivations* arising from basic psychological needs. These are universal organismic necessities, rather than acquired motives, since they have been found across cultures and countries at any age over the human life cycle (Ryan 1991; Ryan and La Guardia 2000). Deci and Ryan (2000a) point out that whereas physiological needs are deficit motives, since they restore quiescence as the set point of human physical organism, basic psychological needs trigger the growth of mental processes and structures as the set point. With different methods and in different contexts, they have found that there are three of these needs: autonomy, competence, and relatedness. The satisfaction of each of these

---

[16] For a partial attempt at formalization see Pugno (2008).

[17] For an economist's original point of view on human imagination, see Shackle (1961).

needs is necessary, and the satisfaction of all of them is sufficient for ongoing psychological growth, integrity, and well-being.

Competence encompasses people's striving to control outcomes and to experience effectance of their action. It is the accumulated result of one's interactions with the environment, of one's exploration, learning, and adaptation. *Autonomy* encompasses people's striving to feel themselves as originating their action. This need better specifies the conditions for personal freedom. *Relatedness* is the need to feel authentic relationships with others.

These needs primarily trigger motivations called "intrinsic" because the reward is the satisfaction of the need itself. By contrast, an external reward like a monetary incentive, which implies an exchange, is called an "extrinsic" motivation. If the reasons for extrinsically motivated activities are felt to be external by the individual, basic psychological needs are not satisfied. On the contrary, intrinsic motivations may be thwarted if extrinsic motivations are superimposed because the need for autonomy may be not satisfied (Deci et al. 1999; Frey 1997). This crowding-out effect can be avoided if the locus of causality, which is originally external in the extrinsic motivations, is internalized. Internalization takes place when "an individual acquires an attitude, belief, or behavioral regulation and progressively transforms it into a personal value, goal, or organization" (Deci and Ryan 1985:130).

One of the most interesting aspects of Deci and Ryan's approach is the dynamics of the individual's self and well-being. The self develops through "the dialectic . . . involv[ing] the integrating tendency of the self as it meets the forces and events that arise internally from organismic conditions and externally from contextual circumstances" (Deci and Ryan 1991:244). Well-being is the outcome of a successful process of integration, which takes place if the basic needs are satisfied. However, "if people's need for relatedness is substantially thwarted when they are young, they might compensate by attempting to gain approval or sense of worth by pursuing image-oriented goals, such as accumulating money or material possession" (Deci and Ryan 2000a:249). In this case, people usually withdraw concern for others, increase extrinsic motivations, and reduce intrinsic motivations, thus deteriorating well-being.[18]

Deci and Ryan's approach to the study of the self is thus interesting for various reasons. First, it points to the content of goals of human development, rather than to cognitive or rational processes pursuing unspecified goals. Secondly, it selects goals as basic psychological needs, while it considers natural drives like hunger, need for security, and so on, as deficit motives for restoring the conditions before the drives, so qualifying human development as development of the mind.[19] Thirdly, it shows that the satisfaction of

---

[18] For evidence on this point see Richins (1994); Rindfleisch et al. (1997); Kasser and Ryan (2001).

[19] "People do not have an eating drive, they have a need for sustenance. Eating behaviors may satisfy that need or drive, but eating can also satisfy a variety of other motives or need substitutes" (Deci and Ryan 2000b:328).

psychological needs leads to well-being, while aspiring to substitute them with material goals brings lower well-being. The systematic evidence on this point, which is consistent with the previous evidence arising from rich countries, suggests that humans may be induced by uncontrollable mechanisms within the self to fail in maximizing well-being. Fourthly, it also suggests the reason for this failure, by showing that those who particularly aspire after material well-being are tendentially those who have experienced an unsatisfied need of relatedness.

Deci and Ryan's approach is strengthened by the psychology literature on self-deception. In fact, it has been observed that in order to enjoy the benefits from controlling the environment and the self, individuals may self-deceive themselves by presuming to have close control, thus raising their self-esteem. The consequences may be beneficial, insofar as the illusion triggers a renewed motivation and action determinacy (Baumeister 1998:716–7).[20] However, the consequences may be negative (or even very negative), if deception is not met by outcomes (Baumeister 1998:720–3). This case opens the way for an explanation of the "bias" in rational choice, since it introduces the analysis of emotions in decision-making, and, more generally, the analysis of that part of the self which is not under the control of cognition.

Deci and Ryan's approach thus appears powerful in explaining the mental causes of well-being and the underlying changes in fundamental preferences over the life cycle, that is, whether people are oriented more to satisfying basic psychological needs like personal growth and social relations, or substitute needs like wealth and fame.

Unfortunately, the approach also leaves some key points unclear. Defining the self as "integrated processes and structures" is vague. Also the process of internalization is hard to detect independently from its positive effects on need satisfaction and well-being. But an economist would typically ask why people do not learn from past experience to satisfy the needs appropriate eventually to maximizing well-being. The next two subsections will show that other studies in the psychology literature can help remedy these weak points.

4.2 Conscious and Non-Conscious Self, and Well-Being

The second root of selfhood, that is, the reflexive self, concerns the problem of self-consciousness, and hence the distinction between conscious and unconscious self. In this chapter the term "consciousness" is used in a rather strict sense as the ability to describe the self distinctly from the outside world in a temporal context inclusive of past and future, and usually by means of verbal language. This meaning of consciousness is also implied by the

---

[20] This has also been analyzed in the recent economic literature (Benabou and Tirole 2002).

"methodological individualism" adopted by mainstream economics, where rationality addresses the well-defined problem of utility maximization.

Neuroscience has recently begun to study the emergence of consciousness from the brain and from the body, which is originally used to perform automatic processes. The most interesting study is Damasio's (1994, 1999, 2003) proposal of three levels of self. The *proto-self* non-consciously collects information from the body, and records it temporarily in neural sites of the brain so as to represent the current state of the organism. The *nuclear self* is the process of perceiving both the body through the proto-self and the environment, or, more precisely, the spontaneous change in the body caused by the stimulus of the environment: what Damasio calls "emotion". This process of linking the emotion to the stimulus also has a permanent effect on other sites of the brain, since it fixes "somatic markers" of the stimuli, or what are more generally called "feelings". It produces the instantaneous dimension of consciousness. The *autobiographic self* elaborates current stimuli on the bases of the memory of past feelings and the nuclear self. It connects current with retrieved feelings to form new ones. It is thus able to project possible future states, and to imagine novelties. One may refer to the terms of "imagination" or "intuition", until "creation". No awareness is necessarily implied by this activity, which is nevertheless typically human and included in human thought. Consciousness[21] is that particular activity whereby the individual directs his attention contemporaneously to the selected and clearly perceived stimulus (or piece of information), and to the related feelings that he is able clearly to recall (preferences). Consciousness is a slow and very limited activity, since it works sequentially, and it is very selective. But it is also powerful, since, together with verbal language, it is able to produce results which can be communicated unambiguously, and which can be replicated.

Damasio's contribution is manifold. He underlines that the human mind is unceasingly (even during sleep) elaborating and developing information as non-conscious processes, and it is structurally rooted in a single and stable body. Non-conscious processes, and feelings in particular (somatic markers), are crucial for individuals' decisions, even if they follow rational evaluation and choice. Patients with traumatized prefrontal lobes, who maintain logical abilities, appear unable to form somatic markers and then to take decisions. It has also been observed that these patients are similar to sociopaths, since both are affected by disorders in social relationships (Tranel et al. 2000).

Various studies in psychology are consistent with Damasio's contribution. Much research is currently devoted to *non-consciousness*, moving along new lines since Freud's works.[22] The starting point may be Wilson's (2002:24)

[21] Called "extended consciousness" by Damasio.
[22] This is why the term "non-consciousness" is used here instead of "unconsciousness", which is used by Freud with a rather restrictive meaning (Damasio 1999:ch.7; Wilson 2002: ch.1).

observation that the brain of an individual receives through the five senses more than 11,000,000 pieces of information every second, whereas it is able to process consciously about 40 pieces of information. What happens to the other 10,999,960, Wilson wonders.

One line of inquiry in psychology, which it shares closely with neuroscience, studies phenomena closely linked to Damasio's proto-self. Implicit perception, implicit appreciation, implicit memory, implicit attitudes, implicit motivations, implicit learning, and automatic processes of goal activation and behaviors emerge from a variety of both robust and weak evidence, as nonconscious dispositions or processes which can influence current judgments, feeling, or behaviors (Kihlstrom 1999; Ansfield and Wegner 1996; Bargh and Chartrand 1999; Forgas 2000; LeDoux 1996).

In economics this evidence is recognized in a rather reductionist way. In fact, "behavioral economics" assumes that humans are motivated by "visceral factors" which tend to be out of control and to bias rational choice (Loewenstein 1996; Gifford 2002). Humans would be thus characterized by rational consciousness and by contrasting animal visceral motives. By contrast, both neuroscience and psychology show that "most of moment-to-moment psychological life must occur through nonconscious means" also for humans. More specifically, it is possible to identify "an automatic effect of perception on action, automatic goal pursuit, and a continual automatic evaluation of one's experience" (Bargh and Chartrand 1999:462). This means that although human individuals are characterized by consciousness and rationality, they acquire information, evaluate, and choose in non-conscious ways (Zajonc 1980, 2000).

These considerations bring us to the second line of inquiry, which focuses on the relationships between non-conscious processes and the self conceived as a construct built up by the individual in relation to others through the accumulation of beliefs (Baumeister 1998:687). Non-conscious processes are recognized as undoubtedly important for construction of the self, since they contribute to forming and changing individuals' beliefs, judgments, and preferences over their life cycles, thereby guiding choices and behaviors. However, as mentioned below, also recognized as important is the feedback of the agentic self onto the non-conscious processes.

Wilson (2002) reviews and presents a variety of evidence that human individuals are far from consciously learning about their non-conscious processes. They also appear far from attempting to maximize knowledge about themselves. On the contrary, self-deception and similar practices like self-serving memory, attention lowering, and inflating self-esteem are found to be frequent. As Duval and Wicklund (1972) point out, people may feel so bad when outcomes reveal their self-deception that they are induced to escape from the aversive state of self-awareness. The typical example is alcoholism, but also other techniques can accomplish the result of deconstruction of the self by shifting attention to narrow and relatively concrete, unemotional stimuli. This process may lead to psychological vulnerability to stressful events, to psychopathology and suicide (Baumeister 1998:686; Rhodewalt and Sorrow 2003). Therefore, conscious learning about self, including beliefs, judgments, and preferences, thus appears to be actively hindered by individuals themselves (Dunning 2005). Even the argument that conscious learning should be pursued by individuals for well-being is at odds with several experiments showing that attempts consciously to introspect may have perverse effects (Schooler et al. 2003). Other evidence shows that people are happier when their conscious and non-conscious goals correspond than when they do not. Similarly, the dissociation between explicit and implicit self-esteem seems to give rise to problems in interpersonal relationships, mental and physical health (Wilson and Dunn 2004).

This brief survey yields two interesting conclusions. First, people do not systematically learn from past errors in their choices and behaviors for various reasons. They do not recognize errors when remembered, because of biased and self-serving memory. They may recognize errors but they may suppress them. They may change beliefs, preferences, and attitudes to reduce dissonance. They fail to predict changes in their preferences, and to disentangle systematic affective experiences from the past (Gilbert and Wilson 2000). Secondly, people who are particularly inclined to repress unfavorable outcomes, to self-deceive, to inflate self-esteem, that is, to build a self on dissociate beliefs, also tend to exhibit ill-being (see also Wenzlaff and Wegner 2000).

4.3 The Self in Human Relationships and Well-Being

Interpersonal relatedness, which is the third root of selfhood considered by social psychology (Baumeister 1998), is important for people's well-being because it deeply influences both the agentic self, for example, through changing autonomy and competence as seen above (4.1), and the reflexive self, particularly by activating implicit processes (see 4.2).

The best-known approach to the problem of the self and interpersonal relatedness in connection to well-being is the "attachment approach" (Bowlby 1969; Ainsworth et al. 1978).[23] This is based on a wide range of evidence, and is especially included in developmental psychology, which is used to attempt at measuring unobservable psychological dimensions.

In this approach, by "attachment" is meant an innate system that induces the infant to seek to establish communication with the mother or other caregiver on whom s/he is entirely dependent for satisfaction of her/his basic needs, both material and psychological.[24] One can say that the infant is short

---

[23] Note that the "attachment approach" is not extraneous to CA, since Nussbaum (2001) discusses it at length.

[24] Deci and Ryan specify which are the basic psychological needs (see Section 4.1).

of information about her/his being in the world, and s/he makes demands for new information, especially to the caregiver, without the use of verbal language. The caregiver's ability to feel, understand, and respond with body language shapes the kind of interaction with the infant. On this basis, the infant builds an "internal working model" of relationships (or "attachment styles"), that is, expectations about the caregiver's responsiveness, and the representation of self as (un)worthy of love and care.[25]

Three main attachment styles can be distinguished: "secure", "preoccupied", and "avoidant". *"Secure" attachment* occurs when the caregivers are able to satisfy both the infant's material and mental needs, especially the need for relatedness. Consequently, the infant develops security in coping with external reality, vitality, and the mindsight which enables her/him to understand people without the use of verbal language. Therefore, the infant's internal working model built upon well-being in relatedness brings her/him to positive expectation, feeling, and disposition to others. S/he can draw great well-being from relationships, while her/his vitality helps her/him overcome stressful events, thus to maintain the original style of attachment. *"Preoccupied" attachment* occurs when the caregivers perform hyperprotection and incoherent emotional responses to the infant's needs, so that s/he is partially disappointed since her/his need for relatedness is unsatisfied by confused communication. The infant becomes dependent on the caregivers, short of mindsight, and anxious about new relationships. Therefore, her/his internal working model is negative about the self, but positive about others. A lack of vitality makes her/him vulnerable to stressful events, thus to maintain the original style of attachment. *"Avoidant" attachment* occurs when the caregivers are unable adequately to feel and respond to the infant's needs because they control emotionality in relationships. The infant is seriously disappointed, short of understanding, and learns to control emotions. This induces the infant to "solve" her/his insecurity by building an internal working model of no expectation, reduced feeling and understanding, and a reduced disposition to others. S/he rapidly learns not to base well-being on relationships and is thus unable to appreciate positive experiences with others, which reinforces the original style of attachment.

Attachment styles may be maintained in adulthood by the above-mentioned stabilizing mechanisms, which can be briefly reworded in economic terminology. The "secure" person bases her/his prior belief on the probability of experiencing future rewarding relationships on an ample positive information set, although this is non-consciously acquired during infancy. Information updating is applied on a particular self-service basis: by selecting favorable close relation-

---

[25] Neuroscientists observe that an infant's brain is especially plastic, so that the attachment pattern may be viewed as a set of information, only partially accessible, correlated with neuronal connections (Siegel 1999, 2001).

ships, and by under-weighting the effects of possible negative information. The "preoccupied" person maintains a prior belief about relationships which is negative but very uncertain because it is based on disappointed expectations and ambiguous information. S/he updates with a negative bias, and without the ability to collect information from favorable relationships. The "avoidant" person maintains a definite negative prior belief about relationships which is constrained by the particular self-agency to avoid updating.

Therefore, self-serving information may induce some people to display an unhealthy identity. This may be called a "rationality failure" insofar as a non-conscious process of management of information about the self in relation to others and to the world violates the Bayesian updating of information, and thus does not maximize well-being (see Pugno 2005).

Bartholomew and Horowitz (1991) propose a further distinction within "avoidant" persons between "fearful", who display negative models of both self and others, and "dismissive", who display a positive model of self close to narcissism, and a negative model of others. With this study the attachment approach allows a distinction to be drawn between two positive models of self, both of which apparently produce great self-esteem, but with opposite outcomes in well-being: the "secure" person and the "avoidant dismissive" person. Moreover, it also becomes clear that direct management of one's own self-esteem to maximize well-being is not possible.

The major weakness of the attachment approach is that it is basically conceived as a system of an individual's defensive reactions to external threats, or simply stressful events, which gives rise to a search for a reliable attachment figure, who will be subsequently internalized (Mikulincer et al. 2003).[26] However, this approach seems only able to explain the unhealthy functioning of the individual's mind, this being due to the inability of her/his attachment figure to provide security, but it does not fully explain the healthy *development* of the human mind. "The ability to use an attachment figure as a secure base", Waters and Cummings (2000:167) argue, " . . . provides the confidence necessary to explore and master ordinary environments." However, this does not appear to be a *sufficient* condition. The approach suggests that the individual attempts to learn the mind functioning of the attachment figure, thus "incorporat[ing] the partner's resources into the self" (Mikulincer et al. 2003:94), but again this cannot explain the development of the mind in humans with respect to other animals.

The major strength of the attachment approach is that it provides much evidence on how basic non-conscious processes form during childhood and characterize adults. The understanding of non-conscious processes in individuals' well-being is an especially difficult task owing to the obvious problem of direct unobservability. The attachment approach attempts indirect observa-

---

[26] This reveals the origin of the attachment approach in ethology (Bowlby 1969).

tions through inference from experimental tests and from observation of the behavior of, for example, the mother–infant relationship.

A different line of research is pursued by the psychiatrist Fagioli, who proposes the psychotherapeutic relationship in order to understand the meaning of non-conscious communications. In fact, his theoretical work is backed by a very large amount of clinical experience, and it provides explanations for the development of the human mind.

Fagioli's (1972, 1974, 1975) theory argues that at birth the infant must cope with an environment very different from that of the fetal state, for the stimuli to which the infant is subject are new and very intense. The homeostasis of the previous state, which ensures that the body and vitality develop in balance with the environment, this being the amniotic fluid, no longer exists at birth. This change stimulates a twofold reaction in the infant: s/he makes the new environment (light, cold, etc.) non-existent in her/his mind ("annulment drive"), and creates a mental image of her/his previous relationship with the amniotic fluid. This is really a creation, a product of the fancy, because the infant did not see any clear object before birth, but afterwards, on this basis, s/he can enjoy the attachment to the breast. Hence, separation from the mother after birth forces the infant to experience an "annulment drive" against the natural world, to create a new psychical activity necessary for the formation of the self, and to intuit what is healthy for her/him.

Since the infant is totally dependent on other human beings, s/he learns that the search for well-being—which confirms its capacity to relate to the environment and therefore to develop his/her self—can be satisfied by human relatedness. In fact, an infant's search for satisfaction of her/his material needs arises jointly with her/his search for human relatedness. If both these searches are satisfied, the self is strengthened and becomes able to relate to others and the world. But if the search for human relatedness is not satisfied, the infant may be allowed to develop in the body, but s/he is induced to enact the "annulment drive" against the relationship, and hence against the healthy formation of her/his self. If this experience repeats itself, the infant learns this reaction, and when adult s/he will thus react non-consciously, with the consequence that s/he will have poor relationships, and a weak, or even harmed non-conscious self.

Therefore, Fagioli's theory proposes that the origin of the psychical activity necessary for the self is at birth (i.e. the self is neither innate nor introjected from the mother),[27] that this activity is essentially non-conscious, and that it develops through feelings and intuitions of the others' self. If primary rela-

---

[27] As is well known, Freud believed that at birth an infant has instincts alone, and that s/he only acquires the self with verbal language—that is, only with acquisition of consciousness. A similar view has been put forward in neurobiology by Rolls (2000) and criticized by various colleagues in *Behavioral and Brain Sciences* (2000). Freud's position has been developed by Klein, who maintains that an infant acquires the self by introjection of the mother's image.

tionships are unsatisfactory, the non-conscious self weakens since the annulment drive deteriorates any ability to self-feeling. However, if the person is induced to recognize this dynamic, the non-conscious self can be recovered and strengthened.

5. Attempting to Revise the Capability Approach

The main result of the search for a theory of self in psychology and related disciplines is that well-being can be obtained only if the non-conscious processes in the self are healthy. Naturally, a healthy non-conscious self may bring the person to well-being, although s/he is not aware of this. However, if non-conscious processes do not work well the person is induced to collect and elaborate information on self-serving bases, which affects preferences, judgments, and evaluations. S/he may largely sub-optimize, or even lapse into destructive behavior and mental illness.

This is not recognized by the CA, and it may explain why the CA does not meet the challenge arising from rich countries. The mental malaise in these and other countries cannot be cured if the measures inspired by the CA are taken as a guide. The apparent problem is that mental malaise is difficult to measure, but the real problem is that there is no mainstream theory of the self which embodies non-conscious processes.

Let us attempt to revise the CA in the light of the research on the theory of self as briefly reviewed in the previous section, doing so in three steps.

The first step is to distinguish between well-being as due to health and satisfaction in the body, and well-being due to health and satisfaction in the mind. This distinction evinces that the body develops by nature, and must be nourished, defended against injuries, and cured of diseases. The healthy development of the body is well-known, and medicine attempts to maintain it. The human body can be thought of as a particular machine, similar to the body of other animals, with specific needs for goods characteristics to be satisfied, and specific functionings and capabilities. The CA fits this restricted domain well. Even the rational principle of efficiency may be applied if the goal is to maximize health and comfort of the body over time.

By contrast, the person's mind develops at a rhythm that largely depends on the person her/himself, and on her/his relation with the environment, especially with the human environment. The development of the mind of a human individual is not completely predictable, because motivations arising from basic psychological needs are only partially distinguishable from unhealthy motivations, and especially because it is typically human to do

However, both the neurobiologist Damasio and the motivational-approach psychologists Deci and Ryan contest the idea that the mind of a newborn child is a *tabula rasa*.

243

new things, even apparently useless things, like climbing a mountain, making a painting, having a romantic relationship, or even writing and providing open-source software. The CA attempts to make the mind's functioning similar to the body's functionings and capabilities by extending the types of goods consumed. However, the quality and the amount of goods required to maximize the development of the mind is crucially more difficult to determine. Rich countries clearly fail on this crucial account.[28]

The second step is to recognize that healthy development in the functionings of the human mind is not simply an accumulation of knowledge with which to increase personal skill, or even to appreciate music. It rather implies a special functioning: the ability to choose. Psychology, psychiatry, and neuroscience provide evidence and theories on how the ability to choose for an individual's overall well-being depends on the functionings of the self, inclusive of the non-conscious processes. The contribution of these disciplines is important because malfunctioning of the self due to perverse non-conscious processes may explain ill-being also where opulence and legal rights prevail.

These extra-economic disciplines show that non-conscious processes largely inform the conscious self, since perceptions of stimuli and reactions in the body are largely non-conscious also in human individuals. But typical of humans is the elaboration of their reactions, so that the non-conscious self also changes endogenously. In fact, consciousness emerges as effortful attention to selected accessible information drawn from the entire set of perceived stimuli from outside and from memory, thus being affected by non-conscious inputs. The chosen behavior provides further stimuli, so that the conscious and the non-conscious self interact.

The interaction between the conscious and non-conscious self may give rise to a stable pattern of behavior which may be studied by economists in the conventional way even if it is not restricted to economic behavior alone. Healthy interaction provides all the information relevant to forming preferences and judgments, and to supporting choices and improving behavior, thus leaving individuals largely satisfied with their well-being. However, if the interaction is unhealthy, behavior may become puzzling for economists, since it does not appear to achieve satisfaction with well-being.

In order to understand the unhealthy functioning of the mind, psychology and related disciplines suggest that the non-conscious process of self-serving information should be investigated. This process alters the perception of both external and internal stimuli, their recall, and hence their elaboration, with

---

[28] The problem of explaining how the human mind can be kept healthy and satisfied appears to be solved in mainstream economics by Becker (1976) and Stigler and Becker (1977), who assume stable individual preferences concerning "fundamental aspects of life, such as health, prestige, sensual pleasure, benevolence, or envy" (Becker 1976:5). However, the most interesting aspects of the problem are avoided by the vagueness of this list, and by the assumption that the individual is perfectly informed on all items of the list, and s/he is perfectly able to predict their future effects on her/his utility.

the consequence of changing the information set for behavior. On this basis, in turn, behavior may be induced, or even rationally chosen, in order to favor that altered process. Over time, well-being may thus deteriorate because of an unhealthy functioning of the mind, and particularly of the non-conscious self.

Therefore, the CA should take account of the functioning of the self and the underlying non-conscious processes, not just as additional to the other functionings and capabilities but as performing a primary role. This is especially evident in the evaluation stage of a person's functionings and capabilities. Since the self is the evaluation maker, even when deciding the group of people to be subject to standard evaluation, its functioning is crucial. If non-conscious processes are not healthy, the evaluation is not a reliable guide to well-being, so that a person may freely choose the quantity and quality of goods without enjoying the expected well-being.

The third step in revising the CA is to recognize that healthy non-conscious processes require healthy relatedness with others. The importance of close personal relationships for well-being is also recognized in the economic literature (Bruni and Stanca 2008; Frey and Stutzer 2002; Layard 2005; Bartolini et al. 2007). Drawing from developmental psychology and psychiatry, it is possible to show that close personal relationships are important for well-being because they can heavily affect non-conscious processes.

There is no agreement among researchers on the origin and development of the non-conscious self, but the primary relationships during infancy appear to play a crucial role.[29] These should be satisfactory for a healthy non-conscious self, without education being limited to material and cognitive concerns. According to the attachment approach, caregivers should provide adequate personal care to the infant so that they represent reliable figures to be internalized by her/him. If primary relationships are not satisfactory, the infant is induced to fear or to avoid relationships. By contrast, according to Fagioli, caregivers should avoid annulment toward the infant's demand for relatedness, and allow for her/his autonomous mental development. If primary relationships are not satisfactory, the infant is induced to annul the relationships with others generally, and hence to loose her/his ability to feel others and her/himself. The origin of the non-conscious self as being in relation with others is thus crucial in order to develop the individual's ability to choose.

6. Concluding with Some Policy Implications

The CA provides only a partial account of well-being, since it concentrates on body-like functionings and capabilities, or to be more precise, on functionings and capabilities with observable and clear constraints. To provide a complete

---

[29] This point has been recently recognized also by authoritative economists like James Heckman (Cunha et al. 2006).

description of well-being, the functioning of the human mind inclusive of non-conscious processes should be considered. In fact, unhealthy functioning of the mind may involve self-destructive behavior in the body, while healthy functionings and capabilities of the body are not guarantees of a healthy mind. Secondly, the aspect of freedom in the concept of capability acquires full meaning only if the self, as organizer of the mind's processes, is considered. In fact, a healthy self implies a successful ability to choose, that is, a successful attainment of capabilities.

Therefore, revising the CA to include the functioning of the mind implies a theory to explain the central role of the self in decision-making. The evidence from rich countries suggests that the self of significant parts of the population is not able to guarantee them well-being, although they enjoy substantial liberties. A theory should thus also explain this failure.

Contributions in psychology, neuroscience, and psychiatry point out that non-conscious processes of the self must be considered in order to explain well-being, and that the self develops over the individual's life-cycle. The functioning of the mind may be internally constrained by something which is not observable but still very effective. In fact, the self is a subjective construct built up through the accumulation of beliefs based on external and internal information as a largely non-conscious process. Since this collection and the elaboration of information are self-serving, they may inflate or deflate the self-image, thereby impairing the functioning of the self in relation to the world. This seems to arise when primary close relationships thwart the feeling of the infant's non-conscious processes necessary to the formation of the self, although the material care may be guaranteed. The development of the healthy self requires instead the satisfaction of the basic psychological needs. Adults' choices thus become neither necessarily self-serving nor self-centered, because individuals' well-being will include enjoyment in other-regarding actions.[30]

Therefore, the study of the self can explain people's vulnerability to making sub-optimal choices for their overall well-being, being attracted by material rewards in the attempt to substitute primary psychological needs. In rich countries, where the organization of social relations, of production and commerce is shaped by the market, people's vulnerability to "wrong" choices is exploited. In fact, industrial and commercial firms pursue the goal of maximizing returns and selling goods, thus attracting people toward materialism and away from healthy relationships (Bowles 1998; Lane 1991). An unequal competition thus emerges, because only successful industrial and commercial firms tend to survive in the market, whereas no comparable selection mech-

---

[30] This result is obtained without conflicts within the self—according to Deci and Ryan's argument as briefly discussed in Section 4.1—since the basic psychological needs can be satisfied by adequate experiences. By contrast, according to Nussbaum (2001) the conflict between the individual's need for others and her/his need to be self-centered is an irreducible human characteristic.

anism governs the ability to run healthy relationships within the family, and society as a whole.[31] It is ironic that this process of deterioration in people's ability to choose occurs when globalization is especially demanding for this kind of ability, since the information and option sets are enlarging at unprecedented rates.

The main policy implication from revising the CA along these lines is that the educational system should be seriously reconsidered, from nursery to households, from schools to television programs. It is in fact organized around the coupling of accumulation of knowledge of the cognitive and material world with consumption for comfort during free time, thus emphasizing extrinsic motivations. Little attention is paid to relatedness, to intrinsic motivations generally, and to the underlying non-conscious processes.

The gap in the resources between the market system, which is designed to attract children and youth toward materialism, and their parents and families, who attempt to provide healthy relationships, should be reduced. A new system of caregiving should be conceived as shaping not only educational policy, but also urban policy and media policy. The organization of the city should be designed as more children- and youth-friendly; television and other media should observe professional standards comparable to those of the educational services. Such enlarged educational policies would also favor health policies in monitoring mental health and in preventive actions.

A society and an economy more oriented to caring and stimulating children and youth will also affect adults in their relationships, and in managing their time towards a more healthy life.

References

Ainsworth MDS, MC Blehar, E Waters, and S Wall (1978) *Patterns of Attachments: A Psychological Study of the Strange Situation*, Hillsdale, NJ: Erlbaum.

Akerlof GA and RE Kranton (2000) Economics and identity, *Quarterly Journal of Economics*, 115(3), 715–53.

Amato PR, DR Johnson, and A Booth (2003) Continuity and change in marital quality between 1980 and 2000, *Journal of Marriage & Family*, 65(1), 1–22.

Ansfield ME and DM Wegner (1996) The feeling of doing, in PM Gollwitzer and JA Bargh (eds) *The Psychology of Action*, New York: Guilford, pp. 482–506.

Banaji MR and DA Prentice (1994) The self in social context, *Annual Review of Psychology*, 45, 297–332.

---

[31] The law usually sanctions individuals' behavior when they are "able to understand and to will", whereas non-conscious processes are not sanctioned. Unfortunately, non-conscious processes may bring people to persist in constraining psychological functionings of others, especially children (Fagioli 1975).

Bargh JA and TL Chartrand (1999) The unbearable automaticity of being, *American Psychologist*, 54(7), 462–79.

Bartholomew K and LM Horowitz (1991) Attachment styles among adults: a test of a four-category model, *Journal of Personality and Social Psychology*, 61, 226–44.

Bartolini S, E Bilancini, and M Pugno (2007) Did the decline in social capital decrease American happiness? A relational explanation of the happiness paradox, *Quaderni del Dipartimento di Economia Politica* n°513, Siena.

Baumeister RF (1998) The self, in Daniel T Gilbert and Susan T Fiske (eds) *Handbook of Social Psychology*, Vol. 2 (4th edn), New York: McGraw-Hill, pp. 680–740.

Becker GS (1976) *The Economic Approach to Human Behavior*, Chicago: Chicago University Press.

Behavioral and Brain Sciences (2000) 23, 191–234.

Benabou R and J Tirole (2002) Self-confidence and personal motivation, *Quarterly Journal of Economics*, 117(3), 871–916.

Blanchflower DG and AJ Oswald (2004) Well-being over time in Britain and the US, *Journal of Public Economics*, 88(7–8), 1359–86.

Bowlby J (1969) *Attachment and Loss*, New York: Basic Books.

Bowles S (1998) Endogenous preferences, *Journal of Economic Literature*, 26, 75–111.

Bruni L and L Stanca (2008) Watching alone: relational goods, television and happiness, *Journal of Economic Behavior and Organization*, 65(3), 506–28, March.

Camerer CF, G Loewenstein, and R Rabin (eds) (2003) *Advances in Behavioral Economics*, Princeton: Princeton University Press.

Chishti P, DH Stone, P Corcoran, E Williamson, and E Petridou (2003) Suicide mortality in the European Union, *European Journal of Public Health*, 13, 108–14.

Clark AE, P Frijters, and MA Shields (2007) Relative income, happiness and utility: an explanation for the Easterlin paradox and other puzzles, *IZA Discussion Papers* 2840, Institute for the Study of Labor (IZA).

Cunha F, JJ Heckman, LJ Lochner, and DV Masterov (2006) Interpreting the evidence on life cycle skill formation, in EA Hanusheck and F Welch (eds) *Handbook of the Economics of Education*, Amsterdam: North-Holland.

Cutler DM, EL Glaeser, and KE Norberg (2000) Explaining the rise in youth suicide, *NBER Working Paper*, no.7713, May.

Damasio AR (1994) *Decartes' Error: Emotion, Reason and the Human Brain*, New York: Grosset/Putnam.

—— (1999) *The Feeling of What Happens: Body and Emotion in the Making of Consciousness*, New York: Harcourt, Brace and Jovanovich.

—— (2003) *Looking for Spinoza: Joy, Sorrow and the Feeling Brain*, Heinemann: London.

Davis JB (2003) *The Theory of the Individual in Economics*, London: Routledge.

—— (2004) Identity and commitment, *Tinbergen Institute Discussion Paper*, 055/2.

Deci E, R Koestner, and R Ryan (1999) A meta-analytic review of experiments examining the effects of extrinsic rewards on intrinsic motivation, *Psychological Bulletin*, 125(6), 627–68.

Deci EL and RM Ryan (1985) *Intrinsic Motivation and Self-determination in Human Behavior*, New York: Plenum.

—— —— (1991) A motivational approach to self: integration in personality, in RA Dienstbier (ed.) *Perspectives on Motivation*, Lincoln (Neb): University of Nebraska Press, pp. 237–88.

—— —— (2000a). The "what" and "why" of goal pursuits: Human needs and the self-determination of behavior. *Psychological Inquiry*, 11, 227–68.

—— —— (2000b). The darker and brighter sides of human experience, *Psychological Inquiry*, 11, 319–38.

Diener E and MEP Seligman (2004) Beyond money, *Psychological Science in the Public Interest*, 5(1), 1–31.

Duane WC, RM Houts, TL Huston, and LJ George (2002) Compatibility, leisure, and satisfaction in marital relationships, *Journal of Marriage and Family*, 64(2), 433–49.

Dunning D (2005) *Self-Insight*, New York: Psychology Press.

Duval S and RA Wicklund (1972) *A Theory of Objective Self-awareness*, New York: Academic Press.

Easterlin RA (1974) Does economic growth improve the human lot? Some empirical evidence, in PA David and MW Reder (eds) *Nations and Households in Economic Growth*, New York: Academic Press, pp. 89–125.

European Commission (2004) *The State of Mental Health in the European Union*, DG Health and Consumer Protection, Brussels.

Fagioli M (1972), *Istinto di morte e conoscenza [Instinct of Death and Knowledge]*, 12th edn, 2007, Rome: Nuove Edizioni Romane [partially translated in <http://www.nuoveedizioniromane.it/catalogo/libri_mf1.html>].

—— (1974) *La marionetta e il burattino [The Marionette and the Puppet]*, 8th edn, 2002, Rome: Nuove Edizioni Romane.

—— (1975) *Psicoanalisi della nascita e castrazione umana* [now *Theory of Birth and Human Castration*], 8th edn, 2005, Rome: Nuove Edizioni Romane.

Fombonne E (1998) Increased rates of psychosocial disorders in youth, *European Archives of Psychiatry and Clinical Neuroscience*, 248(1), 14–21.

—— H Simmons, H Meltzer, and R Goodman (2003) Prevalence of pervasive developmental disorders in the British nationalwide survey of child mental heath, *International Review of Psychiatry*, 15(1–2), 158–65.

Forgas JP (2000) (ed.) *Feeling and Thinking: The Role of Affect in Social Cognition*, Cambridge: Cambridge University Press.

Frey BS (1997) On the relationship between intrinsic and extrinsic work motivation, *International Journal of Industrial Organization*, 15(4), 427–39.

—— and A Stutzer (2002) *Happiness and Economics: How the Economy and Institutions Affect Well-being*, Princeton, NJ: Princeton University Press.

Gasper D (2007) What is the capability approach?, *Journal of Socio-Economics*, 36, 335–59.

Gifford A Jr (2002) Emotion and self-control, *Journal of Economic Behavior & Organization*, 49, 113–30.

Gilbert DT and TD Wilson (2000) Miswanting. Some problems in the forecasting of future affective states, in JP Forgas (ed.) *Feeling and Thinking: The Role of Affect in Social Cognition*, Cambridge: Cambridge University Press, pp. 178–97.

Glenn N and CN Weaver (1998) The changing relationship of marital status to reported happiness, *Journal of Marriage and the Family*, 50(2), 317–24.

Goldstein K (1934/1995) *The Organism: A Holistic Approach to Biology Derived from Pathological Data in Man*, New York: Zone Books.

Halli SS and Z Zimmer (1991) Common law union as a differentiating factor in the failure of marriage in Canada, 1984, *Social Indicator Research*, 24(4), 329–45.

Huang W-C (1996) Religion, culture, economic and sociological correlates of suicide rates, *Applied Economics Letters*, 3, 779–82.

Huppert FA (2005) Positive mental health in individuals and populations, in FA Huppert, B Keverne, and N Baylis (eds) *The Science of Well-being*, Oxford: Oxford University Press.

Joiner TE (2000) Depression: current developments and controversies, in SH Qualls and N Abeles (eds) *Psychology and the Aging Revolution*, Washington, DC: American Psychological Association, pp. 223–37.

Jungeilges J and G Kirchgaessner (2002) Economic welfare, civil liberty, and suicide, *Journal of Socio-economics*, 31, 215–31.

Kamp Dush CM, CL Cohan, and PR Amato (2003) The relationship between cohabitation and marital quality and stability: change across cohorts?, *Journal of Marriage and Family*, 65(3), 539–49.

Kasser T and RM Ryan (2001) Be careful what you wish for, in P Schmuck and KM Sheldon (eds) *Life Goals and Well-being*, Goettingen, Germany: Hogrefe und Huber, pp. 116–31.

Keyes CLM (2003) Complete mental health, in CLM Keyes and J Haidt (eds) *Flourishing: Positive Psychology and the Life Well-Lived*, Washington, DC: American Psychological Association, pp. 293–312.

Kihlstrom JF (1999) The cognitive unconscious, in LA Parvin and OP John (eds) *Handbook of Personality: Theory and Research*, New York: Guilford, 2nd edn, pp. 424–42.

Kirman A and M Teschl (2004) On the emergence of economic identity, *Revue de Philosophie Economique*, 1(9), 59–86.

Klerman GL (1988) The current age of youthful melancholia, *British Journal of Psychiatry*, 152, 4–14.

—— (1993) The postwar generation and depression, in Ghadirian Abdu'l, A Missagh, and HE Lehmann (eds), *Environment and Psychopathology*, New York: Springer Publishing Co, pp. 73–86.

Kobak RR and A Sceery (1988) Attachment in late adolescence, *Child Development*, 59(1), 135–46.

Kuklys W and I Robeyns (2005) Sen's capability approach to welfare economics, in Wiebke Kuklys, *Amartya Sen's Capability Approach: Theoretical Insights and Empirical Applications*, Berlin: Springer Verlag, pp. 9–30.

Kyprianou M (2005) Mental illness is Europe's unseen killer, European Commission, Press Release <http://europa.eu.int/rapid/pressReleasesAction.do?reference=IP/05/27&format=HTML&aged=0&language=EN&guiLanguage=en>.

Lane RE (1991) *The Market Experience*, New York: Cambridge University Press.

—— (2000) *The Loss of Happiness in Market Democracies*, New Haven and London: Yale University Press.

Lavori PW, M Warshaw, GL Klerman, and TI Mueller (1993) Secular trends in lifetime onset of MDD stratified by selected sociodemographic risk factors, *Journal of Psychiatric Research*, 27(1), 95–109.

Layard R (2005) *Happiness: Lessons from a New Science*, New York: Penguin Press.

Leary MR and JP Tangney (2003) (eds) *Handbook on Self & Identity*, New York: The Guilford Press.

LeDoux J (1996) *The Emotional Brain: The Mysterious Underpinnings of Emotional Life*, New York: Simon & Schuster.

Lester D and B Yang (1997) *The Economy and Suicide: Economic Perspectives on Suicide*, Commack, NY: Nova Science.

Levi F, C La Vecchia, and B Saraceno (2003) Global suicide rates, *European Journal of Public Health*, 13, 97–8.

Loewenstein G (1996) Out of control: visceral influences on behavior, *Organizational Behavior and Human Decision Processes*, 65(3), 272–92.

Maughan B, AC Iervolino, and S Collishaw (2005) Time trends in child and adolescent mental disorders, *Current Opinion in Psychiatry* 18(4), 381–5.

Merrick J, I Kandel, and G Vardi (2003) Trends in adolescent violence, *International Journal of Adolescent Medicine and Health*, 15(3), 285–7.

Mikulincer M, PR Shaver, and D Pereg (2003) Attachment theory and affect regulation, *Motivation and Emotion*, 27(2), 77–102.

Nickerson AB and RJ Nagle (2004) The influence of parent and peer attachments on life satisfaction in middle childhood and early adolescence, *Social Indicators Research*, 66, 35–60.

Nickerson C, N Schwartz, E Diener, and D Kahneman (2003) Zeroing in on the dark side of the American dream, *Psychological Science*, 14(6), 531–6.

Nussbaum M (2000) *Women and Human Development: The Capabilities Approach*, Cambridge: Cambridge University Press.

—— (2001) *Upheavals of Thought: The Intelligence of Emotions*, Cambridge: Cambridge University Press.

—— (2003) Capabilities as fundamental entitlements: Sen and social justice, *Feminist Economics*, 9(2–3), 33–59.

Olfson M, MJ Gameroff, SC Marcus, and PS Jensen (2003) National trends in the treatment of attention deficit hyperactivity disorder, *American Journal of Psychiatry*, 160(6), 1071–7.

—— SC Marcus, MM Weeissman, PS Jensen, and S Peter (2002) National trends in the use of psychotropic medications by children, *Journal of the American Academy of Child and Adolescent Psychiatry*, 41(5), 514–21.

Pritchard C and A Butler (2003) A comparative study of children and adult homicide rates in the US and the major Western countries 1974–1999, *Journal of Family Violence*, 18(6), 341–50.

Pugno M (2005) The happiness paradox: a formal explanation from psycho-economics, Economics Department, University of Trento (Italy), *Discussion Paper*, no.1.

—— (2007a) The subjective well-being paradox: a suggested solution based on relational goods, in L Bruni and PL Porta (eds) *Handbook on the Economics of Happiness*, London: Elgar, pp. 263–89.

—— (2008) Economics and the self: a formalisation of Self-Determination Theory, *Journal of Socio-Economics*, 37, 1328–46.

Putnam RD (2000) *Bowling Alone*, New York: Simon & Schuster.

Rhodewalt F and DL Sorrow (2003) Interpersonal self-regulation: lessons from the study of narcissism, in MR Leary and JP Tangney (eds) *Handbook on Self & Identity*, New York: The Guilford Press, pp. 519–35.

Richins ML (1994) Special possession and expression of material values, *Journal of Consumer Research*, 21, 522–33.

Rindfleisch A, JE Burroughs, and F Denton (1997) Family structure, materialism, and compulsive consumption, *Journal of Consumer Research*, 23(4), 312–25.

Robeyns I (2005) The capability approach—a theoretical survey, *Journal of Human Development*, 6(1), 93–114.

Rogers SJ and PR Amato (1997) Is marital quality declining? Evidence from two generations, *Social Forces*, 75, 1089–100.

Rolls ET (2000) Précis of the "Brain and Emotion", *Behavioral and Brain Sciences*, 23, 177–91.

Rutter M and DJ Smith (eds) (1995) *Psychosocial Disorders in Young People: Time Trends and Their Causes*, Chichester: Wiley.

Ryan RM and EL Deci (2001) On happiness and human potentials, *Annual Review of Psychology*, 52(Feb.), 141–66.

—— and J La Guardia (2000) What is being optimized? in SH Qualls and N Abeles (eds), *Psychology and the Aging Revolution*, Washington, DC: American Psychological Association, pp.145–72.

Schokkaert E (2007) Capabilities and Satisfaction with Life, *Journal of Human Development*, 8(3), 415–30.

Schooler JW, D Ariely, and G Loewenstein (2003) The pursuit and assessment of happiness can be self-defeating, in I Brocas and JD Carrillo (eds) *The Psychology of Economic Decisions*, Oxford: Oxford University Press, pp. 41–72.

Sen A (1984) *Resources, Values and Development*, Oxford: Blackwell.

—— (1985a) *Commodities and Capabilities*. Amsterdam: North Holland.

—— (1985b) Goals, commitment, and identity, *Journal of Law, Economics and Organization*, 1(2), 341–55.

—— (1987) The standard of living, in G Hawthorn (ed.) *The Standard of Living*, Cambridge: Cambridge University Press.

—— (1992) *Inequality Reexamined*, Oxford: Clarendon Press.

—— (1999a) *Development as Freedom*, New York: Knopf.

—— (1999b) *Reason before Identity*, New Delhi: Oxford University Press.

—— (2002) *Rationality and Freedom*, Cambridge, MA: Belknap Press.

—— (2006) *Identity and Violence*, New York: Norton & Company.

Shackle GLS (1961) *Decision, Order and Time*, Cambridge: Cambridge University Press.

Siegel DJ (1999) *The Developing Mind: Toward a Neurobiology of Interpersonal Experience*, New York: Guilford.

—— (2001) Toward an interpersonal neurobiology of the developing mind, *Infant Mental Health Journal*, 22(1–2) 67–94.

Simon HA (1976) From substantive to procedural rationality, in SJ Latsis, *Method and Appraisal in Economics*, Cambridge: Cambridge University Press, pp. 129–48.

Stigler GJ and GS Becker (1977) "De Gustibus non est disputandum", *American Economic Review*, 67(2), 76–90.

Tranel D, A Bechara, and AR Damasio (2000) Decision making and the somatic marker hypothesis, in MS Gazzaniga (ed.) *New Cognitive Neurosciences*, Cambridge: MIT Press, pp. 1047–61.

Twenge JM (2000) The age of anxiety? The birth cohort change in anxiety and neuroticism, 1952–1993, *Journal of Personality and Social Psychology*, 79(6), 1007–21.

UNDP (1990–2004), *Human Development Reports*, New York: Oxford University Press.

Vansteenkiste M, RM Ryan, and EL Deci, Self-Determination Theory and the explanatory role of psychological needs in human well-being, Ch. 8 (this volume).

Waters E and EM Cummings (2000) A secure base from which to explore close relationships, *Child Development*, 71 (Feb.) 164–72.

Wenzlaff RM and DM Wegner (2000) Thought suppression, *Annual Review of Psychology*, 51, 59–91.

Wilson TD (2002) *Strangers to Ourselves: Discovering the Adaptive Unconscious,* Cambridge, MA: Belknap Press/Harvard University Press.

—— and EW Dunn (2004) Self-knowledge, *Annual Review of Psychology*, 55, 493–518.

World Health Organization (2001) *The WHO Report 2001: Mental Health, New Understanding New Hope,* Report on Mental Health.

Zajonc RB (1980) Feeling and thinking, *American Psychologist*, Feb., 151–75.

—— (2000) Feeling and thinking: closing the debate over the independence of affect, in JP Forgas (ed.) *Feeling and Thinking*, Cambridge: Cambridge University Press, pp. 31–58.

10

Subjective Measures Of Agency*

Sabina Alkire

Introduction

Quite a few studies indicate that durable poverty reduction or enduring social change occurs when some poor persons, as well as others in their society, participate actively in development processes. Such is the strength of this finding that it has become a truism to advocate the "participation" and "empowerment" of persons in many dimensions—such as women's empowerment in the market and at home, or the empowerment of local communities to hold school teachers accountable, or the inculcation of democratic practices such that communities and marginalized groups are able to articulate political demands and make their voices heard.

In Amartya Sen's work, the term "human agency" represents people's ability to act on behalf of goals that matter to them, and this aspect of freedom, he argues, is a core ingredient of positive social change. "The people have to be seen . . . as being actively involved—given the opportunity—in shaping their own destiny, and not just as passive recipients of the fruits of cunning development programs."[1]

Until recently, agency seemed to elude measurement. The dynamic phenomenon of human action, innovation, determination, and leadership could not be easily captured by the same kinds of questions that chart nutritional status, schooling, agricultural activities, and savings practices. Yet "quantitative" or survey-based measures of agency, in the sense of people's self-evaluation of whether or not they are free to act as agents, is by no means uncharted empirical territory. Furthermore, some such measures seem to be comparable and robust across cultures.[2]

* I am very grateful for the comments of Richard Ryan, Carol Ryff, Valery Chirkov, Ed Deci, Shalom Schwartz, Ron Inglehart, Séverine Deneulin, and Sebastian Silva Leander, and for the research assistance of Afsan Bhadelia.
[1] 1999a: 53.
[2] Alsop (2005), Alsop et al. (2005), Narayan-Parker (2005), Alkire (2005), Alkire (2008).

Table 10.1.

Author(s)	Theory	Method/Scale	Assessment
Schwartz	Self direction is one of ten universal values that motivate human action. Self direction is **independent thought and action—choosing creating exploring.**	Rate how each value fares as a guiding principle in my life from 0 to 7. FREEDOM (freedom of action and thought) CREATIVITY (uniqueness, imagination) INDEPENDENT (self-reliant, self-sufficient) CHOOSING OWN GOALS (selecting own purposes) CURIOUS (interested in everything, exploring)	Definitions are local but may not be comparable across cultures. Measures relative value of agency *in comparison* with other goals (not its instrumental use in furthering such goals). Might not be policy responsive. Might conflate agency with individualism/independence.
Welzel, Inglehart	**Mass liberty aspirations** are a measurable intermediate variable. They are (partly) created by economic development and in turn provide a source of public pressure for democratization.	Code and sum 3 items, each ranked 0–2, to give an ordinal index 0–5. 1. Seeing that people have more say about how things are done at their jobs and in their communities 2. Giving people more say in important government decisions 3. Protecting freedom of speech	Measures agency with respect to public space only (political agency). Might pick up values of individualism (in freedom of speech question). Would need other measures for women's agency etc.
Ryff	**Psychological well-being** across cultures includes six domains, two of relevance: **Environmental mastery** (being able to choose or create contexts suitable for personal needs and values); and **Autonomy** (is self-determining and independent).	Indicate agreement with statements along a 6-point scale (there are different survey forms, with 3, 9, or 14 statements per domain). **Environmental mastery:** 1. In general, I feel I am in charge of the situation in which I live. 2. The demands of everyday life often get me down. 3. I am quite good at managing the many responsibilities of my daily life.	Source lists for psychological well-being were biased. Questionnaires require adaptation across cultures. Looks at global rather than domain-specific agency, and the practical relevance of such evaluations is unclear. Better to study agency with respect to certain domains rather than life as a whole.

(Continued)

Table 10.1. Continued

Author(s)	Theory	Method/Scale	Assessment
		Autonomy: 1. I tend to be influenced by people with strong opinions. 2. I have confidence in my opinions, even if they are contrary to the general consensus. 3. I judge myself by what I think is important, not by the values others think are important.	
Self-Efficacy Bandura et al.	**People's agency** has internal and external determinants; people can learn to increase their own agency.	Measures people's belief in their capabilities to exercise control over given events with respect to a specific domain (health, sport, collective action).	Cannot discern if agents value the goals they can advance efficaciously. May be policy-responsive.
	Perceived self-efficacy refers to "people's belief in their capabilities to mobilise the motivation, cognitive resources, and courses of action needed to exercise control over given events" Ozer and Bandura (1990: 472).	Constructs scales, 5–20 items per scale. Each item is ranked 0–10 (or 0–5). Scale is the sum of item rankings. Items vary depending on the domain with respect to which self-efficacy is measured.	Can be used for different domains. May be good predictors across cultures. In some settings collective-efficacy may be a more useful scales than self-efficacy because they are less individualist.
Self-Determination Theory Ryan, Deci et al.	Humans have 3 basic psychological needs: autonomy, competence, and relatedness.	Identifies practice(s) that pertain to a given domain. Asks persons to rate, from 1 to 5, the following possible reasons why they felt/believe/engage in the practice.	Explores agency that people value and have reason to value. May be policy-responsive.
	Autonomy is the experience of integration and freedom.	*External regulation:* Because of external pressures.	Distinguishes autonomy from individualism.
	Autonomy can be distinguished from dependence/independence and from individualism/collectivism.	*Introjected regulation:* To obtain approval or avoid guilt. *Identified regulation:* Because it is important and worthwhile. *Integrated regulation:* Because I have thoughtfully considered and fully chosen this.	Appears to identify a relevant and valued variable across cultures. Can be used with respect to different domains.

This chapter begins by introducing Amartya Sen's concept of agency, as well as the term "empowerment", and identifies some considerations in choosing measures for these. The chapter then surveys three subjective measures of human agency considered as a domain of well-being (Schwartz, Welzel/Inglehart, Ryff) and two other multidomain measures of agency (Self-Efficacy Theory, and Self-Determination Theory). The measures reflect people's perceptions of their autonomy, and in some cases their subjective evaluations of the importance of agency. The measures surveyed are introduced in Table 10.1.

The studies and approaches here surveyed have developed along an independent academic path from economics or development literature. Yet the survey instruments, and the research on the nature of subjective quantitative data, may be useful in crafting subjective indicators of individual agency or empowerment. As Ruut Veenhoeven observed with respect to the subjective well-being literature, "the research effort is highly redundant" because different groups (including economists and those working in development) have begun to undertake subjective studies without properly reviewing the literature and techniques. Hence the purpose of this chapter is to draw the attention of those engaged in multidimensional measures of poverty, or quality of life, or capability expansion, to some literature on agency measures. The hope is that a preliminary conversation between disciplines might help to clarify and advance measurement options both in the capability approach and in development practice.

Agency

Sen's well-known Dewey Lectures, "Well-being, Agency, and Freedom," articulate "a moral approach that sees persons from two different perspectives: well-being and agency. Both the 'well-being aspect' and the 'agency aspect' of persons have their own relevance in the assessments of states and actions. Each also yields a corresponding notion of freedom."[3]

Sen defines agency freedom as "what a person is free to do and achieve in pursuit of whatever goals or values he or she regards as important."[4] The agency aspect is important "in assessing what a person can do in line with his or her conception of the good."[5] Unlike well-being, which refers to the person's own state, agency is general; it is "not tied to any one type of aim. Agency freedom is freedom to achieve whatever the person, as a responsible agent, decides he or she should achieve." Sen argues that "Persons should

---

[3] 1985: 169 (opening sentences). Note that Sen's Arrow lectures use instead the terminology of process and opportunity freedoms, with personal process freedoms relating most closely to empowerment (2002: chs 19–21).

[4] 1985: 203.   [5] 1985: 206.

enter the moral accounting by others not only as people whose well-being demands concern, but also as people whose responsible agency must be recognised."[6] We can identify several characteristics of Sen's account of agency that are relevant for measurement: (i) agency is exercised with respect to goals the person values; (ii) agency includes effective power as well as direct control; (iii) agency may advance well-being or may address other-regarding goals; (iv) to identify agency also entails an assessment of the value of the agent's goals; (v) the agent's responsibility for a state of affairs should be incorporated into his or her evaluation of it.[7]

Agency may be exercised at the individual level, or in groups, or through democratic participation. For example Dréze and Sen directly identify participation as an expression of agency, and argue that it can have intrinsic value:

Participation also has intrinsic value for the quality of life. Indeed being able to do something not only for oneself but also for other members of the society is one of the elementary freedoms which people have reason to value. The popular appeal of many social movements in India confirms that this basic capability is highly valued even among people who lead very deprived lives in material terms.[8]

In addition to intrinsic importance and instrumental value Sen argues that joint forms of agency also have constructive importance because the information and perspectives people exchange can change their values and preferences: "the practice of democracy gives citizens an opportunity to learn from one another, and helps society to form its values and priorities. In this sense, democracy has constructive importance."[9] He cites the example of declining fertility rates, which have been "much influenced by public discussion of the bad effects of high fertility rates on the community at large and especially on the lives of young women."[10]

An "informational analysis" of Sen's own work would lead to the conclusion that information on human agency—whether agency is exercised individually or together with others—is indeed required for an adequate assessment of social arrangements.[11] But how do we obtain this information? Can we measure expansions in agency in a sensitive and policy-relevant manner? Before addressing this question, we pause briefly to acknowledge a related concept.

[6] 1985: 204 both quotes.
[7] Alkire (2008).
[8] 1995: 106. See also 1989.
[9] 1999b: 10. See also India: Development and Participation 2002, "Participation also plays a crucial role in the formation of values and in generating social understanding." p 10.
[10] 1999b: 11.
[11] The first of Sen's Dewey Lectures, on the moral role of information, makes this point (Sen 1985) as does Sen 1979.

Empowerment

The term "empowerment" is related to, although not synonymous with, an increase in human agency. The measures surveyed here may pertain to empowerment, a term that is currently used in poverty reduction efforts. However definitions of empowerment vary widely; indeed over thirty definitions appear to be in present use.[12]

The *World Development Report 2000/1* draws attention to the "sense of voiceless and powerlessness" poor persons highlighted when they discussed social and public institutions. "Those materially deprived feel acutely their lack of voice, power, and independence."[13] The words "sense of'" and "feel" suggest that empowerment refers to persons' own judgments and recurrent emotional states. Furthermore, the *Voices of the Poor* study and participatory poverty assessments like it rely on people's own definitions of powerlessness and voicelessness. Hence one aim of poverty reduction, these argue, might be to improve these subjective self-evaluations or perceptions so that in a later round of meetings persons report an increase in empowerment. Such an increase would have an intrinsic value and would also enable communities to advance their own concerns effectively. This aspect of empowerment could similarly be analyzed using subjective indicators of human agency.

Empowerment is never defined conceptually or directly in the *World Development Report 2000/1* but rather operationally. The paragraph that introduces empowerment in the framework for action is as follows:

Empowerment means enhancing the capacity of poor people to influence the state institutions that affect their lives, by strengthening their participation in political processes and local decision-making. And it means removing the barriers—political, legal, and social—that work against particular groups and building the assets of poor people to enable them to engage effectively in markets.[14]

This definition suggests that a considerable part of empowerment measurement and evaluation will be associated with the discrete elements of political processes, awareness-raising, decentralization, legal structures, democracy, and so forth that are instrumentally effective in a particular situation. Thus measures of empowerment could reflect the instrumental strength of agency in the relevant spheres.

Sen argues that well-being and agency are distinctive, and both of intrinsic value. Earlier I have argued, following Finnis, Nussbaum, and others, that

---

[12] Ibrahim and Alkire (2007).

[13] 2000/1: 34, 35 respectively.

[14] 2000/1: 39. The World Bank's (2002) manual defines empowerment as: "the expansion of assets and capabilities of poor people to participate in, negotiate with, influence, control, and hold accountable institutions that affect their lives."

insofar as agency is of intrinsic value, it can be considered to be one dimension of human well-being.[15] Yet active agents are able to affect their ability to enjoy other dimensions of well-being more fully, so agency may also be a cause of well-being. But person A's agency is not limited to person A's well-being but may advance other aspects of his or her conception of the good (saving the seals or changing a government policy to be more equitable). Further, Sen points out that agency can also conflict with aspects of well-being. For example, a drowning child in the river beside which one is having a picnic causes one's agency freedom to expand by giving one the occasion to save the child's life—which one deems a worthwhile project. But that same occasion may reduce one's actual well-being in other respects (by making one cold and wet and worried if one dives in) and also one's well-being freedom (as one is not free to finish one's lunch in peace).[16] Thus the relationship between well-being and agency is complex and they are best studied independently.

Given the diverse conceptions of empowerment, no attempt is made to choose one. However in many definitions, empowerment is an increase in certain kinds of agency that are deemed particularly instrumental to the situation at hand. For example, the World Bank's "empowerment sourcebook" identified four activities that were, in their view, preconditions for empowerment, and also activities that development agencies could proactively advance.

Subjective Agency Measures

This chapter limits its focus to self-reported or "subjective" studies of human agency. I have observed elsewhere that, if agency describes people's ability to act on behalf of what they "value and have reason to value", then two kinds of measures might be appropriate. One set of objective measures would reflect their *ability* to act on behalf of what it might be argued they have reason to value (for example, the income over which women have decisive spending authority).[17] A complementary set of subjective measures, which I have elsewhere referred to as *autonomy* measures, would probe their own values, in regards the agency they did and did not enjoy.[18]

---

[15] Alkire (2002a, 2002b), Grisez et al. (1987), Nussbaum (2000).

[16] 1985: 207–8.

[17] Cummins (2000b). See also Cummins (2002a) and Schulz (2000). In quality of life measures, Cummins and others found the intracorrelations among subjective and among objective measures of individual quality of life to be much stronger than the intercorrelations between the two types of measures, except among the very poor. This led to a hypothesis that subjective satisfaction may be under "homeostatic control"(see Cummins 2003) and that subjective measures should accompany and not replace objective measures.

[18] Alkire (2008).

The subjective studies here reviewed have several identifying characteristics.[19] First, they are intended to reflect the internal experience of the respondent—including their own judgments and values about how well they are functioning in various dimensions. Second, they may include positive as well as negative experiences. Third, they focus on enduring evaluations rather than fleeting emotional states (a different literature focuses on fleeting happiness[20]). These aspects of subjective well-being studies make them particularly appropriate for engaging with the capability approach, which stresses practical reason and seeks information on valuable states of being and doing, which may be distinct from transitory states of emotional bliss.

Clearly, as Diener and Suh's introduction to their excellent collection *Culture and Subjective Well-Being* points out, the methodological issues for comparable research (whether participatory or survey in method) on subjective or self-reported data across multiple cultures are momentous.[21] Are qualitative scales comparable across individuals? Are they comparable across societies? How does one aggregate data for samples that include multilingual, or literate and illiterate populations? What measurement artifacts are introduced by translation into different languages and by the associated need to translate concepts across cultures? What self-report artifacts are introduced in cultures that value humility rather than overt success, or teamwork rather than individual gain? To these recent studies of empowerment add one further question: How can subjective data be corrected for "adaptive preferences"?

A further hoard of issues surround the causality of subjective states, and are important in situations where policy-responsive indicators are required. Do subjective indicators track deliberate changes in agency outcomes better than (or differently from) proxy indicators such as parents' education, women's employment, and so on? And how do we assess the margins of error (created by, for example, the impact of current events, of moods, of personality, of the "reference point", of the impression given by the facilitator or enumerator, of a limited knowledge set, and other transient, situational factors)? Can subjective data accurately track long-term trends in agency expansion?

Twenty years into research on subjective well-being, methodologies for checking data characteristics such as the cross-cultural comparability of

---

[19] Diener and Suh (2000).

[20] See Argyle and Martin (1991), and Argyle et al. (1991). Argyle and Martin find the "causes of joy"—joy being fleeting emotional happiness—to be social contacts with friends, or others in close relationship, sexual activity; success, achievement; physical activity, exercise, sport; nature, reading, music; food and drink; alcohol. This list does not include health, education, or other "basic needs" with which poverty reduction is primarily concerned, and does include activities in which development professionals do not have an evident comparative advantage. The domains of well-being conceived of as life satisfaction are more similar to the domains that comprise "multidimensional" poverty, and have been selected for that reason.

[21] Diener and Suh (2000), Diener et al. (1999). See also Smith and Bond (1993). Van de Vijver and Leung (2000).

subjective scales have been developed; a few thousand preliminary studies have been completed, substantial survey articles and collective volumes are appearing, and some findings appear robust. While this chapter focuses on conceptual matters, the measures surveyed here could not be accurately deployed without these methodological tools and background studies.

Agency as a Dimension of Well-Being

Agency measures may be broadly divided into two types: those that view agency as one dimension among others of human well-being, and those that consider agency with respect to different dimensions of well-being. Broadly speaking, the first measures look at agency as a component of well-being; the second measures look at agency as a process of freedom.

While perhaps the most visible of subjective well-being studies conceives of subjective well-being as a whole, another avenue of well-being and quality-of-life research measures different "domains" of multidimensional well-being. That is, the surveys collect information on a number of different dimensions of well-being, and may or may not later provide weighted aggregates for overall well-being. Researchers may also study intercorrelations between objective and subjective data on the same dimension.

Aspects of human agency are often, although by no means always, included in multidimensional accounts of well-being, whether these be philosophical or empirical. So John Finnis refers to practical reason or authentic self-direction; Martha Nussbaum refers to practical reason and control over one's environment; Doyal and Gough to autonomy; Max-Neef to participation; Ryan and Deci to autonomy; Narayan et al. to freedom of choice and action; Schwartz to self-direction; Galtung to being an active subject; Allardt to self-determination; Andrews and Withey to independence; Lasswell to power; Qizilbash to autonomy or self-determination.[22] While the definitions of terms differ and consideration of these differences is beyond the scope of this chapter, it is still interesting to note that different disciplinary approaches recognize the validity of an agency-related dimension of well-being.

What must be signaled from the start is that measures of agency as a "dimension of well-being" face a conceptual difficulty that is relevant for measurement. Sen rejects the view that agency can adequately be represented only as a dimension of well-being. He acknowledges that agency can have intrinsic value, and insofar as it does, I have argued that it can take its place alongside other incommensurable actions and states that have intrinsic value, such as friendship, meaningful work, or being healthy.[23] Sen's capabil-

---

[22] These and other approaches are surveyed in Alkire (2002a, 2002b).
[23] Alkire (2002a) ch. 5.

ity approach argues that process freedoms must be evaluated with respect to each valuable functioning—agency also plays an architectonic role with respect to the other dimensions of well-being.[24] It would seem consonant with this approach to suggest that, similarly, agency might be best evaluated not only as a general capability but also with respect to different functionings that people might wish to advance.

Agency is often exercised with respect to distinct dimensions and indeed it is precisely the dimension-specific agency levels that may be of policy interest. A person who is "empowered" as a wife and mother may nonetheless be hesitant to participate in village meetings because of her low educational and social status. Furthermore, she may be excluded from the labor market because of her gender. While some psychologists focus on enabling persons to develop inner global agency resources for coping with a variety of external circumstances, it is more practical for development to address the external constraints that inhibit agency—such as legal, economic, or social barriers. In these cases, for practical reasons, a measure of dimension-specific expansions in human agency could identify dimensions in which agency might be constrained by external barriers.

Still, there might be occasions in which agency-related measures that were not specific to one domain could be informative. For example, it might be hoped and also expected that increases in agency in one domain might have positive "spillover" effects as persons applied the organizational or leadership skills in new contexts, and it would be interesting to identify which interventions produce larger spillover effects. It would also be interesting to identify which domains are related and which seem relatively independent. Thus it does seem fruitful to consider indicators that measure agency with reference to agency-related dimension(s) of well-being. Shalom Schwartz's Universal Value of Self-Direction, Welzel and Inglehart's analyses of the World Values Survey, and Carol Ryff's work are chosen as examples.

A further question is whether to measure agency and empowerment, or, rather, to measure disempowerment and oppression. It might be assumed that agency and disempowerment are polar opposites: a low score on disempowerment would inevitably indicate a high score empowerment. However Kahneman's work among others cautions against such assumptions. Thus empirical work would be needed to probe whether measures of one or both are necessary.

It may be worth signaling in advance that the approaches introduced here and in the following section might usefully be explored and assessed along at least four axes, only one of which is undertaken. First, often the work is guided by a theoretical perspective that may be distinct from the capability approach. For example, some theories hold that agency is valued only by individualistic societies, or that it only emerges as a value in post-material societies in which

---

[24] See also Nussbaum (2000).

material needs are largely satisfied. This chapter mentions, but does not scrutinize these diverse theoretical motivations. Second, each has developed survey instruments for obtaining information on agency freedom, which are presented and discussed. Third, in some cases researchers have also developed or made improvements upon statistical techniques for analyzing the data—such as internal tests for robustness and accuracy of the instruments across cultural, age, and language groups. These techniques are of considerable interest, but are not covered in this chapter. Fourth, each approach has also generated a body of data and empirical findings, some of which may be of considerable interest and relevance. Again, while these are mentioned in passing, the chapter restricts its focus to the measurement instruments.

Self-Direction as a Universal Value

Shalom Schwartz has proposed and revised a "theory of the universal content and structure of human values" based on empirical cross-cultural research. In developing a framework for the empirical research, Schwartz et al. have tried to formulate (i) "the substantive content" of values, (ii) the "comprehensiveness" of the values identified, (iii) whether the values have some equivalence of meaning across groups of people, and (iv) whether there is a meaningful and identifiable structure of relations among different values.

Schwartz defines values as "desirable trans-situational goals, varying in importance, that serve as guiding principles in the life of a person or other social entity. Implicit in this definition of values as goals is that (i) they serve the interests of some social entity, (ii) they can motivate action, giving it direction and emotional intensity, (iii) they function as standards for judging and justifying action, and (iv) they are acquired both through socialisation to dominant group values and through the unique learning experiences of individuals."[25] His current set of comprehensive[26] value dimensions include the following:

Power (social status and prestige, control or dominance over people and resources)
Achievement (personal success through demonstrating competence according to social standards)
Hedonism (pleasure and sensuous gratification for oneself)
Stimulation (excitement, novelty, and challenge in life)
Self-direction (independent thought and action—choosing, creating, exploring)
Universalism (understanding, appreciation, tolerance, and protection for the welfare of all people and for nature)

[25] 1994: 21. See also Schwartz and Bilsky (1987, 1990) and Schwartz (1992).
[26] For an explanation of the test of comprehensiveness see 1992: 37.

Benevolence (preservation and enhancement of the welfare of people with whom one is in frequent personal contact)

Tradition (respect, commitment, and acceptance of the customs and ideas that traditional culture or religion provide)

Conformity (restraint of actions, inclinations, and impulses likely to upset or harm others and violate social expectations or norms)

Security (safety, harmony, and stability of society, of relationships, and of self)

Of particular interest in this list is self-direction. Self-direction, like Schwartz's other values, is recognized to have both terminal or intrinsic value, as well as instrumental value. Sagiv and Schwartz argue that self-direction on their scale corresponds to the term "autonomy" in the self-determination theory that we will explore below. Further, the ability to think, act, choose, create, and explore would seem to relate to agency and to empowerment. What does turn out to introduce some complexities are the "independence" factors of the description, which make it seem to capture views on individualism as well as views on agency as we have defined it.

Schwartz has measured values in two ways: first, via a long and rather abstract questionnaire, and second, via a "portraits questionnaire" which is appropriate among people of widely varying ages and levels of education.

In the first measure, respondents are presented with a list of about fifty-seven values, each identified by two or three brief phrases. Respondents "set their scale" by choosing and rating the most important value as 7 ("of supreme importance"), the value most opposed to their principles as 1 or, if there is no such value, the least important value as 0. They then rate how each value fares "as a guiding principle in my life" on a scale from negative 1 to 7.[27] Schwartz selected the list of values by drawing on previous studies[28] and modified his substantive list of value dimensions in response to evidence from about 200 surveys in 64 countries involving well over 60,000 respondents.[29] The values items relating to self direction are:

FREEDOM (freedom of action and thought)
CREATIVITY (uniqueness, imagination)
INDEPENDENT (self-reliant, self-sufficient)

[27] Scaled thus: 7: of supreme importance; 6: very important; 5, 4 unlabeled; 3: important; 2, 1 unlabeled; 0: not important; −1: opposed to my values.

[28] Schwartz cites Rokeach (1973), Braithwaite and Law (1985), Chinese Culture Connection (1987), Hofstede (1980), Levy and Guttman (1974), Munro (1985), and the "examination of texts on comparative religion and from consultations with Muslim and Druze Scholars" 1992: 17.

[29] Schwartz (1994) summarizes progress until that date. His work also cross-references other values theories and research. The 64 countries include 2 African, 2 North American, 4 Latin American, 8 Asian, 2 South Asian, 8 Eastern European, 1 Middle Eastern, 14 European, 2 Mediterranean, Australia, and New Zealand.

CHOOSING OWN GOALS (selecting own purposes)
CURIOUS (interested in everything, exploring)

Subsequently Schwartz designed a ten-minute instrument specifically for less educated populations 13 years old or above (used initially in Uganda, South Africa, Italy and Israel).[30] This instrument, called the Portrait Values Questionnaire (PVQ), presents brief descriptions of 29 different people. Each portrait consists of two sentences that characterize the person's goals, aspirations, and wishes, all expressive of a single value type.[31] For example, one of the three self-direction descriptions on the "male" version of the questionnaire describes a self-directed man in these two ways: "He thinks it's important to be interested in things." And "He is curious and tries to understand everything." Respondents are then asked, "How much like you is this person?" They indicate their response in one of six boxes, which are labeled: 6 = very much like me/like me/somewhat like me/a little like me/not like me/1 = not like me at all. The four questions are below (with genders alternating):

- Thinking up new ideas and being creative is important to him. He likes to do things in his own original way.
- It is important to her to make her own decisions about what she does. She likes to be free to plan and to choose her activities for herself.
- He thinks it's important to be interested in things. He likes to be curious and to try to understand all sorts of things.
- It is important to her to be independent. She likes to rely on herself.

What is not apparent is when Schwartz's value items would measure peoples' values with respect to agency as we are using the term. Schwartz leaves the definition of the values to the respondents—the descriptions are deliberately vague. For example, the word "freedom" has diverse connotations (as Sen has shown vigorously), and it is not clear how persons who were part of a family and found "freedom of action" in acting as a member of that group would interpret the second question above. In this as in all approaches, further work would be required in order to determine either which aspect(s) of agency the instrument(s) measured, or, how they could be modified to provide accurate agency measures.

Schwartz's Portrait Values Questionnaire in particular presents an interesting methodology and does, it would seem, reflect assessments even among junior respondents (those in Uganda were 13–14 years old). Self-direction is measured as a value, to be rated in comparison with other values. That is, Schwartz's approach evaluates people's assessments of the relative value of self-direction in comparison with other values (benevolence, universalism, power, achievement). The conceptual problem with this aspect of the measure is that

---

[30] See Schwartz et al. (2001), Munene and Schwartz (2000).
[31] Schwartz et al. (2001: 521).

a primary reason to expand agency might be to further these or other valued goals such as health, or security, or a higher standard of living. Also, a change in measures of self-direction would indicate a change in values but might not be policy responsive to changes in empowerment. Furthermore, the definition of self-direction conflates "autonomy" with "independence" which means that the measure would seem to combine assessments of agency as Sen understands them with assessments of the value of individual independence. But whereas agency may be of value across communities, clearly the value of individualism differs between people and between cultures. As we shall see in Self-Determination Theory, autonomy may fruitfully be distinguished from individualism.

World Values Survey

Welzel and Inglehart are two of a number of writers who have used the World Values Survey to study value priorities in societies that are undergoing modernization. Inglehart's central thesis is that "economic, cultural, and political change go together in coherent patterns that are changing the world in predictable ways."[32] He studies the changes in values that accompany material and economic transformations during modernization. Of particular note is the work by Inglehart and Welzel on "liberty aspirations" and how these link to democracy.

The World Values Survey includes 259 questions (wave four) on economic, political, and cultural variables. While the core questions remain constant, the survey has been modified four times, and carried out in four "waves", 1990 (originally conducted by the European Values Survey in 1981), 1995, 2000, and 2005. The WVS has completed representative national surveys of basic values and beliefs in 79 independent countries whose combined populations account for 80 percent of the world's inhabitants. Initially most participating countries were European, but the last two waves of surveys have included developing countries to a much greater extent. This database is an empirical resource for many analyses of values and value changes; its web page states that over 300 publications in 20 languages analyze its data.[33] Certain questions contained in the WVS may themselves be of independent interest for agency studies.

Drawing on Sen's work among others, Welzel and Ingelhart identify the importance of civil and political freedoms to human development. However countering an empirical study by Przeworski and Limongi,[34] Welzel and Inglehart argue that "Economic development does contribute to the

---

[32] 1997: 7.
[33] <http://margaux.grandvinum.se/SebTest/wvs/articles/folder_published/article_base_51> accessed 12 May 2008.
[34] 1997.

emergence of democracy and it does so dramatically." Drawing on their empirical study in Eastern Europe, Welzel and Inglehart argue that the values form an intermediate variable between economic development and democratization. Economic development "reshapes prevailing public preferences"[35] including preferences relating to liberty or freedom. In turn these new "mass priorities provide a source of public pressure that can favor democratization."[36] Welzel and Inglehart then try to measure the intermediate values term.

To measure changes in pro-freedom preferences, Welzel and Inglehart create an index of "mass liberty aspirations" that draws on data from the WVS.[37] The question upon which they draw is below:

There is a lot of talk these days about what the aims of this country should be for the next 10 years. On this card are listed some of the goals which different people would give top priority. Would you please say which one of these you, yourself, consider the most important? And which one would be the next most important?[38]

The respondent is then shown cards with four items on them.

Card 1

1-1 A high level of economic growth

1-2 Making sure this country has strong defense forces

1-3 Seeing that people have more say about how things are done at their jobs and in their communities

1-4 Trying to make our cities and countryside more beautiful

Card 2

2-1 Maintaining order in the nation

2-2 Giving people more say in important government decisions

2-3 Fighting rising prices

2-4 Protecting freedom of speech

The "mass liberty aspirations" index is created from the emboldened entries (1–3, 2–2, and 2–4) in the following way. Each respondent gave a value of "top priority" (=2) "second priority" (=1) or "no priority" (=0) to each of these items. The responses for the selected three items are coded and summed, to make an ordinal index from 0 to 5, with 0 being lowest priority and 5 being the highest. Aggregating these at the national level creates a continuous scale from 0 to 5, of "mass liberty aspirations", which can then be subjected to the various data tests before use.

---

[35] mimeo p. 8.

[36] mimeo p. 7, drawing on Inglehart and Wenzel (2004) Again, p. 12: "Mass liberty aspirations give rise to public pressure for growing freedom—and to public resistance against the curtailment of freedom."

[37] Welzel and Inglehart (2005).

[38] Inglehart (1997: 108).

The mass liberty aspirations by Welzel and Inglehart probes people's agency aspirations with respect to public space. The index was created in order to evaluate how changes in individual aspirations relate to formal democratization processes; implicit in this is the description of political agency as a dimension of well-being. Changes in a woman's agency within the household, or changes in agency derived from an NGO microcredit or savings program, might not be captured very directly by these measures. Similarly, as indeed Inglehart found in other work, responses to terms such as "Freedom of speech" reflect to some extent the individualism or collectivism of the culture. As in the case of Schwartz, it would be desirable for agency measures to be distinct from measures of the value of individualism.

Other questions within the WVS may, upon closer inspection and analysis, also pertain to agency and/or empowerment. The questions raise issues such as perceptions of free choice and control, perceptions of the freedom to make decisions at the workplace, attitudes towards change, and how others perceive the respondent. The extent to which any of these throw light on an agency domain would need careful scrutiny and testing. These are reproduced in Box 1.

Psychological Well-Being

Carol Ryff[39] and colleagues have developed an approach to measuring domains of psychological well-being which complement research on subjective well-being or life satisfaction. Subjective well-being leaves it entirely up to the individual to define their values, thus is relativist and open to adaptive preferences. In contrast, Ryff and other authors such as Ryan in this survey take a normative approach, in which they seek to identify elements that characterize psychological well-being across cultures. First, she identified six domains of well-being by synthesizing domains from three schools of psychology that had developed normative conceptions of psychological well-being.[40] These domains are

1. *Self-acceptance:* having a positive attitude towards oneself and one's past life.
2. *Purpose in life:* having goals and objectives that give life meaning.

---

[39] Carol Ryff is the Director of the Center for Aging at the University of Wisconsin-Madison, and has over forty academic papers on this topic. Hazel Markus, the David-Brack Professor of Psychology at Stanford, has adapted Ryff's domains in her own investigation of how gender, ethnicity, social class, cohort, or region or country of national origin may influence self-concept and self-esteem.

[40] She consulted three theoretical schools. Life-span developmental theories—Erikson's 1959 psycho-social stage model, Buhler's basic life tendencies (Buhler 1935, Bulher and Massarik, 1968), Neugarten (1968, 1973); clinical theories of personal growth—Maslow (1968), Rogers (1961), Jung (1933, von Franz 1964), Allport (1961); and mental health literature—Jahoda (1958).

Box 1 WORLD VALUES SURVEY: SELECTED QUESTIONS

V95 Some people feel they have completely free choice and control over their lives, and other people feel that what they do has no real effect on what happens to them. Please use the scale to indicate how much freedom of choice and control you feel you have over the way your life turns out.

    1   2   3   4   5   6   7   8   9   10
None at all   A great deal

V 117 How free are you to make decisions in your job? Please use this card to indicate how much decision-making freedom you feel you have.

    1   2   3   4   5   6   7   8   9   10
None at all   A great deal

Now I want to ask you some questions about your outlook on life. Each card I show you has two contrasting statements on it. Using the scale listed, could you tell me where you would place your own view? 1 means you agree completely with the statement on the left; 10 means you agree completely with the statement on the right, or you can choose any number in between.

                        1 2 3 4 5 6 7 8 9 10
V 323 A) One should be cautious about making   You will never achieve much unless you
major changes in life   act boldly

                        1 2 3 4 5 6 7 8 9 10
V 324 B) Ideas that have stood the test of time   New ideas are generally better than old
ones are generally best   ones

                        1 2 3 4 5 6 7 8 9 10
V 325 C) When changes occur in my life I worry   When changes occur in my life, I welcome
about the difficulties they may cause   the possibility that something new is beginning

A variety of characteristics are listed here. Could you take a look at them and select those which apply to you?

    V326 A)   I usually count on being successful in everything I do
    V327 B)   I enjoy convincing others of my opinion
    V328 C)   I often notice that I serve as a model for others
    V329 D)   I am good at getting what I want
    V330 E)   I own many things others envy me for
    V331 F)   I like to assume responsibility
    V332 G)   I am rarely unsure about how I should behave
    V333 H)   I often give others advice
    V334   None of the above.

---

3. *Environmental mastery*: **being able to manage complex demands of daily life.**

4. *Personal growth*: having a sense of continued development and self-realization.

5. *Positive relations with others*: possessing caring and trusting ties with others.

6. *Autonomy*: **being able to follow one's own convictions.**

The domains are measured by surveys of variable length (the three forms of surveys have 14, 9, and 3 statements per domain). Respondents are asked to indicate their agreement with each statement along a 6-point scale. The 3-question form is being used for international comparisons, which are underway in 18 language groups.

Expansions of agency freedom might be detected by at least two of Ryff's dimensions. For example, consider the definition of a "high scorer" in two areas (the three questions that appear on the shortest questionnaire are below):

Environmental mastery: "Has a sense of mastery and competence in managing the environment; controls complex array of external activities; makes effective use of surrounding opportunities; able to choose or create contexts suitable to personal needs and values."[41]

1. In general, I feel I am in charge of the situation in which I live.
2. The demands of everyday life often get me down.
3. I am quite good at managing the many responsibilities of my daily life.

Autonomy: "is self-determining and independent; able to resist social pressures to think and act in certain ways; regulates behavior from within; evaluates self by personal standards."[42]

1. I tend to be influenced by people with strong opinions.
2. I have confidence in my opinions, even if they are contrary to the general consensus.
3. I judge myself by what I think is important, not by the values of what others think is important.

Ryff and colleagues use this work in hierarchical regression analyses with different age cohorts to ascertain how people's conceptions of well-being change with age.[43] They also track which aspects of their well-being people cultivate at different stages of life.[44] For example, Ryff and Heidrick (1997) study whether different normative and non-normative life events "were significant predictors of multiple aspects of present and future wellness" among different age cohorts. Thus their measures are sensitive to change over time, although it is not known whether they are sufficiently sensitive to be used as policy instruments.

Ryff's work has been criticized for cultural bias, arising from the cultural surroundings and presuppositions of her source authors (the synthesis domains did not temper the cultural values and assumptions of the original authors).[45] Certainly the questions would require adaptation for cross-cultural

---

[41] Ryff (1989b: 1072).   [42] Ibid.
[43] For example, Ryff (1989c).   [44] Ryff (1991).
[45] Christopher (1999): 146–7 details criticisms of each subscale.

comparability. The concepts are also distinct: "Self-mastery" measures control, and "autonomy" measures independence rather than valued agency. The survey also is problematic, as signaled above, because people's agency may be quite variable in different domains and it is precisely these differences that may be of interest, yet a global response will mask such differences. Consider the question, "In general, I feel I am in charge of the situation in which I live." In order to choose a number, a woman who answers this question may need to balance, fleetingly, her home life and relation to her husband and in-laws, her political life, and outlets of local or national political expression, her women's cooperative, and the women's willingness to lend her personal or material support in times of need. She may answer this question with relation to one of these domains—the one that popped into mind. Or she may try to give an aggregate of her different domain-specific agencies (medium low at home; low politically, but very high with reference to the women's group, so on balance, four out of six). What might be of interest for many purposes would be to disaggregate this, and ascertain agency or empowerment changes with respect to certain dimensions. For this reason, we turn to Self-Efficacy Scales, and Self-Determination Theory, as each of these do so, albeit in different ways.

Multidomain Agency Measures

This section introduces two further approaches to measuring human agency, which comprise perhaps the most appropriate avenues for further exploration. These measures can be used with respect to different domains or dimensions of well-being (work, health, education, political participation, gender relations, etc.), some of which might be quite narrow, and others of which might track broader shifts.

Self-Efficacy

The first significant empirical approach is the self-efficacy approach initiated by Albert Bandura.[46] Bandura sometimes refers to this approach as a "theory of human agency" and also discusses it using the language of capabilities and of empowerment:

Converging lines of evidence reveal that personal and social change rely extensively on methods of empowerment.[47] These approaches achieve their effects by equipping people with the requisite knowledge, skills, and resilient self-beliefs of efficacy to alter aspects of their lives over which they can exercise some control. Studies of various

---

[46] Bandura's and related work has been collected in Bandura (1997). See also Bandura (1977, 1986, 1988, 1989, 1991, 1995, 2000, 2001a, 2001b, 2002a, and 2002b).

[47] Bandura (1988); Rappaport and Hess (1984); Ratcliff (1984); Silbert (1984).

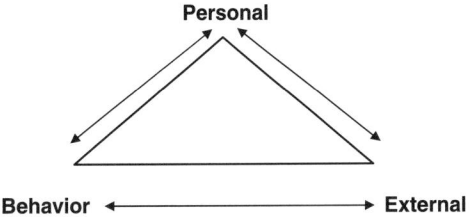

Figure 10.1. Determinants in reciprocal causation

aspects of personal change indicate that methods of empowerment operate through the self-efficacy mechanism.[48] However, the mode of operation and the generality of this mediating mechanism require further verification.[49]

The self-efficacy theory holds that empowerment or human agency has internal as well as external determinants: if people perceive themselves to be more capable of accomplishing certain activities, they are more likely to undertake them. "Because judgments and actions are partly self-determined, people can effect change in themselves and their situations through their own efforts."[50] Of course people's efficacy is limited by the external environment, as well as by their own behaviors. Bandura sketches "three major classes of determinants in triadic reciprocal causation. B represents behaviour; P the internal personal factors in the form of cognitive, affective, and biological events; and E the external environment" (Figure 10.1).[51]

A key question is how people can causally contribute to their own motivation to act—how they can increase their agency or freedom? Note that "Freedom is not conceived negatively as the absence of external coercion or constraints. Rather, it is defined positively in terms of the exercise of self-influence."[52] Some might learn new information, skills or behaviors; but some contributors are internal and personal—they relate to P.

The self-efficacy approach argues that people's perceived self-efficacy comprises a key determinant of people's motivation, their level of effort, and their perseverance in a task. Perceived self-efficacy is a "judgment of capability"[53] in that it concerns "people's beliefs in their capabilities to exercise control over their own functioning and over events that affect their lives."[54] A second way in which people exercise personal agency is through goal representations and the capacity of forethought. "People anticipate the likely consequences of their prospective actions, they set goals for themselves, and they plan courses

[48] Bandura (1986).　　　　　　　　　[49] Ozer and Bandura (1990), opening paragraph.
[50] Bandura (1989: 1175).　　　　　　[51] Ibid. (1997: 6). See also Bandura (1986).
[52] Ibid. (1989: 1182).　　　　　　　　　　　[53] Ibid. (2001a: 1).
[54] Bandura (1994) gives four different titles to ways by which people increase their perceived self-efficacy: by having successful "mastery experiences", by the vicarious experiences provided by social models, by social persuasion, and by learning to manage negative stress responses (pp. 72–4).

of action likely to produce desired outcomes."[55] Anticipated outcomes form a third agency mechanism related to people's "ability to envision the likely outcomes of prospective actions."[56] "People's perceptions of their efficacy influence the types of anticipatory scenarios they construct and reiterate."[57] People with strong self-efficacy beliefs imagine positive outcomes more easily. Finally, people's self-efficacy beliefs, their goal representations, and their anticipated outcomes are also modulated by feedback mechanisms. Yet to sustain motivation, self-efficacy beliefs must not only learn from failure; they must also be positive enough to override some negative feedback. Failures are natural, yet optimistic humans can improve and accomplish tasks they failed in earlier: "Forethought often saves us from the perils of a foreshortened perspective,"[58] writes Bandura, citing the persistence, in the face of rejection and failure, exhibited by Gertrude Stein, James Joyce, Van Gogh, Rodin, Stravinsky, Frank Lloyd Wright, and the Beatles (whose recording contract Decca Records turned them down with the remark: "We don't like their sound. Groups of guitars are on their way out"[59]).

Empirically, measures are constructed of people's perceived self-efficacy, which "is concerned with people's belief in their capabilities to mobilise the motivation, cognitive resources, and courses of action needed to exercise control over given events."[60] Bandura and colleagues have used these measures with respect to cognitive functioning, health functioning, clinical (psychological) functioning, athletic functioning, organizational functioning, and collective efficacy.[61]

Perceived self-efficacy is measured by constructing scales, with 5–20 items each.[62] The scale is the simple average of responses. The items in each scale each refer to efficacy with respect only to one domain, because this approach argues that perceived self-efficacy "is not a global trait but a differentiated set of beliefs linked to distinct realms of functioning. Multi-domain measures reveal the patterning and degree of generality of people's sense of personal efficacy."[63] The measures are intended to isolate self-efficacy from related but distinct topics such as self-esteem, locus of control, and outcome expectancies.

Respondents are asked to rate the strength of their perceived efficacy, or their perceived capability to execute a certain activity. The scale ranged from complete uncertainty (0) to complete certitude (10)—or sometimes (5). Respondents may "practice" using the scale with a simple question (such as, "can you lift an object weighing x pounds") before completing the questionnaire. Normally self-efficacy scales would only be one set of variables collected in a study.

---

[55] Ibid. (1989: 1179).   [56] Ibid. 1180.   [57] Ibid. 1176.
[58] Ibid. 1181.   [59] Ibid. 1177 citing White (1982).   [60] Ozer and Bandura (1990: 472).
[61] Bandura (1997).   [62] Bandura (2001a).   [63] Ibid. 307.

The scales are designed to be sensitive to variations in the generality, strength, and level of self-efficacy, and to track changes in quite short intervening periods. For example, Ozer and Bandura (1990) developed three scales, which were administered at four points in time, each being five weeks apart. Between the second and third administration, participants (who were women) received a 22.5-hour class in self-defense training. The efficacy scales were used to study changes in perceived self-efficacy with respect to self-defense, as well as changes in wider forms of self-efficacy with respect to interpersonal relationships and leisure activities. In this example self-defense, interpersonal relationships, and leisure activities are the "domains" with respect to which perceived self-efficacy is measured.

In addition to measuring individual self-efficacy, two kinds of measures can be constructed to represent "perceived collective efficacy." Perceived collective efficacy is defined as "a group's shared belief in its conjoint capabilities to organise and execute the courses of action required to produce given levels of attainments."[64] The social-cognitive theory Bandura uses distinguishes between personal agency, and proxy, and collective forms of agency. Similar questions enable individuals to rank each kind of "efficacy" on scales from 1 to 5. In addition to the perceived personal efficacy introduced above (handling activities in family, in partnership, at work, managing personal finances and health), questions address proxy or individual social efficacy (perceived capabilities to contribute individually to improvements in social problems, or to functions they perform in a group) and collective social efficacy (capabilities of society or a group operating as a whole to effect desired improvements—e.g. in unemployment, corruption, criminal and drug activities, economic crises, and terrorism).[65] While Bandura's own interest focuses on the way that individuals' efficacy beliefs can be cultivated in order to increase efficacy itself, the measures may also be of interest to those whose primary variables are external to the person or community.

Self-efficacy scales have been criticized for not being able to distinguish between activities that agents undertake because they pertain to the agent's conception of the good, and "the activities they feel coerced or seduced into doing."[66] This distinction would be important for a measure that adequately represented Sen's concept of human agency. Critics have also observed that a positive measure of self-efficacy might reflect greater functional skills and competence rather than only, or even mainly, agency freedom. This could make the self-efficacy measures of interest for measuring some aspects of empowerment, but less accurate as a pure agency measure.

---

[64] Bandura (1997: 477). Political efficacy is, he argues, a subset of collective efficacy (pp. 482–504). See also Bandura (1995, 2000, 2001a, 2002b).

[65] Fernandez-Ballesteros and Diez-Nicolas Bandura (2002). See Bandura (2001a).

[66] Deci and Ryan (2000: 257).

Others have explored whether Bandura's claim to the universality of self-efficacy scales across cultures is empirically validated, or whether self-efficacy reflects a more "Western" mental construct. In a careful survey of twenty such studies, Klassen found that "it is clear... that efficacy beliefs operate differently in non-Western countries than they do in Western cultures."[67] He found that efficacy scales were lower in collectivist cultures (who achieved high levels of performance while holding more realistic efficacy beliefs) than in individualist cultures, but also that they were a good predictor of performance across countries. It may be that collective efficacy scales should replace self-efficacy in some cultural settings.

The self and collective efficacy scales are potentially interesting for the purposes of describing subjective perceptions of efficacy, which are clearly a contributing factor to human agency, and one which is not captured by measures of external barriers. Bandura views self-efficacy as an instrumental intervening variable, one of multiple determinants of human motivation, and thus one explanatory factor for empowerment or disempowerment. Self-efficacy scales are relatively straightforward, and potentially policy-responsive. Their comparability across cultures has raised interesting issues, although they have not been used with poor or illiterate populations. While the scales might potentially track important attitudinal shifts, they would not provide information on external barriers to empowerment—and these are the main barriers which are of interest to other disciplines. Also, the scales would not reflect a key aspect of agency, namely the degree to which the "efficacious" activity was valued by the respondent.

Self-Determination Theory

The Self-Determination Theory (SDT) of Ryan and Deci and colleagues arises out of a school of psychologists who understand human beings to have a few "basic developmental propensities and psychological needs, supports for which are essential to well-being."[68] On the basis of empirical study Self-Determination Theory identified the three basic psychological needs that, its authors argue, are prerequisites to well-being that pertain across cultures: autonomy, competence, and relatedness.[69] These needs are "innate psychological nutriments that are essential for ongoing psychological growth, integrity, and well-being."[70]

SDT describes autonomy—the variable of interest to this chapter—in the following way:

---

[67] 2004: 224. See Bandura (2002b).
[69] Ryan and Deci (2000).

[68] Chirkov et al. (2003: 97).
[70] Deci and Ryan (2000: 229).

a person is autonomous when his or her behaviour is experienced as willingly enacted and when he or she fully endorses the actions in which he or she is engaged and/or the values expressed by them. People are therefore most autonomous when they act in accord with their authentic interests or integrated values and desires. (Deci and Ryan, 1985, 2000; Ryan et al. 1995)[71]

SDT contrasts autonomy with its (presumed) opposite, heteronomy, "in which one's actions are experienced as controlled by forces that are phenomenally alien to the self, or that compel one to behave in specific ways regardless of one's values or interests."[72]

As is immediately apparent, this definition is the closest to Sen's concept of agency, because it focuses on capabilities that the person values (in contract to self-efficacy, which identifies capabilities a person understands herself to have—whether or not she values them).

The attention within SDT to autonomy, which Deci and Ryan describe as "the experience of integration and freedom, and... an essential aspect of healthy human functioning"[73] generated a vigorous empirical debate within the field. Some argued and attempted to demonstrate empirically that autonomy is not universally valued, but is rather valued by, and useful in, more individualist cultures and societies alone. In a powerful rebuttal to this attack, Chirkov et al. distinguished autonomy—conceptually as well as empirically— from several related concepts: dependence/independence, individualism/collectivism, and vertical/horizontal.[74]

It is worthwhile to note their distinction between dependence and independence. Of particular interest, given the other measures surveyed, is the possibility that a person could be autonomously dependent. The basic terms are defined as follows:

SDT defines dependence as reliance on others for guidance, support, or needed supplies (Ryan and Lynch, 1989). Within SDT, the opposite of dependence is not autonomy but rather independence, the circumstance of not relying on others for support, help, or supplies.

Thus SDT argues that a person can be autonomously dependent or autonomously independent—that these categories are orthogonal to one another. An autonomous person might, for example, welcome others' influence and be responsive to good advice—or she might be inclined to resist any external influences. Similarly, they argue that an autonomous person may be more individualist (ascribing "relative priority... to the individual's goals and preferences"[75]), or more collectivist (priority placed on the needs, norms, and goals of one's group or collective"[76]). Finally, they argue that individualism

---

[71] Chirkov et al. (2003: 98).   [72] Ibid.   [73] Deci and Ryan (2000: 231).
[74] Following Triandis (1995). See also Oyserman et al. (2002), who does not mention SDT however.
[75] Chirkov et al. (2003: 98–9).
[76] Ibid. 99.

and collectivism can be fruitfully distinguished from horizontal and vertical aspects of culture, where these refer to "practices and norms supporting equality or interchangeability among people versus hierarchical or subordinate social relations."[77]

What threatens autonomy is not verticalism, not individualism, and not dependence, but rather coercion. For example, a person could be acting within rules set by a parent, or by social norms, or by law, and doing so autonomously because the person internally endorsed those rules. Alternatively, one could be acting in the same way but feeling utterly coerced and oppressed by the parent, the norms, or the law. In the first instance, autonomy—and indeed agency—is not compromised; in the second it is.

In order to test whether autonomy was empirically distinguishable from dependence/independence and from individualism/collectivism—and that autonomy was valued in collectivist cultures—Chirkov et al. tested a cross-culturally valid methodology for measuring autonomy.[78] To determine autonomy, the study first asked respondents whether they engaged in certain practices (for the purposes of the study these practices distinguished individualist vs. collectivist and vertical vs. horizontal orientations, but other practices might be chosen).[79] Respondents then were asked to rate, from 1 to 5, four possible reasons why they felt, or believed, or engaged in the practice (1 = not at all because of this reason; 5 = completely because of this reason). The possible reasons ranged from less autonomous (1) to more autonomous (4) and were as follows:

1. **External regulation**: Because of external pressures (to get rewards or avoid punishments). I would engage in this behavior because someone insists on my doing this, or I expect to get some kind of reward, or avoid some punishment for behaving this way.
2. **Introjected regulation**: To get approval or avoid guilt. I would engage in this behavior because people around me would approve of me for doing so, or because I think I should do it. If I didn't do this I might feel guilty, ashamed, or anxious.
3. **Identified regulation**: Because it is important. I would engage in this behavior because I personally believe that it is important and worthwhile to behave this way.
4. **Integrated regulation**: Because I have thoughtfully considered and fully chosen this. I have thought about this behavior and fully considered

---

[77] Chirkov et al. (2003: 99)

[78] Chirkov et al. (2003) explicitly tested for "measurement invariance and latent construct comparability" using the Means and Covariance Structure Analysis (MACS) of Little (1997 and 2000), and this methodology may be of independent interest for subjective quantitative measures of agency.

[79] This follows the Self-Regulatory Questionnaire of Cultural Practices, based on Ryan and Connell (1989), Vallerand (1997), and Sheldon and Houser-Marko (2001).

alternatives. It makes good sense to me to act this way. I feel free in choosing and doing it.[80]

Testing autonomy thus defined across four countries (Turkey, Russia, the US, and Korea) produced a series of interesting findings that broadly supported the SDT claims, and established that autonomy can be distinguished from individualism,[81] as well as from horizontal vs. vertical outlooks, and that autonomy is correlated with well-being for persons in individualist as well as collectivist cultures.[82]

The SDT approach to measuring autonomy is of considerable interest for several reasons. First, previous empirical studies have apparently been able to use variants of this instrument to discern changes in autonomy, so the instrument has the potential of being sensitive to policy changes. Second, the concept of autonomy is carefully distinguished, and empirically distinguishable from, individualism and independence, and thus potentially relevant across cultures and societies much in the same way that Sen understands agency to be relevant across cultures. Third, the self-regulation scales can be adapted to measure autonomy with respect to different practices or to different dimensions of well-being. Indeed the SDT psychologists have developed separate questionnaires for autonomy related to education (from elementary age and above, including persons with learning disorders), health-related behaviors, religion, pro-social behaviors, friendship, and exercise. Agency can be differently exhibited in different spheres—within the household, in gender relations, in health practices, in political domains. The SDT autonomy tool could, conceivably, be used to map agency in different domains. Fourth, the tool is relatively brief, which improves feasibility and reduces costs. Fifth, the MACS technique provides ways to test the comparability of the constructs across cultures, thus improving the potential robustness of the tool. While each of the measures surveyed in this article challenges the view that agency freedoms are intangible, the effort to distinguish agency from individualism and independence makes SDT a particularly rich vein of work (see Table 10.1).

Conclusion

The overall thrust of Sen's Dewey lectures was to argue that greater information should be brought to bear in the assessment of states and actions, including

---

[80] Chirkov et al. (2003: 102). These four are explained at greater length in Deci and Ryan (2000).

[81] See Oyserman et al. (2002), whose in-depth review of empirical psychological studies of individualism and collectivism between European Americans and non-Americans or African/Latino/Asian Americans, found that "these differences were neither as large nor as systematic as often perceived."

[82] Chirkov et al. (2003).

information on agency. This chapter has addressed one of the pedantic difficulties of doing so, namely the methods by which information on agency freedom might be gathered directly. Admittedly, the magpie approach of venturing into other disciplinary gardens to collect glittering measurement objects with but passing regard for their setting and significance can seem hasty or ill-advised, and certainly intrusive. It is hoped, however, that explorations such as this will encourage interactions between those working in these areas, or perhaps the sharing of sturdy cuttings in place of flimsy tinsel.

Bibliography

Alkire, S.: 2002a, *Valuing Freedoms: Sen's Capability Approach and Poverty Reduction* (Oxford University Press: Oxford).

—— 2002b, "Dimensions of human development", *World Development* 30, pp. 181–205.

—— 2005, "Subjective quantitative studies of human agency", *Social Indicators Research*, 74(1), pp. 217–60.

—— 2007, "Measuring freedoms alongside well-being", in I. Gough and J. A. McGregor (eds) *Well-Being in Developing Countries: New Approaches and Research Strategies* (Cambridge: Cambridge University Press).

—— 2008, "Concepts and measures of agency", ch. 24 in K. Basu and R. Kanbur (eds), *Arguments for a Better World: Essays in Honor of Amartya Sen. Vol. I: Ethics, Welfare, and Measurement* (Oxford: Oxford University Press).

Alsop, R., M. Bertelsen, and J. Holland: 2006, *Empowerment in Practice From Analysis to Implementation* (Washington, DC: World Bank).

—— and N. Heinsohn: 2005, "Measuring empowerment in practice: Structuring analysis and framing indicators", in Policy Research Working Paper (Washington, DC: World Bank).

Argyle, M. and M. Martin: 1991, "The psychological causes of happiness", in M. Argyle, F. Strack, and N. Schwartz (eds), *Subjective Well-Being* (New York: Pergamon Press).

—— F. Strack, and N. Schwartz (eds): 1991, *Subjective Well-Being: An Interdisciplinary Perspective* (Oxford: Pergamon Press).

Bamberger, M. (ed.): 2000, *Integrating Quantitative and Qualitative Research in Development Projects* (Washington DC: World Bank).

Bandura, A.: 1977, "Self-efficacy: Toward a unifying theory of behavioral change", *Psychological Review* 84(2), pp. 191–215.

—— 1986, *Social Foundations of Thought and Action: A Social Cognitive Theory* (Englewood Cliffs, NJ: Prentice Hall).

—— 1988, "Perceived self-efficacy: Exercise of control through self-belief", in J. P. Dauwalder, M. Perez, and V. Hobi (eds), *Annual Series of European Research in Behavior Therapy* (Lisse, The Netherlands: Swets & Zeitlinger) Vol. 2, pp. 27–59.

—— 1989, "Human agency in social cognitive theory", *American Psychologist*, 44(9) pp. 1175–84.

—— 1991, "Human agency: The rhetoric and the reality", *American Psychologist*, 46(2) pp. 157–62.

—— 1994, "Self-efficacy", in V. S. Ramachandran (ed.), *Encyclopedia of Human Behavior* (San Diego, CA: Academic Press) Vol. 4, pp. 72–81.

—— (ed.): 1995, *Self-Efficacy in Changing Societies* (New York: Cambridge University Press).

—— 1997, *Self-efficacy: The Exercise of Control* (New York: Freeman).

—— 1998, "Exercises of agency in personal and social change", in E. Sanavio (ed.), *Behavior and Cognitive Therapy Today* (Oxford: Elsevier), pp. 1–29.

—— 2000, "Exercise of human agency through collective efficacy", *Current Directions in Psychological Science* 9(3), pp. 75–8.

—— 2001a, "Guide for Constructing Self-Efficacy Scales", in F. Pajares and T. C. Urdan (eds), *Self-Efficacy Beliefs of Adolescents* (Greenwich, CT: Information Age Publishing), pp. 307–37.

—— 2001b, "Social cognitive theory: An agentic perspective", *Annual Review of Psychology* 52, pp. 1–26.

—— 2002a, "Growing primacy of human agency in adaptation and change in the electronic era", *European Psychologist* 7(1), pp. 1–16.

—— 2002b, "Social cognitive theory in cultural context", *Journal of Applied Psychology: An International Review* 51(2), pp. 269–90.

Biswas-Diener, R. and E. Diener (eds): 2001, "Making the best of a bad situation: Satisfaction in the slums of Calcutta", *Social Indicators Research* 55(3), pp. 329–52.

Carvalho, S. and H. White: 1998, "Combining the quantitative and qualitative approaches to poverty measurement and analysis", World Bank Technical Paper 366.

Chirkov, V. I., R. M. Ryan, Y. Kim, and U. Kaplan: 2003, "Differentiating autonomy from individualism and independence: A self-determination theory perspective on internalization of cultural orientations and well-being", *Journal of Personality and Social Psychology* 84(1), pp. 97–110.

Christopher, J. C.: 1999, "Situating psychological well-being exploring the cultural roots of its theory and research", *Journal of Counseling & Development* 77, pp. 141–52.

—— 2001, "Culture and psychotherapy: Toward a hermeneutic approach", *Psychotherapy* 38(2), pp. 115–28.

Christopher, S., J. C. Christopher, and T. Dunnagan: 2000, "Culture's impact on health risk appraisal psychological well-being questions", *American Journal of Health Behavior* 24(5), pp. 338–48.

Cummins, R. A.: 1996, "The domains of life satisfaction: An attempt to order chaos", *Social Indicators Research* 38(3), pp. 303–28.

—— 1997, "The Comprehensive Quality of Life Scale—Adult", 5th edn, ComQol-A5, Manual, (Melbourne: School of Psychology, Deakin University).

—— 2000a, "Personal income and subjective well-being: A review", *Journal of Happiness Studies* 1(2), pp. 133–58.

—— 2000b, "Objective and subjective quality of life: An interactive model", *Social Indicators Research* 52(1), pp. 55–72.

—— 2002, "Proxy responding for subjective well-being: A review", *International Review of Research in Mental Retardation* 25, pp. 183–207.

—— 2003, "Normative life satisfaction: Measurement issues and a homeostatic model", *Social Indicators Research* 64(2), pp. 225–56.

Deci, E. L. and R. M. Ryan: 1985, *Intrinsic Motivation and Self-Determination in Human Behavior* (New York: Plenum Press).

Deci, E. L. and R. M. Ryan: 1987, "The support of autonomy and the control of behaviour", *Journal of Personality and Social Psychology* 53(6), pp. 1015–23.

—— —— 1995, "Human autonomy: The basis for true self-esteem", in M. Kemis (ed.), *Efficacy, Agency, and Self-Esteem* (New York: Plenum), pp. 31–49.

—— —— 2000, "The 'What' and 'Why' of goal pursuits: Human needs and the self-determination of behaviour", *Psychological Inquiry* 11(4), pp. 227–68.

Diener, E.: 1995a, "Subjective well-being in cross-cultural perspective", in H. Grad, A. Blanco, and J. Georgas (eds), *Proceedings of the 12th International Congress of Cross-Cultural Psychology* (Lisse, The Netherlands: Swets & Zeitlinger).

—— 1995b, "A value-based index for measuring national quality of life", *Social Indicators Research* 36(2), pp. 107–27.

—— and E. Suh (eds): 2000, *Culture and Subjective Well-Being* (Cambridge, Mass.: MIT Press).

—— —— R. E. Lucas, and H. L. Smith: 1999, "Subjective well-being: Three decades of progress", *Psychological Bulletin* 125(2), pp. 276–302.

Drèze, Jean, and Amartya Kumar Sen: 1989, *Hunger and Public Action* (Oxford: Clarendon Press).

—— —— 2002, *India, Development, and Participation* (New Delhi and New York: Oxford University Press).

Fernandez-Ballesteros, R. and J. A. Diez-Nicolas Bandura: 2002, "Determinants and structural relation of personal efficacy to collective efficacy", *Journal of Psychology: An International Review* 51(1), pp. 107–25.

Frey, B.: 1997, *Not Just for Money: An Economic Theory of Personal Motivation* (Aldershot: Edward Elgar Publishing).

Gore, C.: 1997, "Irreducibly social goods and the informational basis of Amartya Sen's capability approach", *Journal of International Development* 9(2), pp. 235–50.

Grisez, G., J. Boyle, and J. Finnis: 1987, "Practical principles, moral truth and ultimate ends", *American Journal of Jurisprudence* 32, pp. 99–151.

Ibrahim, S. and S. Alkire: 2007, "Agency and empowerment: a proposal for internationally comparable indicators", *Oxford Development Studies* 35(4), pp. 379–403.

Inglehart, R.: 1997, *Modernization and Postmodernization: Cultural, Economic, and Political Change in 43 Societies* (Princeton: Princeton University Press).

—— 2000, "Globalization and postmodern values", *The Washington Quarterly* 23(1), pp. 215–28.

—— and W. E. Baker.: 2000, "Modernization, cultural change, and the persistence of traditional values", *American Sociological Review* 65(1), pp. 19–51.

—— and C. Welzel: 2005, *Modernization, Cultural Change and Democracy: The Human Development Sequence* (Cambridge: Cambridge University Press).

Kabeer, N.: 1999, "Resources, agency, achievements: Reflections on the measurement of women's empowerment", *Development and Change* 30(3), pp. 435–64.

Kahneman, D.: 1999, "Objective happiness", in D. Kahneman, E. Diener, and N. Schwartz (eds.), *Well-Being: The Foundations of Hedonic Psychology* (New York: Russell Sage Foundation), pp. 3–25.

—— 2002, "Maps of bounded rationality: A perspective on intuitive judgement and choice", Nobel Prize Lecture, <http://nobelprize.org/economics/laureates/2002/kahnemann-lecture.pdf>.

Kanbur, R. (ed.): 2003, *Q-Squared: Qualitative and Quantitative Methods of Poverty Appraisal* (Delhi: Permanent Black).

Klassen, R. M.: 2004, "Optimism and realism: A review of self-efficacy from a cross-cultural perspective", *Journal of Psychology* 39(3), pp. 205–30.

Little, T. D.: 1997, "Mean and covariance structure (MACS) analysis of cross-cultural data: Practical and theoretical issues", *Multivariate Behavioral Research* 32(1), pp. 53–76.

—— 2000, "On the comparability of constructs in cross-cultural research: A critique of Cheung and Rensvold", *Journal of Cross-Cultural Psychology* 31(2), pp. 213–19.

Malhotra, A., S. Schuler, and C. Boender: 2002, *Measuring Women's Empowerment as a Variable in International Development Draft* (Washington, DC: The World Bank, PRMGE).

Munene, J. C., and S. H. Schwartz: 2000, *Cultural Values and Development in Uganda* (Amsterdam, The Netherlands: Royal Tropical Institute).

—— —— G. Kibanja, and J. Kikooma: 2005, *Escaping From Behavioural Poverty in Uganda: The Role of Culture and Social Capital* (Kampala, Uganda: Fountain Publishers).

Narayan, D. (ed.): 2002, *Empowerment and Poverty Reduction: A Sourcebook* (Washington, DC: The World Bank, PREM).

—— R. Chambers, M. K. Shah, and P. Petesch: 2000, *Voices of the Poor: Crying Out for Change* (New York: Oxford University Press for the World Bank).

Narayan-Parker, D., 2005, *Measuring Empowerment: Cross-Disciplinary Perspectives* (Washington, DC: World Bank).

Nussbaum, M. C.: 2000, *Women and Human Development: The Capabilities Approach* (Cambridge: Cambridge University Press).

Oyserman, D., H. Coon, and M. Kemmelmeier: 2002, "Rethinking individualism and collectivism: Evaluation of theoretical assumptions and meta-analyses", *Psychological Bulletin* 128(1), pp. 3–72.

Ozer, E. and A. Bandura: 1990, "Mechanisms governing empowerment effects: A self-efficacy analysis", *Journal of Personality and Social Psychology* 58(3), pp. 472–86.

Pattanaik, P.: 1998, *Cultural Indicators of Well-Being: Some Conceptual Issues* (Paris: UNESCO Publishing), pp. 333–9.

—— and Y. Xu: 1998, "On preference and freedom", *Theory and Decision* 44(2), pp. 173–99.

Przeworski, A. and F. Limongi: 1997, "Modernization: Theories and Facts," *World Politics* 49(2), pp. 155–83.

Rappaport, J. C. and S. R. Hess (eds): 1984, *Studies in Empowerment: Steps Toward Understanding and Action* (New York: Haworth).

Ratcliff, R. E. (ed.): 1984, *Research in Social Movements, Conflicts and Change*, Vol. 6. (Greenwich, CT: JAI Press).

Rosenbaum, E. F.: 2000, "On measuring freedom", *Journal of Theoretical Politics* 12(2), pp. 205–27.

Ryan, R. M., V. I. Chirkov, T. D. Little, K. M. Sheldon, E. Timoshina, and E. L. Deci: 1999, "The American dream in Russia: Extrinsic aspirations and well-being in two cultures", *Personality and Social Psychology Bulletin* 25(12), pp. 1509–24.

—— and J. P. Connell: 1989, "Perceived locus of causality and internalization", *Journal of Personality and Social Psychology* 57(5), pp. 749–61.

Ryan, R. M. and E. L. Deci: 2000, "Self-Determination Theory and the facilitation of intrinsic motivation, social development, and well-being", *American Psychologist* 55(1), pp. 68–78.

—— —— 2001, "On happiness and human potentials: A review of research on hedonic and eudaimonic well-being", *Annual Review of Psychology* 52, pp. 141–66.

—— E. L. Deci, and W. S. Grolnick: 1995, "Autonomy, relatedness, and the self: Their relation to development and psychopathology", in D. J. Cicchetti Cohen (ed.), *Developmental Psychopathology: Theory and Methods* (New York: Wiley), pp. 618–55.

—— J. Kuhl, and E. L. Deci: 1997, "Nature and autonomy: Organizational view of social and neurobiological aspects of self regulation in behavior and development", *Development and Psychopathology* 9(4), pp. 701–28.

—— and J. Lynch: 1989, "Emotional autonomy versus detachment: Revisiting the vicissitudes of adolescence and young adulthood", *Child Development* 60(2), 340–56.

Ryff, C. D.: 1989a, "Beyond Ponce de Leon and life satisfaction: New directions in quest of successful ageing", *International Journal of Behavioral Development* 12(1), pp. 35–55.

—— 1989b, "Happiness is everything, or is it? Explorations on the meaning of psychological well-being", *Journal of Personality and Social Psychology* 57(6), pp. 1069–81.

—— 1989c, "In the eye of the beholder: Views of psychological well-being among middle-aged and older adults", *Psychological Aging* 4(2), pp. 195–210.

—— 1991, "Possible selves in adulthood and old age: A tale of shifting horizons", *Psychological Aging* 6(2), pp. 286–95.

—— and S. M. Heidrick: 1997, "Experience and well-being: Explorations on domains of life and how they matter", *International Journal of Behavioral Development* 20(2), pp. 193–206.

—— and C. L. M. Keyes: 1995, "The structure of psychological well-being revisited", *Journal of Personality and Social Psychology* 69(4), pp. 719–27.

Sagiv, L. and S. H. Schwartz: 2000, "Value priorities and subjective well-being: Direct relations and congruity effects", *European Journal of Social Psychology* 30(2), pp. 177–98.

Schmutte, P. S. and C. D. Ryff: 1997, "Personality and well-being: Reexamining methods and meanings", *Journal of Personality and Social Psychology* 73(3), pp. 549–59.

Schulz, W.: 2000 "Explaining quality of life—The controversy between objective and subjective variables", EUReporting Working Paper No.10.

Schwartz, S. H.: 1992, "Universals in the content and structure of values: Theoretical advances and empirical tests in 20 countries", *Advances in Experimental Social Psychology* 25, pp. 1–65.

—— 1994, "Are there universal aspects in the structure and contents of human values?", *Journal of Social Issues* 50(4), pp. 19–45.

—— and W. Bilsky: 1987, "Toward a universal psychological structure of human values", *Journal of Personality and Social Psychology* 53(3), pp. 550–62.

—— —— 1990, "Toward a theory of the universal content and structure of values: Extensions and cross-cultural replications", *Journal of Personality and Social Psychology* 58(5), pp. 878–91.

—— G. Melech, A. Lehmann, S. Burgess, M. Harris, and V. Owens: 2001, "Extending the cross-cultural validity of the theory of basic human values with a different method of measurement", *Journal of Cross-Cultural Psychology* 32(5), pp. 519–42.

Sen, A. K.: 1979, "Informational analysis of moral principles", in Ross Harrison (ed.), *Rational Action* (Cambridge: Cambridge University Press), pp. 115–32.

—— 1985, "Well-being agency and freedom: The Dewey Lectures 1984", *Journal of Philosophy* 82(4), pp. 169–221.

—— 1999a, *Development As Freedom* (New York: Knopf Press).

—— 1999b, "Democracy as a universal value", *Journal of Democracy* 10(3), pp. 3–17.

—— 2002, *Rationality and Freedom* (Cambridge, Mass.: Belknap Press).

Sheldon, K. M. and L. Houser-Marko: 2001, "Self-concordance, goal-attainment, and the pursuit of happiness: Can there be an upward spiral?", *Journal of Personality and Social Psychology* 80(1), pp. 152–65.

Silbert, M. H.: (1984), "Delancy Street Foundation–Process of mutual restitution", in E. Riessman (ed.), *Community Psychology Series* (New York: Human Sciences Press) Vol. 10, pp. 41–52.

Smith, F. and S. Deneulin: 2002, "Amartya Sen's contribution to development thinking", *Studies in Comparative International Development* 37(2), pp. 61–70.

Smith, P. B. and M. H. Bond: 1993, *Social Psychology Across Cultures: Analysis and Perspectives* (Hemel Hempstead: Harvester Wheatsheaf).

Suh, E. M.: 2002, "Culture, identity consistency, and subjective well-being", *Journal of Personality and Social Psychology* 83(6), pp. 1378–91.

—— E. Diener, S. Oishi, and H. Triandis: 1998, "The shifting basis of life satisfaction judgements across cultures: Emotions versus norms", *Journal of Personality and Social Psychology* 74(2), pp. 482–93.

Suzumura, K.: 1999, "Consequences, opportunities, and procedures", *Social Choice and Welfare* 16(1), pp. 17–40.

Taillefer, M. C., G. Dupuis, M. A. Roberge, and S. Le May: 2003, "Health-related quality of life models: Systematic review of the literature", *Social Indicators Research* 64(2), pp. 293–323.

Tashakkeri, A. and C. Teddlie: 1998, *Mixed Methodologies: Combining Qualitative and Quantitative Approaches* (London: Sage Publications).

Triandis, H. C.: 1995, *Individualism and Collectivism* (Boulder, CO: Westview Press).

Vallerand, R. J.: 1997, "Toward a hierarchical model of intrinsic and extrinsic motivation", in M. P. Zanna (ed.), *Advances in Experimental Social Psychology* (New York: Academic Press), pp. 271–360.

Van de Vijver, F. J. R. and K. Leung: 2000, "Methodological issues in psychological research on culture", *Journal of Cross-Cultural Psychology* 31(1), pp. 33–51.

Welzel, D and R. Inglehart: 2005, "Liberalism, postmaterialism and the growth of freedom: The human development perspective", *International Review of Sociology* 15(1), pp. 81–108.

—— —— and H. D. Klingemann: 2003, "The theory of human development: A cross-cultural analysis", *European Journal of Political Research* 42(3), pp. 341–79.

White: 1982, *Rejection* (Reading, MA: Addison-Wesley).

World Bank: 2000/1, *World Development Report 2000/2001* (Washington, DC: The World Bank).

—— 2002, *Empowerment and Poverty Reduction: A Sourcebook* (Washington, DC: The World Bank).

World Values Survey: 2006, *Building a Worldwide Network of Social Scientists* (Sweden: WVS).

11

The Philosophical Foundations of Subjective Measures of Well-Being*

Erik Angner

Introduction

The goal of this chapter is to make explicit fundamental theoretical commitments of the effort to develop subjective measures of well-being, that is, measures based on answers to questions such as "Taking things all together, how
would you say things are these days—would you say you're *very happy, pretty
happy*, or *not too happy* these days?" (Gurin, Veroff, and Feld 1960, 411, italics in
original). My main thesis is that increased attention to these commitments—
which can also be called philosophical foundations—can help us improve
our understanding of the nature, strengths, and weaknesses of these measures.
I will focus on two fundamental commitments, namely, the answers to the
following two questions. First: what, more precisely, are subjective measures of
well-being designed to represent? Second: what, more exactly, makes proponents of subjective measures think that they can measure it? Although it is
perfectly reasonable for social and behavioral scientists to be wary of spending
too much time thinking about the philosophical foundations of their enterprise, there are moments when it is eminently useful to do so. In this case, I will
maintain, the philosophical foundations of the enterprise are directly relevant
to the assessment of subjective measures. Attending to those foundations is
therefore well worth the effort.[1]

* I am grateful to Luigino Bruni and Pier Luigi Porta for the opportunity to contribute to
their workshop on capabilities and happiness at the University of Milan–Bicocca, and to the
participants—especially Jon Fahlander and Robert Sugden—for comments. I thank Marshall
Abrams and Laurence James for feedback on an earlier draft. Errors are my own.
    [1] See Angner (forthcoming) for a longer discussion about some of these themes.

Background

The concept of well-being plays prominent roles in a variety of disciplines, including philosophy—especially in ethics and in social and political philosophy—but also in economics, psychology, psychiatry, public health, gerontology, and elsewhere. Although the exact function of the concept varies across authors and disciplines, it is typically expected to play several important roles. Thomas M. Scanlon (1998) articulates these roles as follows:

> It is commonly supposed that there is a simple notion of individual well-being that plays the following three roles. First, it serves as an important basis for the decisions of a single rational individual, at least for those decisions in which he or she alone is concerned (that is to say, in which moral obligations and concerns for others can be left aside). Second, it is what a concerned benefactor, such as a friend or parent, has reason to promote. Third, it is the basis on which an individual's interests are taken into account in moral argument. (Scanlon 1998, 93)[2]

Whatever the exact function of the concept of well-being in various disciplines, it certainly is often assumed to play a role in determining both what I should pursue in my own life and what I should promote in the lives of others. Incidentally, the concept of well-being is often applied to groups and nations as well as to individuals, and it is supposed to play a role as a basis for the deliberations by governments regarding public policy.

The philosophical literature refers to this "simple notion" of well-being in a variety of ways. For example, in his book *Welfare, Happiness, and Ethics*, L. W. Sumner (1996) writes that "a person's welfare is more or less the same as her well-being or interest or (in one of its many meanings) her good" (Sumner 1996, 1). Similarly, in the words of Andrew Moore and Roger Crisp (1996): "At a minimum, a life of well-being is a life going well. The numerous near-equivalents to well-being include a person's good, benefit, advantage, interest, prudential value, welfare, happiness, flourishing, *eudaimonia*, and utility" (Moore and Crisp 1996, 599). Other terms that could have been added to this list include "quality of life" and "thriving" (Nussbaum and Sen 1993, 1). Though all these terms may be used slightly differently in ordinary language (Keller 2004, 39), these quotes support Scanlon's contention that philosophers, psychologists, economists, and others who try to think systematically about well-being tend to use these terms to denote one simple notion rather than a multiplicity of related ones.

The concept of well-being, as it is used here, needs to be sharply distinguished from the concept of financial well-being, or economic welfare, where the latter is understood in terms of access to economic resources (Sen 1987, 16). While it

---

[2] Though Scanlon proceeds to criticize the view outlined in this passage, his characterization of the role that the concept of well-being is often supposed to play is useful.

is plausible to assume that some economic resources are necessary for a life of well-being, such resources are not constitutive of it. The concept of well-being, as it is employed in this chapter, also needs to be distinguished from the concept of welfare used, for example, in Nicholas Rescher's book *Welfare* (1972):

On closer scrutiny, it emerges that welfare relates to the *basic requisites of a man's well-being* in general, but most prominently includes those basic concerns with health and economic adequacy to which we have become accustomed by such presently current terms as the "welfare state" or a "welfare worker." (Rescher 1972, 3–4, italics in original)

The concept of welfare as it is used in this passage is broader than that of economic welfare, as used above, since it has many dimensions of which economic welfare is but one (Rescher 1972, 4–5).

Unsurprisingly, there have been many attempts to measure well-being. As a working definition of "measurement," I will adopt the following classic statement: "When measuring some attribute of a class of objects or events, we associate numbers (or other familiar mathematical entities, such as vectors) with the objects in such a way that the properties of the attribute are faithfully represented as numerical properties" (Krantz et al. 1971, 1). A measure of well-being, then, is a mapping from individuals (or groups) to numbers that is designed to represent the well-being of those individuals (or groups). In what follows, we will see that there have in fact been many efforts to develop measures of well-being so defined, and that these efforts were often motivated by a desire to help governments and other decision makers design policy so as to promote people's well-being.

Although it can be argued that efforts to measure well-being have a longer history, a prominent effort in this direction is evident in the work of A. C. Pigou, who is commonly considered the father of welfare economics. In *The Economics of Welfare* ([1920] 1952), Pigou was explicit about his desire to develop a measure of welfare that could be used in practice. In his own words, the goal was "to make more easy practical measures to promote welfare—practical measures which statesmen may build upon the work of the economist" (Pigou 1952, 10). Measures like those favored by Pigou, such as Gross National Product (GNP), continue to be widely used as a guide to public policy (Nussbaum and Sen 1993, 2).

The social indicator movement—so identified by Otis Dudley Duncan (1969, 1)—arose as a reaction to the widespread use of economic measures of well-being (Carley 1981, 1).[3] Thus, the authors of the *Human Development Report*, published by the United Nations Development Programme (UNDP) and probably the best-known expression of the social indicator movement,

---

[3] Robert J. Rossi and Kevin J. Gilmartin (1980) trace the history of the social indicator movement back to William Ogburn's work at the University of Chicago during the 1920s and 1930s (Rossi and Gilmartin 1980, 1).

wrote: "Caught up with the rise and fall of national incomes, economists often lost sight of the real end of development—people's well-being. Economic growth is merely a means—albeit an important one—for achieving this end" (UNDP 2004, 127). By contrast, the social indicator movement sought to find "a broader and more sensitive set of measures that will provide a fuller description of people's lives" (Campbell 1976, 118). These measures were supposed to play the very same role as traditional economic accounts had come to play, including as a guide to public policy. Indeed, some proposed the development of a comprehensive index of Gross National Welfare, analogous to the GNP (Rossi and Gilmartin 1980, 27).

Though subjective measures of well-being have recently achieved a certain prominence, they cannot, in fact, be described as a novel invention.[4] They go back at least to the early part of the twentieth century. One of the pioneers was Goodwin Watson (1930), who lamented that it is "extraordinary almost beyond belief that so few attempts have been made to apply the techniques of psychological study to the understanding of happiness" (Watson 1930, 79). Since the late 1920s, psychologists (including Watson) developed a fascinating variety of measures of happiness and satisfaction, and using these measures, established a range of empirical results. Summarizing the early research, Warner Wilson (1967) concluded: "The happy person emerges as a young, healthy, well-educated, well-paid, extroverted, optimistic, worry-free, religious, married person with high self-esteem, high job morale, modest aspirations, of either sex and of a wide range of intelligence" (Wilson 1967, 294). These measures were often presented as suitable guides for policy (Campbell, Converse, and Rodgers 1976, 8–9). More recently, some psychologists have promoted a "set of national indicators of well-being" to be used for public policy purposes (Diener and Seligman 2004, 21).

The brief review of efforts to measure well-being suggests that it is fair to think of traditional economic measures, social indicators, and subjective measures of well-being as—at least as described by some of their proponents—in some sense trying to represent the same thing.[5] The fact that economists and psychologists argue about which is the best measure of well-being supports this contention. So does the fact that proponents of measures of all three kinds argue that their measures are best suited as guides for public policy. Nevertheless, I will argue that these approaches to the measurement have radically different philosophical foundations. Moreover, I will claim that a clearer view of what these foundations are can help us better understand the various efforts to measure well-being and identify their relative strengths and

---

[4] This paragraph draws on Angner (manuscript).

[5] Though it is possible to think of subjective measures merely as measures of something like happiness, satisfaction, or the like, and not at the same time as measures of well-being, they are often presented as both (e.g. in Diener and Seligman 2004), and this is how I will treat them here.

weaknesses. Because subjective measures are frequently offered as alternatives to the more widely used economic measures, I will focus on the ways in which the foundations of subjective measures differ from those of economic measures. Hence, I will leave social indicators aside from now on.

Accounts of Well-Being

Because the concept of well-being has been part of the Western philosophical tradition for a long time, it is not surprising that philosophers should have developed many accounts of well-being. In accordance with standard practice, I divide accounts of well-being into three main classes: *mental state accounts*, *preference-satisfaction accounts*, and *objective list accounts*.[6] This division is sometimes traced to Derek Parfit (1984), who writes:

> What would be best for someone, or would be most in this person's interests, or would make this person's life go, for him, as well as possible? Answers to this question I call *theories about self-interest*. There are three kinds of theory. On *Hedonistic Theories*, what would be best for someone is what would make his life happiest. On *Desire-Fulfilment Theories*, what would be best for someone is what, throughout his life, would best fulfil his desires. On *Objective List Theories*, certain things are good or bad for us, whether or not we want to have the good things, or to avoid the bad things. (Parfit 1984, 493, italics in original)

In what follows, I will discuss the three kinds of account in order.

On the first kind of account, well-being is a "mental state" or a "state of mind." According to these accounts, people are well off to the exact degree that they are in the relevant mental state, be it happiness, satisfaction, elation, or similar. What defines these accounts is that they all see well-being "as having to enter our experience" (Griffin 1986, 13). This requirement is sometimes referred to as the *experience requirement* (Griffin 1986, 13), and accounts that satisfy it as *experiential accounts* (Scanlon 1998, 99). According to such accounts, "something contributes to well-being if, but only if, it affects the quality of one's experience" (Scanlon 1998, 100). There are, of course, many kinds of mental state account, depending (among other things) on what specific mental state is to count.

According to the second kind of account—variously referred to as *state of the world*, *desire fulfillment*, or *preference satisfaction accounts*—well-being is a matter of preference satisfaction (Griffin 1986, 7). According to these accounts, people are well off to the exact extent that their preferences are satisfied.

---

[6] This tri-partite division is perfectly standard. The division appears not only in Parfit (1984, 493–502) but also in James Griffin (1986, section 1), and Daniel M. Hausman and Michael S. McPherson (1996, chapter 6). The taxonomy is not unproblematic (cf. Scanlon 1993), but it is good enough for present purposes.

These accounts do not satisfy the experience requirement, because people can be made better or worse off by changes in the world that satisfy their preferences but do not in any way enter their consciousness (Scanlon 1993, 186). Since people can feel happy (or whatever) even though their preferences are not satisfied, and vice versa, these accounts imply that well-being "can, and it frequently does, come apart from any satisfaction or enjoyment. When you get what you want, you might like it, or you might not. You might not even know you've got it" (Moore and Crisp 1996, 599). Again, there are many kinds of preference satisfaction account, depending (among other things) on what preferences are to count.

The two kinds of account described so far are collectively referred to as *subjective accounts*, because they describe a person's well-being as (at least partly) a function of his or her feelings, experiences, desires, and so on (Scanlon 1975, 656). By contrast, we can identify what we may call *objective—*or *objective list—accounts*, according to which a person's well-being does not depend on such subjective factors. Hence: "Objective accounts of welfare appeal to the thought that there are features of the circumstances, position, or characteristics of persons that enable us to judge how well off they are" (Weale 1998, 704). On this view, then, "certain things are good or bad for beings, independently in at least some cases of whether they are desired or whether they give rise to pleasurable experiences" (Chappell and Crisp 1998, 553). There are many different objective list accounts, depending (among other things) on the exact list of things that are included on the list. Candidates for membership are controversial but include "moral goodness, rational activity, the development of one's abilities, having children and being a good parent, knowledge, and the awareness of true beauty" (Parfit 1984, 499).[7]

It should be clear, even from a relatively casual examination, that subjective measures of well-being typically presuppose some mental state account of well-being.[8] We can tell this, in part, from the fact that psychologists interested in the measurement of well-being largely appear to adopt the experience requirement. For example, David G. Myers (1992) quotes Madame de la Fayette as saying: "If one thinks that one is happy, that is enough to be happy," and adds that "like Madame de La Fayette, social scientists view well-being as a state of mind. Well-being, sometimes called 'subjective well-being' to emphasize the point, is a pervasive sense that life is good" (Myers 1992, 23; cf. p. 27). Similarly, Ed Diener and Eunkook Suh (1997) write: "Subjective well-being research . . . is concerned with individuals' subjective experiences of their lives. The underlying assumption is that well-being can

---

[7] Not all accounts of well-being fit neatly in this taxonomy. For example, some accounts are best seen as composite or hybrid views (cf. Parfit 1984, 502).

[8] This is not to deny that proponents of subjective measures may have different ideas about the nature of well-being.

be defined by people's conscious experiences—in terms of hedonic feelings or cognitive satisfactions" (Diener and Suh 1997, 191). The fact that Diener and Suh argue that well-being is not only *concerned* with individuals' subjective experiences, but is *defined* by them, strongly suggests that Diener and Suh accept the experience requirement.[9]

By contrast, proponents of economic measures tend to favor preference satisfaction accounts. In the words of Hausman and McPherson (1997): "Welfare economics identifies welfare with the satisfaction of preferences. This identification is so automatic and ubiquitous that economists seldom realize how controversial it is" (Hausman and McPherson 1997, 17). Notice that the satisfaction of preferences is different from feeling satisfied; economic measures are intended to represent the former rather than the latter. Economists also tend to identify well-being with utility, which is interpreted as an index of preference satisfaction (Mongin and d'Aspremont 1998, 382). This means that economists can legitimately talk about utility—even as identical to well-being—without making any reference to subjective states like happiness, pleasure, and satisfaction. Indeed, economists take a certain amount of pride in eschewing references to such subjective notions (Angner and Loewenstein, forthcoming).

Thus, there is a fundamental difference between the accounts of well-being adopted by proponents of subjective measures and traditional economic measures. The difference has not always been explicitly acknowledged. Consider, for example, some psychologists' criticism of economic measures for being too indirect, in the sense that they do not get directly at "what really matters," which is clearly assumed to be some subjectively experienced mental state (cf. Kahneman, Diener, and Schwarz 1999). Although this line of criticism may be correct, it will strike economists as misguided, because it does not explicitly acknowledge that economic measures—whatever their flaws—are not intended to reflect any subjectively experienced mental state. Similarly, economists who criticize subjective measures of well-being often fail to acknowledge that proponents of such measures operate with a different account of well-being from that of mainstream economists.

As the previous paragraph suggests, the fact that different measures of well-being presuppose different accounts of well-being is highly relevant to the assessment of those measures. If it turned out that mental state accounts are inadequate, this would constitute *prima facie* evidence against the subjective measures of well-being (since they were designed to represent mental states). It would not constitute proof, however, since it would remain possible for subjective measures also to represent well-being properly understood.

---

[9] Some proponents of subjective measures of well-being can be understood as defending hybrid views (see note 7 above). For example, Daniel Kahneman (2000, 691) suggests that subjectively experienced happiness is but one of several constituents of well-being properly understood.

Analogously, if it turned out that preference satisfaction accounts of well-being are inadequate, this would constitute *prima facie* evidence against the economic measures (as they were designed to represent preference satisfaction). Again, it would not constitute proof, since it would remain possible for economic measures also to represent well-being properly understood. Either way, the plausibility of underlying accounts of well-being is eminently relevant to the adequacy of given measures.

Approaches to Measurement

In social and behavioral science, there are (broadly speaking) two different approaches to measurement.[10] As Krantz (1991) puts it: "One, which may be termed the *psychometric* approach, introduces latent [unobservable] variables to explain behavioral orderings. The second . . . treats the numerical representation of behavioral orderings axiomatically" (Krantz 1991, 2, my italics). The second approach is sometimes referred to as the *representational* approach (e.g. in Dawes and Smith 1985, 511). For the reason identified by Dawes and Smith (1985, 512)—the fact that all measurement is at bottom about representation—I will call it the *measurement-theoretic* approach.

The psychometric approach—due in large part to the American Psychological Association's 'Technical Recommendations' (1954) and developed by Lee J. Cronbach and Paul E. Meehl (1955) (cf. John and Benet-Martínez 2000, 351–7)—is largely centered around the concepts of "construct" and "construct validation." A construct is "a variable [that] is abstract and latent rather than concrete and observable" (Nunnally and Bernstein 1994, 85). Meanwhile, construct validation is often described as an instance of ordinary hypothesis testing (Johnson 2001, 11316). On this approach, you start off by simultaneously hypothesizing the existence of a construct and proposing a measure of the construct. On the basis of these assumptions, you derive the prediction that (informally speaking) the measure of the construct will "behave as expected." By exploring differences in the measure of the construct across conditions, and relationships between the measure of the construct and measures of other constructs and overt behavior, you can test whether the prediction is true. If it is, you infer that the construct as well as the proposed measures of it have been validated; if it is not, you infer that either the construct does not exist, or the proposed measure is invalid.

The measurement-theoretic approach was first articulated by Dana Scott and Patrick Suppes (1958) but received its canonical statement in David

[10] For more on the difference between the two approaches, see Robyn M. Dawes and Tom L. Smith (1985), David H. Krantz (1991), Charles M. Judd and Gary H. McClelland (1998), and Oliver P. John and Veronica Benet-Martínez (2000).

Krantz, R. Duncan Luce, Patrick Suppes, and Amos Tversky' *Foundations of Measurement* (1971). Instead of constructs, this approach emphasizes observable orderings and representation theorems (Krantz 1991, 1). On this approach, you start off with a set A of objects (e.g. rods, commodity bundles), which can be ordered with respect to some property (e.g. length, preference) by applying a simple observable operation. Then, you prove that if the empirical relation $\succ$ satisfies certain properties, then there is a function ϕ $(\cdot)$ from A into some set of numbers such that ϕ $(\cdot)$ is a *homomorphism*, that is, an assignment of numbers to each member of A such that one object bears relation $\succ$ to another just in case the former is associated with a greater number than the latter.

There is a great deal of evidence that proponents of subjective measures operate within the psychometric approach. First, there is a purely historical connection in that both subjective measures and psychometrics grew out of personality psychology during the early twentieth century (Angner manuscript; Winter and Barenbaum 1999, 5). Second, proponents of subjective measures often refer to "psychometric criteria" (Lyubomirsky and Lepper 1999, 140) and "psychometric properties" (Diener et al. 1999, 277). More importantly, the manner in which these psychologists defend their measures exhibit all the hallmarks of the psychometric approach to measurement. Among other things, they reveal an obvious desire to establish construct validity in the manner described above (cf. Lyubomirsky and Lepper 1999, 145; Diener et al. 1999, 277). Finally, within contemporary psychology, the measurement-theoretic approach is widely regarded as a failure and is not commonly used (John and Benet-Martínez 2000, 341).[11]

Meanwhile, there is much evidence that proponents of economic measures operate within the measurement-theoretic approach. First, there is a purely historical connection, in that measurement theory was motivated in part by issues relating to utility measurement (Krantz et al. 1971, 9). Second, proponents of economic measures tend to defend their measures precisely in the manner described above (cf. Mas-Colell et al. 1995, 80–2). Thus, economists infer that a given measure has been justified when it has been shown to be computed on the basis of market choices assumed to satisfy the relevant axioms, in conjunction with a formal proof that shows that the measure is an index of preference (i.e. a utility function). This procedure, if successful, in fact establishes that the measure is a homomorphism, just as the measurement-theoretic approach requires. Finally, economists make no effort to validate their measures in the manner favored by the psychometric approach.

Thus, there is a fundamental difference between the approach to measurement adopted by proponents of subjective measures as compared to that adopted by proponents of traditional economic measures. This difference—

---

[11] See Norman Cliff (1992) for a discussion about why the measurement-theoretic approach is not more widely used in psychology.

like the difference in accounts of well-being—is rarely explicitly acknowledged. For example, economists often reject subjective measures of well-being by saying that mental states like happiness simply cannot be measured: "[the] concept of happiness is one for which there can be no scientific objective measure" (Beckerman 1974, 53). The objection is best understood as based on the claim that the measurement of happiness does not proceed from an observable ordering, as the measurement-theoretic approach suggests that it should. This line of criticism does not acknowledge that subjective measures—whatever their flaws—are justified in the manner of the psychometric approach, not the measurement-theoretic one. Similarly, psychologists sometimes criticize economists for failing properly to validate their measures in the manner of the psychometric approach, without mentioning that economists validate their measures in accordance with the measurement-theoretic one.

As the last paragraph suggests, the fact that proponents of subjective and economic measures adopt different approaches to measurement is directly relevant to the assessment of those measures. If it turned out that the psychometric approach is a failure, this would constitute *prima facie* evidence against subjective measures (since they are justified in the manner of the psychometric approach). It would not constitute proof, however, since it might still be possible to validate subjective measures in some other way. Analogously, if it turned out that the measurement-theoretic approach is a failure, this would constitute *prima facie* evidence against the economic measures (since they are justified in the manner of the measurement-theoretic approach). Again, it would not constitute proof, since it might still be possible to validate economic measures in some other way. Either way, it should be clear that the adequacy of different approaches to measurement is eminently relevant to the adequacy of measures of well-being.

Conclusion

Though the discussion in this chapter has been brief, we have seen that subjective and economic measures of well-being rest on radically different philosophical foundations. First, whereas subjective measures are typically understood as representing some mental state account of well-being, economic measures are typically understood as representing some preference-satisfaction account. Second, whereas subjective measures are typically justified in accordance with the psychometric approach to measurement, economic measures are typically justified in accordance with the measurement-theoretic approach. The discussion suggests that attention to the philosophical foundations of measures of well-being can shed light on the nature of as well as the differences between alternative measures.

A better understanding of the philosophical foundations of measures of well-being could help clarify the strengths and weaknesses of such measures. As I have suggested, the assessment of a measure of well-being depends to some extent on its philosophical foundations: on both the underlying account of well-being and the relevant approach to measurement. The connection between the measures and their philosophical foundations is of course more complicated than I have indicated here, and could only be explored in a much longer study. Still, the discussion has important implications. One such implication is that some attention to the philosophical foundations of measures of well-being is unavoidable: a complete defense of a given measure will have to say something about the nature of well-being and approaches to measurement.

In conclusion, I hope to have shown that there is much to be gained from exploring philosophical foundations. By taking explicit account of philosophical foundations of our efforts to measure well-being, we can hope to gain a better understanding of the nature, strengths, and weaknesses of our measures.

References

American Psychological Association (1954) 'Technical Recommendations for Psychological Tests and Diagnostic Techniques,' supplement, *Psychological Bulletin* 51: 1–38.

Angner, Erik (forthcoming) 'Subjective Measures of Well-Being: Philosophical perspectives,' in Harold Kincaid and Don Ross (Eds) *Handbook on the Philosophical Foundations of Economics as a Science* (Oxford: Oxford University Press).

—— (manuscript) 'The Evolution of Eupathics: The historical roots of subjective measures of well-being.'

—— and George Loewenstein (forthcoming) 'Behavioral Economics,' in Uskali Mäki (Ed.) *Philosophy of Economics*, Vol. 13 of Dov Gabbay, Paul Thagard, and John Woods (Eds) *Handbook of the Philosophy of Science* (Amsterdam: Elsevier).

Beckerman, Wilfred (1974) *Two Cheers for the Affluent Society: A spirited defense of economic growth* (New York: St. Martin's Press).

Campbell, Angus (1976) 'Subjective Measures of Well-Being,' *American Psychologist* 31: 117–24.

—— Philip E. Converse, and Willard L. Rodgers (1976) *The Quality of American Life: Perceptions, evaluations, and satisfactions* (New York: Russell Sage).

Carley, Michael (1981) *Social Measurement and Social Indicators: Issues of policy and theory* (Boston: George Allen & Unwin).

Chappell, Tim, and Roger Crisp (1998) 'Utilitarianism,' in Edward Craig (Ed.) *The Routledge Encyclopedia of Philosophy*, Vol. 9 (London: Routledge), pp. 551–7.

Cliff, Norman (1992) 'Abstract Measurement Theory and the Revolution that Never Happened,' *Psychological Science* 3: 186–90.

Cronbach, Lee J., and Paul E. Meehl (1955) 'Construct Validity in Psychological Tests,' *Psychological Bulletin* 52: 281–302.

Dawes, Robyn, and Tom L. Smith (1985) 'Attitude and Opinion Measurement,' in Gardner Lindzey and Elliot Aronson (Eds) *Handbook of Social Psychology*, 3rd Edn, Vol. 1 (New York: Random House), pp. 509–66.

Diener, Ed, and Martin E. P. Seligman (2004) 'Beyond Money: Toward an economy of well-being,' *Psychological Science in the Public Interest* 5: 1–31.

—— and Eunkook Suh (1997) 'Measuring Quality of Life: Economic, social, and subjective indicators,' *Social Indicators Research* 40: 189–216.

—— —— Richard E. Lucas, and Heidi L. Smith (1999) 'Subjective Well-Being: Three decades of progress,' *Psychological Bulletin* 125: 276–303.

Duncan, Otis Dudley (1969) *Toward Social Reporting: Next steps* (New York: Russell Sage).

Griffin, James (1986) *Well-Being: Its meaning, measurement, and moral importance* (Oxford: Clarendon).

Gurin, Gerald, Joseph Veroff, and Sheila Feld (1960) *Americans View Their Mental Health: A nationwide interview survey* (New York: Basic Books).

Hausman, Daniel M., and Michael S. McPherson (1996) *Economic Analysis and Moral Philosophy* (Cambridge: Cambridge University Press).

—— —— (1997) 'Beware of Economists Bearing Advice,' *Policy Options* 18: 16–19.

John, Oliver P., and Veronica Benet-Martínez (2000) 'Measurement: Reliability, Construct Validation, and Scale Construction,' in Harry T. Reiss and Charles M. Judd (Eds) *Handbook of Research Methods in Social and Personality Psychology* (Cambridge: Cambridge University Press), pp. 339–69.

Johnson, J. A. (2001) 'Personality Psychology: Methods,' in Neil J. Smelser and Paul B. Baltes (Eds) *International Encyclopedia of the Social and Behavioral Sciences*, Vol. 16 (Amsterdam: Elsevier), pp. 11313–17.

Judd, Charles M., and Gary H. McClelland (1998) 'Measurement,' in Daniel T. Gilbert, Susan T. Fiske, and Gardner Lindzey (Eds) *The Handbook of Social Psychology*, 4th Edn (Boston: McGraw-Hill), pp. 180–232.

Kahneman, Daniel (2000) 'Experienced Utility and Objective Happiness,' in Daniel Kahneman and Amos Tversky (Eds) *Choices, Values and Frames* (Cambridge: Cambridge University Press), pp. 673–92.

—— Ed Diener, and Norbert Schwarz (Eds) (1999) *Well-Being: The foundations of hedonic psychology* (New York: Russell Sage).

Keller, Simon (2004) 'Welfare and the Achievement of Goals,' *Philosophical Studies* 121: 27–41.

Krantz, David H. (1991) 'From Indices to Mappings: The representational approach to measurement,' in Donald R. Brown and J. E. Keith Smith (Eds) *Frontiers of Mathematical Psychology: Essays in honor of Clyde Coombs* (New York: Springer), pp. 1–52.

—— R. Duncan Luce, Patrick Suppes, and Amos Tversky (1971) *Foundations of Measurement*, Vol. 1 (New York: Academic Press).

Lyubomirsky, Sonja, and Heidi S. Lepper (1999) 'A Measure of Subjective Happiness: Preliminary Reliability and Construct Validation,' *Social Indicators Research* 46: 137–55.

Mas-Colell, Andreu, Michael D. Whinston, and Jerry R. Green (1995) *Microeconomic Theory* (Oxford: Oxford University Press).

Mongin, Philippe, and Claude d'Aspremont (1998) 'Utility Theory and Ethics,' in Salvador Barberà, Peter J. Hammond, and Christian Seidl (Eds) *Handbook of Utility Theory*, Vol. I (Dordrecht: Kluwer), pp. 371–481.

Moore, Andrew, and Roger Crisp (1996) 'Welfarism in Moral Theory,' *Australasian Journal of Philosophy* 74: 598–613.

Myers, David G. (1992) *The Pursuit of Happiness: Who is happy and why?* (New York: William Morrow).

Nunnally, Jum C., and Ira H. Bernstein (1994) *Psychometric Theory*, 3rd Edn (New York: McGraw-Hill).

Nussbaum, Martha, and Amartya Sen (Eds) (1993) *The Quality of Life* (Oxford: Oxford University Press).

Parfit, Derek (1984) *Reasons and Persons* (Oxford: Clarendon).

Pigou, A. C. ([1920] 1952) *The Economics of Welfare*, 4th Edn (London: Macmillan).

Rescher, Nicholas (1972) *Welfare: The social issues in philosophical perspective* (Pittsburgh: University of Pittsburgh Press).

Rossi, Robert J., and Kevin J. Gilmartin (1980) *The Handbook of Social Indicators: Sources, characteristics, and analysis* (New York: Garland).

Scanlon, Thomas M. (1975) 'Preference and Urgency,' *The Journal of Philosophy* 72: 655–69.

—— (1993) 'Value, Desire, and Quality of Life,' in Nussbaum and Sen (1993), pp. 185–200.

—— (1998) 'The Status of Well-Being,' in Grethe B. Peterson (Ed.) *The Tanner Lectures on Human Values*, Vol. 19 (Salt Lake City: The University of Utah Press), pp. 91–143.

Scott, Dana, and Patrick Suppes (1958) 'Foundational Aspects of Theories of Measurement,' *The Journal of Symbolic Logic* 23: 113–28.

Sen, Amartya (1987) *Commodities and Capabilities* (New Delhi: Oxford University Press).

Sumner, L. W. (1996) *Welfare, Happiness, and Ethics* (Oxford: Clarendon).

United Nations Development Programme (2004) *Human Development Report 2004: Cultural liberty in today's diverse world* (New York: United Nations Development Programme).

Watson, Goodwin (1930) 'Happiness Among Adult Students of Education,' *The Journal of Educational Psychology* 21: 79–109.

Weale, Albert (1998) 'Welfare,' in Edward Craig (Ed.) *The Routledge Encyclopedia of Philosophy*, Vol. 9 (London: Routledge), pp. 702–6.

Wilson, Warner (1967) 'Correlates of Avowed Happiness,' *Psychological Bulletin* 67: 294–306.

Winter, David G., and Nicole B. Barenbaum (1999) 'History of Modern Personality Psychology Theory and Research,' in Lawrence A. Pervin and Oliver P. John (Eds) *Handbook of Personality: Theory and research*, 2nd Edn (New York: Guilford).

12

Capability, Happiness, and Opportunity*

Robert Sugden

For much of the twentieth century, there was a consensus in economics that normative analysis should use the "welfarist" (or "ordinal utilitarian") approach. In welfarism, the concern is with social welfare—the overall good of a society. Social welfare is taken to be an aggregate of the welfare of individuals; each person's preferences (treated as given) provide the standard by which his or her welfare is assessed. Recently, however, two different approaches to normative analysis have begun to gain ground—the "capability" approach and the "happiness" approach. Each rejects preference-satisfaction as a standard of individual well-being, but for different reasons. Advocates of the capability approach claim that a person's preferences are too malleable—too subject to influences from the social environment—to be a reliable indicator of well-being. They also claim that well-being has many aspects, and that for the assessment of some of these, particularly those related to freedom and autonomy, preferences do not provide the right kind of information. Advocates of the happiness approach claim that individual decision-making is only boundedly rational; because of this, there can be systematic deviations between the *ex ante* judgments that precede choices and the *ex post* experiences that result from those choices. Preferences correspond with *ex ante* judgments while, it is claimed, well-being is a matter of the hedonic quality of actual outcomes.

One of the most salient features of welfarism is that it accepts each individual's own judgments about how to run her own life as decisive in assessing the relative well-being she derives from alternative options. Economists have traditionally treated this feature of welfarism as an important merit—the merit of respecting "consumer sovereignty", of not being paternalistic. In this chapter I argue that neither the capability approach nor the happiness

* This work was supported by the Economic and Social Research Council of the UK (award no. RES 051 27 0146).

approach has this feature. In different ways, each of these new approaches allows the individual's own judgments about her own life to be subordinated to judgments that are imposed from outside, whether by normative analysts, by supposed "experts" in decision-making, or as the outcome of some political process. I argue that each of us, as a citizen, should be wary of allowing his or her own judgments to be overridden in this way.

This chapter is not a defense of welfarism. The normative stance from which it is written is contractarian. In a contractarian approach, social arrangements must be justified to each individual separately, as a fair and mutually advantageous agreement, rather than to a neutral moral observer or impartial spectator. I argue that the capability and happiness approaches lead to policy proposals which cannot be justified to the individuals whose judgments about their own lives are being overridden. To keep the chapter within bounds, I do not try to formulate a contractarian alternative to the capability and happiness approaches: I confine myself to the easier task of criticism. My tentative attempts at developing such an approach can be found in other work (Sugden, 2004, 2005, 2006).

1. The Capability Approach

The capability approach was first proposed by Amartya Sen, and Sen has remained its most prominent advocate. In describing and interpreting this approach, I refer to a series of works by Sen, particularly his books *Commodities and Capabilities* (1985), *Inequality Reexamined* (1992) and *Development as Freedom* (1999). I also make some use of Martha Nussbaum's *Women and Human Development: The Capabilities Approach* (2000). As Nussbaum's subtitle suggests, she presents her work as a development of Sen's approach. She writes in the Aristotelian tradition that Sen (e.g. 1992, p. 39; 1999, p. 24) acknowledges as one of his own philosophical starting points.

This section of my essay draws heavily on a previous paper I wrote for a *Utilitas* symposium on John Stuart Mill and Amartya Sen (Sugden, 2006). In his contribution to that symposium, Sen (2006, pp. 87–90) is—to put it mildly— very critical of my reading of his work on capability. Calling this reading a "total misrepresentation" of his position, he claims that I am attributing to him views which are "absolutely—and emphatically—*not* mine", "absurd", "inane", "despotic", "tyrannical", and "monstrous". I will try to explain more carefully why I think Sen's work does indeed imply a commitment to these positions. Of course, it is not I but Sen who characterizes them as absurd, inane, despotic, tyrannical, and monstrous. I merely urge my readers to consider the risks involved in endorsing them.

As a starting point, it is important to distinguish between, on the one hand, the capability approach as a specific normative theory and, on the other, the *oeuvres* of Sen the economic philosopher, Sen the practicing development economist, and Sen the political commentator. A normative theory, as I understand it, is an attempt to *systematize* a body of normative judgments, intuitions, or sentiments. (I leave open the meta-ethical question of whether the theory claims to be about objective moral truth or subjective moral perceptions.) Inevitably, systematization requires simplification and abstraction: that is how theories work. It should not be surprising, then, if a particular normative theory fails to capture every relevant aspect of its creator's moral intuitions—any more than it is surprising if a descriptive theory of human behavior fails to capture every relevant regularity known to the scientist who proposes it.

If it is to be useful, a normative theory has to have an existence independent of the beliefs of its creator: the theory cannot just be everything to which that person is morally committed, just as the scientist's theory cannot just be everything that the scientist knows. So, I maintain, the capability approach should be understood as a specific theory, one that was first proposed by Sen and which has subsequently been developed by others. It is not a synonym for the collected works of Amartya Sen. In this essay, I am concerned with the implications of this particular theory. If it turns out that there are implications that Sen himself has reservations about, that may point to limitations of the theory; it doesn't show that these are not implications of the theory after all. Conversely, the fact that Sen is strongly committed to some normative proposition or policy proposal does not show that that proposition or proposal is implied by the capability approach. When I assess the possible risks of following this approach, my interest is in those policy proposals that might be justified by the theory, whether or not Sen himself would favor them. Thus, for example, Nussbaum's political proposals are relevant to the extent that she can show them to be justifiable within the capability approach, whether or not Sen supports them.

So what *is* the capability approach?[1] The core of the theory is an attempt to answer the question "as to how a person's interests may be judged and his or her personal 'state' assessed" (Sen, 1985, p. 1). This is presented as the first step in assessing alternative states of a society. Since Sen is an egalitarian, this latter assessment depends on the answer to one of his favorite questions, "Equality of what?" (e.g. 1992, pp. 12–30). The idea is that if we can find the right dimension—or, more generally and less ambitiously, the right "informational base"—for assessments of individuals' personal states, that will also be the dimension in which equality should be sought. In assessing personal states, Sen takes account of many different aspects of well-being, but always from the viewpoint of a *moral observer*, making "judgments", "assessments", or "evaluations" of a person's state from outside.

---

[1] The following paragraphs are adapted from Sugden (2006).

Sen's commitment to this viewpoint is nicely illustrated by the "parable" he uses in *Development as Freedom* to introduce a comparison between alternative methods of assessing a person's state. The story is of a woman hiring an unemployed laborer to work in her garden. There are three applicants, each of whom would do much the same work for the same payment, but "being a reflective person, she [the employer] wonders who would be the right person to employ." Sen imagines the employer asking herself how, in choosing between the applicants, she can do the most good. Should she choose the poorest applicant (thus doing as much as she can to reduce poverty)? Or should she choose the applicant who would gain most happiness from being employed (thus doing as much as she can to increase happiness)? Or should she choose the applicant for whom the job would make the biggest difference to "the quality of life and freedom from illness"? (1999, p. 54). The story is about alternative ways of distributing a valuable resource among three needy individuals. Notice how Sen presents this problem through the eyes of a fourth person who, from a neutral position, "reflectively" asks which solution would be best.

Sen introduces his own approach to normative social theory by presenting a critique of utilitarianism, summed up in the following claim: "The mental metric of pleasure or desire is just too malleable to be a firm guide to deprivation and disadvantage" (1999, p. 63). Sen is particularly concerned with the mechanisms by which a person's desires and capacities for pleasure adapt to unfavorable circumstances. Among his examples of such "persistently deprived" people are "perennially oppressed minorities in intolerant communities, traditionally precarious sharecroppers living in a world of uncertainty, routinely overworked sweatshop employees in exploitative economic conditions, hopelessly subdued housewives in severely sexist cultures" (1999, pp. 62–3; see also 1985, p. 53; 1992, p. 55). The idea is that a moral observer should recognize the evil or unjustness of entrenched deprivation, even if, because of adaptation, the deprived people themselves do not feel unhappy about their situation and feel no desire to change it. Sen allows that subjective experiences of happiness may be part of the informational base on which the moral observer makes her assessments, but insists that they are not the whole of it.

Sen's own approach starts from the idea that an assessment of well-being must be concerned with the quality of whatever is "constitutive of a person's being". He describes these constitutive elements, or "beings and doings", as *functionings* (1992, p. 39). The suggestion is that functionings can be defined sufficiently generally that they are realizable in, and have value in, just about any human society. One of Sen's favorite examples of a functioning is "appearing in public without shame": this is something that matters in every society, even though the particular items of clothing that allow a person to avoid shame are specific to particular societies (1992, p. 115; 1999, pp. 73–4).

A person's actual state of being is represented by a vector of functionings. The opportunity or effective freedom that a person enjoys is then represented by the set of functioning vectors from which she is able to choose; this is her *capability set*.

Sen proposes that the capability set should be the informational base for the assessment of a person's well-being. By focusing on objective functionings, rather than on happiness or desire, Sen is able to separate a moral observer's judgments of a person's well-being from that person's own subjective experiences. By taking account of capabilities, rather than only of achieved functionings, Sen expresses his commitment to the value of freedom.

Summing up his proposal, Sen says: "The basic concern ... is with our capability to lead the kind of lives we have reason to value" (1999, p. 285). Similar expressions, always couched in terms of what a person has reason to value, appear throughout *Development as Freedom*. Why is it so important for Sen that a person's capabilities are assessed in terms of what she *has reason to* value? The answer, I suggest, is that, given Sen's critique of utilitarianism, he cannot assess capability entirely by reference to an individual's actual desires: they are too malleable, too susceptible to adaptation. He needs to be able to say that certain functionings are valuable for all human beings, whether they are desired or not. But, I take it, he does not want to assess a person's capability in terms of a standard of value that is wholly external to her. His solution is to invoke a concept of "reason" that is in some way universal: the suggestion is that the standard of value is one which, in the light of reason, each individual would endorse.

Usually, and particularly in his later work, Sen avoids making concrete proposals about how one capability set should be valued in relation to another. However, the "reason to value" formula implies that a capability set has value for a person to the extent that it provides her with opportunities to choose vectors of functionings that she has reason to value.[2] If the question of what a person has reason to value does not have a unique answer, then an appropriate kind of diversity within the capability set (that is, diversity which caters to the various conceptions of a good life that the person might reasonably endorse) can have value too. But even singleton capability sets can be ranked in terms of how far they answer to what people have reason to value.

For example, Sen defends the legitimacy of expressions such as "freedom from malaria". The problem that such a defense has to overcome is that the eradication of an infectious disease is a public good, typically brought about by

---

[2] In addition—and, from a theoretical point of view, somewhat awkwardly—Sen (1992, pp. 41, 51–2) allows that the activity of choosing can be a valuable part of living in itself. Thus, the extent to which a person is free to choose how to live her life appears in the theory both in the evaluation of capability sets (larger sets may be judged more valuable than smaller ones) and in the content of those sets (since choosing is a functioning in itself, the extent of choice is a property of the functioning vectors which are the elements of capability sets).

collective action at a national or international level. At the level of the individual, there is no choice in the matter: in effect, a public decision determines which of two singleton capability sets {x} and {y} applies to each individual, where x stands for "exposed to danger of epidemics" and y for "not exposed to danger of epidemics". Sen argues that each individual has greater freedom (and not merely greater well-being) with {y} than with {x}. The crucial step in the argument is the claim that "Being able to live as one would value, desire and choose *is* a contribution to one's freedom ... [T]he relation of the results to what one would have chosen (and would have had reasons to choose) is a matter of direct relevance to freedom." Given the natural assumption that people prefer not to be exposed to epidemics, and given the apparently uncontroversial claim that this preference is supported by reason, we immediately arrive at the conclusion that each person is more free with {y} than with {x}. This allows Sen to arrive at what he calls a "momentous perspective": that "the available data regarding the *realization* of disease, hunger, and early mortality tell us a great deal about the presence or absence of certain central basic *freedoms*" (1992, pp. 64–9). The suggestion seems to be that, in cases in which we are sufficiently confident about what people have reason to value, what matters most, both for well-being *and for freedom*, is that people achieve those functionings they have reason to value.

Sen's approach puts great stress on the concept of reason. What does it mean to say that someone has reason to value something, or reason to desire it, or reason to choose it? In *Commodities and Capabilities* and *Inequality Reexamined*, Sen sometimes hints at an objective account of well-being. For example, he reports his own belief that "the 'limits' of objectivity extend well into the assessment of well-being", while saying that his theoretical analysis does not depend on this belief (1985, p. 35). He suggests that the fact that people sometimes disagree about assessments of well-being may reflect the "fundamental incompleteness" of well-being comparisons: the concept of well-being is "broad and partly opaque" (1992, pp. 46–9). I take this to mean that well-being may be an objective but vague concept. But more commonly, and particularly in *Development as Freedom*, the emphasis is on reflective moral judgment, interpreted without any presumption about the existence or otherwise of "objective" moral truth.

In deciding which functionings to take into account, and how to weight functionings relative to one another, what is required, according to Sen, is "reasoned evaluation". Sen distinguishes between an individual person making her own moral judgments and a political entity making a collective judgment. In the first case, reasoned evaluation is a matter of "reflection". The implication seems to be that for one person j to say that another person i has reason to value some thing x is simply for j to say that, after reflection, she has come to believe that x is valuable for i. In the case of collective judgment: "[T]here has to be some kind of a reasoned 'consensus' ... This is a 'social choice' exercise, and it requires public discussion and a democratic under-standing and acceptance" (1999, pp. 78–9). Sen is a firm advocate of collective decision-making processes based on democratic participation, reasoned dis-cussion, and openness to public scrutiny. In the case of collective judgment, then, the statement that *i* has reason to value *x* reports that, after appropriate public discussion, the proposition "*x* is valuable for *i*" has been approved by a democratic political process.

Given Sen's emphasis on democratic judgment, it would be wrong to suggest that his concept of "reason to value" is paternalistic or elitist. He is not proposing a capability analogue of Government House utilitarianism, in which wise and benevolent rulers decide what is valuable in human life, and then structure the social environment so that ordinary people have effective freedom only with respect to what (according to the rulers) they have reason to value. For the most part, he does not offer hypotheses about the substantive content of the consensus that (according to his account) will emerge from the democratic process. He presents his own work as a contribution to "[t]he theory of evaluation and assessment", and maintains a sharp distinction between theory and politics: "[P]ure theory cannot 'freeze' a list of capabilities for all societies for all time to come, irrespective of what the citizens come to understand and value" (2004, p. 78). But he *is* committed to the position that a majority judgment about what is valuable in human life, if arrived at through democratic discussion, provides a warrant for determining what (for political purposes) everyone can be deemed to have reason to value, and hence what effective freedoms each person should be given. And at least some substantive claims about what there is reason to value are deeply embedded in Sen's account of his theory—in particular, the repeated emphasis on the malleabil-ity of the desires of the persistently deprived. In these passages, I take it, Sen is addressing us as fellow-citizens, seeking to persuade us that the persistently deprived have reason to value things that they do not in fact desire.

It might be objected on Sen's behalf that he is assuming that reasoned debate will produce a *consensus*, and not merely a majority opinion. A simple response is that he is not entitled to assume this. We can require people to defend their political judgments in public; if we are prepared to accept a specification of the status quo as a default position, we can even require that collective decisions require unanimous approval; but we cannot require that distinct and autono-mous individuals, each playing the role of moral observer, arrive at common judgments. If democratic discussion means what it says, we cannot stipulate that it ends in agreement. But there is more to be said. If Sen is read as assuming literal unanimity of judgments, it is not clear why he needs to discuss adaptive desires at all. He wants to be able to say that his hopelessly subdued housewife lacks desires for freedoms that she has reason to value. But it is hard to see how she could have no desire for these freedoms, while *at the same time* assenting to the judgment that she has reason to value them.

It seems that Sen is asking us to consider a democratic process which results in the collective judgment that certain freedoms are valuable for everyone in a society, even though some members of that society do not recognize the value of those freedoms. In other words, we are being asked to consider a "consensus" that is not shared by those people whose adaptive desires Sen tells us not to take at face value.

Thus, I claim, Sen's theory licenses collective decisions about capabilities to override some individuals' actual desires about how to live their own lives, in favor of other people's judgments about what those individuals have reason to desire. It is to this characterization of his theory that Sen (2006) objects so strongly. Relatedly, and even more strongly, he objects to my having said, apropos of his general approach: "The idea that 'we', as ethical theorists, can claim to know better than some particular individual what is good for her seems to open the door to restrictions on freedom" (Sugden, 2006, p. 34). This was intended as a reference to Sen's treatment of adaptive desires, which surely *does* rest on a claim to know better than the persistently deprived which freedoms are good for them. If such claims to superior knowledge are allowed to influence the assignment of freedoms in a society, then the freedom of the individual to act as she chooses—to act on her own desires, as she experiences them—*is* liable to be compromised.

Sen's response is to remind us of some of the evidence in support of the adaptation hypothesis, and to say that adaptation is a "specific problem of some importance that has to be addressed". He then says that he does not advocate the overruling of individual's desires *as a general principle*, but only in special cases. His response to the special problem of adaptation "does not, of course, yield a general case for believing . . . that 'ethical theorists can claim to know better than some particular individual what is good for her'": that would be an "extraordinary *general* belief". Similarly, he denies having "a general inclination to override an individual's own assessment in favor of the assessment of others" (2006, p. 88, italics in original). Notice the repeated emphasis on generality: he is objecting to (what he reads as) the suggestion that he wants to override individuals' desires *in general*, rather than only in the special case of adaptation. But what makes that particular case special? Expressed in general terms, the case is one in which we, the ethical theorists, have what we take to be good grounds for claiming that the relevant individuals desire what they have no reason to desire (or fail to desire what they have reason to desire). If the case is special, it must presumably be because we believe those grounds to be especially strong. But, however strongly grounded *we* think those beliefs are, the fact remains that the people whose desires we are overriding do not agree with us: they still think they have reason to desire what they in fact desire. It may be a special case from our point of view, but is not a special case from theirs.

Sen defends his use of the "reason to value" formula, saying that it involves no more than "the Smithian device of introducing an imagined 'impartial spectator' to assess one's own understanding" or "the Rawlsian device of insisting on 'public reasoning' to assess our own unscrutinized assessments". Presumably the impartial spectator is relevant when an individual person is making moral judgments, while public reasoning is relevant when a political entity is making a collective judgment. Sen says: "I am surprised by the extent to which Sugden sees an odd picture of despotism in the recognition of the need for critical assessment and public reasoning" (2006, pp. 88–9). Again, he is presupposing the viewpoint of the moral observer, assessing a person's state from the outside. If we expect the political process to generate collective judgments about individual well-being, then it is indeed natural to expect those judgments to be based on some form of public reasoning; Sen's arguments about adaptation are legitimate contributions to that reasoning. But, if the aim is to assign opportunities to individuals, why do we need to make collective judgments about the rationality of any individual's desires? In a liberal society, one might think, each individual should be allowed the freedom to act on her own desires, in so far as this is possible without infringing the corresponding freedoms of others; there should be no prior requirement on the individual to show that her desires accord with standards of public reason.[3]

In response to this criticism, Sen replies that he should not be accused of "endorsing collective tyranny over the individual, violating his or her liberty". Over many years, he says, he has "discuss[ed] extensively why the need to guarantee liberties and minority rights has to be part of an acceptable framework of democratic collective choice". He feels a "sense of accomplishment in my having had a role in introducing the consideration of a private and personal domain in social choice theory" (2006, pp. 89–90). Sen is quite right to describe this as a major theme in his work, particularly in the 1970s, when his theorem of the "impossibility of a Paretian liberal" sparked off a whole literature on the formal analysis of liberty and rights: he is fully entitled to his sense of accomplishment.[4] However, the main force of Sen's early work on liberty was part of a larger critique of (what he argued was) the impoverished information base of welfarism; it was not a theory in itself. Subsequently, he presented the capability approach as a means of overcoming the limitations

---

[3] In Sugden (2006) I argue that a sketch of such a form of social organization can be found in the work of John Stuart Mill. Mill is an egalitarian in much the same sense that Sen is. Like Sen, Mill believes that desires are subject to adaptation. But Mill sees no need for collective judgments about what is ultimately valuable in human life.

[4] Sen's work to integrate the concept of individual liberty into social choice theory began with Sen (1970a, chapter 6; 1970b). All social choice theorists must acknowledge the importance of this pioneering work—even those who, like me, have not accepted Sen's analysis of liberty. (For an alternative analysis, see Sugden, 1985.)

of welfarism. Clearly, Sen has intended that the theory of capability should capture his commitment to the value of individual liberty. Nevertheless, my concern is with the implications of this theory, and not with Sen's intentions in proposing it. I still maintain that, because the theory is grounded on the idea of "reason to value", it does not allow a robust formulation of each individual's freedom to choose how to live her own life.

Because Sen usually avoids making strong claims about what people have reason to desire, I cannot use his own texts to illustrate the scope that the capability approach offers for some people to impose on others their understanding of what is worthwhile in life. I shall take my examples from Nussbaum's *Women and Human Development*, which (as I have pointed out already) is written from the perspective of the capability approach. The core of Nussbaum's work is a list of "central human capabilities" which, she proposes, should be guaranteed to every individual. Of course, Sen is not committed to this particular list, or to any other (recall his remarks about "freezing" lists of capabilities). But he *is* committed to a political process that will generate some such list. Nussbaum's list is an example of the kind of proposal that Sen expects to be the subject of public discussion, and around which a consensus might form.

Nussbaum seems to take it as self-evident that humanity has a special *telos* which can somehow be read off from the differences between human beings and other animals: the more distinctively human a faculty is, the more valuable it is taken to be. Thus, the guiding principle for her list of central human capabilities is to find what is "fully human", "truly human", not "merely animal", "worthy of the dignity of the human being", even "somehow awe-inspiringly above the mechanical workings of nature" (2000, pp. 70–80). If these words are to be taken seriously, Nussbaum's list expresses a humanistic metaphysics which many people (myself for one) would not want to endorse. Naturally enough, given these premises, her account of the central human capabilities has a high-minded tone—even if she herself is too high-minded to recognize the fact. As if conscious of this potential criticism, she allows "emotions, desires, and even appetites of a human being" to count as "humanly significant parts of her personality, deserving of respect as such" (p. 155), but the condescending "even" in front of "appetites" is surely revealing. Explaining this concession, she says: "The personality is a unity, and practical reason suffuses all its parts, making them all human rather than animal." I do not know what this means. Nevertheless, the message is clear: *mere* appetites—faculties that we share with other animals—cannot rank as highly as more distinctively human faculties unless they can somehow be shown to have inherited human rationality.

My claim is not that Nussbaum's premises are obviously false, but merely that they are contestable. If the question of which capabilities should be deemed to be central to human life really were to be decided by democratic deliberation, and if Nussbaum's proposal really were to be chosen by majority vote, some people (including my own party of low-minded Humeans) would find that their own assignments of capabilities had been determined by a concept of "reason to value" that they did not share. And conversely: Nussbaum might end up on the losing side, and find that she was being denied what for her were central human capabilities because other people did not value them.

When political philosophy is written from the stance of the moral observer, the reality of these risks is all too easily overlooked. In proposing his own conception of what is valuable, an author has to provide a reasoned defense of his position. In doing this, it is easy to slip into assuming that anyone who understands these reasons will find them convincing. Without noticing, we can make the transition from the belief that we are right to the belief that we will come out on the winning side of a reasoned discussion about what is right. So, we are inclined to think, we have nothing to fear from allowing evaluative issues to be resolved in a properly conducted democratic process. Indeed, it is surprisingly easy to go further, and to imagine that the process has already been carried out, and that everyone *has* agreed with us.

For example, consider how Nussbaum presents her list. Her official position is that this is presented simply as a "good idea" that is not "yet" agreed by everyone, and which her readers can accept or reject: it is "recommended as a good idea to politicians . . . who want to make it the basis of national or local policy" (2000, pp. 103–4). But she characteristically treats it as if it expresses a "public political conception" that is already established, and that individual citizens can be required to uphold, whether they like it or not. Thus, when she considers the possibility that some men may not accept her feminist-inspired list of capabilities, she tells us that this is not a serious problem, since it can be overcome "over several generations" if men are given the right kind of "moral education" (p. 165). She is equally brusque when she considers the possibility that her favored principles might be objectionable to particular religions: "Given that the religion has agreed to sign on to a constitution of a certain type, it will have to figure out how to square this 'overlapping consensus' on public political matters of basic justice with the rest of what it teaches" (p. 232). It seems that she is not thinking about how to design a constitution that can be agreed by everyone, given his or her own ideas about what is valuable. In the case of the recalcitrant males, she seems to be imagining imposing her favored principles, and then instituting some kind of public education program which will eventually eliminate dissent. In the second case, she is imagining that the religion that makes the objections has already agreed to her principles: she then uses that imaginary agreement as grounds for overriding its objections.

Of course, these rather dogmatic statements are not implications of the theory of capability; they seem rather to reflect lapses in Nussbaum's argument. Having refused to allow Sen's liberal intentions to count in favor of the theory, I cannot use Nussbaum's dogmatism as evidence against it. My purpose in examining her argument is to illustrate the following lesson about political argument: If you propose a normative theory which allows democratic judgments about reason to desire to override individuals' actual desires, you are not entitled to assume that those judgments will be the same as yours. It may be you whose desires are overridden, on the warrant of other people's beliefs about what is good for you.

2. The Happiness Approach

The capability approach has had particular appeal for scholars working at the interface of economics and philosophy. In contrast, the recent development of the happiness approach reflects the growth of theoretical, survey, and experimental work carried out at the boundary of economics and psychology. It represents a fusion of two previously distinct research programs.

The program of *behavioral economics* has been concerned with how individuals deal with judgment and decision-making tasks. Until quite recently, this was a wholly descriptive enterprise, seeking to discover and to explain regularities in the actual behavior of economic agents. It was recognized—indeed, emphasized—that this behavior often deviates from the predictions of normative theories of rational behavior, but little attention was given to the question of how normative economics should adapt to these findings. A long-standing but separate research program, the *economics of happiness*, has investigated the determinants of individuals' self-reported "subjective well-being" or happiness. One of the most important early findings of this research program was that, over time, self-reported happiness is only weakly correlated with real income. But despite the efforts of Richard Easterlin (1974, 1995) and Tibor Scitovsky (1976) to point out the significance of this observation, it is only recently that it has become a major topic in economics.[5]

In this chapter, I am particularly concerned with a body of recent work which has discussed the implications for normative analysis of the findings of behavioral economics, confronting the issue of paternalism head-on. My points of reference are the papers by Daniel Kahneman, Peter Wakker, and Rakesh Sarin (1997), Kahneman (2000a, 2000b), Colin Camerer, Samuel Issacharoff, George Loewenstein, Ted O'Donaghue, and Matthew Rabin (2003), and Cass Sunstein and Richard Thaler (2003a, 2003b).[6] The papers by Camerer

[5] For introductions to the literature on the economics of happiness, see Frey and Stutzer (2002) and Bruni and Porta (2005).
[6] This list might be supplemented by Kahneman and Sugden (2005). That paper explores the possibility of basing the economic appraisal of policy options on "experienced utility" (that is, hedonic experience). Such an appraisal method would be consistent with the

et al. and by Sunstein and Thaler make rather similar proposals for an allegedly innocuous form of paternalism—"asymmetric paternalism" or "libertarian paternalism"—that is justified by the findings of behavioral economics. Since the authors of these papers include some of the leading names in behavioral economics, their proposals constitute an important and potentially influential consensus. I focus on the paper by Camerer et al., but where Sunstein and Thaler's argument is significantly different, I comment on their paper too.

Surprisingly, Camerer et al. do not give an explicit statement of the normative foundations of their analysis; we have to read between the lines, in the light of a background knowledge of what is taken for granted in economics. They say that the form of paternalism they are defending takes the form of "forcing, or preventing, choices for the individual's own good"; paternalism can be justified when there is a "fear that even people of sound mind might not act in their best interest in certain predictable situations"; "[b]y cataloging a list of common decision-making errors that even highly competent, well-functioning people make in predictable situations", behavioral economics "potentially broadens the scope of situations in which paternalistic policies could usefully be developed" (pp. 1211–14). Behavioral economics is presented as a third stage in a progressive relaxation of the simplifying assumptions that characterized early neoclassical economics. The first stage, starting from the 1930s, was to relax the assumption of perfect competition. The second stage, starting from the 1970s, was to relax the assumption of perfect information. Behavioral economics relaxes the assumption of perfect rationality (p. 1218). The suggestion seems to be that, at each stage, economists have become aware of additional ways in which unregulated markets might fail to promote welfare, and justifications for new forms of regulation have been discovered. Sunstein and Thaler argue in a similar way, claiming that while anti-paternalist economists typically assume that "people always (usually?) make choices in their best interest", that assumption is now known to be "obviously false" (2003a, p. 175). In support of this claim, they refer to the empirical literature of behavioral economics (2003a, p. 176; 2003b, pp. 1167–70, 1177–80).

It seems clear from all this that, for Camerer et al., the standard of normative analysis—and the proper objective of public policy—is the promotion of individual welfare. Their analysis presupposes a concept of an individual's welfare, "good", or "best interest" that is distinct from her preferences; whether or not preferences coincide with interests is an empirical matter, not a conceptual one. Although they present their concrete proposals as moderate and cautious, they do not seem to recognize any objection *of*

---

arguments of the other papers cited. However, Kahneman and I stopped short of recommending it, partly because he did not feel competent to tell cost-benefit analysts how to do their work, and partly because of my normative reservations about the happiness approach.

principle to paternalism.[7] We are told that all the authors share "trepidations" about supporting paternalistic regulations, but these turn out to be the concerns "that paternalistic policies may impose undue burdens on those people who are behaving rationally" and that, because behavioral economics is at an early stage of development, its findings must be treated with caution; because of these concerns, "caution" is appropriate "at this stage" (p. 1214). Both of these concerns are about the implementation of paternalism, not about its justification.

The sense in which Camerer et al. are cautious is encapsulated in their concept of *asymmetric paternalism*. This concept is defined in relation to a model in which there are two types of consumer, the "fully rational" and the "boundedly rational". Paternalistic policies confer benefits (B) on boundedly rational consumers by "counteract[ing] mistakes", but may impose costs (C) on fully rational consumers by restricting their opportunities to make optimal decisions. Camerer et al. give the following definition: "a policy is *asymmetrically paternalistic* if it creates large benefits for those people who are boundedly rational (B is large) while imposing little or no harm on those who are fully rational (C is small)" (p. 1219). Clearly, this criterion is cautious: it favors paternalistic interventions only when the expected benefit/cost ratio is high. But this is a kind of caution that is commonly exercised in all cost-benefit analysis; there is no hint of doubt about the normative status of the cost-benefit calculus itself. Notice also that it is an intrinsic feature of *all* paternalistic arguments that the restrictions they purport to justify are claimed to have exactly this kind of favorable asymmetry. A paternalistic restriction is intended to prevent only actions that a rational agent would not choose to perform; thus, if it is well-designed, its restrictions will not impinge on the choices of rational agents. Irrational agents benefit by being prevented from making mistakes, while rational agents are unaffected. I conclude that, whatever trepidation they may feel about reporting this, Camerer et al. are fully paid-up paternalists.

Here it should be said that Sunstein and Thaler's endorsement of paternalism is more qualified. The fundamental principle of their *libertarian paternalism* is to design public policies to maximize welfare, subject to the constraint that individual freedom of choice is maintained:

The libertarian aspect of our strategies lies in the straightforward insistence that, in general, people should be free to opt out of specified arrangements if they choose to

---

[7] In a footnote, Camerer et al. allow for the possibility that "people may have an intrinsic taste for free choice", but take the view that "how people perceive limits on free choice should itself be subject to behavioral research, rather than be treated as an axiom of resistance in the exploration of paternalism" (p. 1214, note 11). It is difficult to be sure what this statement means, because the main analysis of the paper does not use the concept of "taste". If I am right that their concept of welfare is experienced utility (see later), I think the best reading is that freedom has normative significance only in so far as it is a source of experienced utility.

do so. Hence we do not aim to defend any approach that blocks individual choices. (2003b, p. 1161)

This constraint gives some normative status to freedom, independently of welfare. Sunstein and Thaler's (2003a, pp. 175–6; 2003b, p. 1164) paradigm of libertarian paternalism is the case of the director of a company cafeteria who is choosing the order in which food is arranged. Knowing that customers' choices are affected by this apparently irrelevant factor, she chooses the order which induces the consumption patterns that she judges to be in the customers' best interests: taking account of the findings of dietary science, she puts the fruit before the desserts. Sunstein and Thaler use this example to illustrate their general claim that, in many cases, there are no "viable alternatives to paternalism": if some planner (the cafeteria director) must make a decision between alternative specifications of some rationally irrelevant but behaviorally relevant variable (the order in which food is arranged), it would be perverse not to be guided by the best interests of the people concerned (the health of the cafeteria customers). The example also illustrates the claim that it is possible to influence the behavior of boundedly rational agents without restricting their freedom of choice (anyone who wants to eat a dessert can do so, whatever the order in which the food is laid out).

Paternalistic interventions which satisfy Sunstein and Thaler's criterion are likely to satisfy the criterion of asymmetric paternalism too, because the fully rational agents of Camerer et al's account will take advantage of the freedom of choice they are given, and choose according to their preferences. However, the converse is not necessarily true: there can be interventions which restrict freedom of choice but which pass a cautious cost-benefit test. (For example, Camerer et al. argue that occupational licensing rules can satisfy their criterion (p. 1237). The implicit assumption is that fully rational agents would not choose to buy the services of suppliers whom the licensing authorities judge to be incompetent. But, even if this assumption is true, there is a real restriction on freedom of choice.)

However, this difference between the two sets of authors may not be as great as it appears at first sight. Sunstein and Thaler's policy proposals do not always respect the principle that individual choices should not be blocked. In a section entitled "How much choice should be offered?", they provide the following answer to their rhetorical question:

Libertarian paternalists want to promote freedom of choice, but they need not seek to provide bad options, and among the set of reasonable ones, they need not argue that more is necessarily better. Indeed that argument is quite implausible in many contexts. In the context of savings plans, would hundreds of thousands of options be helpful? Millions? . . . [O]ne recent study finds that when 401(k) plans [i.e. US retirement savings plans] offer more choice, participants are slower to join, perhaps because they are overwhelmed by the number of choices and procrastinate. (2003b, pp. 1196–7)

313

They go on to discuss how a libertarian paternalist might "decide how much (reasonable) choice to offer". The implication is that Sunstein and Thaler *are* in favor of blocking individual choices in cases in which they judge a reduction in the number of options to be in the individual's interests. The idea that individuals should be prevented from confronting "bad" or "unreasonable" options is unreconstructed paternalism.

On Camerer et al's account, paternalism is justified as a means of correcting "errors" (or, equivalently, "violations of rationality") in decision-making (p. 1218). To say that a class of decisions are in error is to say that they "do not accurately reflect the benefits [the decision-makers] derive" from them (p. 1221). It is a "crucial assumption" that the bounds on rationality which generate such errors "are empirical questions subject to systematic analysis, and thus cost-benefit calculations can be made" (p. 1222). Similarly, Sunstein and Thaler treat the proposition that individuals choose contrary to their best interests as empirical, and propose cost-benefit analysis, where feasible, as the method for reaching decisions about paternalistic interventions (2003a, p. 178).

Clearly, Camerer et al. and Sunstein and Thaler are presupposing some empirically defined concept of benefit and cost. It is only in relation to such a concept that we can define what it is rational for an individual to choose in a given situation, and hence to have an objective criterion of error. But what is that concept of cost and benefit?

Camerer et al. distinguish between two different kinds of findings of behavioral economics, both of which are systematic deviations from the previously received theory of rational choice. The first kind is the discovery that "people's preferences are not what economists had supposed". That is, it is found that individuals' actual preferences take account of some factor which the previously received theory had assumed to be irrelevant. One of Camerer et al's examples is the finding, first exhibited in the paradox discovered by Daniel Ellsberg (1961), that real decision-makers are averse to ambiguity about probability. According to Camerer et al., such findings "challenge the descriptive validity of standard economic models, but they do not raise questions about the rationality of economic behavior. To the extent that such tendencies accurately reflect true preferences, they do not create a need for paternalism." In contrast, the second kind of finding is a discovery of some mechanism by which people "fail to behave in their best interests." It is only this type of deviation from the received theory that can properly be treated as an "error" or "violation of rationality", and that can justify paternalistic intervention (pp. 1217–18).

As these passages show, Camerer et al. are identifying rational choice in terms of some concept of "true preference". But how do we distinguish between true preferences and false ones? Notice that, on Camerer et al's account, a person's true preferences are not necessarily revealed in her choices: errors are defined as those cases in which true preferences are *not* revealed in choices. Further, true preferences do not necessarily satisfy the structural assumptions that economic theory has traditionally imposed, even if those assumptions have previously been justified on grounds of rationality. (For example, the axioms of expected utility theory, as formulated by Leonard Savage (1954), are intended to express normative principles of rational consistency, and those principles deem considerations of ambiguity to be irrelevant for rational decision-making.)

In economics, the standard method for identifying a person's preferences is to study the choices that she makes and to try to infer preferences that are consistent with those choices. In making these inferences, we are also constrained by the structural assumptions imposed by the theory of rational choice. In contrast, Camerer et al's approach has two additional degrees of freedom: it is not constrained by actual choice (the decision-maker might be making mistakes), and it is not constrained by conventional consistency assumptions (these are not treated as necessary for rationality). When we observe some regularity of behavior that violates the standard theory, we seem to be given a choice of modeling options. One option is to retain the standard theory as the model of true preferences, and diagnose the behavior as an error. The other is to construct a new specification of preferences, incorporating the deviation from the standard theory, and deem those preferences to be "true". For example, much of the experimental evidence of violations of expected utility theory can be organized by prospect theory, first proposed by Daniel Kahneman and Amos Tversky (1979). One of the main innovations of prospect theory is that actual probabilities are transformed into "decision weights" in a way that increases the weight given to "outlying" consequences (that is, ones which, relative to the lottery in which they appear, are particularly good or particularly bad). Having accepted prospect theory as descriptively valid, we might interpret this transformation of probability as an error—as a misperception of the "true" weight of probabilities—and define true preferences in terms of expected utility theory. Alternatively, we might claim that expected utility theory has an over-simplified understanding of the subjective significance of probability to rational agents (just as, according to most expected utility theorists, a theory in which rationality is defined as the maximization of expected monetary value has an over-simplified understanding of the subjective significance of consequences).

If, as Camerer et al. intend, error is an empirical and not a normative concept, we need a general empirical criterion for choosing, in any specific case, between these two modeling strategies. I cannot see how we can hope to agree on such a criterion without first agreeing, if only in broad terms, what we mean by "rational" choice. In economics, the traditional understanding is that an agent's choices are rational if they reveal preferences that satisfy (allegedly) normatively defensible principles of internal consistency. Camerer et al's proposal clearly presupposes a different understanding of rationality; but they do not spell out what it is.

One possible understanding seems to be proposed by Sunstein and Thaler when, having said that they intend their concept of "better-off" to be measured as objectively as possible, they define "inferior choices" as "choices that [the agents who make them] would change if they had complete information, unlimited cognitive abilities, and no lack of willpower" (2003a, p. 175). This amounts to a counterfactual definition of rational choice (or, equivalently, of true preference): a putative choice is rational for an individual (or is what he truly prefers) if it is the choice that he would have made, had he been fully informed, and had he not been subject to the kinds of bounds on rationality that behavioral economics has shown to be characteristic of normal human decision-making. Notice that this definition of rationality presupposes the following empirical hypothesis: for any given individual, there is a unique set of true preferences, such that, as the influence of whatever casual factors induce errors is reduced, choice behavior converges to a pattern that reveals those preferences. This requires that different learning processes, with different starting points, tend to converge to the same choice behavior (provided only that each process tends to eliminate known sources of error).[8] Sunstein and Thaler do not offer any evidence to support this hypothesis. In fact, there is strong evidence to the contrary. For example, Dan Ariely, George Loewenstein, and Drazen Prelec (2003) investigate individuals' monetary valuations of some simple consumption experiences that are not normally traded on markets. These valuations are strongly influenced by cues which draw individuals' attention to clearly irrelevant numbers (such as the last digits of their social security numbers); and that influence persists even after repeated experience of both trading and consumption.

I can think of only one other understanding of rationality that coheres with the logic of Camerer et al's paper as a whole. Although they do not endorse this answer explicitly, there are some clues in the paper which suggest that this is what they have in mind.[9] This is the understanding of rationality proposed by Kahneman, Wakker, and Sarin (1997) and by Kahneman (2000a).

Kahneman, Wakker, and Sarin's paper declares its position in its title: "Back to Bentham". The paper makes a fundamental distinction between two concepts of utility. *Decision utility* is utility in the sense of modern decision theory—that is, utility as a representation of preferences, where preferences are attitudes towards (or judgments about) options, and are revealed in choice behavior. *Experienced utility* is utility in the sense of classical

---

[8] This hypothesis is similar to Charles Plott's (1996) "discovered preference hypothesis", about which behavioral economists have generally been skeptical (see, e.g. Loewenstein, 1999). The fact that Loewenstein is a leading skeptic suggests that Camerer et al. would not endorse Sunstein and Thaler's definition of rationality.

[9] Given the number of authors, it is possible that the paper's lack of explicitness about the concept of rationality reflects differences between those authors. In that case, these "clues" may be indications that at least one author takes the view that I am attributing to all of them.

utilitarianism—that is, utility as a measure of the hedonic experience induced by consuming a good. Decision utility is an *ex ante* determinant of choice, while experienced utility is an *ex post* experience that results from choice. Kahneman et al. define rationality in terms of the maximization of experienced utility. Failures of rationality occur when people take decisions in ways that lead to less positive hedonic experiences than are in fact on offer. Such failures may be the product of simplifying decision-making heuristics that are not well-adapted to the problem at hand. Or they may issue from failures of "affective forecasting"—that is, inaccurate predictions of the hedonic experiences that will result from particular choices. Or they may reflect failures of self-control: a person may know that one course of action will produce better consequences than another in the long run, yet be unable to resist the temptation to go for the short-term benefits offered by the second option.

Provided that there is a method of measuring hedonic experience on a one-dimensional scale, this approach gives us the empirical concepts of "true preference" and "error" that Camerer et al. need: the standard of true preference is experienced utility, and failures to maximize experienced utility are classified as errors. Is this what Camerer et al. actually have in mind? Possibly. In one footnote, they point to evidence that "not all 'risk preferences' that manifest themselves in choice behavior seem to be fully rational in the sense of maximizing *experienced* welfare" and interpret this as a potential warrant for paternalism (p. 1217, note 21). And when discussing loss aversion, they say that, in many contexts, "the degree of loss aversion exhibited in people's choices seems inconsistent with their actual experiences of gains and losses", and offer this as another justification for paternalism (p. 1218). This latter example corresponds with a suggestion sometimes made by Kahneman—that a major component of loss aversion can be attributed to a failure of affective forecasting: by focusing on transitions between states rather than on the states themselves, people systematically overestimate the pain of moving away from a status quo position (Kahneman and Sugden, 2005).

On this reading, Camerer et al. are presenting a case for a form of paternalism whose objective is to promote experienced utility. Although their concrete proposals are far from radical—in fact, one of their professed aims is to explain elements of paternalism that are embedded in existing law[10]—taking their approach seriously could have momentous consequences. Recall that one of the main findings of the "economics of happiness" literature is that, in time-series studies, self-reported happiness is only weakly correlated with income. One leading explanation for this phenomenon is hedonic adaptation: an increase in a person's real income increases her happiness for a short period,

---

[10] This part of their argument depends on the hypothesis that legal regulation "gravitate[s] toward socially useful forms even when their logic remains poorly articulated" (p. 1223). They note that this is a common hypothesis in the literature of law and economics, but they do not offer any justification for it. I remain skeptical.

but as she adapts to her new pattern of consumption, that effect is dissipated. One might ask why, if this mechanism is so predictable, people continue to strive for increased income. One leading explanation for that is that there is a systematic failure of affective forecasting: people underestimate the extent of adaptation (e.g. Kahenman, 2000a and 2000b). It seems that there could be a case for paternalistic interventions designed to divert people away from the pursuit of increased income. For good or ill, that is not a minor matter: the pursuit of material wealth has been a constant of human motivation through-out recorded history.[11]

In Section 1, I explained the unease I felt about Sen's capability approach, because of the way it allows individuals' actual desires about how to live their own lives to be overridden. Camerer et al's approach induces a similar unease. (Sunstein and Thaler's libertarian paternalism is not vulnerable to the same objection—provided the constraint on "blocking choices" is maintained. The paternalistic interventions that are allowed by Sunstein and Thaler's official criterion try to steer the individual away from irrational choices, but still leave him free to make them.) Suppose that I, as a private citizen, feel a strong desire to work long hours to earn enough income to buy certain luxury goods. And suppose that Camerer et al's social planners, having taken account of the professional judgments of psychologists and behavioral economists, conclude that this is a form of behavior which does not maximize my long-term happi-ness. Then, according to their model, my "type" is that of the boundedly rational consumer. A paternalistic regulation which prevents me from choos-ing my own hours of work will create net benefits through its effects on me, by preventing me from making an irrational choice. The only countervailing factor in the cost-benefit analysis is the harm that the regulation may do to *other* people whom the planners classify as "fully rational", by preventing them from acting in ways that, in the planners' judgment, would increase their happiness. My own desires, however strong, count for nothing, however cautiously the planners interpret the principle of asymmetric paternalism.[12]

---

[11] Some theorists of the economics of happiness are quite explicit in proposing that public policies should be designed to discourage individuals from pursuing increased income. Layard (2005, pp. 149–65) is a prominent example: he argues that high rates of income tax are socially beneficial, independently of their function in raising revenue, because they discourage effort in the workplace and so promote a better work–life balance. Layard is not opposed in principle to paternalism, provided it is effective in promoting happiness (p. 113). However, his argu-ment for income tax rests on the assumption that, because of competition for status, increases in one person's income reduces the happiness of others. Thus, he claims, everyone can benefit from policies which reduce competition for status.

[12] By "desire", I mean the *ex ante* mental state which supplies the motivating force for action. This is conceptually distinct from the *ex post* hedonic experience (i.e. experienced utility) that is generated by an action. We can desire to perform actions which turn out to have unpleasant hedonic consequences, and we can feel no desire to do what turns out to be pleasurable.

3. Why Sign Up to These Approaches?

The capability approach, as developed by Sen and Nussbaum, and the happiness approach, as implemented in Camerer et al's asymmetric paternalism, have the common feature that a person's actual desires can be overridden by other people's judgments about what he has reason to desire. In the capability approach, the warrant for those judgments is either their claim to be based on objective truths about well-being (as hinted at in some of Sen's earlier writings) or their having received majority support in a deliberative democratic process (as now emphasized by Sen). In the happiness approach, the warrant is their claim to be based on scientific findings about hedonic experience. This down-grading of actual desire stems from a very fundamental property that both approaches share. This property is so fundamental, and for most economists and philosophers so natural, that it is usually overlooked: the presupposition that the right questions for normative analysts to ask are about well-being, and that the viewpoint from which these questions should be asked and answered is that of a neutral moral or scientific observer.

Once we, as analysts, take this viewpoint on the social world, it is natural for us to think that we have an intellectual responsibility to base our normative conclusions on the best judgments *we* can make about people's well-being. If we have good reasons (or what we sincerely take to be good reasons) to believe that some individual's well-being does not correspond with what he in fact desires, then our assessments of his well-being must reflect that belief. That "must" is, it seems, just a requirement of clear thinking: our judgments about his well-being must be *our* judgments, not his. And, of course, that is right—*if we take the viewpoint of the neutral observer*. But there is another viewpoint or, rather, a set of other viewpoints: we can take the viewpoint of each individual in turn. Instead of looking for ways of structuring society that are as good as possible, according to the judgments we make as neutral observers, we can try to find proposals to which each individual, looking at those proposals from his own viewpoint, can assent.

When we look at the world in this contractarian way, the risks of endorsing the capability approach become clear. Suppose that I, as a citizen, ask what opportunities I am assured if the distribution of opportunities is governed by the theory of capability. The answer seems to be this: I am assured opportunities to lead those kinds of lives that a majority of my fellow citizens, after reflective deliberation and open debate, judge to be valuable. I am also assured the opportunity to participate in this debate on equal terms with everyone else. What I am *not* assured is the opportunity to live whatever kind of life *I* desire, within the constraints imposed by other people's having similar opportunities. Presented as the terms of a putative constitution, this does not strike me as a particularly attractive offer. What, in terms of my own understanding of my own good, do I gain by allowing the judgments of a majority to override my own desires about matters that are private to me? What, in terms of your own understanding of your own good, do you gain by allowing majority judgments to override your desires about what is private to you? In advocating the capability approach, Sen is asking each of us to take unnecessary risks.[13]

Similarly, if we think in terms of reaching agreement about general principles that are to govern public policy, asymmetric paternalism does not look like a good deal. What is being proposed to me (as a citizen) is that I can be prevented from acting according to my own desires and judgments, provided that expert opinion judges that the actions I would choose to make would not be conducive to my happiness, and provided that the restrictions that are being imposed in my alleged interests are not too costly for other people who are judged more rational than me. Is this in my interests, *as I perceive them*?

I may recognize specific kinds of situation in which, for psychological reasons I can understand, my decisions are liable to be swayed by causal factors that I would prefer to screen out. Under the influence of alcohol, I may find it difficult to resist the temptation to become dangerously drunk; in a face-to-face interaction with a trained salesperson, I may find it difficult to avoid accepting offers which, if I considered coolly, I would reject; when clinically depressed, I may wish to kill myself. These are all cases in which Camerer et al. are willing to support mandatory cooling-off periods. As a citizen, thinking about these situations from my own point of view and while not under the influence of the causal factors in question, I may agree to these proposals. But notice that such cooling-off periods are designed to support me in making my own considered judgments about my own life. Take the case of a law which allows consumers to rescind purchases made from door-to-door salespersons within a certain number of days of the transaction. This law gives me, as a consumer, the opportunity to consider my purchase decision carefully, out of the influence of what I can recognize to be a psychologically powerful force. But the final decision is still mine. No one is telling me what I must choose, after I have deliberated. I am not even being required *to* deliberate; I am merely being given the opportunity to do so.

In contrast, consider a genuinely paternalistic law which compels people to save for their old age. Looking from the viewpoint of a neutral observer, there are good reasons to think that such a law would increase many people's lifetime happiness. Nevertheless, it is hard to see how any individual can *perceive* the restrictions imposed on him by a compulsory savings law as

---

[13] Sen (2006, pp. 89–90) objects to this characterization of his position, on the grounds that he has written extensively on rights and liberties and on the importance of maintaining protected spheres within which individuals can make their own choices. I emphasize again that I am discussing the implications of the capability approach, and not Sen's views as a whole.

working in his own interests. If I come to the considered judgment that I ought to save for my old age, I can take out a savings plan (perhaps with a built-in cooling-off period for subsequent decisions to terminate the plan); I do not need to be compelled. If I am not in that state of mind, how can I see the compulsory savings regime as serving my interests?

As I have already said, when we look at the world from the viewpoint of a moral observer, it is easy to slip into assuming that our own moral judgments about what is valuable in human life will command general assent among our fellow-citizens. Thus, we are inclined to imagine, we can propose that the definition of fundamental capabilities is determined in a democratic process without putting at risk those of our own capabilities that we value most highly. Similarly, it is easy to slip into assuming that our own scientific judgments will command general assent among whatever community of scientists will provide the knowledge base for paternalistic public policies. Thus, we imagine, we can propose that paternalistic considerations should be treated as legitimate justifications for public policy without putting at risk our own opportunities to act on our own considered judgments. The point of this essay is to urge the reader to recognize these risks, and to be cautious about signing up to normative positions which do not recognize each individual as the locus of authority and responsibility with respect to how she lives her own life.

References

Ariely, Dan, George Loewenstein, and Drazen Prelec (2003). "Coherent Arbitrariness": stable demand curves without stable preferences. *Quarterly Journal of Economics* 118: 73–105.

Bruni, Luigino, and Pierluigi Porta (eds) (2005). *Economics and Happiness: Framing the Analysis*. Oxford: Oxford University Press.

Camerer, Colin, Samuel Issacharoff, George Loewenstein, Ted O'Donaghue, and Matthew Rabin (2003). Regulation for conservatives: behavioral economics and the case for "asymmetric paternalism". *University of Pennsylvania Law Review* 151: 1211–54.

Easterlin, Richard (1974). Does economic growth improve the human lot? Some empirical evidence. In Paul A. David and Melvin W. Reder (eds), *Nations and Households in Economic Growth*. New York: Academic Press, pp. 89–125.

—— (1995). Will raising the incomes of all increase the happiness of all? *Journal of Economic Behavior and Organization* 27: 35–47.

Ellsberg, Daniel (1961). Risk, ambiguity, and the Savage axioms. *Quarterly Journal of Economics* 75: 643–69.

Frey, Bruno, and Alois Stutzer (2002). What can economists learn from happiness research? *Journal of Economic Literature* 40: 402–35.

Kahneman, Daniel (2000a). Experienced utility and objective happiness: a moment-based approach. In Amos Tversky and Daniel Kahneman (eds), *Choices, Values, and Frames*. Cambridge: Cambridge University Press.

Kahneman, Daniel (2000b). Evaluation by moments: past and future. In Amos Tversky and Daniel Kahneman (eds), *Choices, Values, and Frames*. Cambridge: Cambridge University Press.

—— and Robert Sugden (2005). Experienced utility as a standard of policy evaluation. *Environmental and Resource Economics* 32: 161–81.

—— and Amos Tversky (1979). Prospect theory: an analysis of decision under risk. *Econometrica* 47: 263–91.

—— Peter Wakker, and Rakesh Sarin (1997). Back to Bentham? Explorations of experienced utility. *Quarterly Journal of Economics* 112: 375–405.

Layard, Richard (2005). *Happiness: Lessons from a New Science*. London: Allen Lane.

Loewenstein, George (1999). Experimental economics from the viewpoint of behavioural economics. *Economic Journal* 109: F25–34.

Nussbaum, Martha (2000). *Women and Human Development: The Capabilities Approach*. Cambridge: Cambridge University Press.

Plott, Charles R. (1996). Rational individual behaviour in markets and social choice processes: the discovered preference hypothesis. In Kenneth J. Arrow, Enrico Colombatto, Mark Perlman, and Christian Schmidt (eds), *The Rational Foundations of Economic Behaviour*. Basingstoke: Macmillan, pp. 225–50.

Savage, Leonard J. (1954). *The Foundations of Statistics*. New York: Wiley.

Scitovsky, Tibor (1976). *The Joyless Economy: The Psychology of Human Satisfaction*. Oxford: Oxford University Press.

Sen, Amartya (1970a). *Collective Choice and Social Welfare*. San Francisco: Holden-Day.

—— (1970b). The impossibility of a Paretian liberal. *Journal of Political Economy* 78: 152–7.

—— (1985). *Commodities and Capabilities*. Amsterdam: North-Holland.

—— (1992). *Inequality Reexamined*. Cambridge, Massachusetts: Harvard University Press.

—— (1999). *Development as Freedom*. Oxford: Oxford University Press.

—— (2004). Capabilities, lists, and public reason: continuing the conversation. *Feminist Economics* 10: 77–80.

—— (2006). Reason, freedom and well-being. *Utilitas* 18: 80–96.

Sugden, Robert (1985). Liberty, preference and choice. *Economics and Philosophy* 1: 213–29.

—— (2004). The opportunity criterion: consumer sovereignty without the assumption of coherent preferences. *American Economic Review*, 94: 1014–33.

—— (2005). Coping with preference anomalies in cost-benefit analysis: a market-simulation approach. *Environmental and Resource Economics* 32: 129–60.

—— (2006). What we desire, what we have reason to desire, whatever we might desire: Mill and Sen on the value of opportunity. *Utilitas* 18: 33–51.

Sunstein, Cass, and Richard Thaler (2003a). Libertarian paternalism. *American Economic Review, Papers and Proceedings* 93 (2): 175–9.

—— —— (2003b). Libertarian paternalism is not an oxymoron. *University of Chicago Law Review* 70: 1159–202.

Index

AACC (Anglo-American corporate
  capitalism) 213–14, 215
Abbey, E. 63
Abrams, L. 205
achievement 23, 25, 23, 261 n., 264, 266
  aspirations and 62
  minor, chronically deprived learn to
    "celebrate" 145
  overemphasis on 64
  potential 229
  primary goods and 149
  prospects of 150
  social 25
  well-being and 70–1, 72
actualization 189, 190, 200
  see also self-actualization
adaptation 6, 40, 44, 49, 121, 141, 230, 231,
    271, 302, 303, 306
  across domains 45–7
  argument from 145
  extreme view of 84
  hedonic 31, 33, 68, 317
  nuanced view of 108
  people underestimate the extent of 318
  psychological 226
  relational goods less affected by 135
  Sen's arguments about 307
  upward 90
adaptive preferences 2, 6, 9, 116, 144, 145, 152,
    261
  SWB open to 269
addictive behavior 173–6, 227
adding value 211
ADHD (Attention Deficit Hyperactivity
  Disorder) 227
adjustment problems/process 64, 145
  psychological, poorer 209
Adkins, C. L. 209
adolescents 198, 199, 212
  conflicts among peers 225
  homicides among 228
  mental disorders among 227
  promoting engagement and well-being
    in 203
  risky behaviors 207

suicide rate 227
violence among 227
Advanced Quality of Life Index (Diener) 65
advantages 141
  persistent 86
adverse circumstances 142
Aelred of Rielvaulx 128 n.
affect 8
  negative 64, 67, 73, 119, 192
  positive 64, 67, 71, 72, 74, 117, 119, 205
affect balance 28, 31, 116
affection 118
affective forecasting 317, 318
affiliation 188
affluence 61–2, 64, 91, 134
  and life satisfaction 90
African Americans 279 n.
African countries 265 n.
age 30, 38, 43
  decline in happiness with 48
  effects of 71
  negative association of happiness to 31
  positive linear relation of happiness to 47
  pure effect of 46–7, 29, 30, 34, 48, 55
  systematic differences related to 24
  well-being increases with 29
agency 2, 151, 152
  independence, conformity and 197–200
  self as 234, 241
  self-regulation and 200–2
  subjective measures of 254–85
agent relativity 147, 152, 154
agentic self 233, 234–6
  feedback onto non-conscious processes 238
aggregation 17, 151 n.
Ahuvia, A. 118
Ainsworth, M. D. S. 239
Akerlof G. A. 90 n., 116 n., 232 n.
alcohol 207, 238, 261 n., 320
Alesina, A. 63, 101
Alkire, S. 2, 254 n., 258 n., 259 n., 260, 262 n.
Allardt, E. 262
Allen, T. D. 71
allocation of resources 135
Allport, G. W. 269 n.

Index

Index

Index

universities 65
University of Chicago 288 n.
University of Wisconsin-Madison 269 n.
unobservable variables 293
unstable employment 109
updating 233, 240–1
upward mobility 94–5, 103, 104
  perceived prospects of 96, 101–2, 108
Ura, K. 173 n., 183 n.
use-interests 154
Usunov, J. 190
utilitarianism 3, 7, 17, 18, 21, 22, 23, 27, 144,
    146, 167, 178, 181 n.
  CA's general critique of 145
  classical 316–17
  egalitarian 170
  "informational famine" promoted by 6
  limitations of 19
  Sen's critique of 149, 302, 303, 305
  sum-total 170
  welfarism has greater plausibility than 26
  wisdom in 150
Utilitas 300
utility 1, 18, 20, 121, 165, 172, 287
  adding to learning activity 211
  argument for supplementation by rights 151
  cardinal 22
  criticized 225, 229
  decision 316, 317
  defining in material or income terms 89
  derived from a clear conscience 167
  economists tend to identify well-being
    with 292
  expected 315
  experienced 310 n., 312 n., 316–17
  happiness and 145
  hedonistic view of 17
  income-based 106
  interpersonal comparisons of 19, 21, 22,
    23, 26
  maximization of 23, 89, 166, 167, 169, 178,
    232–3, 234, 237, 317
  mental-state metrics of 152
  negative externalities that affect 122
  predicted 144 n.
  predicting future effects on 244 n.
  SWB as proxy measure for 118
  total reliance on 19
  utilitarian-hedonistic conception of 166
utility function 294
utility information 150, 151

Vallerand, R. J. 193, 195, 200, 278 n.
valuable functioning 169, 171, 175, 176, 263
  understanding 179
valuations 316
value judgments 66, 178

values 67, 165, 194, 196, 200, 229, 257, 260,
    261, 271
  basic 267
  clash of 215
  democratic practice helps society
    form 258
  deontological 147
  extrinsic 212
  integrated 277
  intermediate 268
  intrinsic 212, 216
  materialistic 62, 64, 210, 215
  moral 143
  social 182
  traditional 181
  universal 5–6, 264–7
  well-internalized 213
  see also European Values Survey; PVQ; WVS
Van de Vijver, F. J. R. 261 n.
Van den Broeck, A. 207
Van Gogh, Vincent 274
Van Hees, M. 6
Van Praag, B. M. S. 28 n., 32, 33, 43
Vanin, P. 134 n.
Vansteenkiste, M. 188, 189, 190, 191, 193,
    198, 199, 200, 202, 205, 207, 209, 210,
    211, 212, 234
variance 98, 208
Vázquez, C. 74
Veblen, Thorstein 91, 121, 122 n.
Vector View (Sen) 147
Veenhoven, R. 90, 118, 124 n., 166 n., 257
Venezuela 61
verbal language 237, 240, 242 n.
Verkley, H. 71
Veroff, J. 289
vicarious experiences 273 n.
violence 3, 88, 227
  unexpected outbreaks of 108
virtue-friendship 128
virtues 123, 128 n., 130
  tension between happiness and 125–6
visceral factors 238
vitality 240, 242
Voices of the Poor study (2000) 259
Volanth, A. J. 72
volatility 93, 94, 97–8
  macroeconomic 103, 109
volition 191, 192, 193, 194, 195, 197, 198,
    200, 201
  autonomy understood as 199
  lack of 214
  shared sense of 196
volunteer work 72–3, 117
voting behavior 21, 100, 101, 194
Vroom, V. H. 188
vulnerability 239, 240, 246